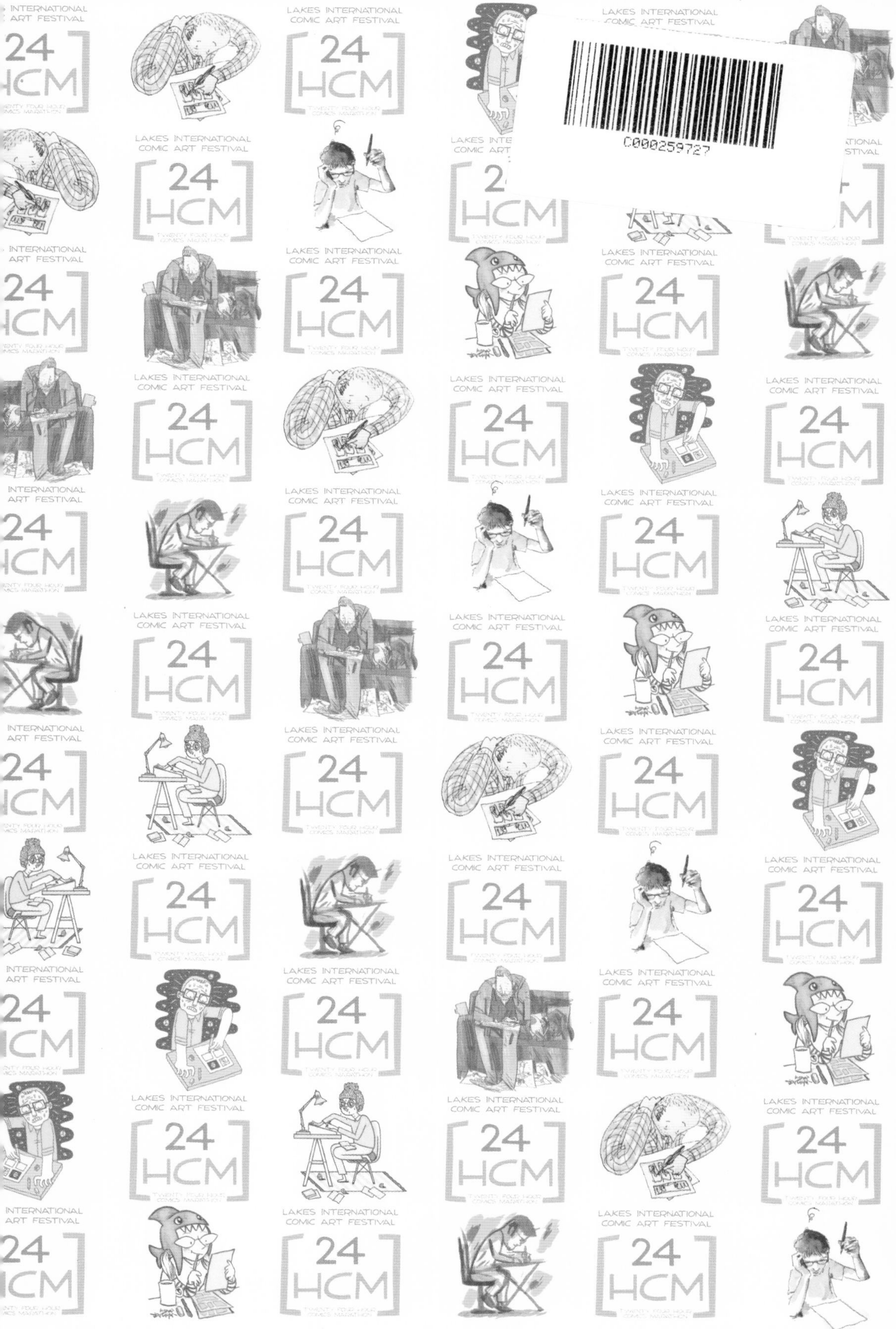
LAKES INTERNATIONAL COMIC ART FESTIVAL
24 HCM
TWENTY FOUR HOUR COMICS MARATHON

Fanfare Presents

24 by 7

Seven comics as diverse as they are witty as they are beautiful to behold, each created within (the same) 24 hours. An extraordinary accomplishment.

Stephen L. Holland, Page 45

Baczynski • Berry • Decie • Johnson-Cadwell
McIntyre • Obata • Teagle

Instigated by the Lakes International Comic Art Festival
Published by Fanfare Presents
Edited by Dan Berry
Layout by Dan Berry
Photography by Sarah McIntyre, Phil Welch, Katie White & Dan Berry
ISBN: 978-0-9932112-0-1

Printed and bound in China by Prolong Press Ltd

© Fanfare Presents 2015 for the anthology arranged with the kind consent
and involvement of all the individual authors (in order of appearance):

    © Sarah McIntyre 2014 for 'Scribble'
    © Joe Decie 2014 for 'I Blame Grandma'
    © Kristyna Baczynski for 'Hand Me Down'
    © Fumio Obata 2014 for 'Anywhere Road'
    © Jack Teagle 2014 for 'Witch Cat'
    © Warwick Johnson Cadwell 2014 for 'Tom Hand – A Tale of Stories'
    © Dan Berry 2014 for 'Nicholas & Edith'

Supported using public funding by

ARTS COUNCIL ENGLAND

Kendal College

glyndŵr

PRIFYSGOL GLYNDŴR WRECSAM
GLYNDŴR UNIVERSITY WREXHAM

absolute°

whether it's a business card, brochure or building wrap

BEST WESTERN PLUS
Castle Green Hotel in Kendal

Gazelle

BABA GANOUSH

The Lakes International Comic Art Festival is a new kind of comic art event for the UK, born in 2013, taking over an entire town on the edge of the English Lake District for a whole weekend. One of the things that makes it different is a programme of commissions which aim to inspire and challenge comic artists, showcase their talent and by doing so bring new audiences to comics.

In our second year one of the ways we decided to do this was by stealing a long-established model of a 24 hour comic marathon (creating an original 24 page comic in 24 hours) and doing it "boutique" style. This meant we curated (i.e. chose!) the artists, created the best possible environment for them to work in and attempted to print all of them as limited editions within 24 hours.

Who better to produce this first LICAF marathon than Dan Berry, a veteran of traditional 24-hour marathons, who was up for the challenge of re-shaping the format and seeing if we could produce 7 comics of real quality which would be as enticing and absorbing as any other comic being produced (at a slightly slower pace) today.

Julie Tait
Director, Lakes International Comic Art Festival.

When people ask how we got this done in 24 hours I always tell them; "we cheated!"

The 24 hour comic event was invented by Scott McCloud in 1990 when he challenged his friend Steve Bissette to create a complete 24 page book; the story, the artwork, the lettering, everything in just one day. Thus the challenge was born. From that point a few variations on this original theme have emerged, including the setting of restrictions that make forward planning futile or imposing further time constraints.

When we were discussing how we were going to make this whole thing work, we decided that we wanted to do something different. We wanted the stories that emerged from this to be the best they could be, so rather than require that everything was completed on the day, we would let our artists plan ahead. The amount of planning that the artists did was entirely up to them, some did more, some did less, but the only stipulation was that they weren't allowed to begin drawing the final artwork before the event. This meant they could spent time writing scripts, designing characters, doing rough layouts and planning, pacing and plotting. Anything they wanted short of putting pen to paper and drawing the final artwork. Now, I know what you are thinking; 'you cheated!'

Well, yes. Given the original rules of the 24 hour comic as set out by Scott McCloud, and the many variations of the 24 hour comics challenge that are run around the world, we cheated. We are a big old stinky gang of dirty rotten cheats.

So how can we live with ourselves, how can we admit to this level of subterfuge and still have the gall to collect these stories in beautiful, sumptuous, glorious print and expect you, the honest rule-abiding, law-respecting reader to put your hand in your pocket and pay good money for this swindle of a book?

Maybe cheating is the wrong word because it makes it all sound easy. It wasn't easy at all. In fact it was difficult, tiring, painful, occasionally miserable, occasionally euphoric and hugely enjoyable. So rather than cheating, let's say we gave ourselves the following unfair advantages;

First, as previously stated, we threw tradition out of the window and had the gall to set our own rules. We chose a group of artists whose work were are excited about, and who we knew would be able to rise to the challenge of making a book in just a day. We then set about finding people to help us. Kendal College very generously gave their time, expertise, equipment and students to help make this happen. Castle Green housed us in their business centre for the duration where we had a seemingly endless supply of snacks and drinks to hand. The restaurant Baba Ganoush sent over care packages of delicious meals.

Katie White & Phil Welch were our boundlessly energetic support crew on the ground, maintaining our event blog, fetching drinks and running errands tirelessly and without complaining once. Donya Todd was on hand to provide invaluable moral and artistic support. We also had a seemingly endless supply of high-profile cartoonists and illustrators dropping in to offer words of encouragement and support including Scott McCloud himself, Junko Mizuno, Bryan & Mary Talbot, Gail Simone, Jeff Smith, Joost Swarte and Nick Abadzis amongst many more.

We also arranged a masseuse to visit and provide a frankly life-changingly good neck, back and shoulder massages to each of the participants. We also knew that we had Absolute Print in Kendal primed and ready to print the first individual runs of each of the books, which we would pick up the same day.

So you can see, we gave ourselves an unfair advantage (cheated) and we ended up with seven astonishing stories that do not at all look like they took a day to draw and I couldn't be more proud.

Dan Berry
Producer/Curator

We are a big old stinky gang of dirty rotten cheats.

SARAH
McINTYRE

SCRIBBLE
BY SARAH McINTYRE

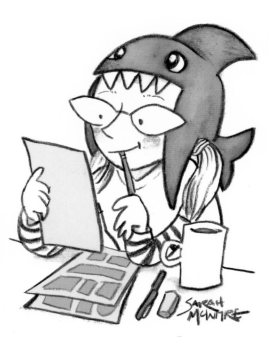

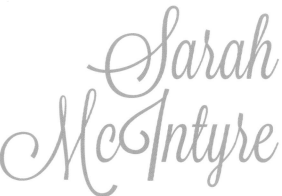

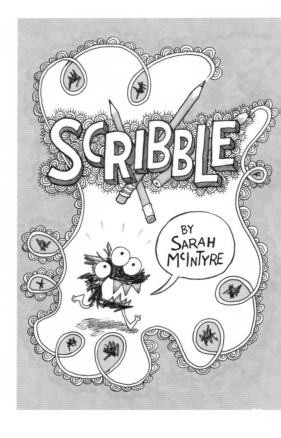

Sarah McIntyre

Six feet tall in pointy specs and silly hats, you can usually spot Sarah McIntyre across a crowded room. Her picture books include ***Dinosaur Police***, ***There's a Shark in the Bath***, ***Jampires*** (with comics artist David O'Connell), ***Morris the Mankiest Monster*** and ***You Can't Scare a Princess***!

She also collaborates with Philip Reeve on highly illustrated chapter books including ***Oliver and the Seawigs*** and ***Cakes in Space***. Her comic book ***Vern and Lettuce*** won the Leeds Graphic Novel Award and she writes and draws a strip called ***Shark & Unicorn*** for The Funday Times.

jabberworks.co.uk
@jabberworks

I WANT TO TELL
YOU ABOUT A
FRIEND OF MINE.
HIS LIFE BEGAN
AS A LITTLE

SCRIBBLE

I MADE ON
MY NAPKIN.

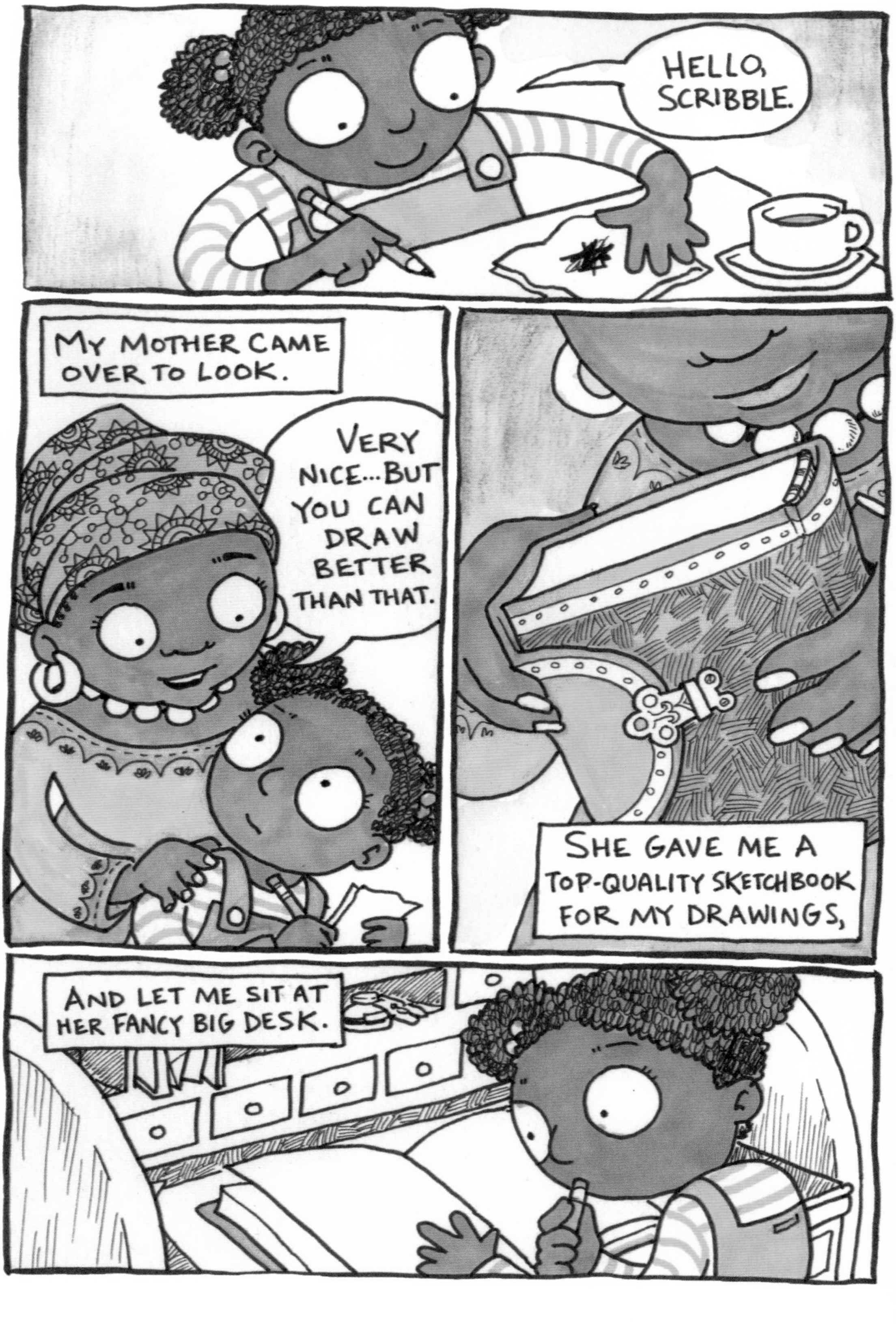
HELLO, SCRIBBLE.
MY MOTHER CAME OVER TO LOOK.
VERY NICE...BUT YOU CAN DRAW BETTER THAN THAT.
SHE GAVE ME A TOP-QUALITY SKETCHBOOK FOR MY DRAWINGS,
AND LET ME SIT AT HER FANCY BIG DESK.

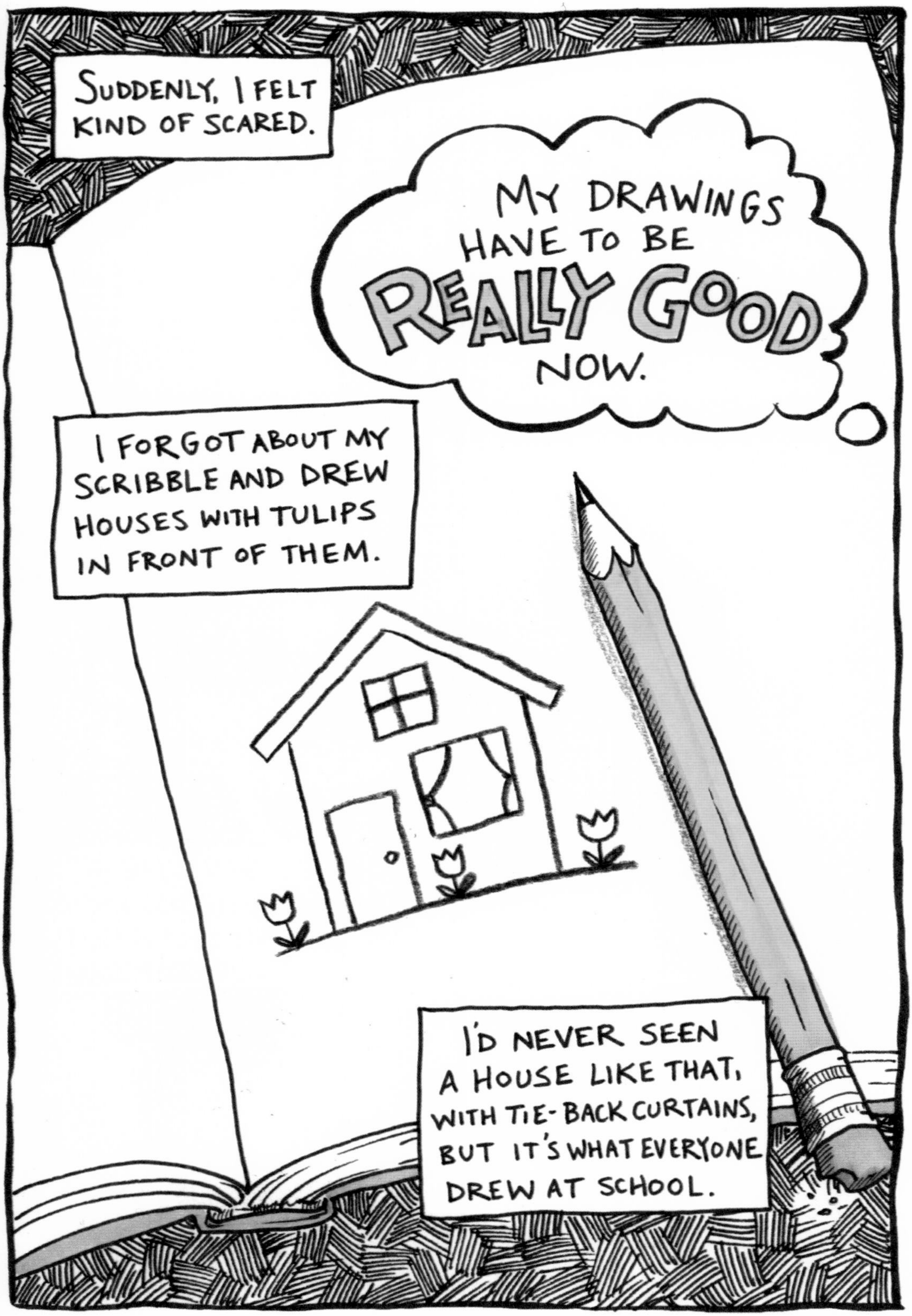
SUDDENLY, I FELT KIND OF SCARED.
MY DRAWINGS HAVE TO BE REALLY GOOD NOW.
I FORGOT ABOUT MY SCRIBBLE AND DREW HOUSES WITH TULIPS IN FRONT OF THEM.
I'D NEVER SEEN A HOUSE LIKE THAT, WITH TIE-BACK CURTAINS, BUT IT'S WHAT EVERYONE DREW AT SCHOOL.

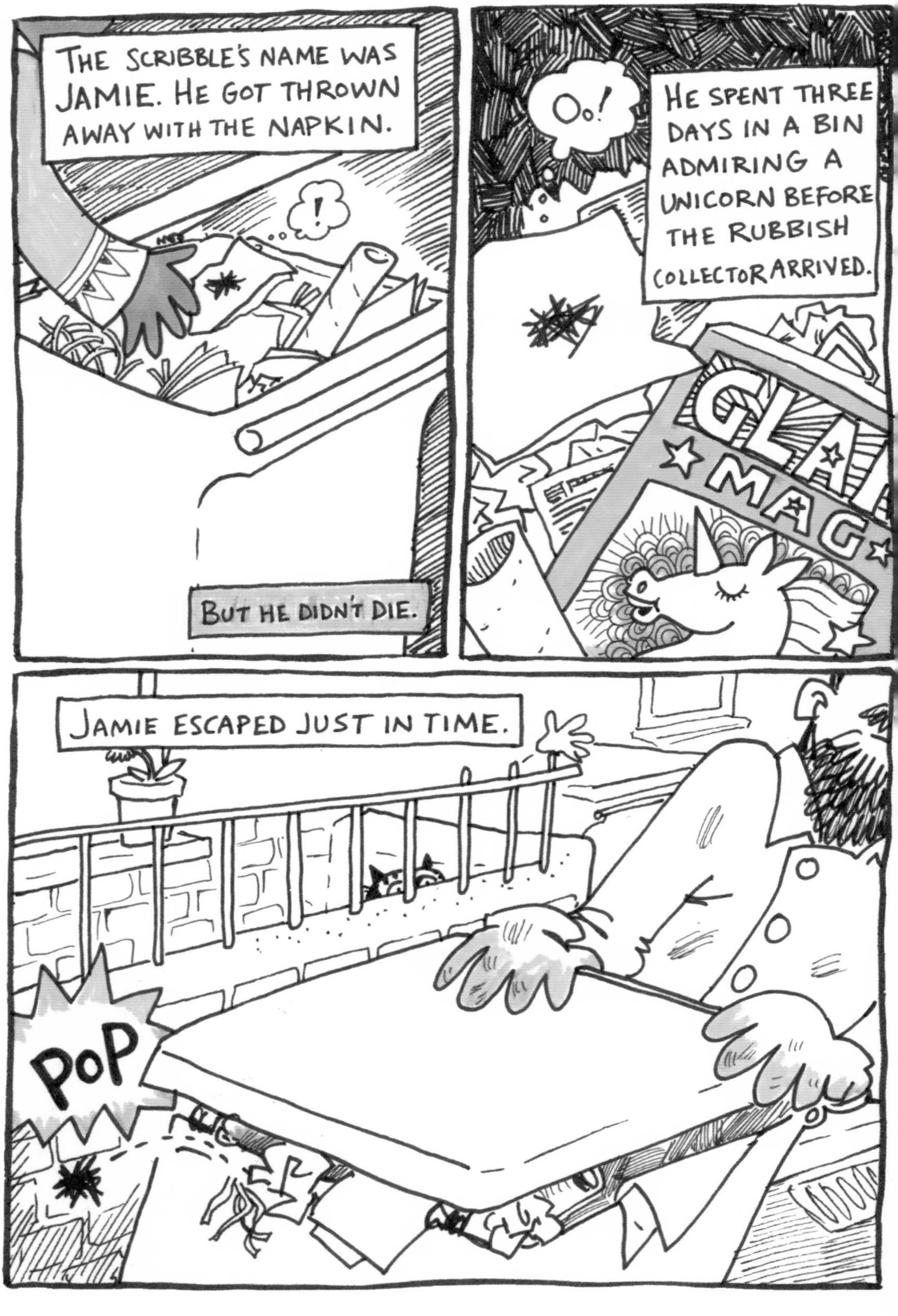
THE SCRIBBLE'S NAME WAS JAMIE. HE GOT THROWN AWAY WITH THE NAPKIN.
!
BUT HE DIDN'T DIE.
Oo!
HE SPENT THREE DAYS IN A BIN ADMIRING A UNICORN BEFORE THE RUBBISH COLLECTOR ARRIVED.
GLA
MAG
JAMIE ESCAPED JUST IN TIME.
POP

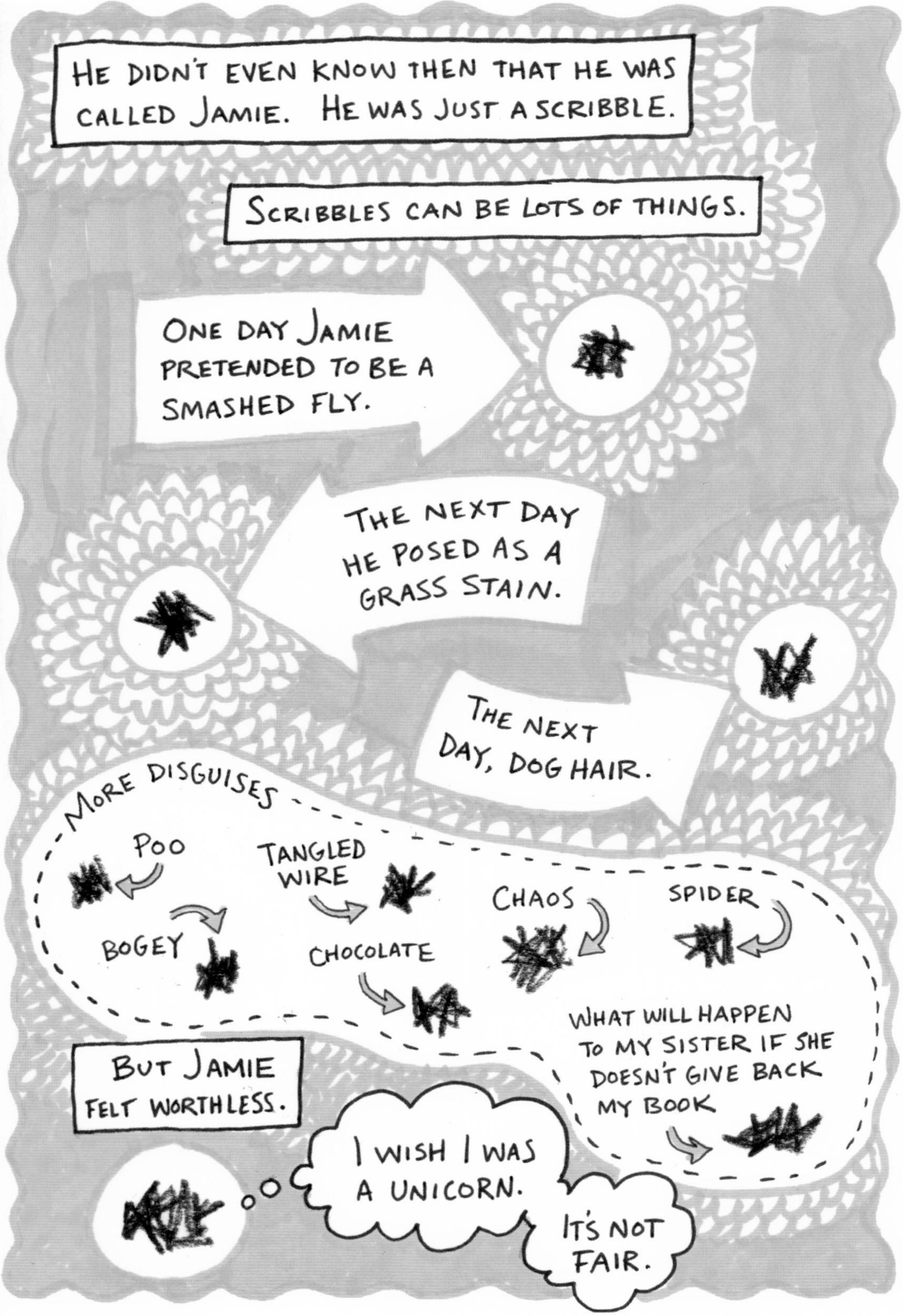
HE DIDN'T EVEN KNOW THEN THAT HE WAS CALLED JAMIE. HE WAS JUST A SCRIBBLE.
SCRIBBLES CAN BE LOTS OF THINGS.
ONE DAY JAMIE PRETENDED TO BE A SMASHED FLY.
THE NEXT DAY HE POSED AS A GRASS STAIN.
THE NEXT DAY, DOG HAIR.
MORE DISGUISES
POO
TANGLED WIRE
CHAOS
SPIDER
BOGEY
CHOCOLATE
WHAT WILL HAPPEN TO MY SISTER IF SHE DOESN'T GIVE BACK MY BOOK
BUT JAMIE FELT WORTHLESS.
I WISH I WAS A UNICORN.
IT'S NOT FAIR.

JAMIE LET
OUT A ROAR

IT'S NOT FAIR THAT I AM JUST A SCRIBBLE!!

HEY, LOOK! JAMIE HAS TEETH! BIG TEETH!

WELL, LOOK AT THAT.
I AM MORE THAN A SCRIBBLE.

I AM A SCRIBBLE WITH TEETH!

BUT NO ONE WANTS TO PLAY
WITH A SCRIBBLE WITH TEETH. JAMIE LOOKED SCARY.

JAMIE WAS LONELY, AND CRIED.

... BUT A SCRIBBLE NEEDS EYES TO CRY,
AND THREE EYES POPPED OUT FROM
SOMEWHERE INSIDE HIM.

HE WAS SO EXCITED
THAT HE RAN AROUND

ON HIS POP LEGS!

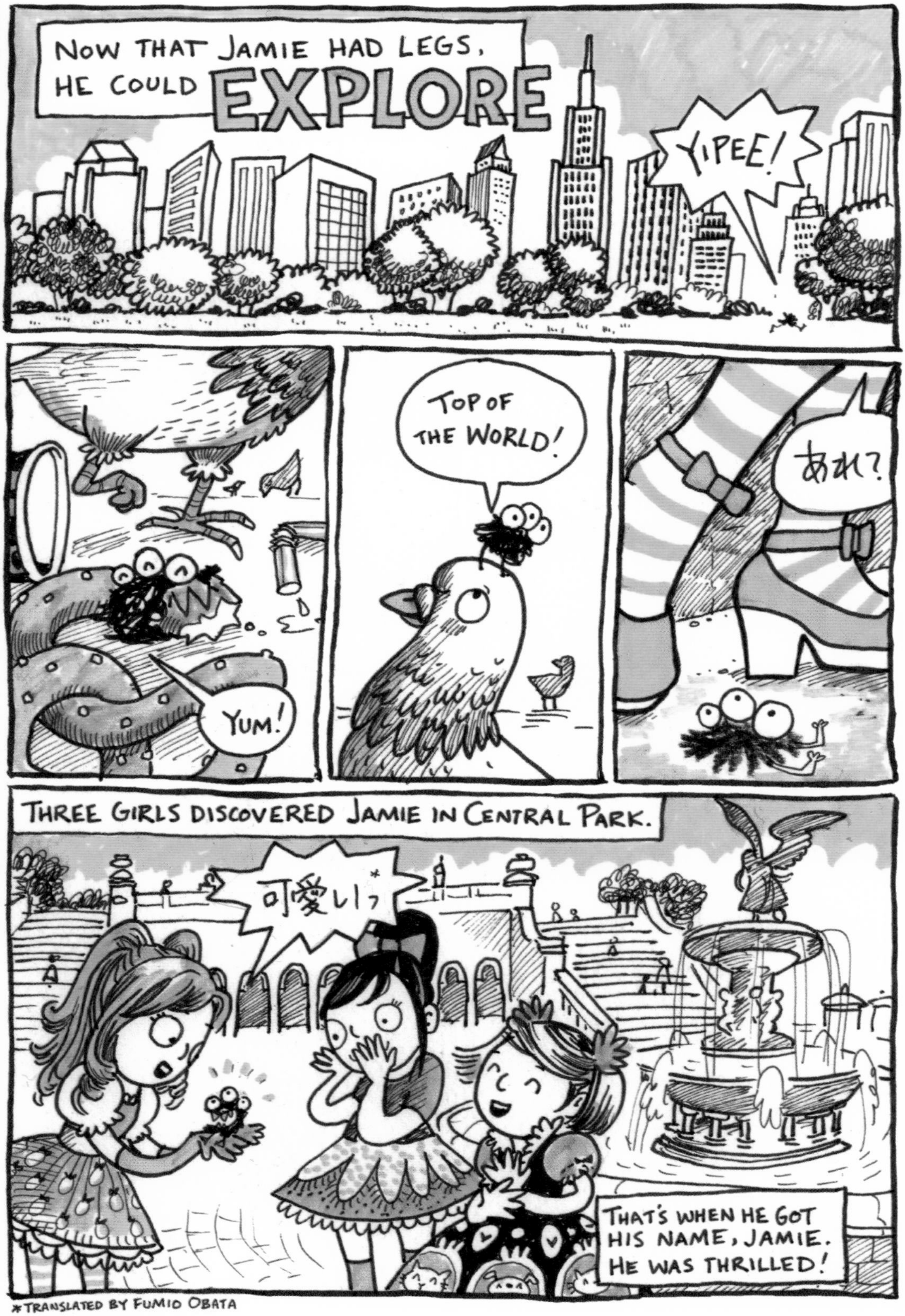

NOW THAT JAMIE HAD LEGS, HE COULD EXPLORE
YIPEE!
YUM!
TOP OF THE WORLD!
あれ?
THREE GIRLS DISCOVERED JAMIE IN CENTRAL PARK.
可愛いっ*
THAT'S WHEN HE GOT HIS NAME, JAMIE. HE WAS THRILLED!
*TRANSLATED BY FUMIO OBATA

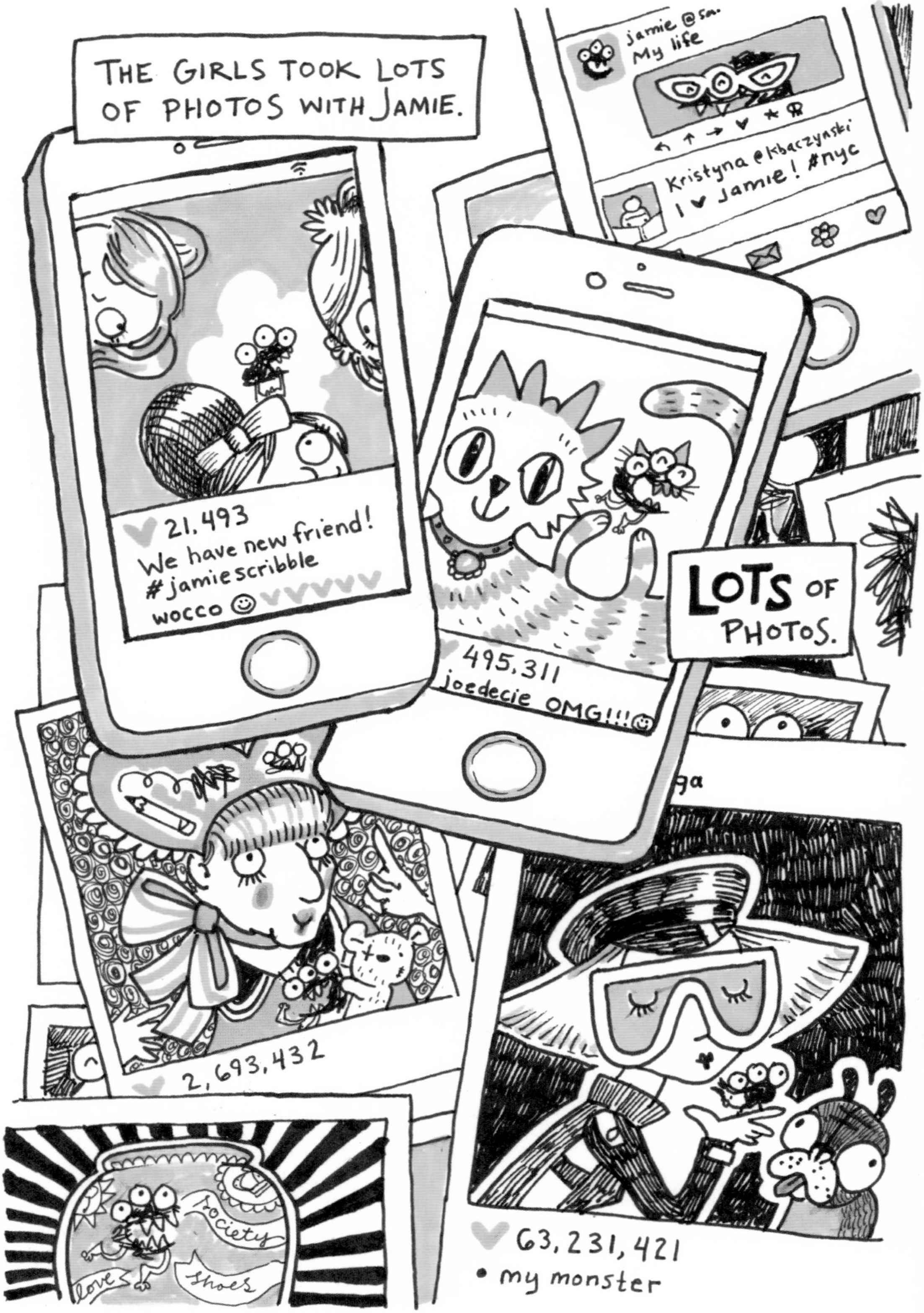
THE GIRLS TOOK LOTS OF PHOTOS WITH JAMIE.
jamie @sa.
My life
Kristyna @kbaczynski
I ♥ Jamie! #nyc
21,493
We have new friend!
#jamiescribble
wocco
495,311
joedecie OMG!!!
LOTS OF PHOTOS.
2,693,432
society
love
shoes
63,231,421
• my monster

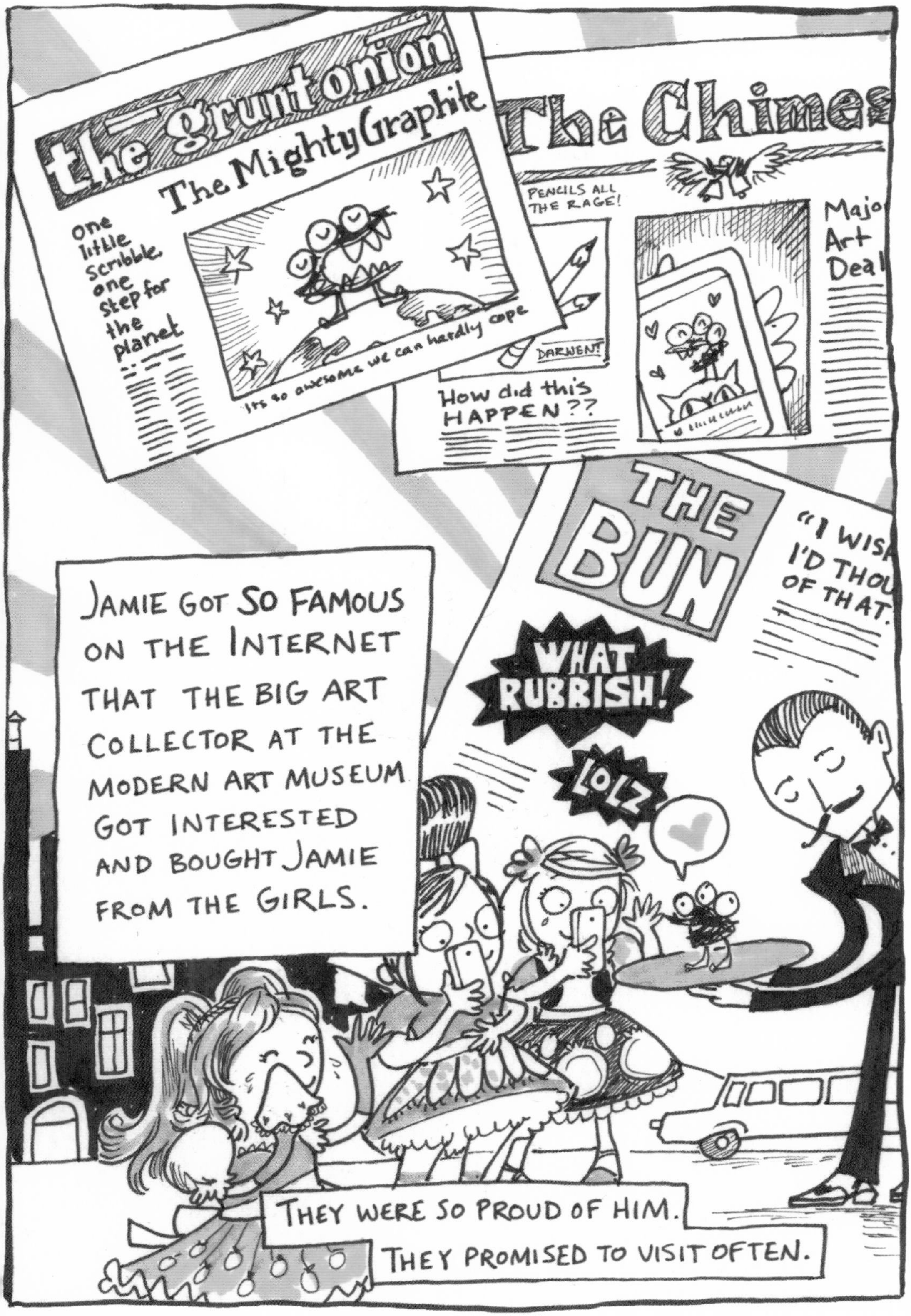

the grunt onion
The Mighty Graphite
one little scribble, one step for the planet
It's so awesome we can hardly cope
The Chimes
PENCILS ALL THE RAGE!
DARWENT
How did this HAPPEN??
Major Art Deal
THE BUN
"I WISH I'D THOUGHT OF THAT."
WHAT RUBBISH!
LOLZ
JAMIE GOT SO FAMOUS ON THE INTERNET THAT THE BIG ART COLLECTOR AT THE MODERN ART MUSEUM GOT INTERESTED AND BOUGHT JAMIE FROM THE GIRLS.
THEY WERE SO PROUD OF HIM.
THEY PROMISED TO VISIT OFTEN.

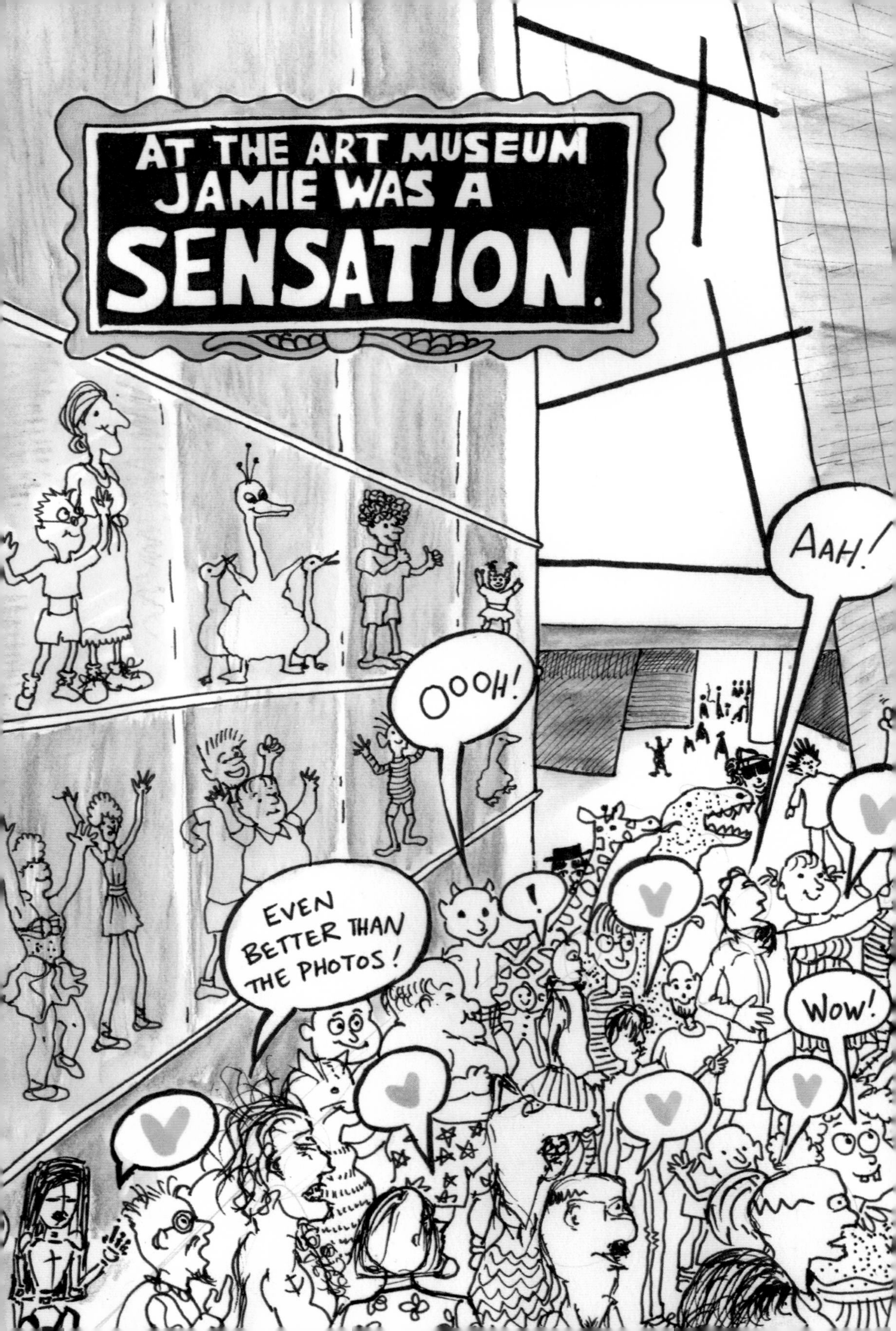
AT THE ART MUSEUM JAMIE WAS A SENSATION.
AAH!
OOOH!
EVEN BETTER THAN THE PHOTOS!
!
WOW!

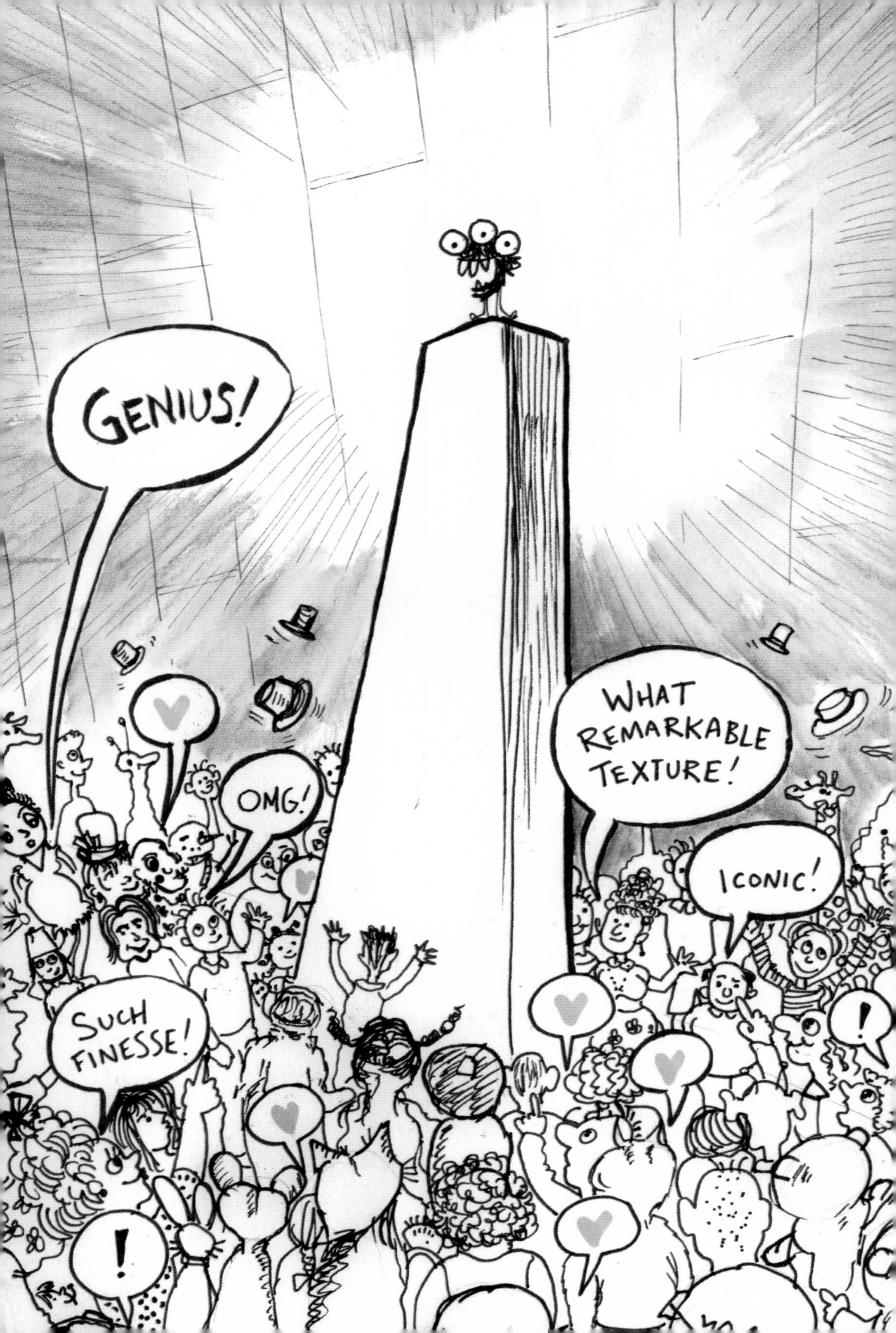
GENIUS!
OMG!
WHAT REMARKABLE TEXTURE!
ICONIC!
SUCH FINESSE!
!
!

JAMIE BECAME **LEGEND.** EVERY HOUSE IN THE COUNTRY HAD A MUG OR A MOUSE PAD OR A CUSHION WITH JAMIE'S PICTURE ON IT.

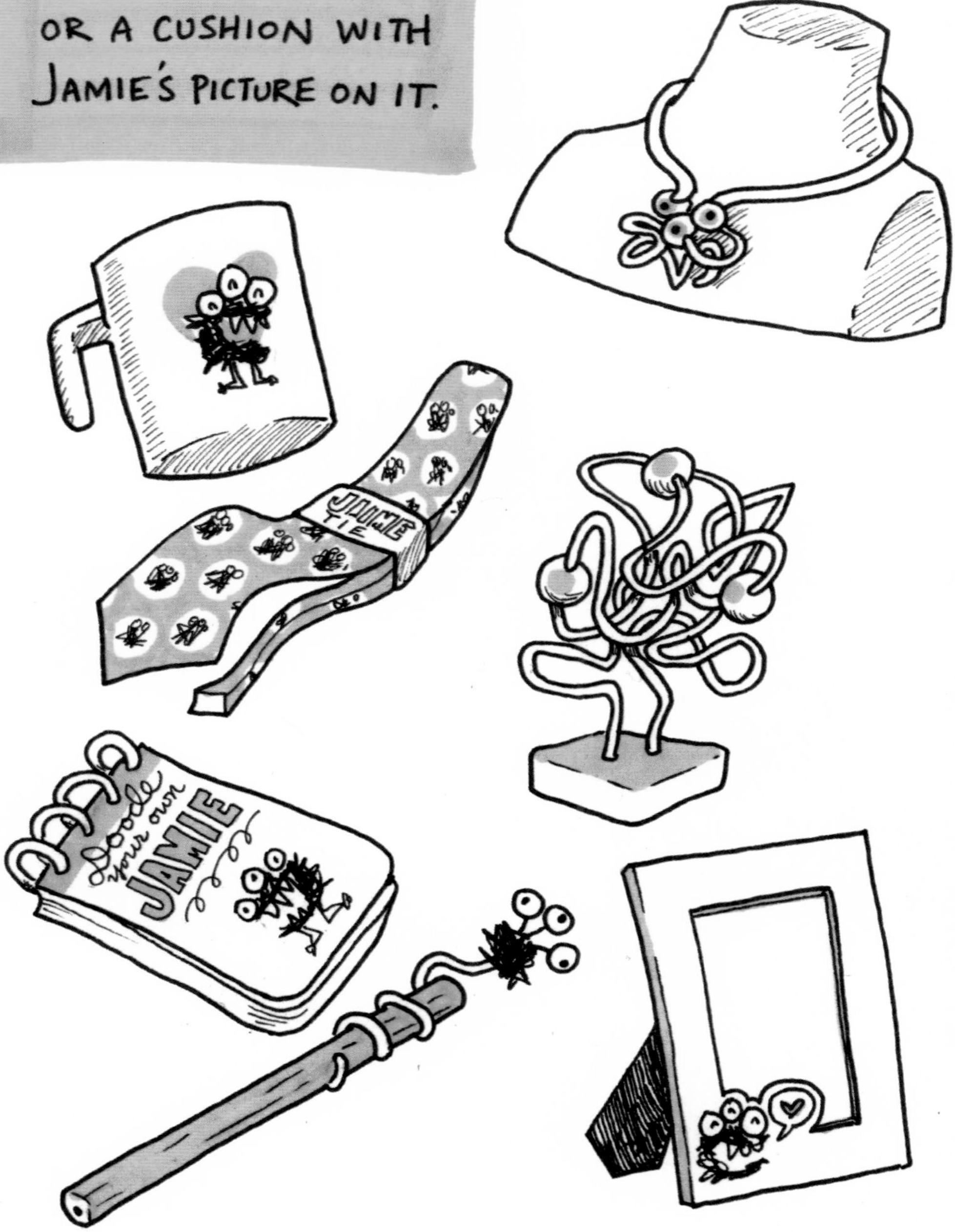
JAMIE
TIE
Doodle your own
JAMIE

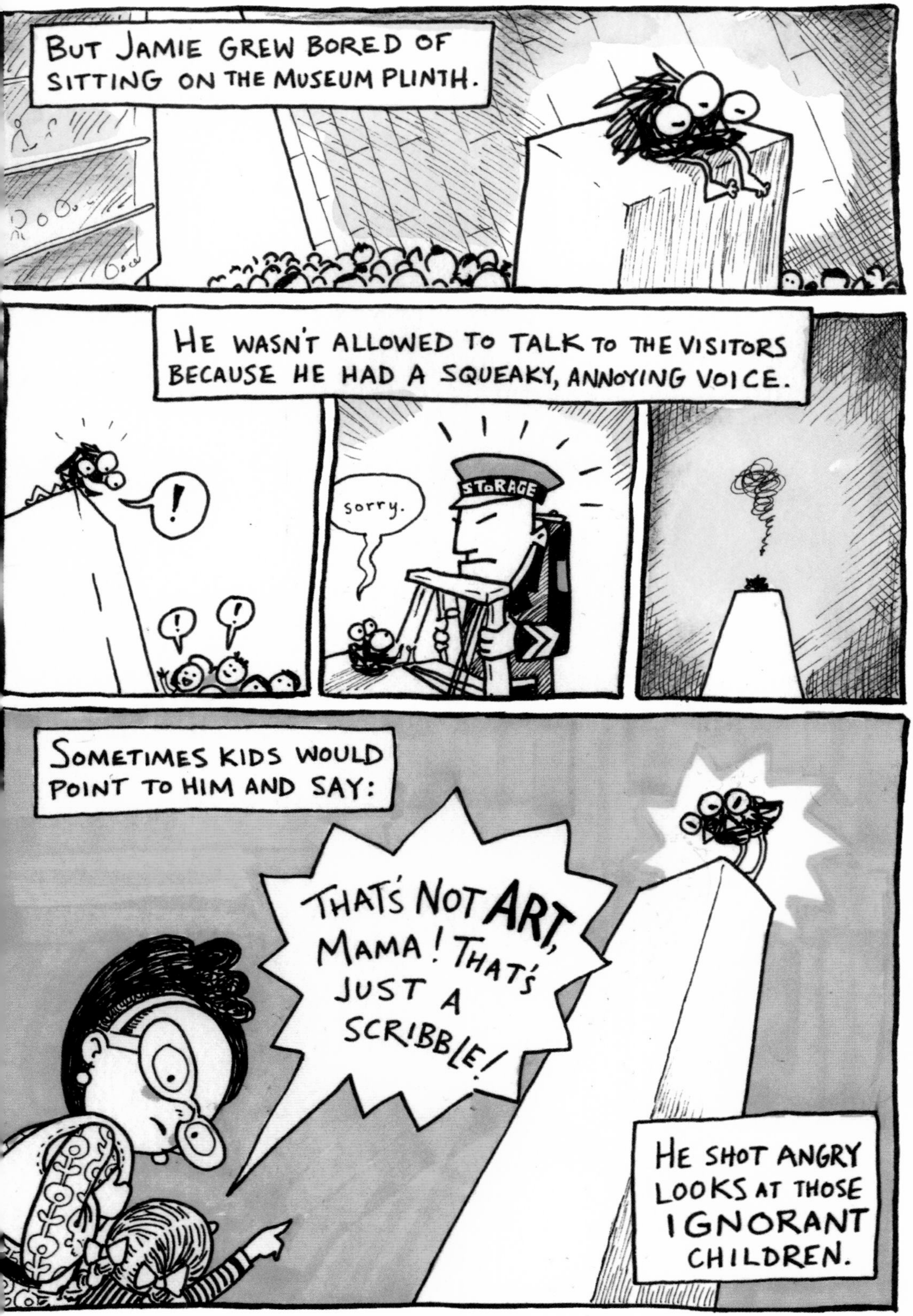
BUT JAMIE GREW BORED OF SITTING ON THE MUSEUM PLINTH.
HE WASN'T ALLOWED TO TALK TO THE VISITORS BECAUSE HE HAD A SQUEAKY, ANNOYING VOICE.
!
!
!
sorry.
STORAGE
SOMETIMES KIDS WOULD POINT TO HIM AND SAY:
THAT'S NOT ART, MAMA! THAT'S JUST A SCRIBBLE!
HE SHOT ANGRY LOOKS AT THOSE IGNORANT CHILDREN.

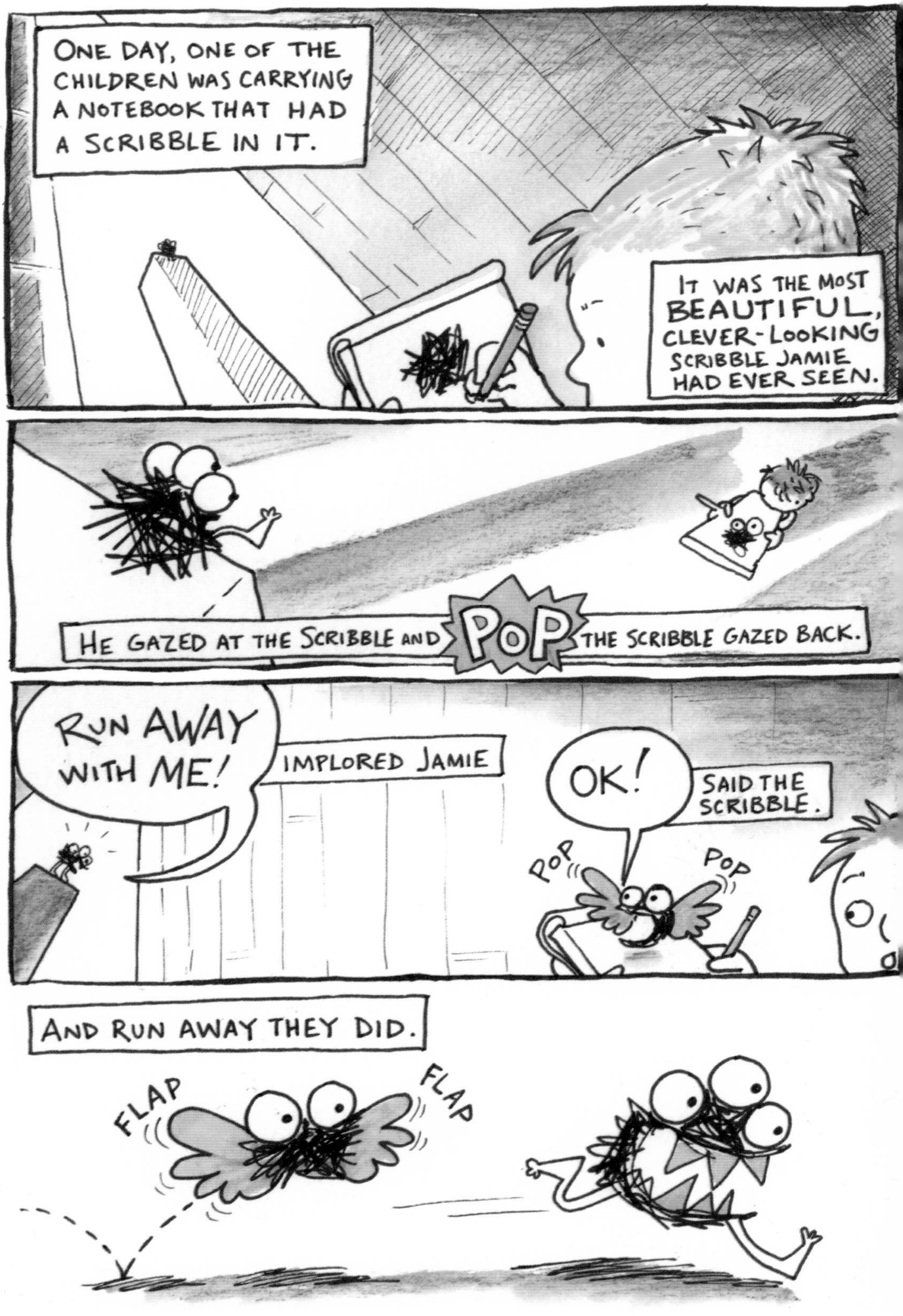
ONE DAY, ONE OF THE CHILDREN WAS CARRYING A NOTEBOOK THAT HAD A SCRIBBLE IN IT.
IT WAS THE MOST BEAUTIFUL, CLEVER-LOOKING SCRIBBLE JAMIE HAD EVER SEEN.
HE GAZED AT THE SCRIBBLE AND
POP
THE SCRIBBLE GAZED BACK.
RUN AWAY WITH ME!
IMPLORED JAMIE
OK!
SAID THE SCRIBBLE.
POP
POP
AND RUN AWAY THEY DID.
FLAP
FLAP

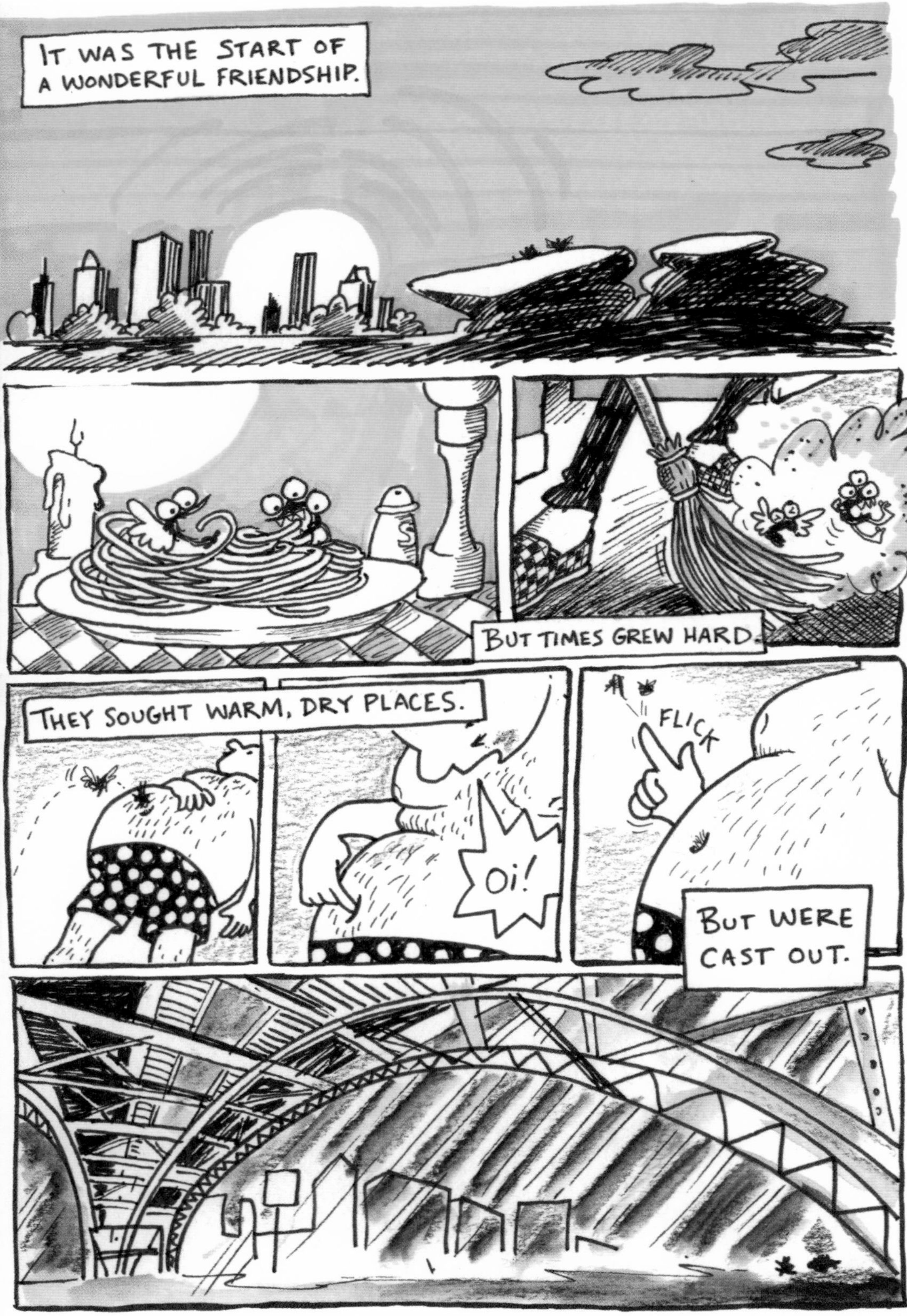
IT WAS THE START OF A WONDERFUL FRIENDSHIP.
BUT TIMES GREW HARD.
THEY SOUGHT WARM, DRY PLACES.
Oi!
FLICK
BUT WERE CAST OUT.

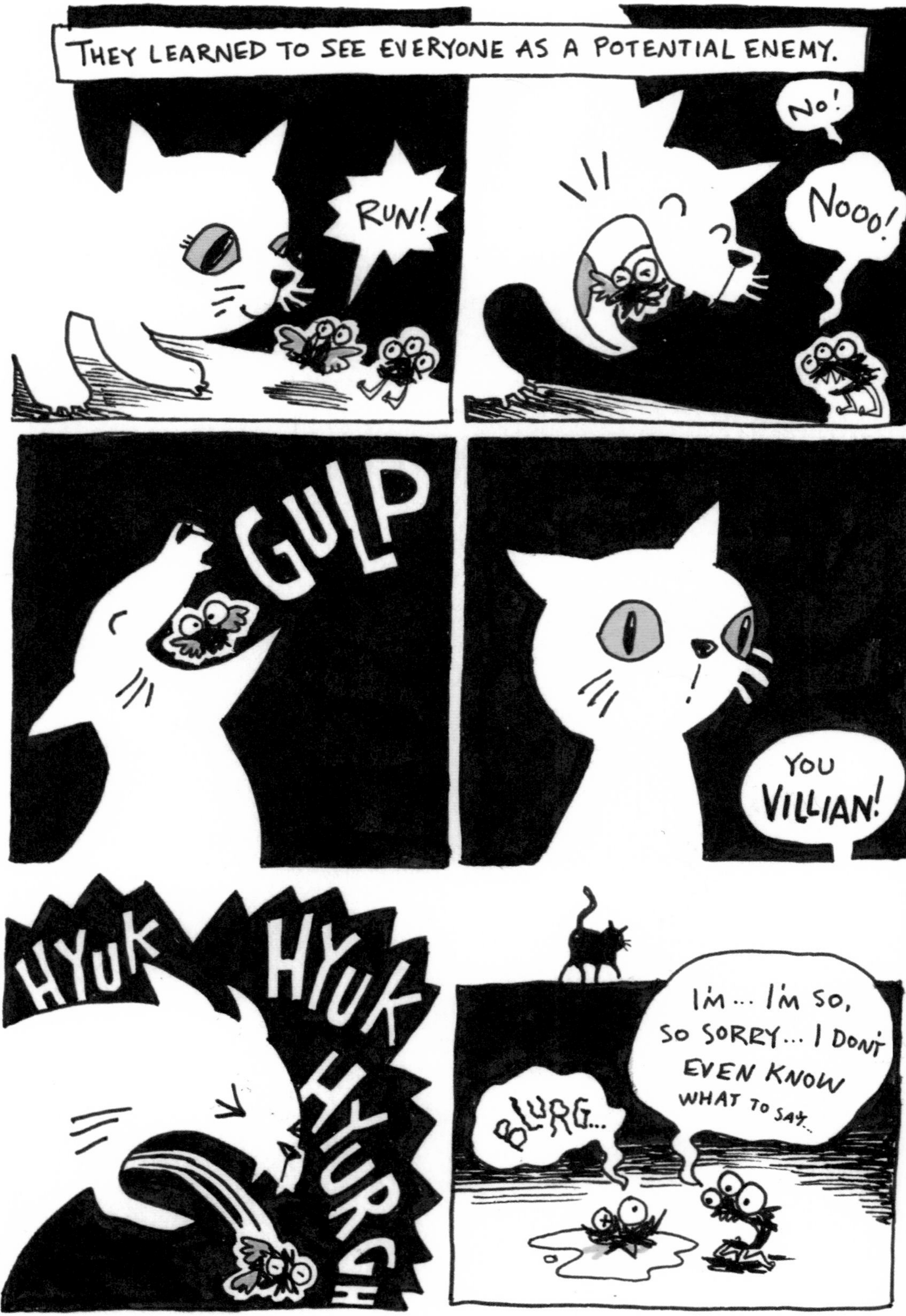
THEY LEARNED TO SEE EVERYONE AS A POTENTIAL ENEMY.
RUN!
No!
Nooo!
GULP
YOU VILLIAN!
HYUK
HYUK
HYURGH
BLURG...
I'M ... I'M SO, SO SORRY... I DON'T EVEN KNOW WHAT TO SAY...

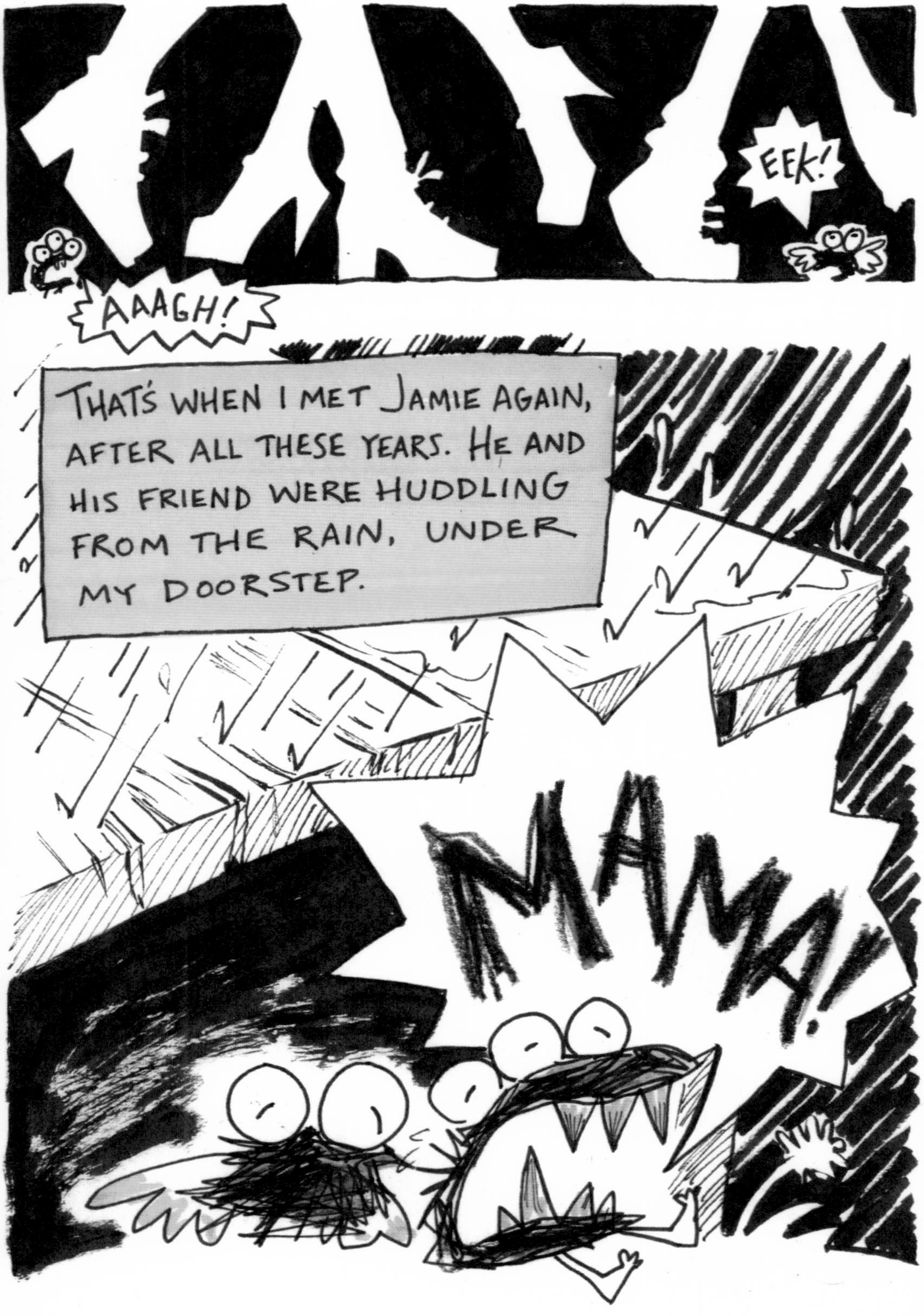
EEK!
AAAGH!
THAT'S WHEN I MET JAMIE AGAIN, AFTER ALL THESE YEARS. HE AND HIS FRIEND WERE HUDDLING FROM THE RAIN, UNDER MY DOORSTEP.
MAMA!

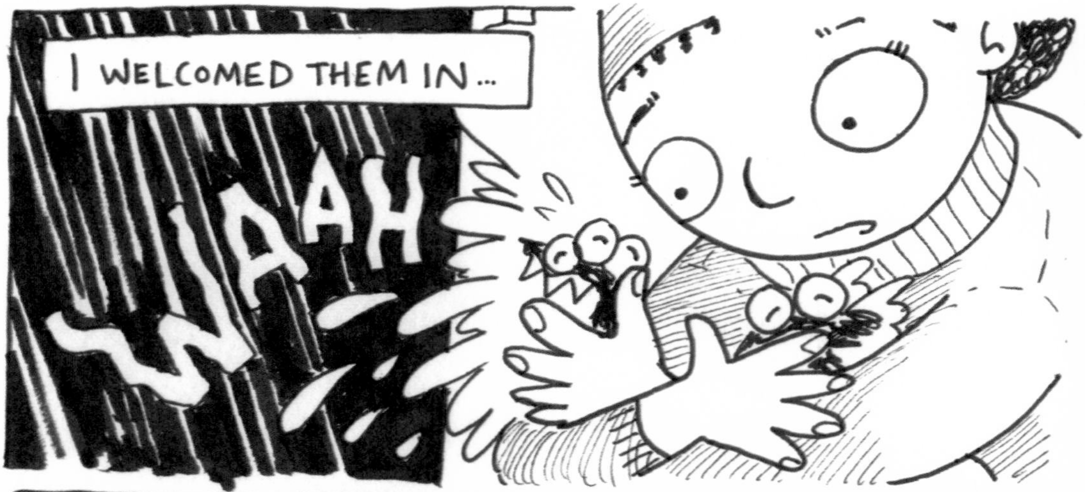
I WELCOMED THEM IN...
WAAH

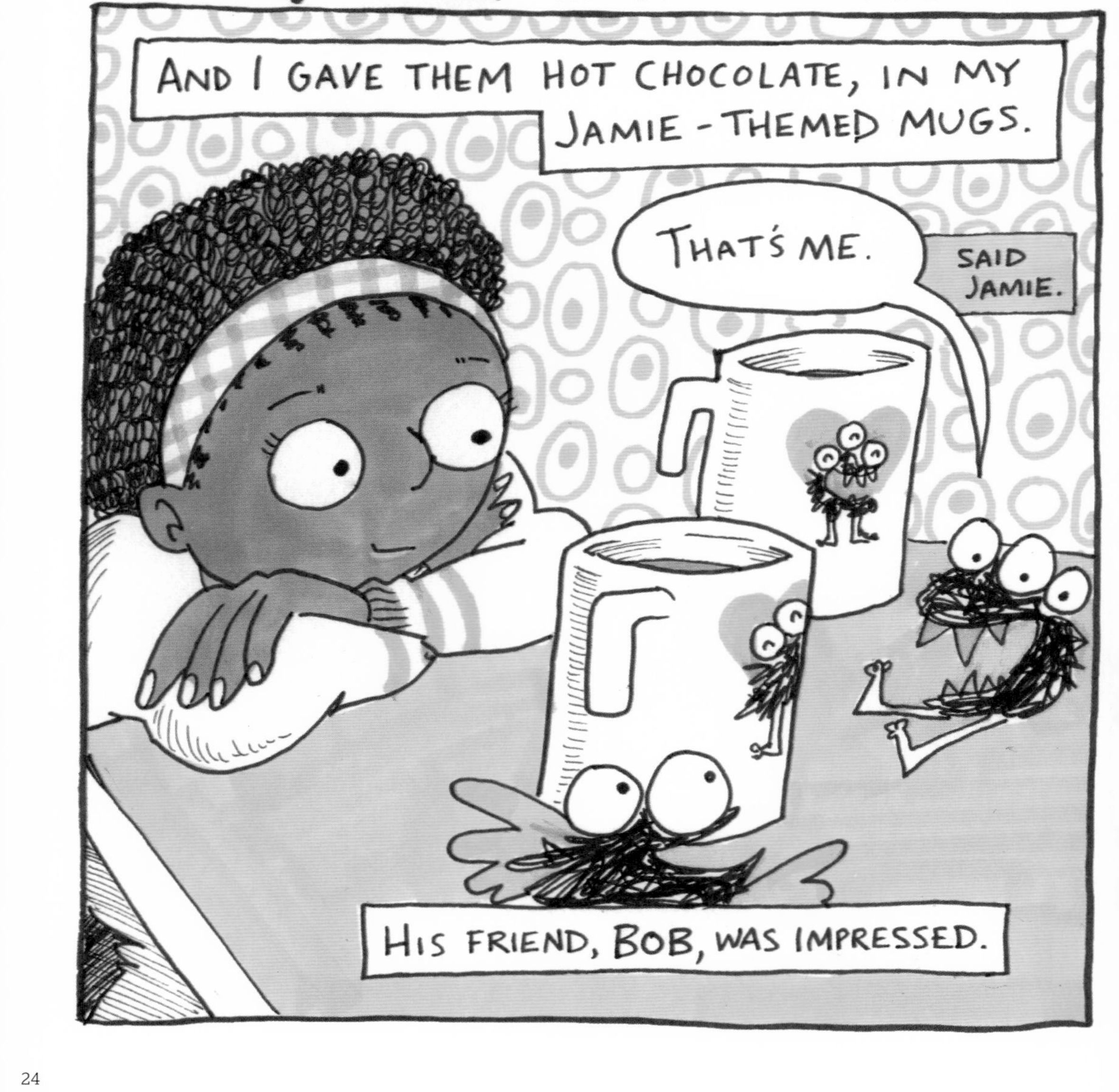
AND I GAVE THEM HOT CHOCOLATE, IN MY JAMIE-THEMED MUGS.
THAT'S ME.
SAID JAMIE.
HIS FRIEND, BOB, WAS IMPRESSED.

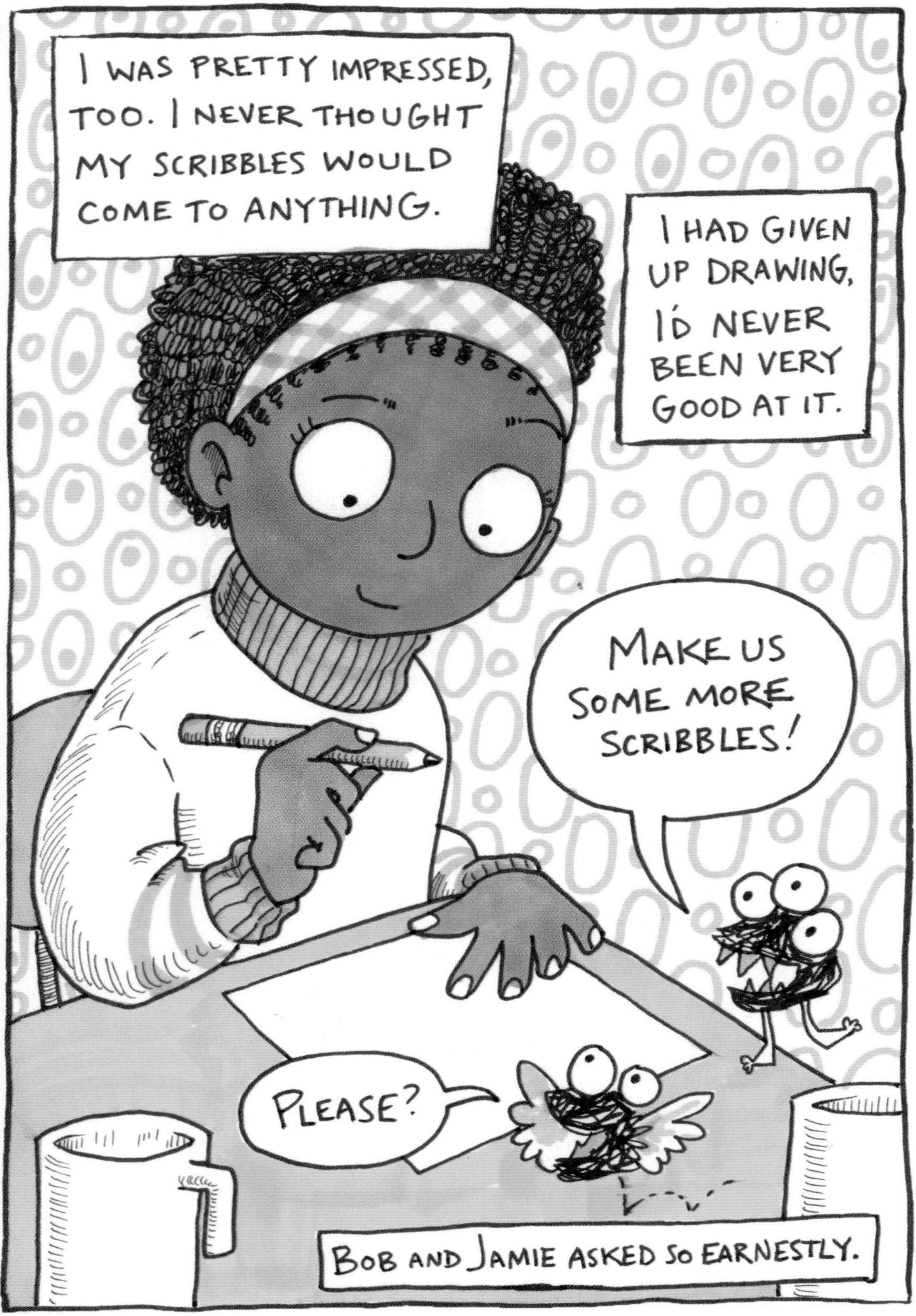
I WAS PRETTY IMPRESSED, TOO. I NEVER THOUGHT MY SCRIBBLES WOULD COME TO ANYTHING.
I HAD GIVEN UP DRAWING, I'D NEVER BEEN VERY GOOD AT IT.
MAKE US SOME MORE SCRIBBLES!
PLEASE?
BOB AND JAMIE ASKED SO EARNESTLY.

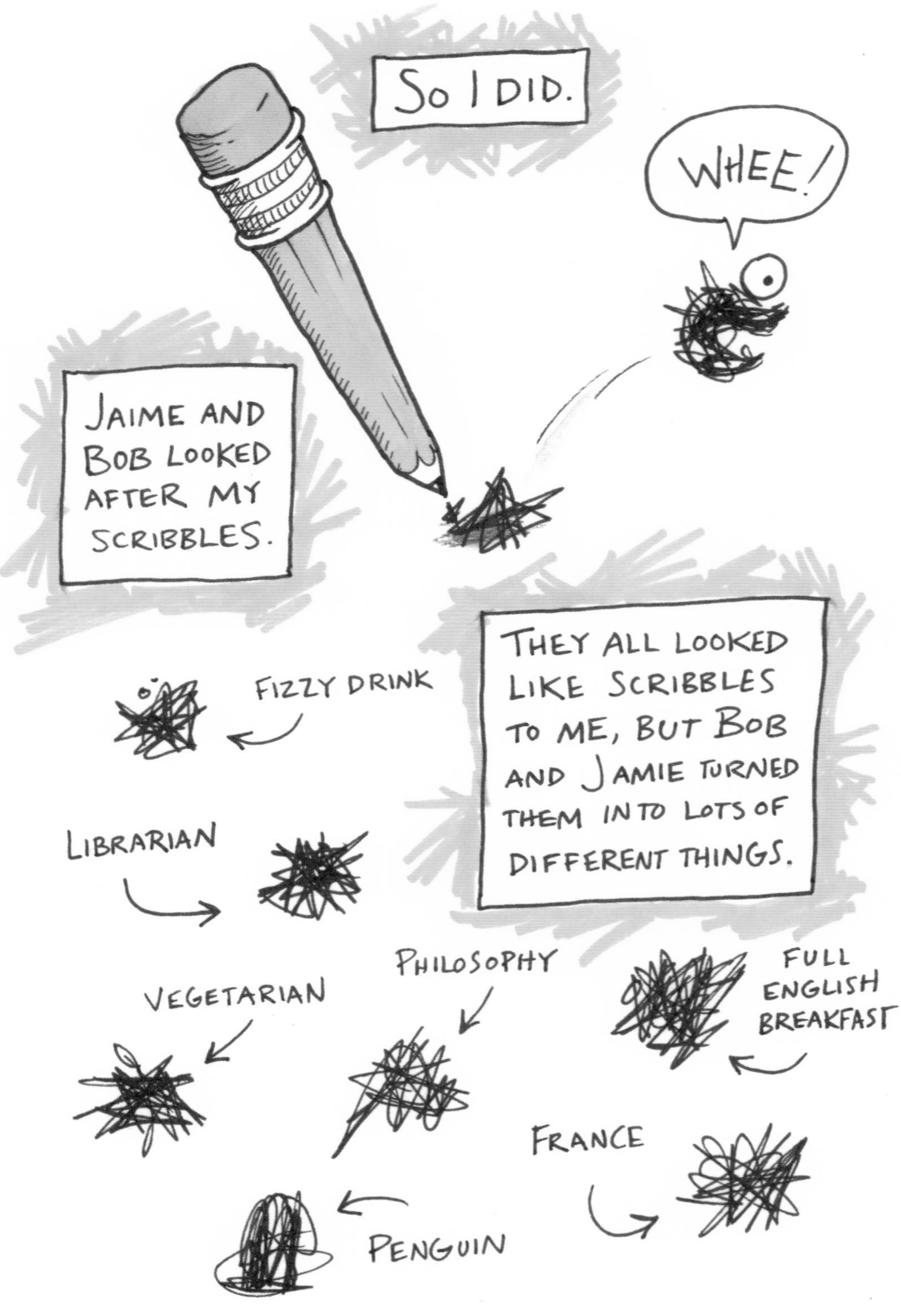

So I DID.
WHEE!
JAIME AND BOB LOOKED AFTER MY SCRIBBLES.
THEY ALL LOOKED LIKE SCRIBBLES TO ME, BUT BOB AND JAMIE TURNED THEM INTO LOTS OF DIFFERENT THINGS.
FIZZY DRINK
LIBRARIAN
PHILOSOPHY
FULL ENGLISH BREAKFAST
VEGETARIAN
FRANCE
PENGUIN

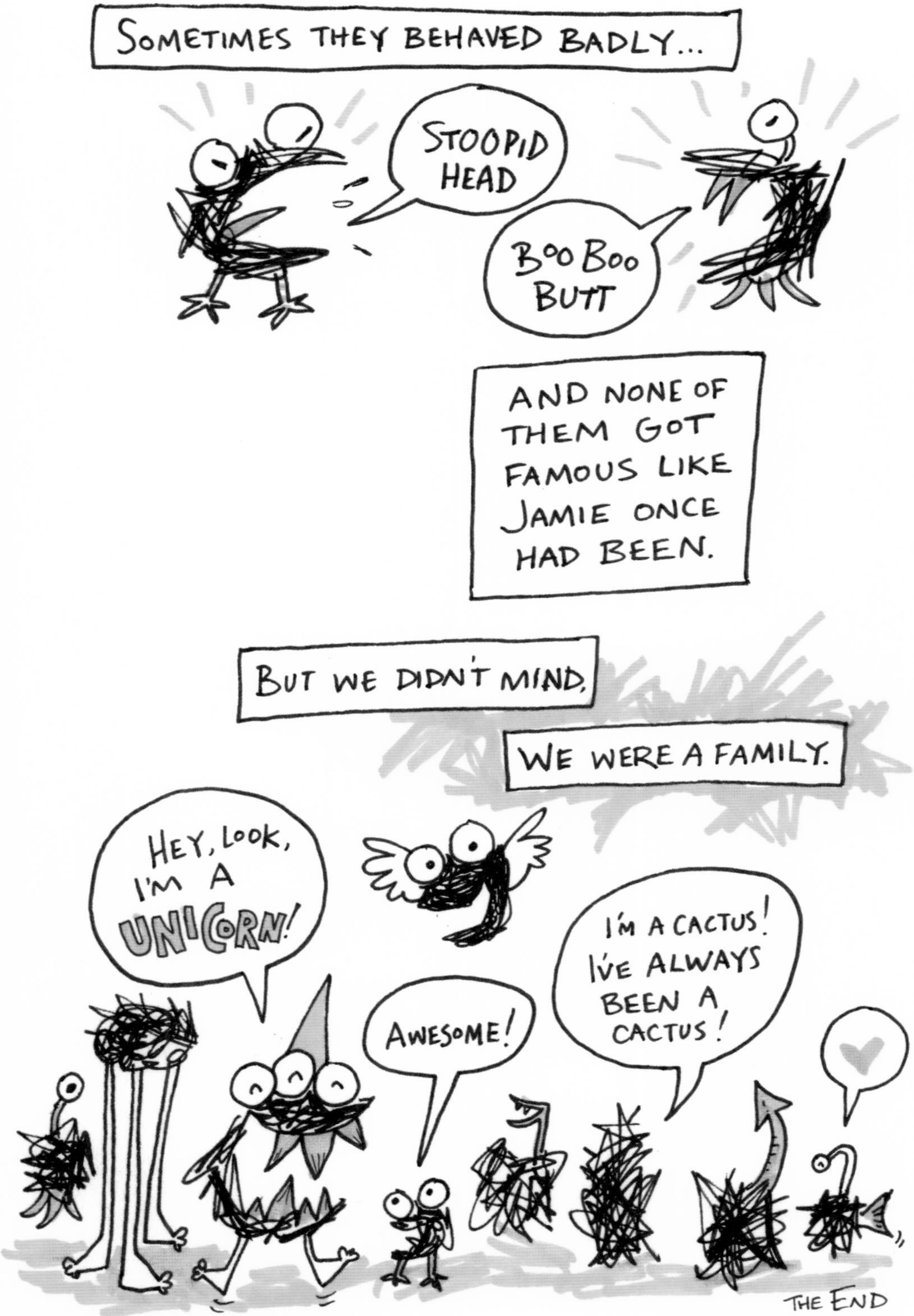
SOMETIMES THEY BEHAVED BADLY...
STOOPID HEAD
BOO BOO BUTT
AND NONE OF THEM GOT FAMOUS LIKE JAMIE ONCE HAD BEEN.
BUT WE DIDN'T MIND.
WE WERE A FAMILY.
HEY, LOOK, I'M A UNICORN!
AWESOME!
I'M A CACTUS! I'VE ALWAYS BEEN A CACTUS!
THE END

CREATE YOUR OWN SCRIBBLE FAMILY!

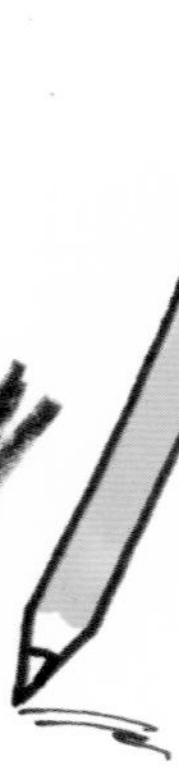

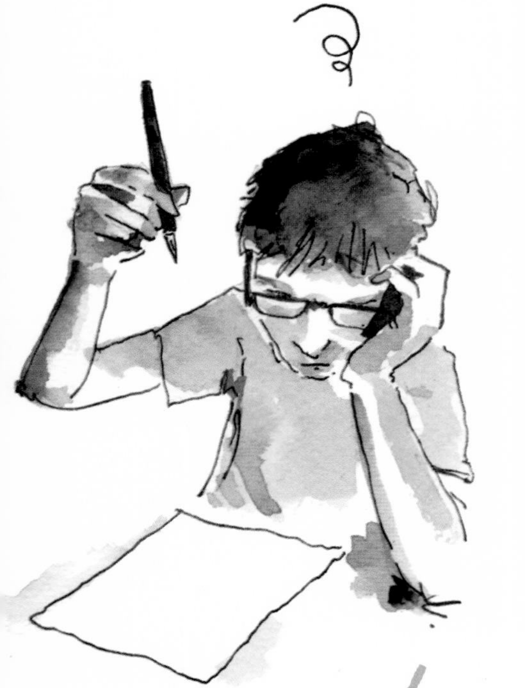

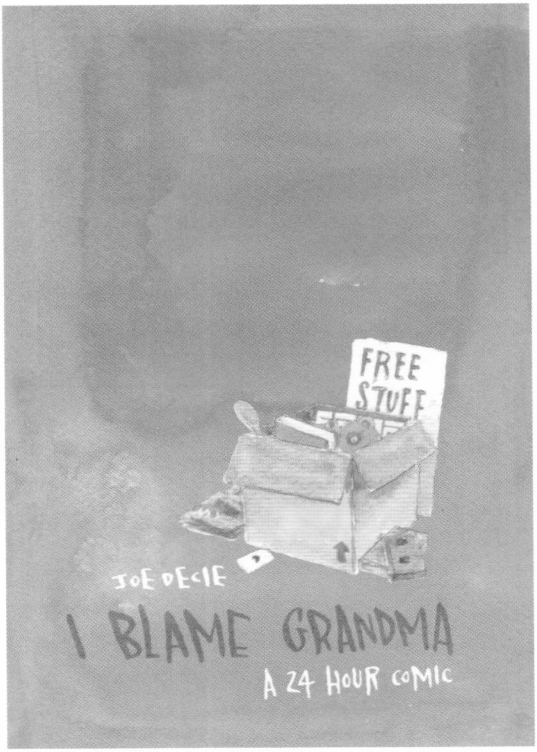
FREE STUFF
JOE DECIE
I BLAME GRANDMA
A 24 HOUR COMIC

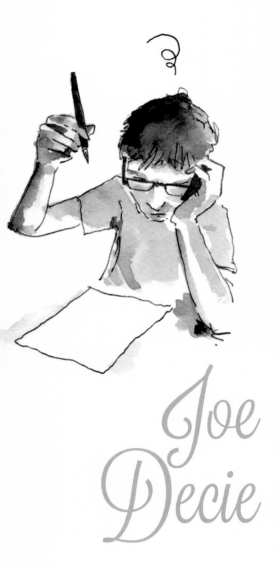

Joe Decie

Joe Decie has been drawing comics and sharing them on the internet since the 15th of January 2008. Both his books, *The Accidental Salad* and
The Listening Agent, were nominated for Best Comic at British Comic Awards.

As well as drawing, Joe teaches comics as communication for young adults with learning disabilities. His favourite curry is the humble tarka dhal.

JoeDecie.com
@joedecie

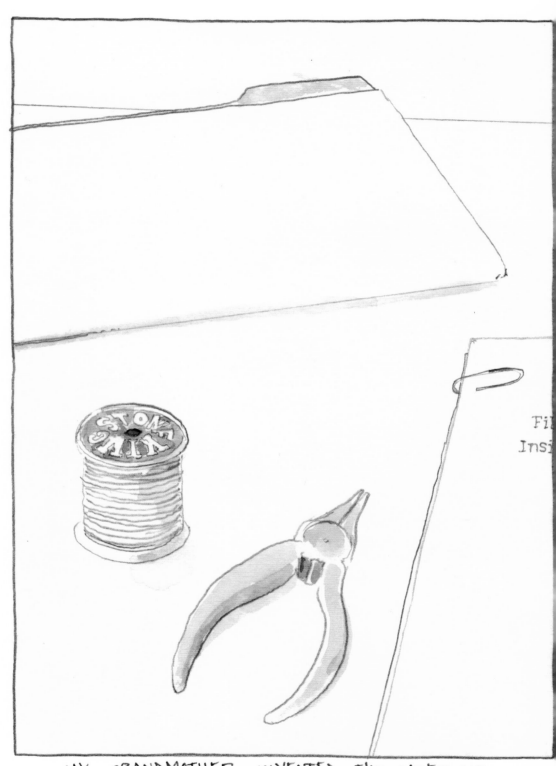

MY GRANDMOTHER INVENTED THE PAPERCLIP.

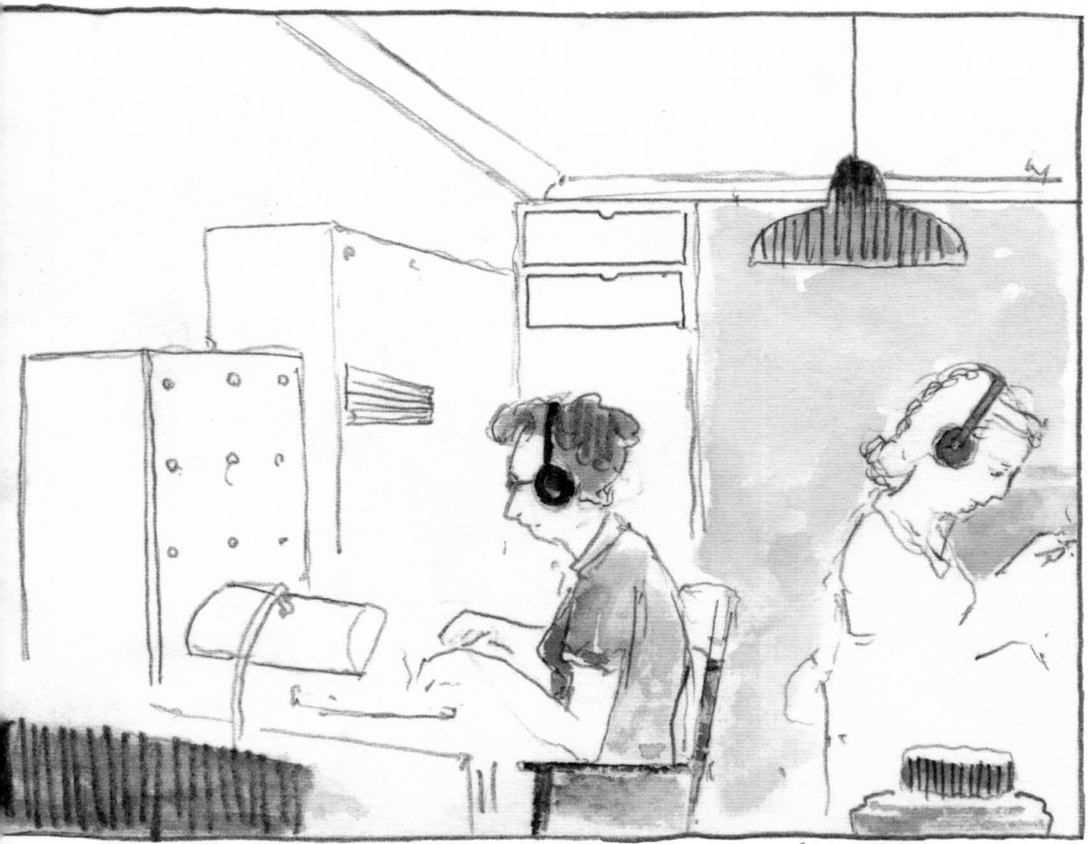

SHE WAS A CLERK IN SIR GERALD PATTEN'S WAR OFFICE
1940 I GUESS?

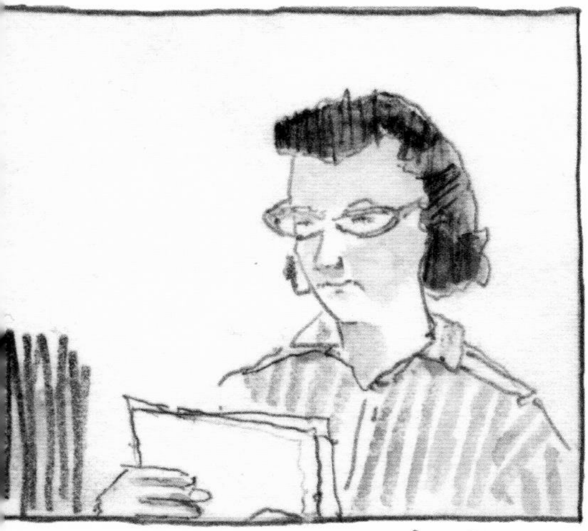

NEEDING TO ORGANISE
HER FILES QUICKER...

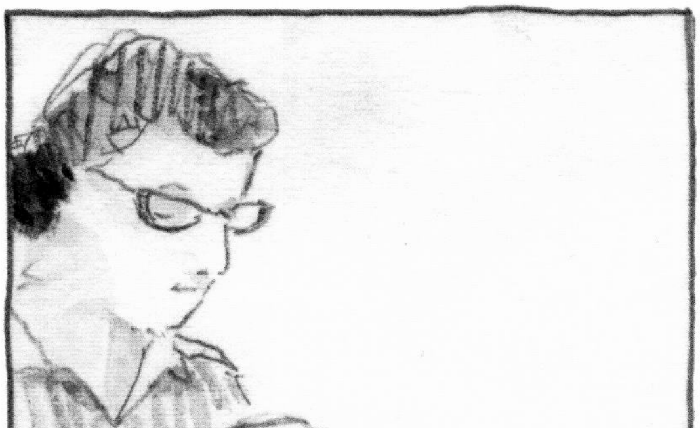

SHE FASHIONED THE CLIP
FROM FUSE WIRE PRETTY
STRAIGHT FORWARD

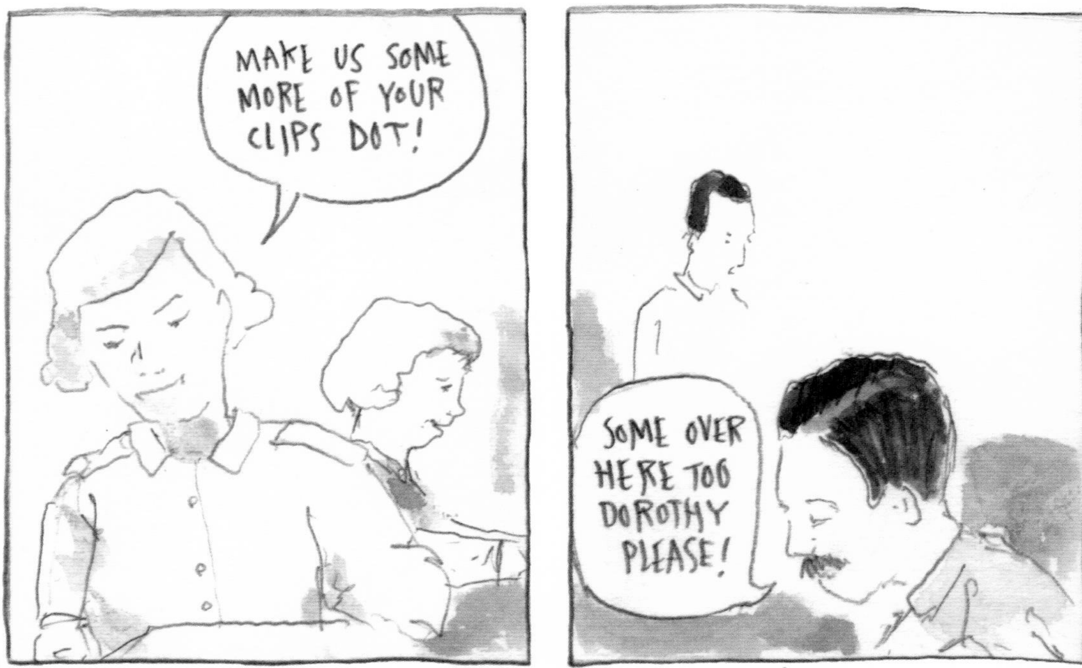
MAKE US SOME MORE OF YOUR CLIPS DOT!
SOME OVER HERE TOO DOROTHY PLEASE!

THE INVENTION (KNOWN THEN AS DOROTHY CLIPS!) QUICKLY CAUGHT ON...

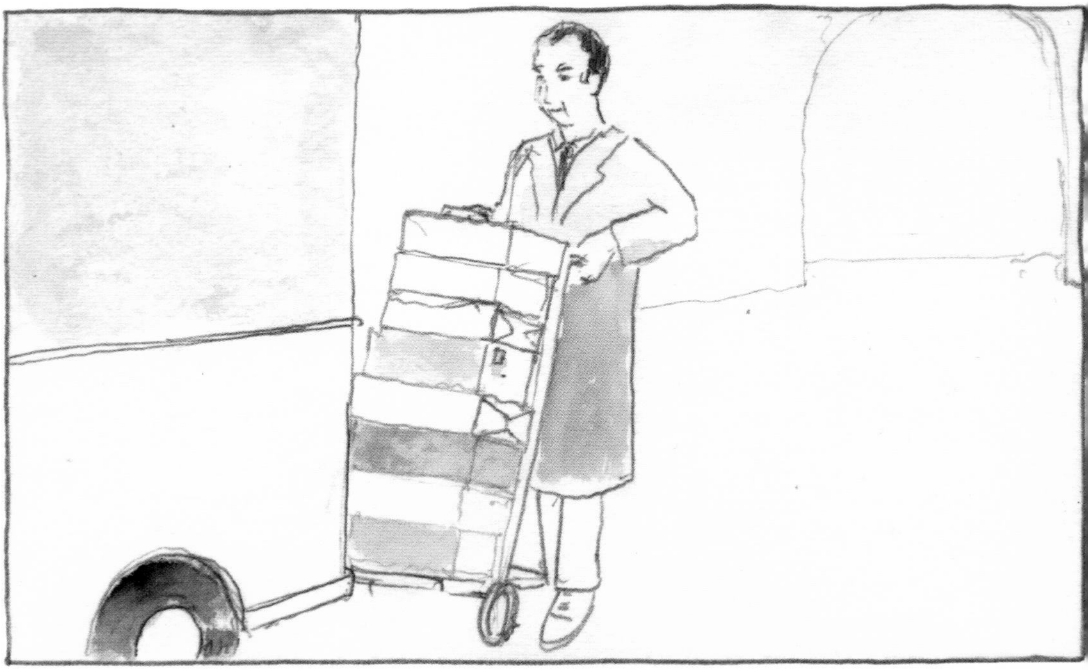

AND SHE WAS ENLISTED TO PRODUCE THEM FOR ALL AREAS OF GOVERNMENT

SHE WAS GIVEN HER OWN OFFICE IN THE REAPPROPRIATED MALVERN ROAD TUBE STATION. SHE TALKED TO ME A FEW TIMES ABOUT THAT BUILDING

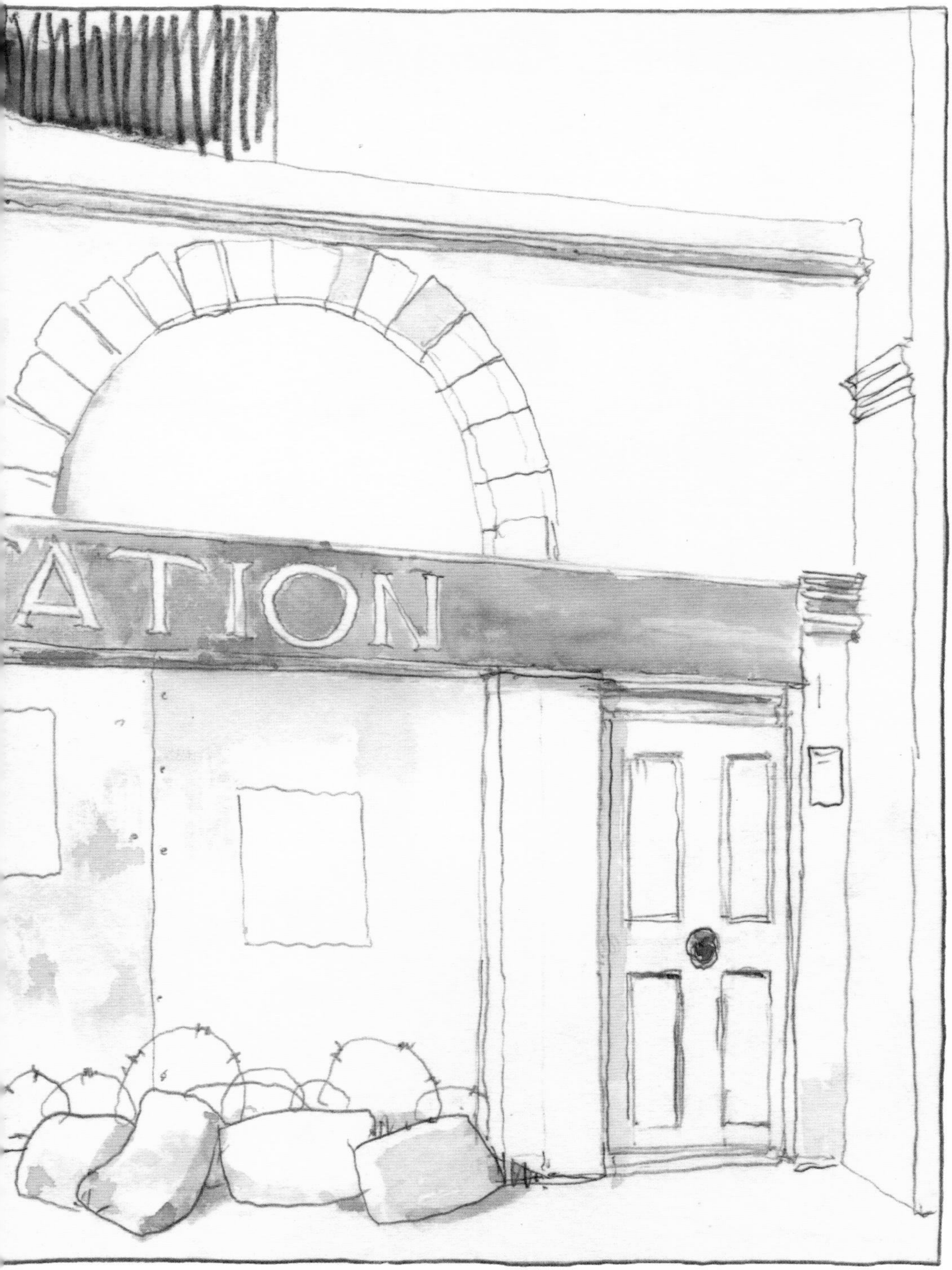
ATION

APPARENTLY IT WAS MOSTLY USED FOR ANTI AIRCRAFT OPERATIONS, BUT GRAN HAD HER OWN BIT, SEPARATE WITH IT'S OWN LIFT!

FROM HER ROOMS SHE HAD DIRECT ACCESS TO THE STATION.

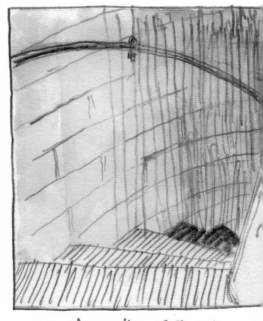

SHE SAID SHE USED TO EAT HER SANDWICHES DOWN THERE. IN THE DAR

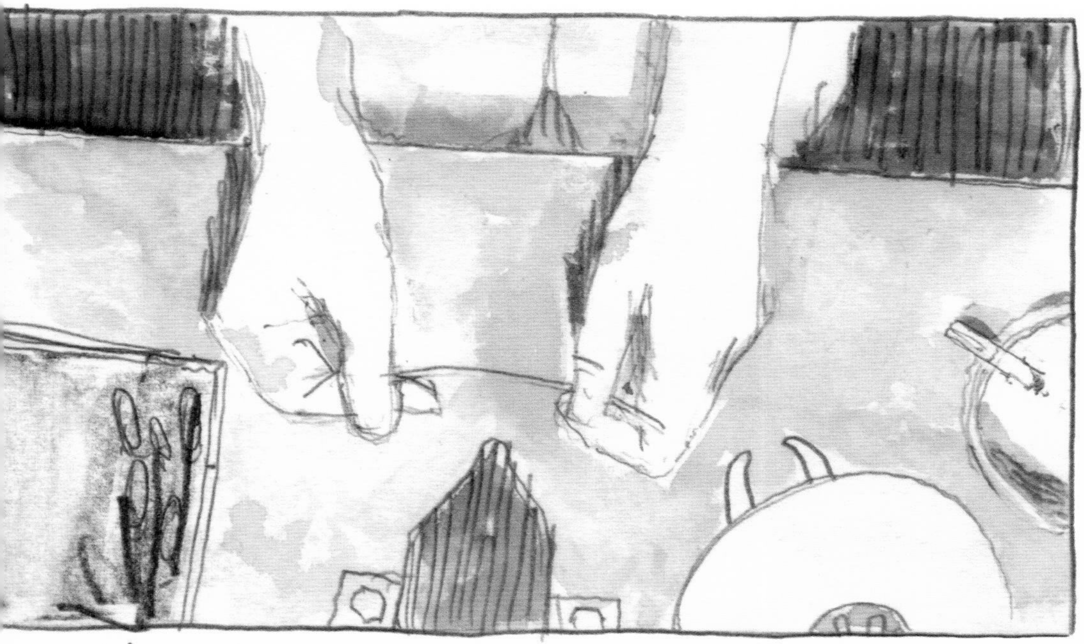

THAT YEAR, SHE ALONE MADE TWO HUNDRED THOUSAND CLIPS.

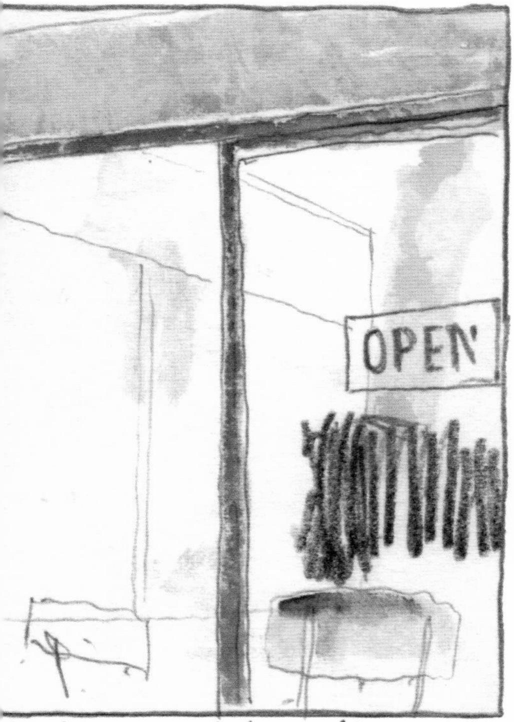
OPEN

YOU KNOW THAT THAI RESTAURANT JUST DOWN THE ROAD?

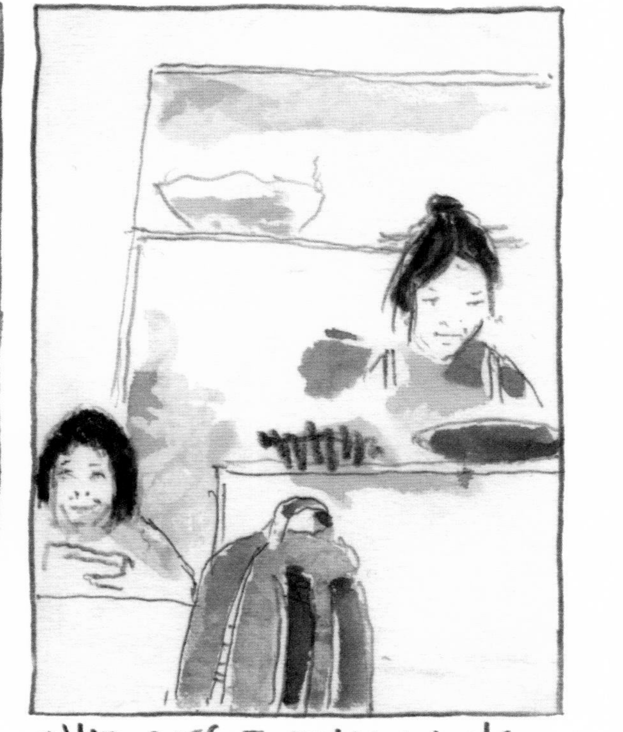

THAT DOESNT REALLY LOOK LIKE A RESTAURANT?

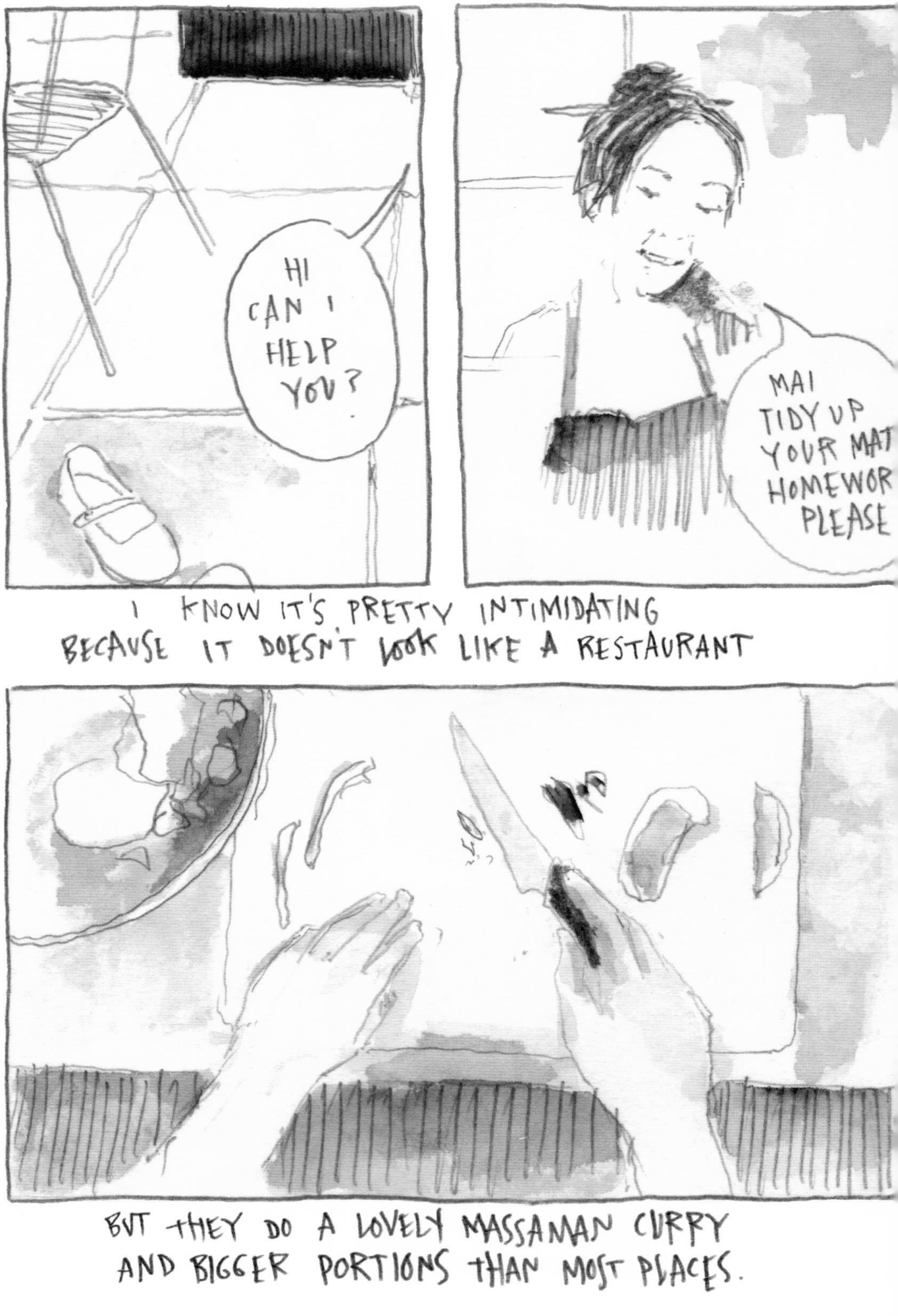
HI CAN I HELP YOU?
MAI TIDY UP YOUR MAT HOMEWOR PLEASE
I KNOW IT'S PRETTY INTIMIDATING BECAUSE IT DOESN'T LOOK LIKE A RESTAURANT
BUT THEY DO A LOVELY MASSAMAN CURRY AND BIGGER PORTIONS THAN MOST PLACES.

WHAT WAS I TALKING ABOUT? OH YEAH GRAN'S PAPERCLIPS. SO ANYWAY...

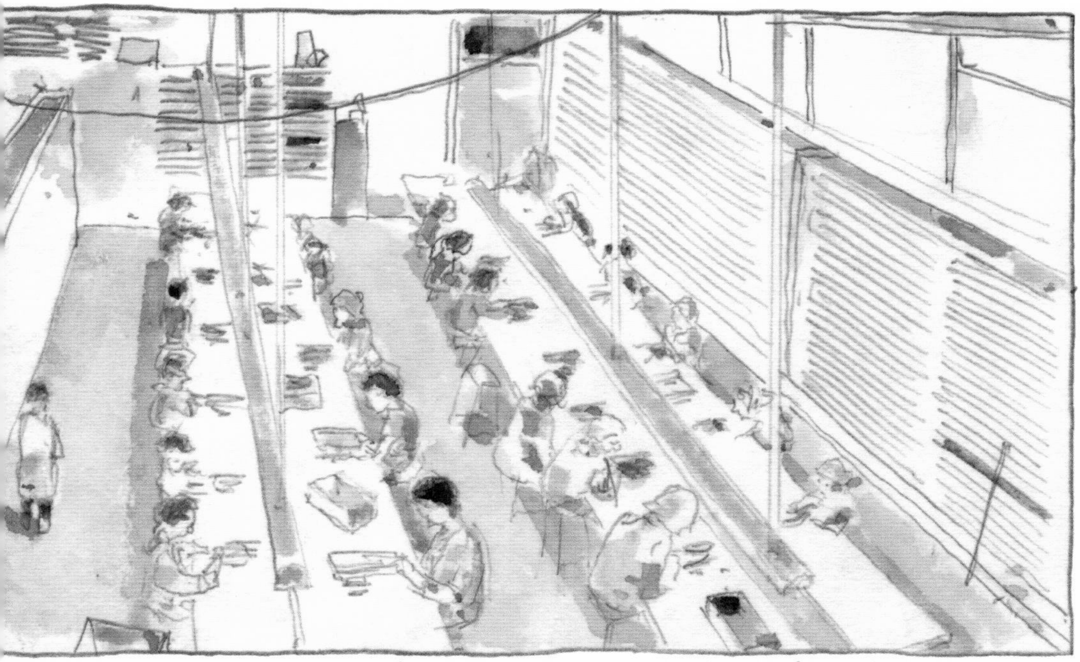

DEMAND GREW TOO HIGH FOR GRANNY AND PRODUCTION WAS EVENTUALLY MOVED TO THREE FACTORIES. TWO IN SHEFFIELD AND ONE IN SUNDERLAND.

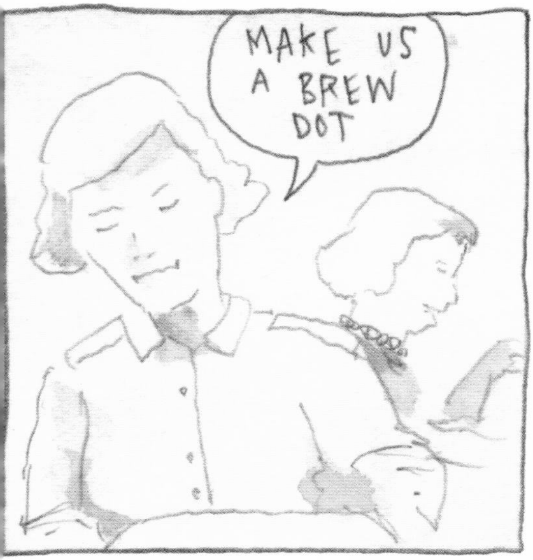
MAKE US A BREW DOT

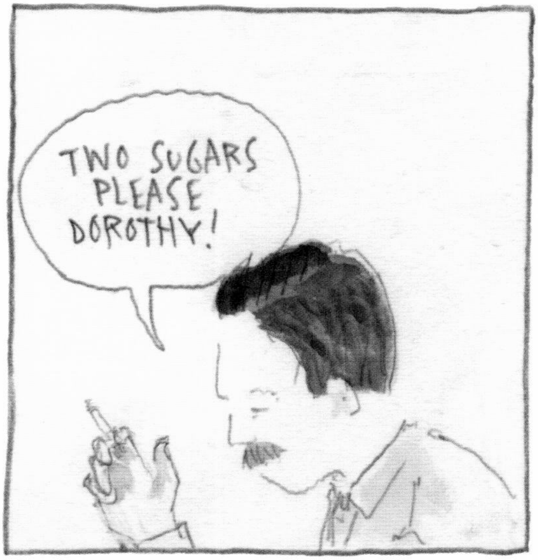
TWO SUGARS PLEASE DOROTHY!

AND MY GRAN WENT BACK TO HER FILING JOB

AFTER THE WAR SHE WAS AWARDED THE ST HUBBINS CROSS MEDAL FOR "INNOVATION IN BUREAUCRATIC ADVANCEMENT AND DEDICATION TO KING AND COUNTRY"

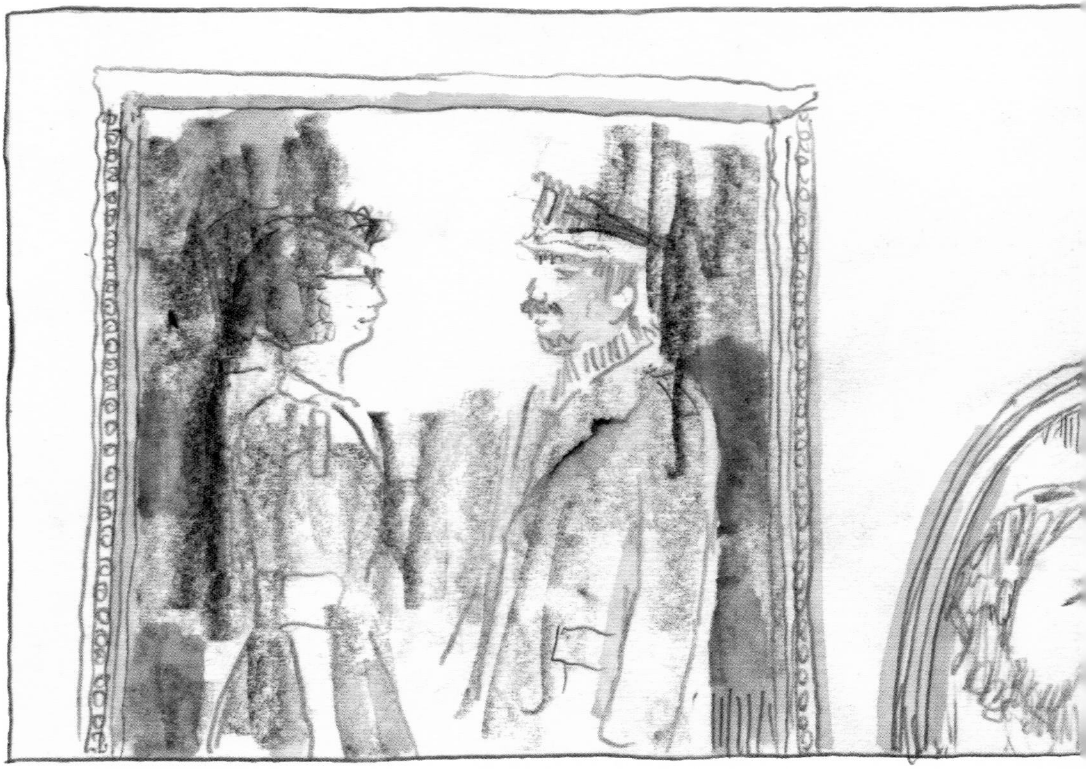

SHE KEPT IT IN A BOOT POLISH TIN...

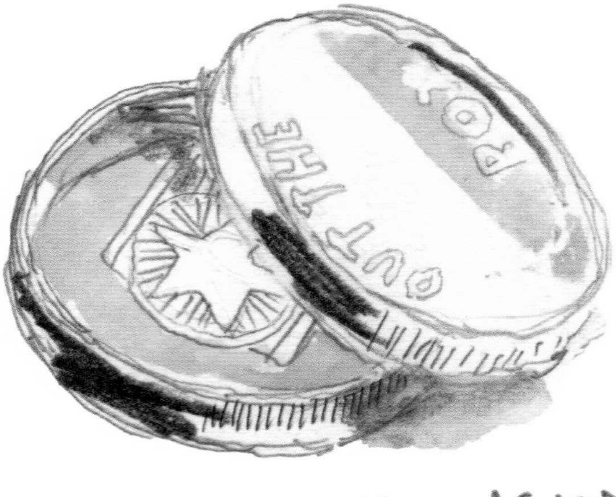

...UNDER HER MATTRESS.

SHE LET US PLAY WITH IT AS KIDS.

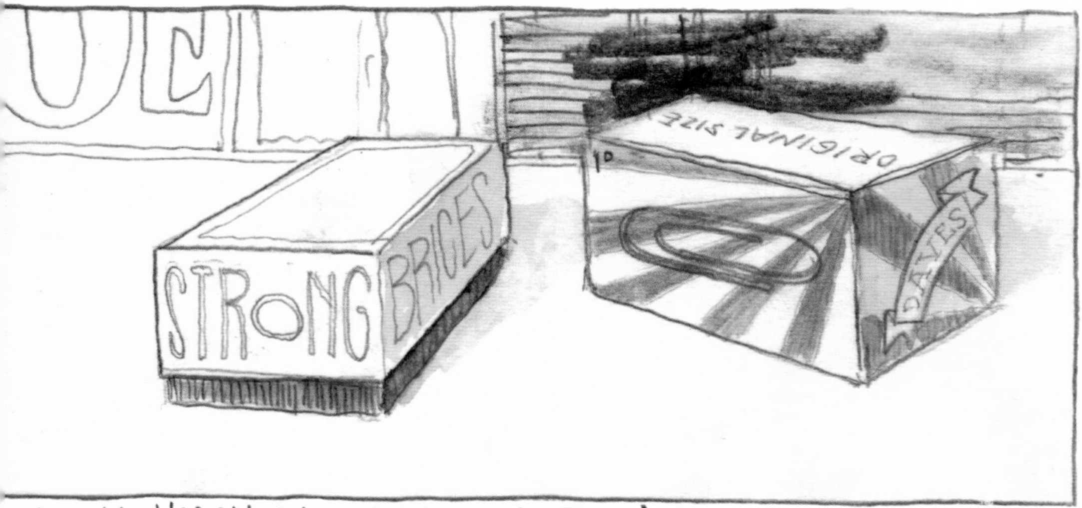
STRONG
BRICES
ORIGINAL SIZE

SO ALTHOUGH PATENTED IN HER NAME, DUE TO THE WAR, SHE DIDN'T MAKE A PENNY FROM THE INVENTION.

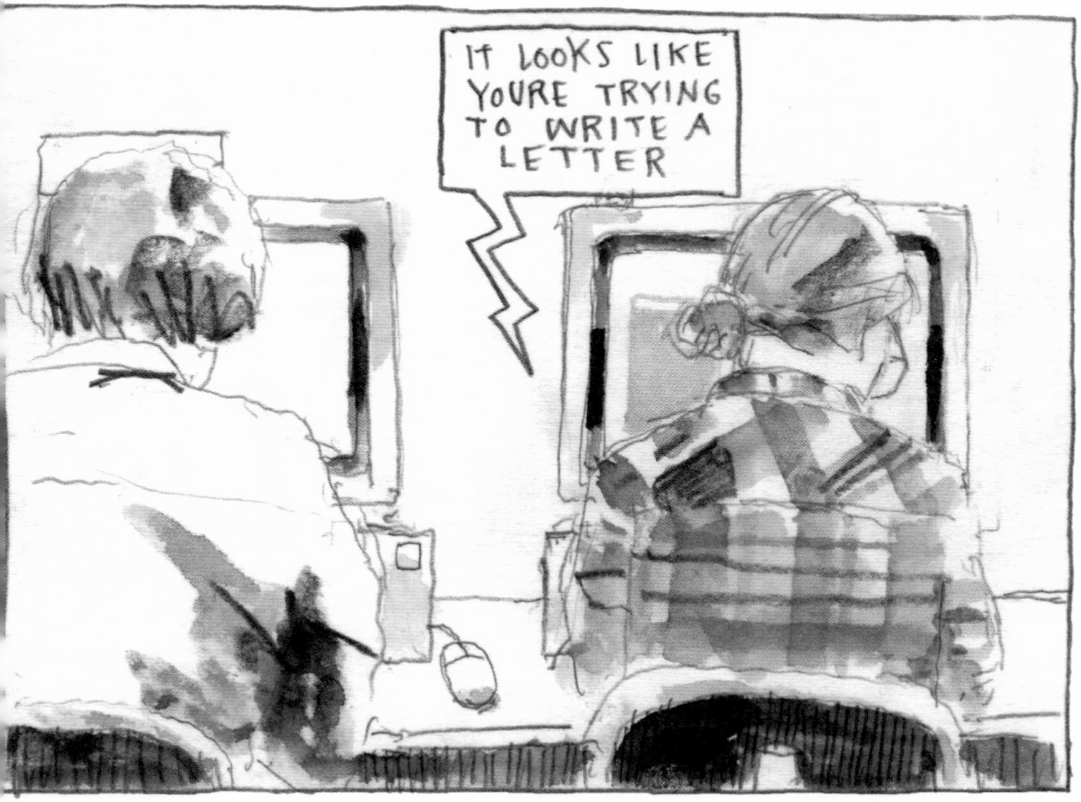
IT LOOKS LIKE YOURE TRYING TO WRITE A LETTER

HOWEVER, FAST FORWARD TO 1992 AND A POPULAR SOFTWARE COMPANY STARTED USING A PAPERCLIP DESIGN AS THEIR "FRIENDLY LOGO"

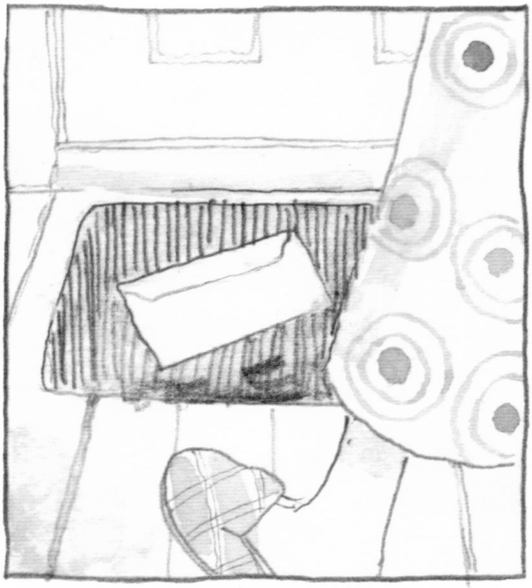

AND MY GRAN WOULD GET A SMALL ROYALTY ON EVERY COPY SOLD.

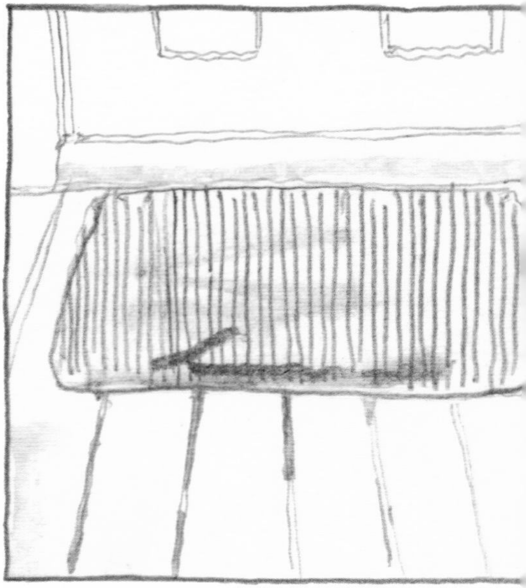

THEY MUST HAVE SOLD QUITE A LOT. AS WITHIN A YEAR, SHE HAD A MILLION POU

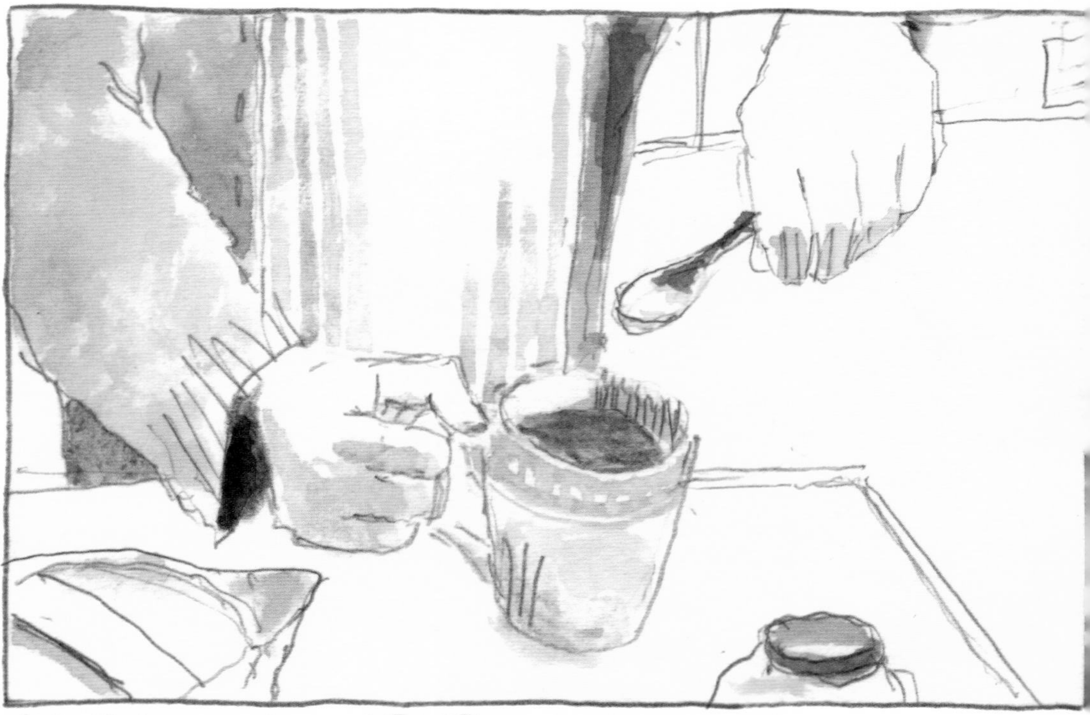

SHE BOUGHT AN ELECTRIC KETTLE AND PAID OFF THE WASHING MACHINE.

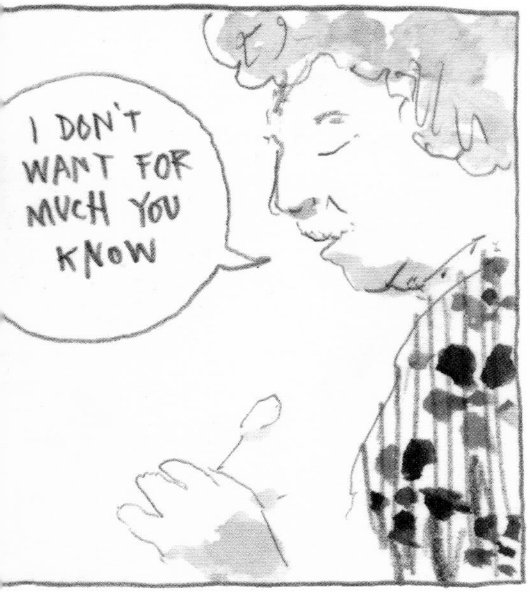
I DON'T WANT FOR MUCH YOU KNOW

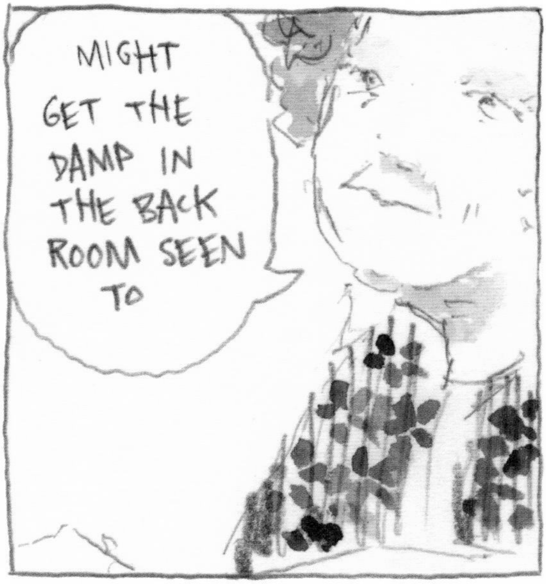
MIGHT GET THE DAMP IN THE BACK ROOM SEEN TO

SO THERE YOU GO

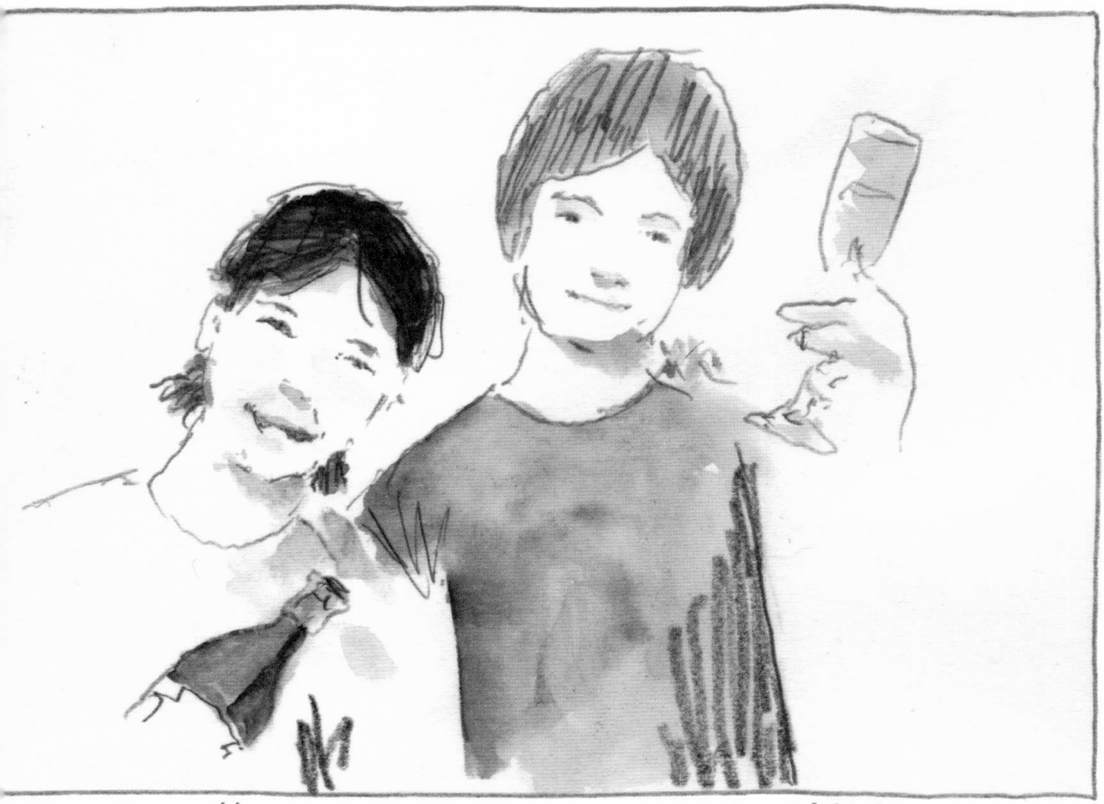

A LARGE CHUNK OF THAT FORTUNE WAS PASSED ON TO ME AND MY BROTHER JACK.

I WAS SIXTEEN YEARS OLD WITH A MULLET

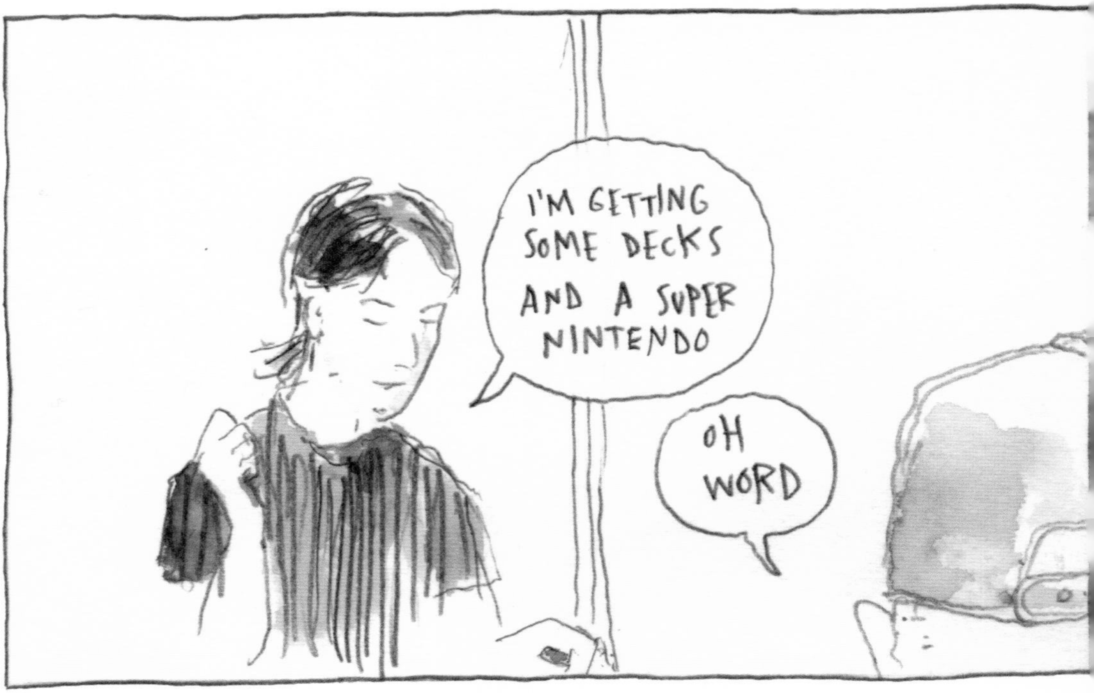
I'M GETTING SOME DECKS
AND A SUPER NINTENDO
OH WORD

AND A MILLION POUNDS

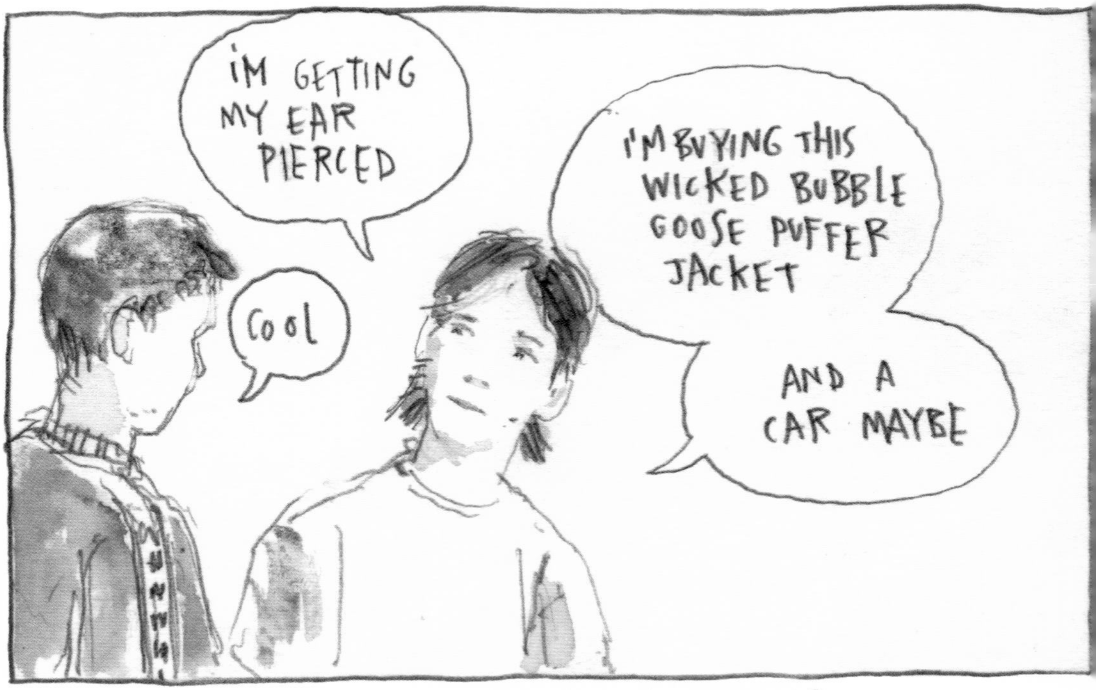
IM GETTING MY EAR PIERCED
I'M BUYING THIS WICKED BUBBLE GOOSE PUFFER JACKET
AND A CAR MAYBE
COOL

WHAT WERE THEY THINKING?

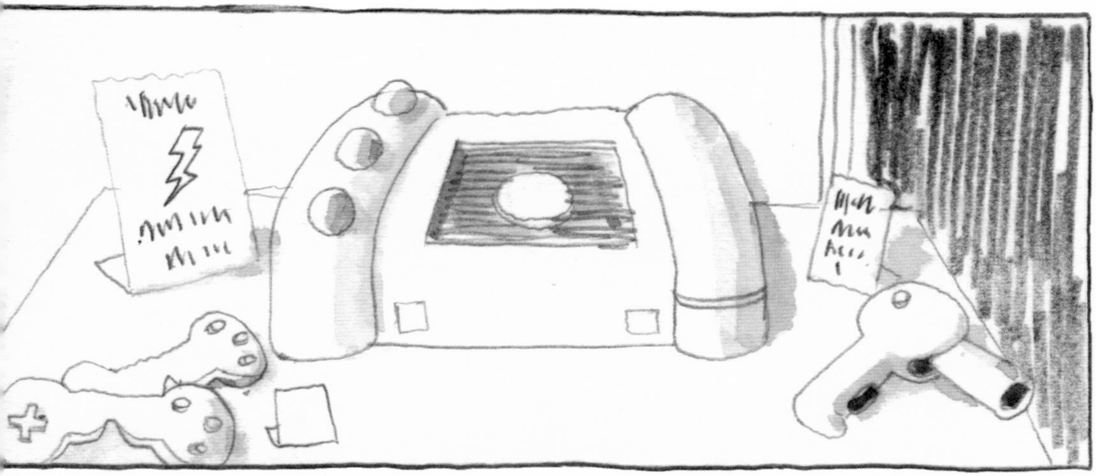

I INVESTED ALL MY SHARE IN BULIDING A GAMES CONSOLE

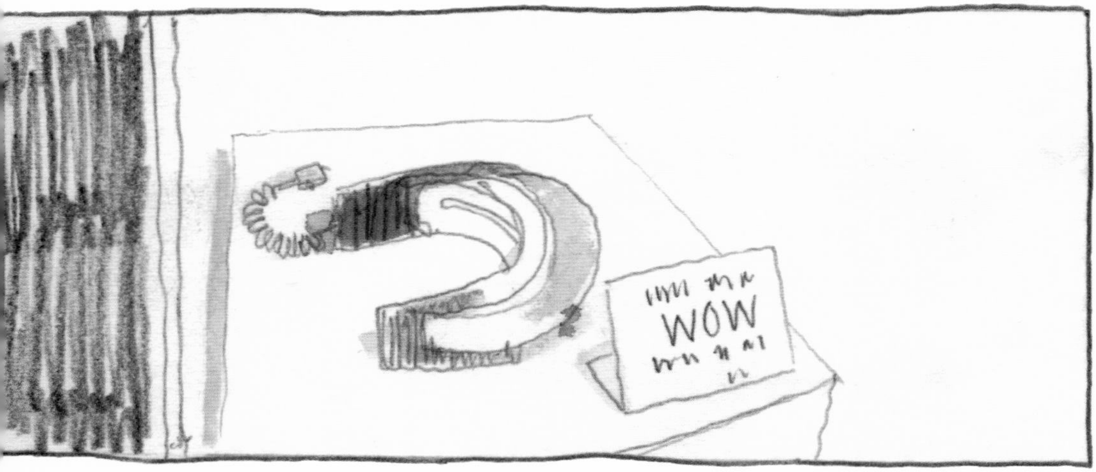
WOW

"THE NEO JOE" IT CAME WITH A VR HEADSET.

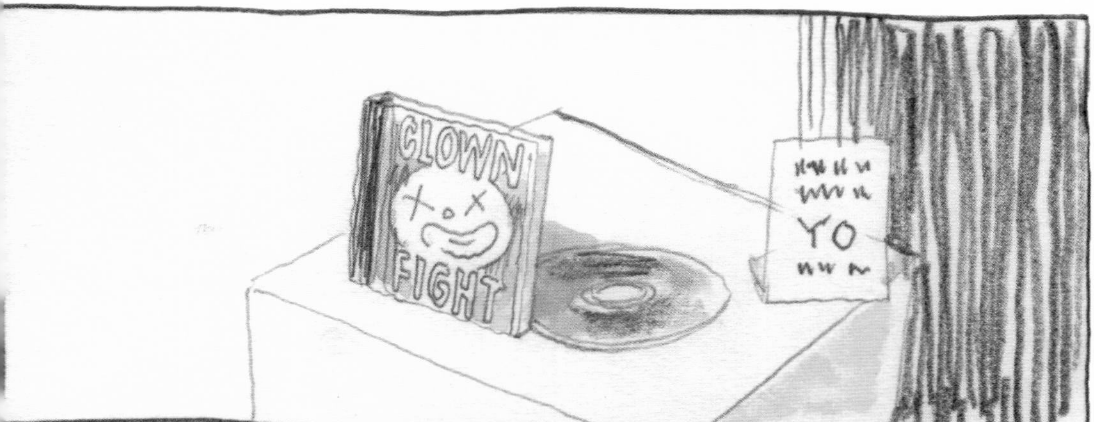
CLOWN FIGHT
YO

AND STATE OF THE ART CD ROMS.

I BECAME A MINOR CELEBRITY IN THE CONSOLE WORLD.

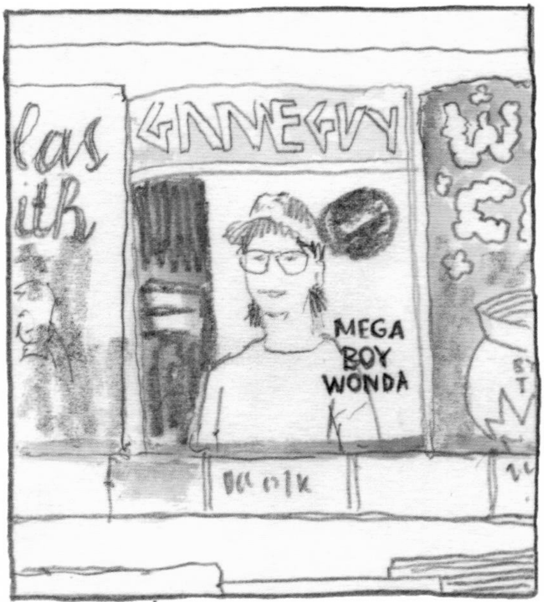
GAMEGUY
MEGA BOY WONDA

MADE THE COVER OF GAME GUY MAGAZINE

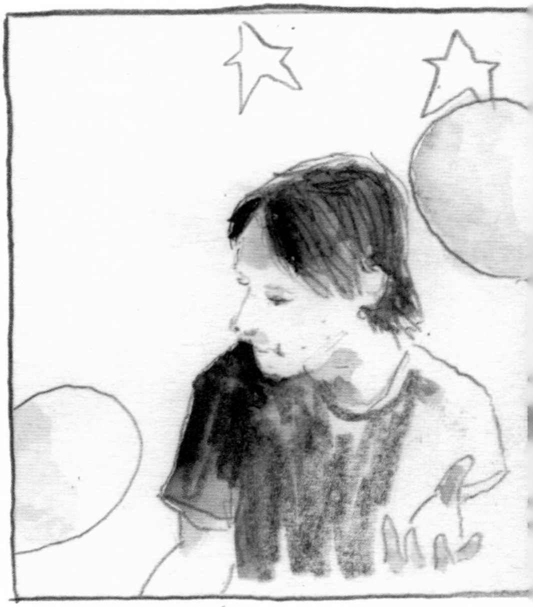

INTERVIEWED ON SUPER SATURDAY SPECIAL SHOW

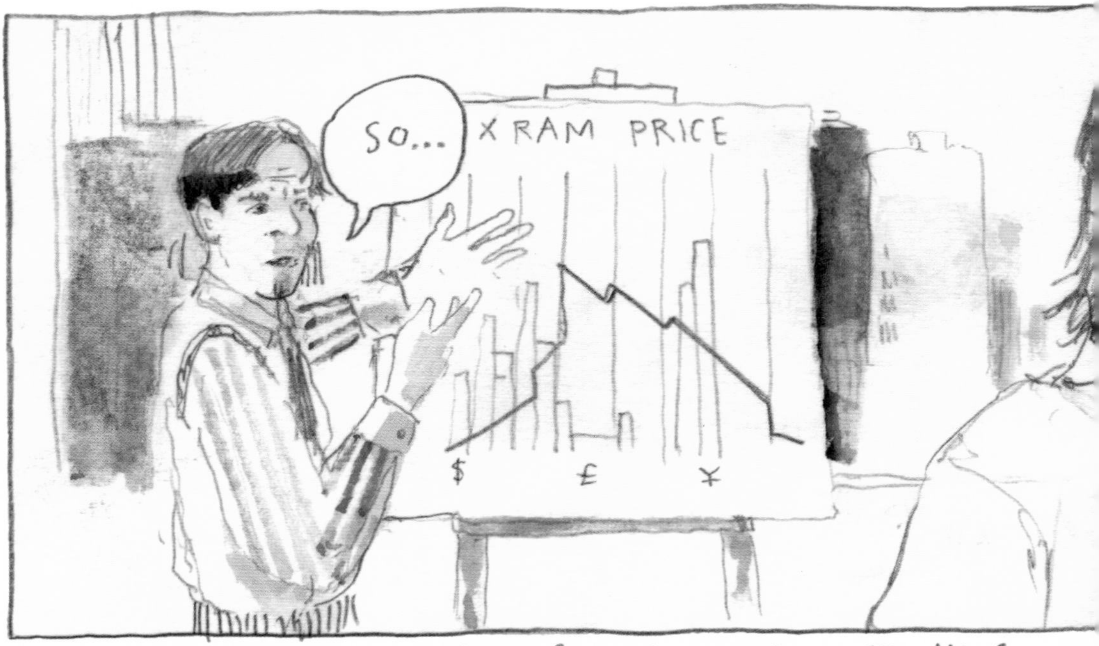
SO...
XRAM PRICE
$ £ ¥

THEN THE COMPANY WENT BUST AND I LOST EVERYTHING

THERE WERE CHARTS EXPLAINING THIS.

MY BROTHER, HE BOUGHT A GERMAN FOOTBALL TEAM.

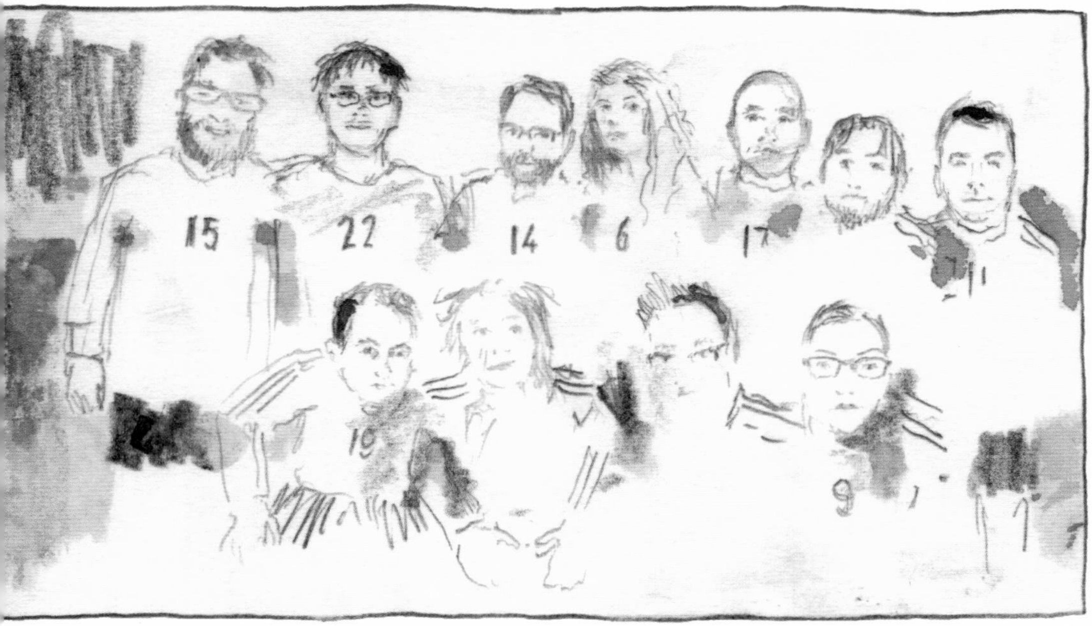

HE NOW OWNS A PRIVATE JET, A (SMALL) ISLAND IN THE OUTER HEBRIDES AND A SUMMER HOUSE IN THE HAMPTONS

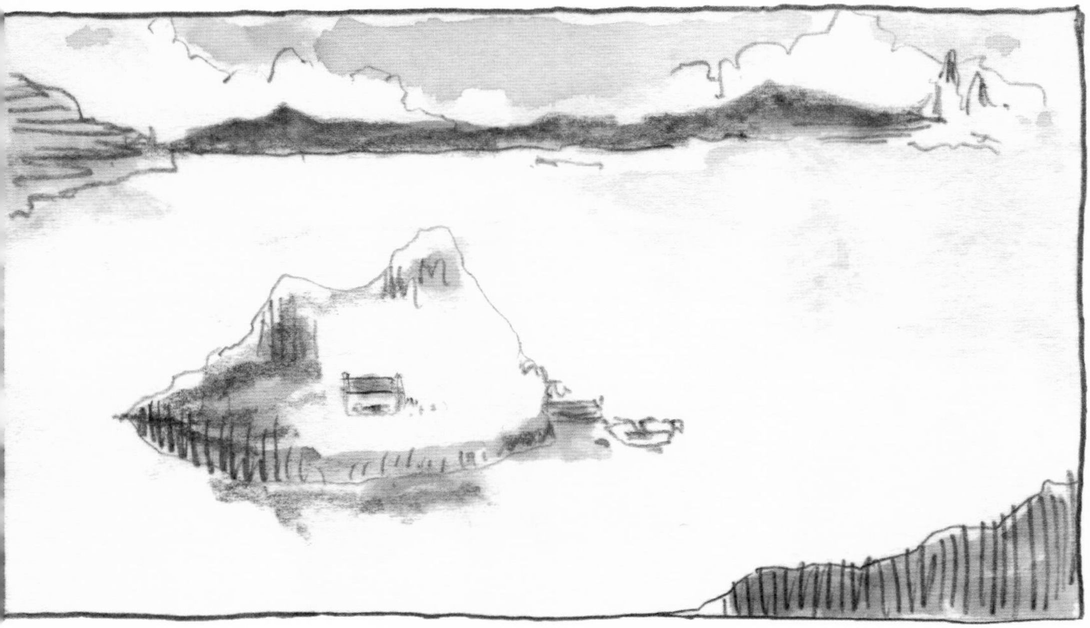

WHAT A GIT.

OH MUSTN'T FORGET, I'VE LEFT MY RAINCOAT ON THE LINE

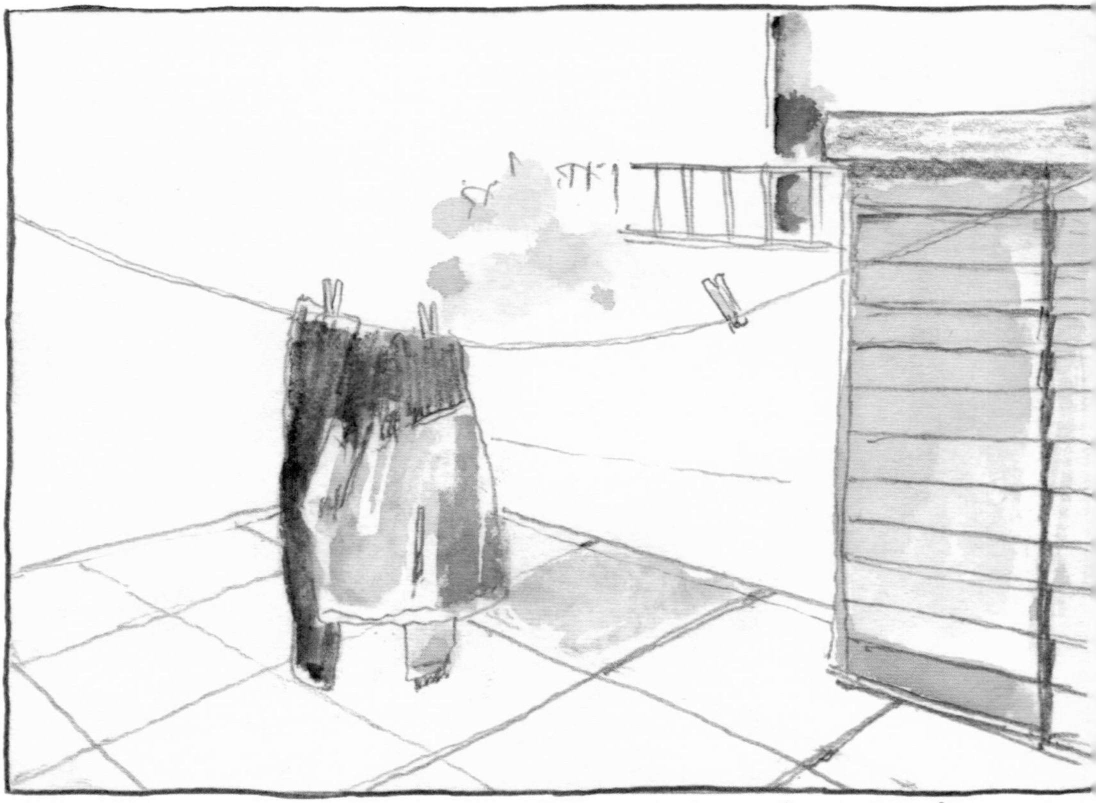

TWO DAYS IT'S BEEN OUT THERE. IN THE RAIN. SHOULD PROBABLY BRING IT IN. OR IT'LL NEVER DRY

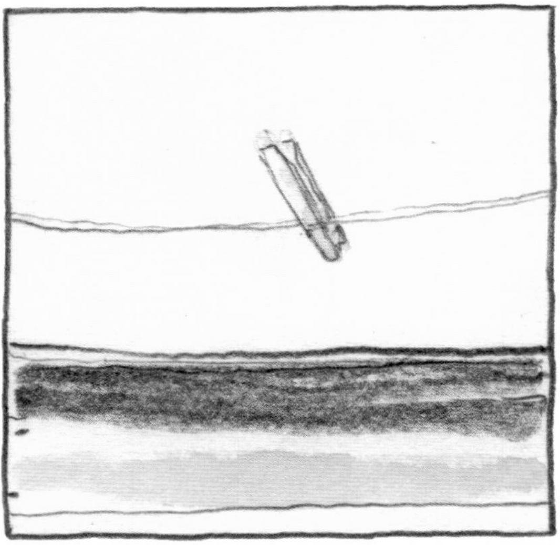

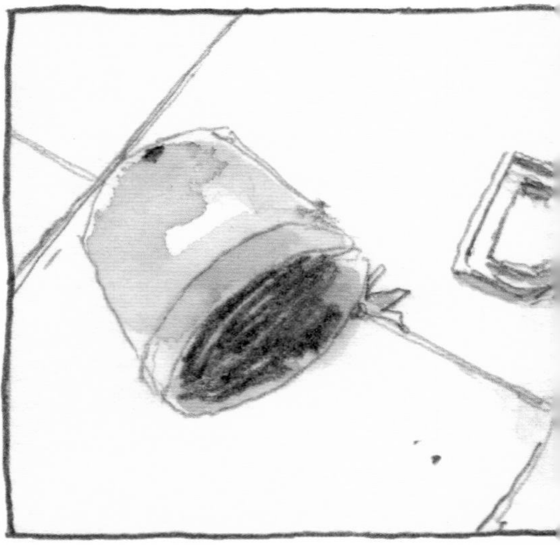

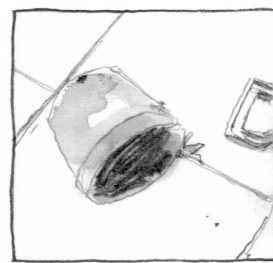

SO MUCH WEATHER EH?

ANYWAY, UM. SO I LOST ALL OF MY SHARE OF THE PAPERCLIP MONEY.

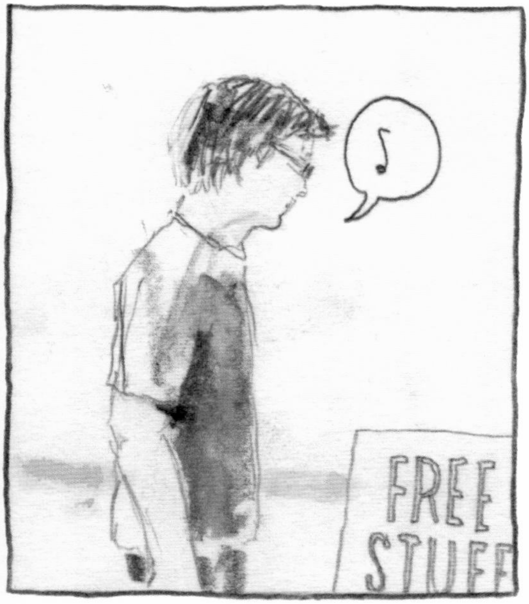
FREE
STUFF

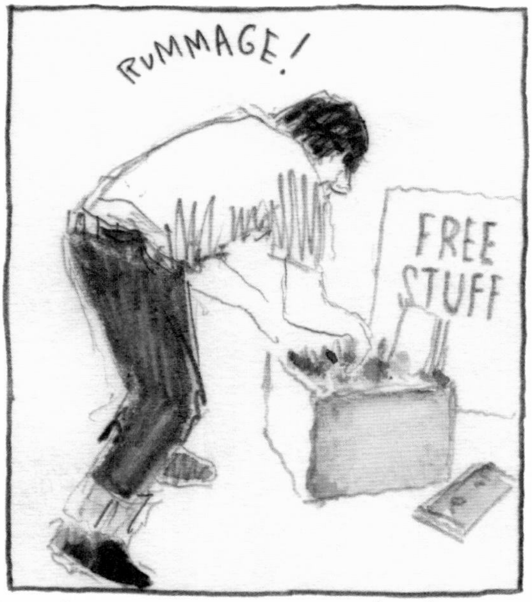
RUMMAGE!
FREE
STUFF

I LIKE TO SHRUG IT OFF, I WAS YOUNG AND FOOLISH
NO DAMAGE DONE

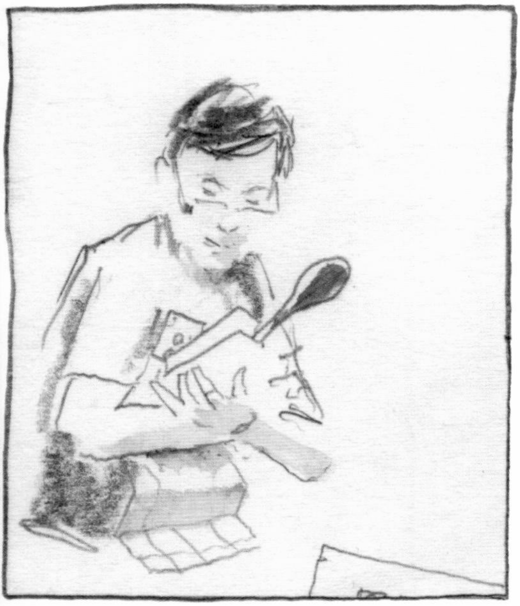

BUT MAYBE

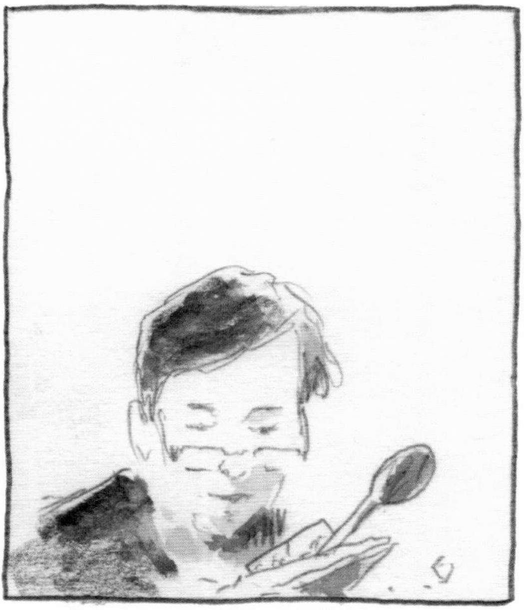

MAYBE THERE WAS A CHANGE IN ME.

OH I LOVE TO COLLECT

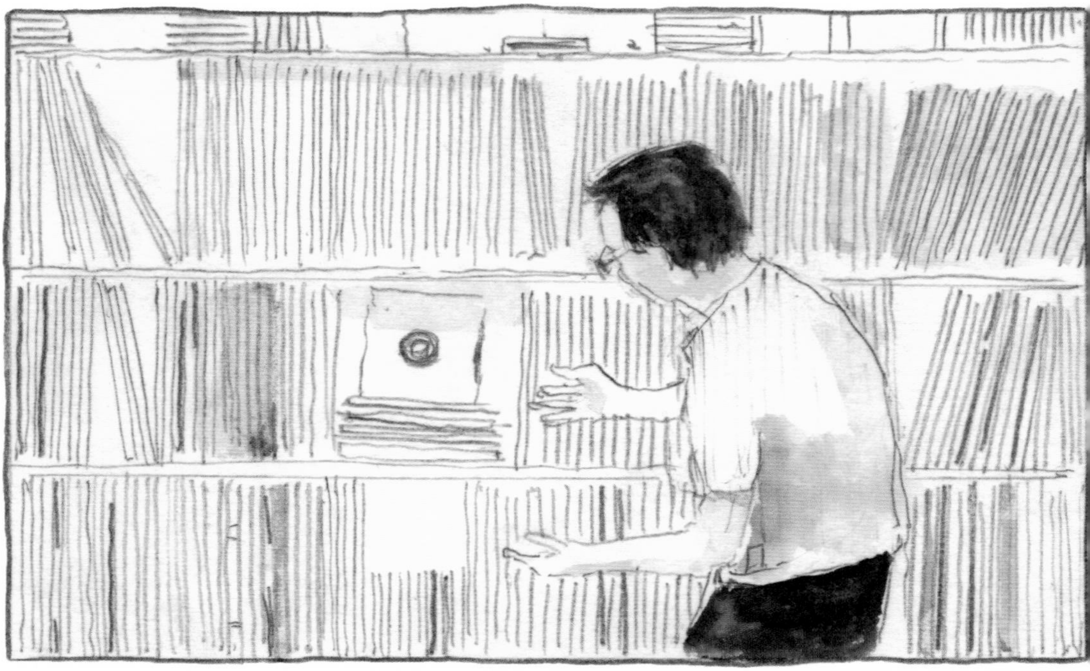

I HAVE TO TAKE THINGS HOME

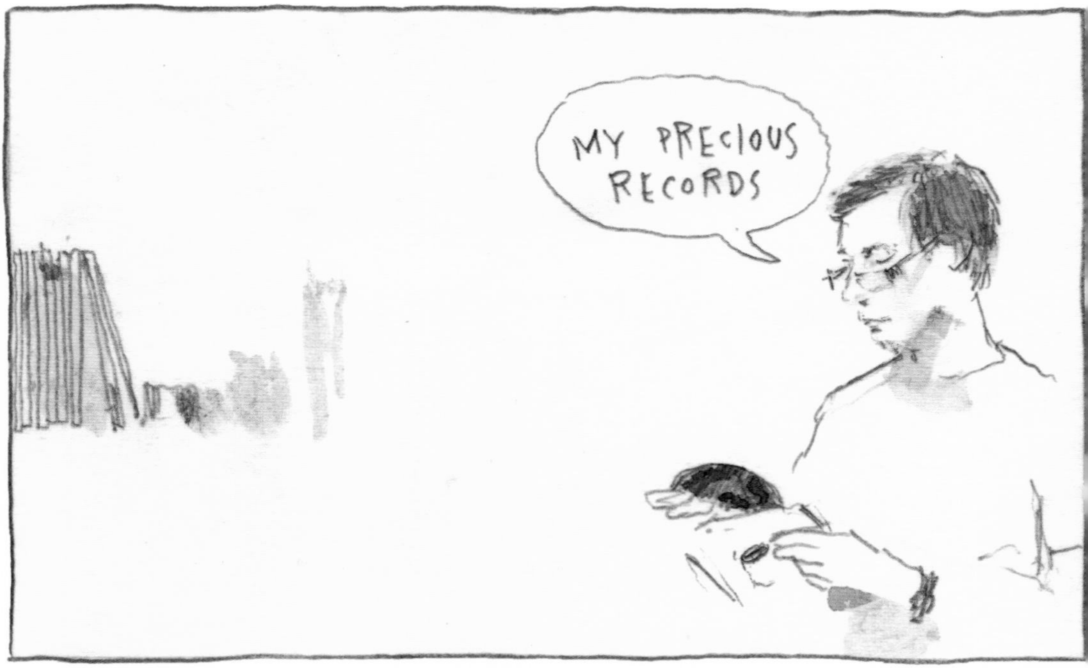
MY PRECIOUS RECORDS

TO KEEP

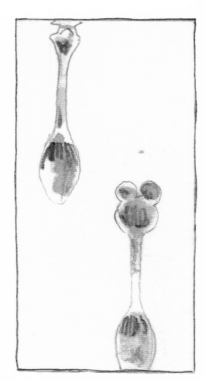

TO ORGANISE

AND, LIKE DEAR OLD GRAN, TO COLLATE

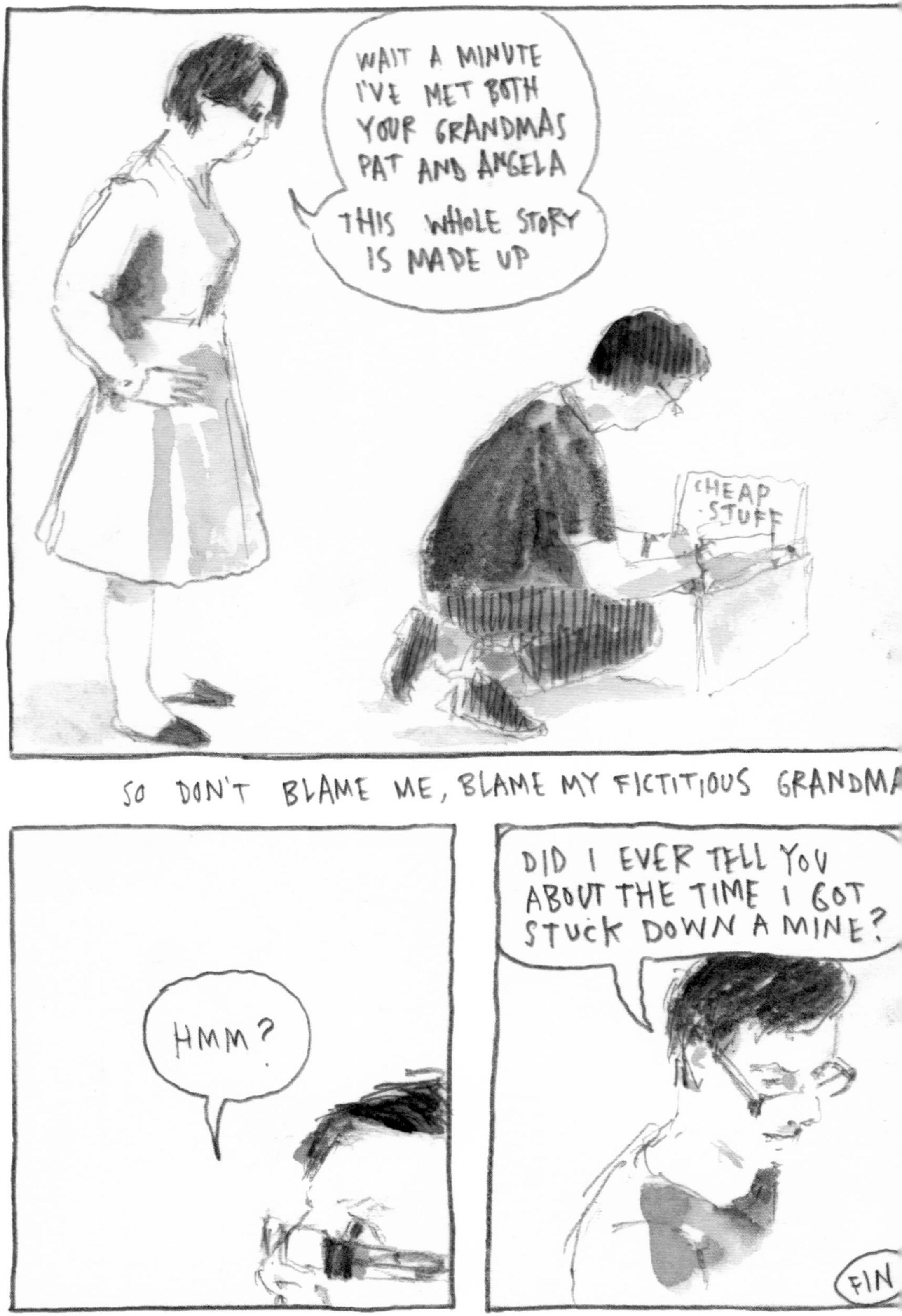
WAIT A MINUTE I'VE MET BOTH YOUR GRANDMAS PAT AND ANGELA
THIS WHOLE STORY IS MADE UP
CHEAP STUFF
SO DON'T BLAME ME, BLAME MY FICTITIOUS GRANDMA
HMM?
DID I EVER TELL YOU ABOUT THE TIME I GOT STUCK DOWN A MINE?
FIN

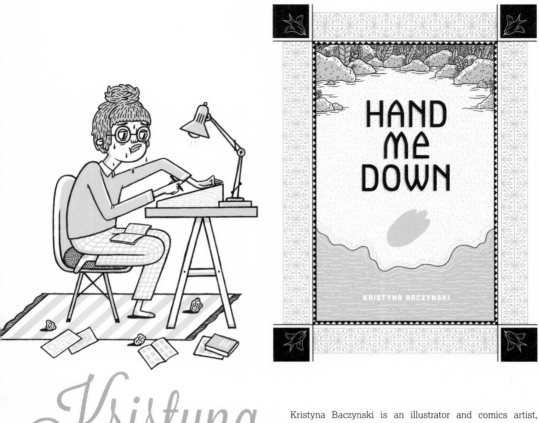

HAND
ME
DOWN
KRISTYNA BACZYNSKI

Kristyna Baczynski

Kristyna Baczynski is an illustrator and comics artist, working from her studio in Leeds, UK. She produces artwork for books, comics, packaging, posters, apparel, stationery and more for a wide range of clients including Chipotle, Anorak, Digital Arts and NME.

As well as creating her own comics, Kristyna has worked with publishers in the UK and internationally such as Fantagraphics, Image, Blank Slate Books, Solipsistic Pop, Bimba and Hic + Hoc.

Kristyna.co.uk
@kbaczynski

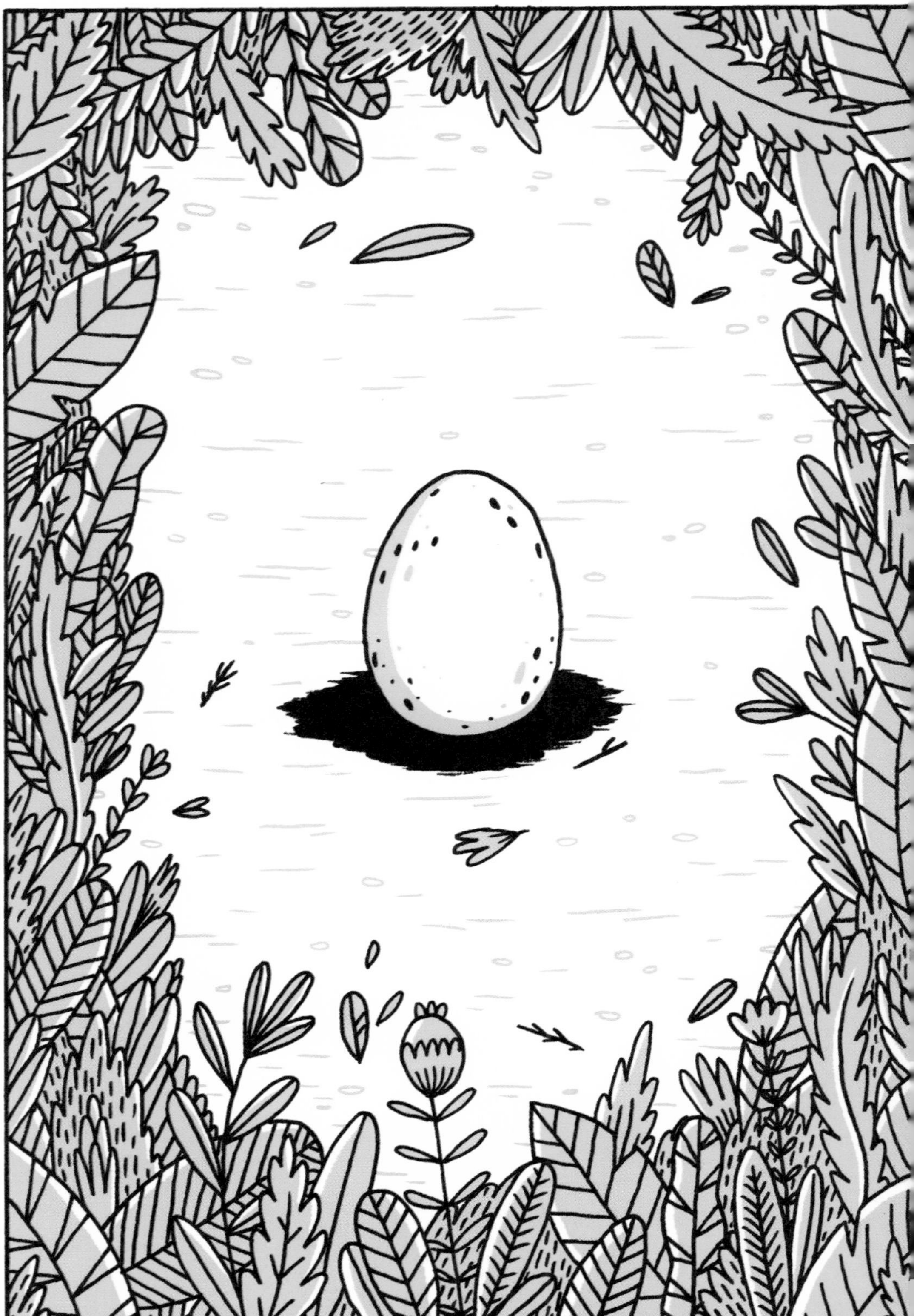

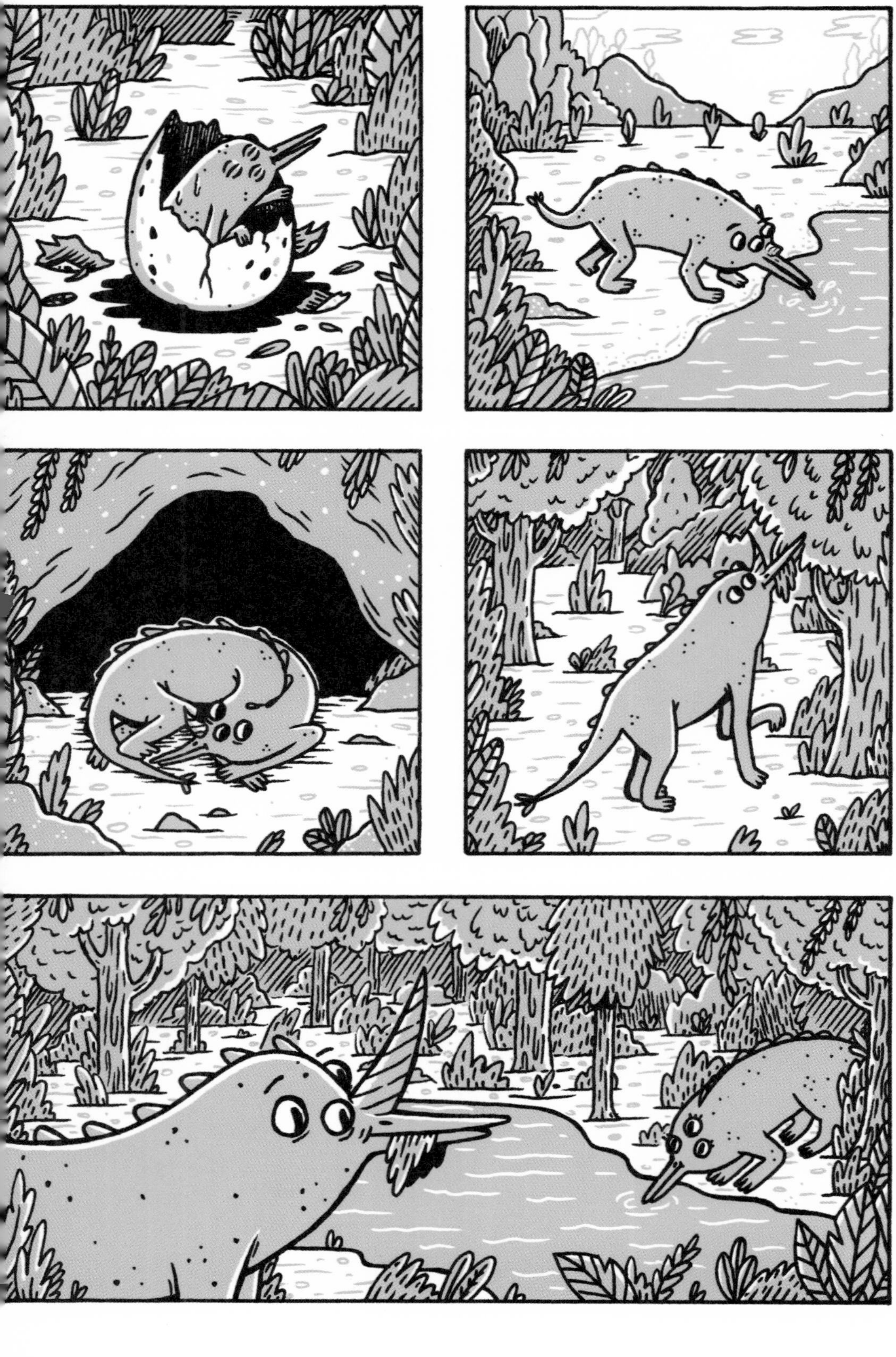

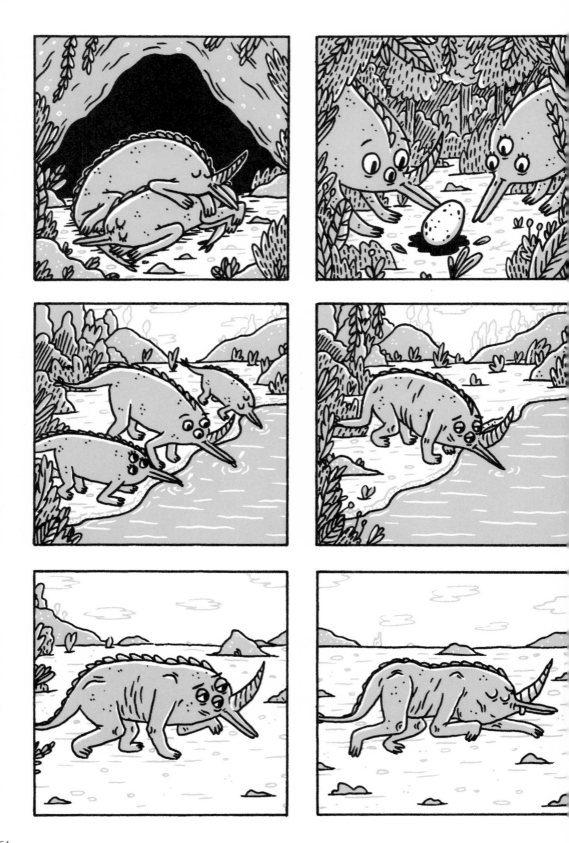

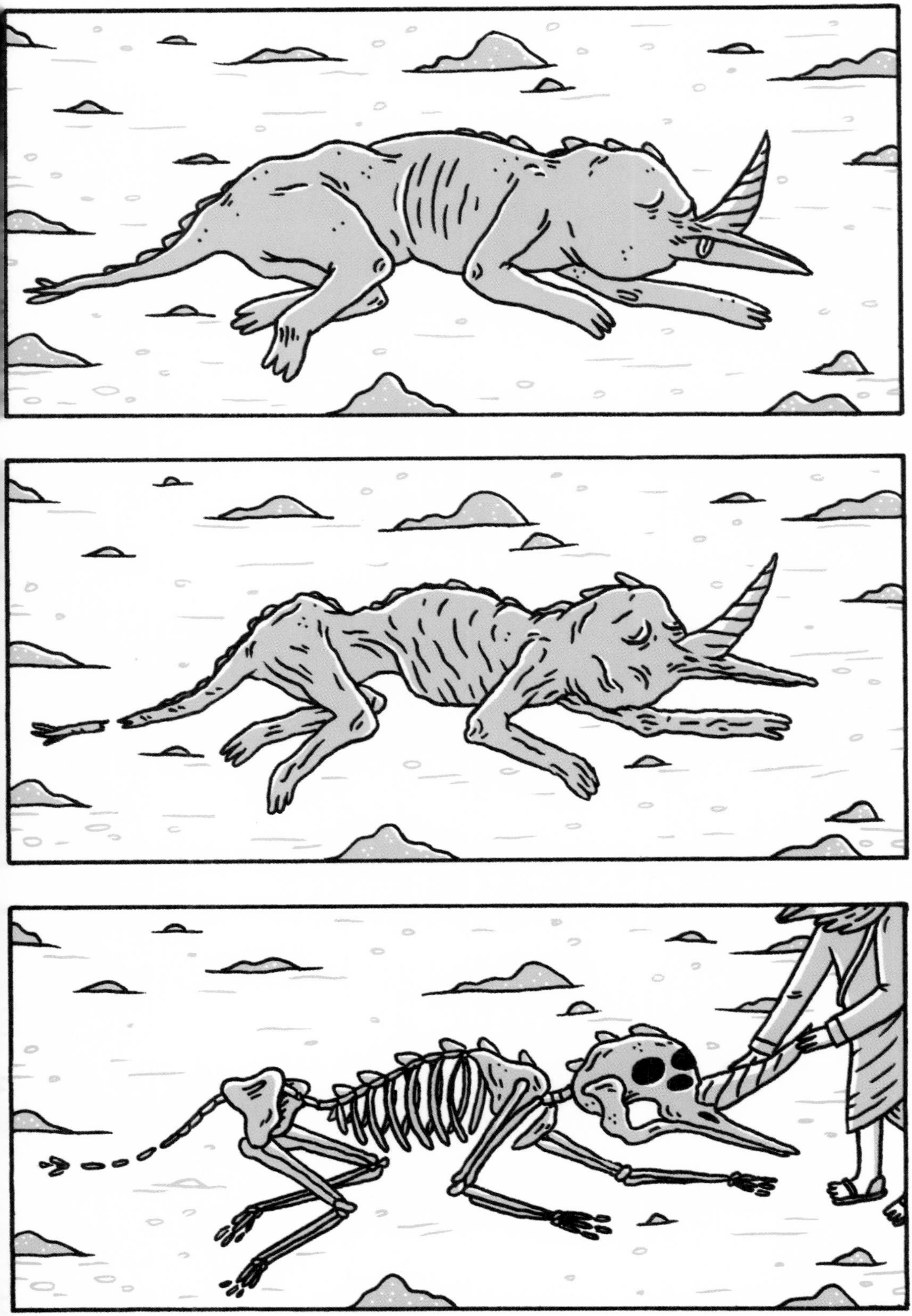

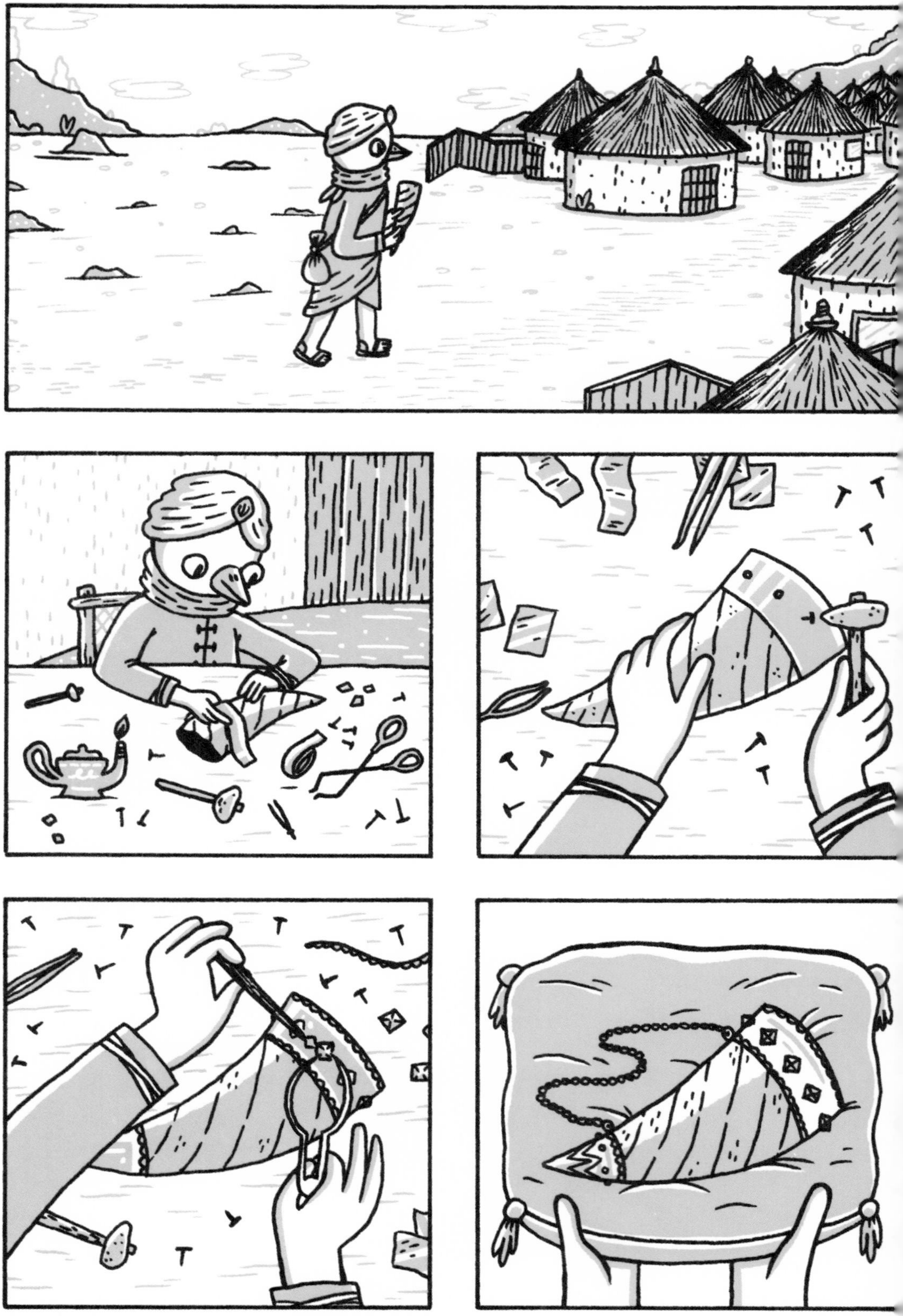

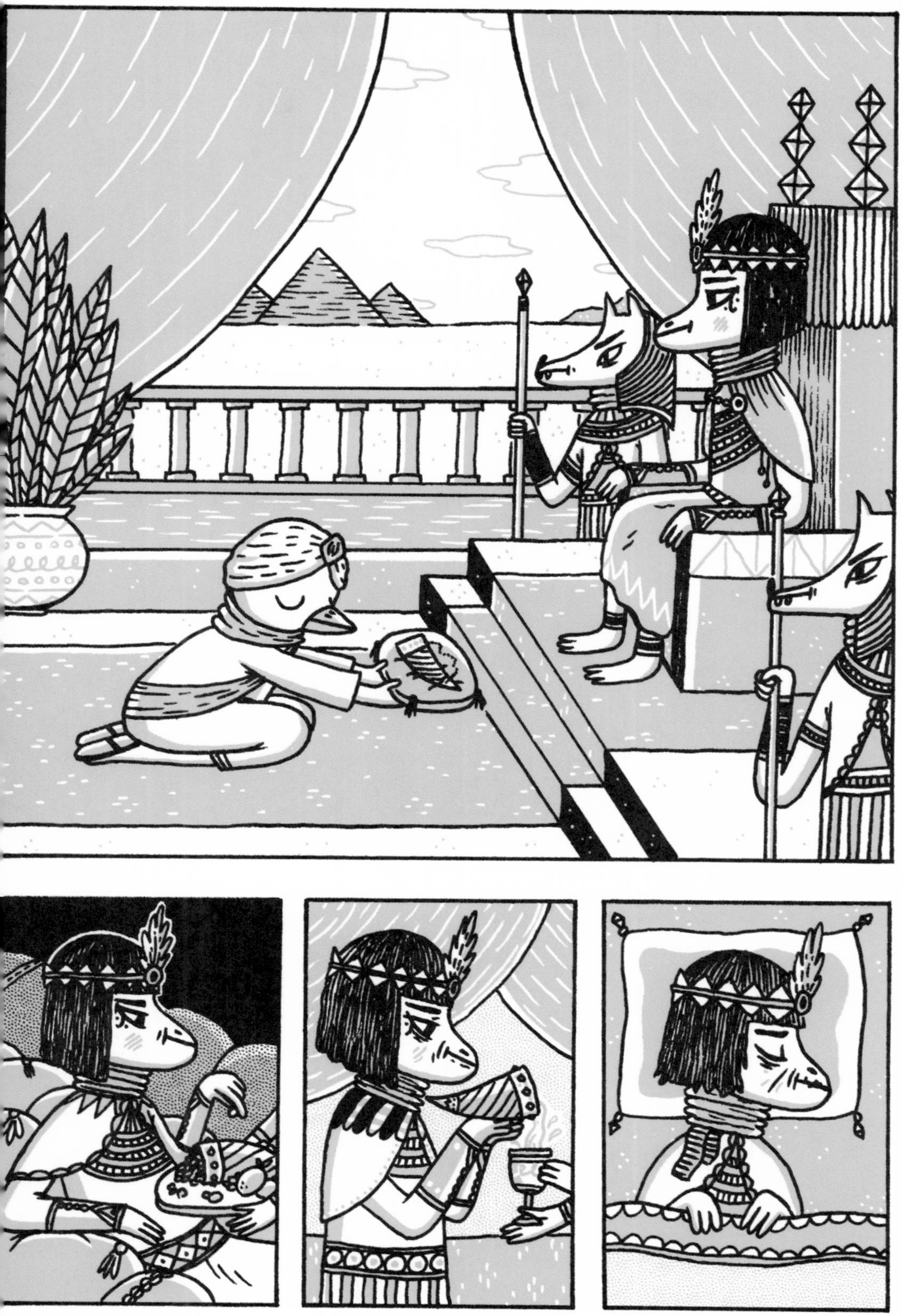

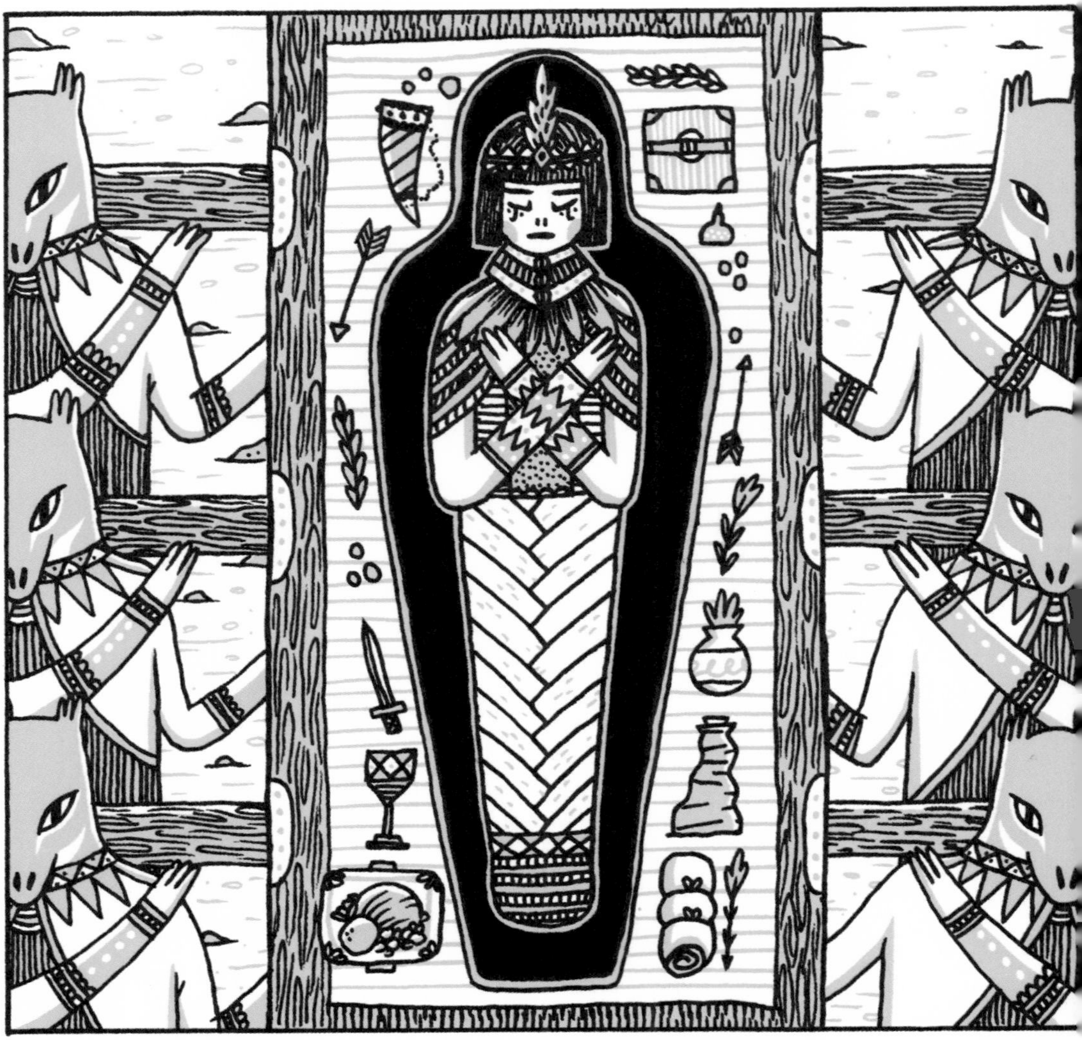

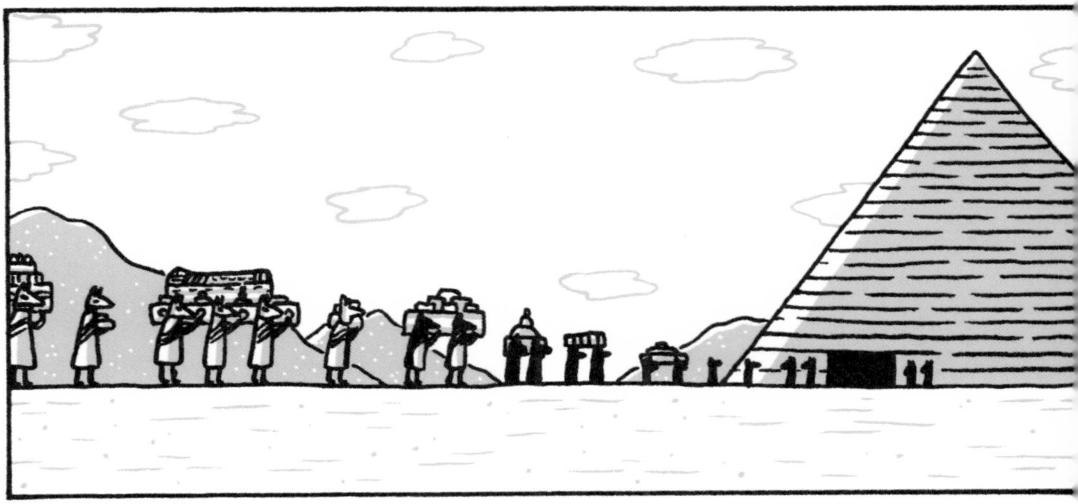

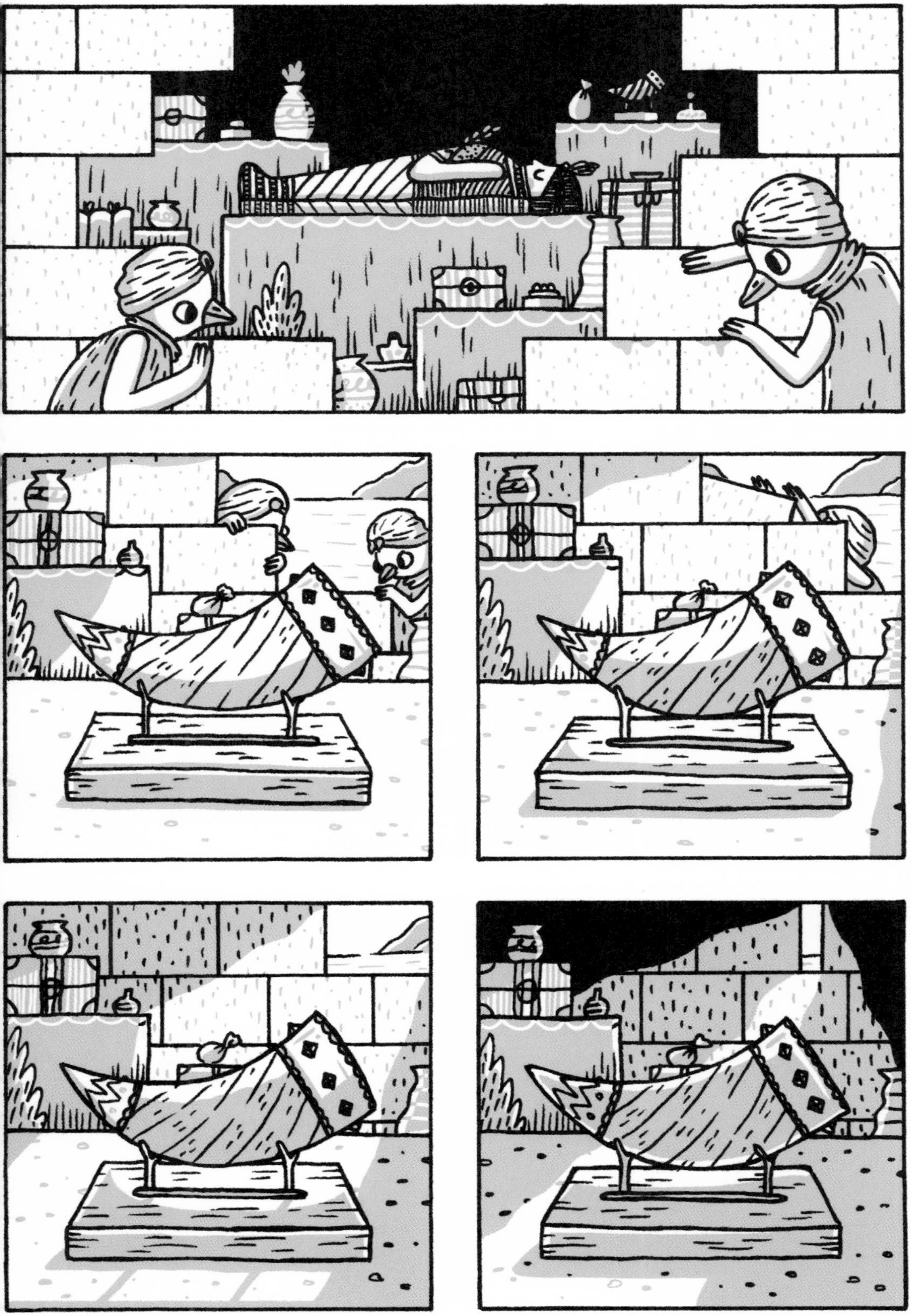

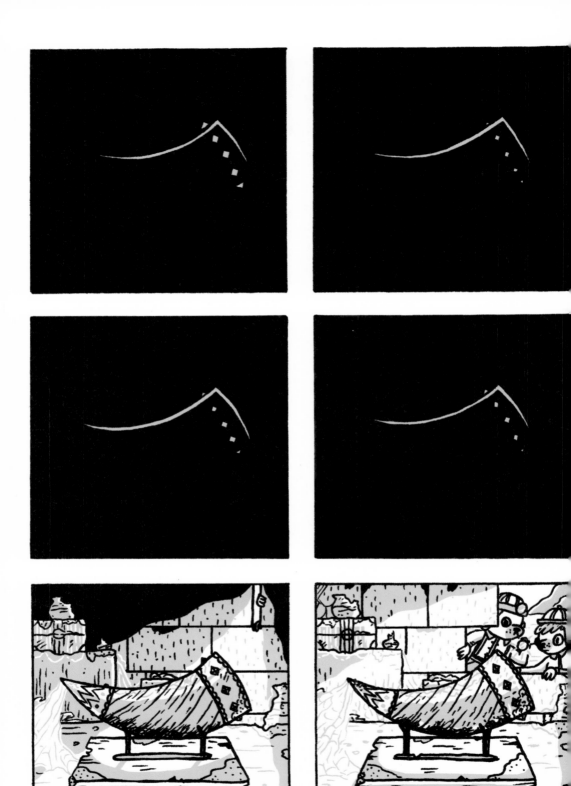

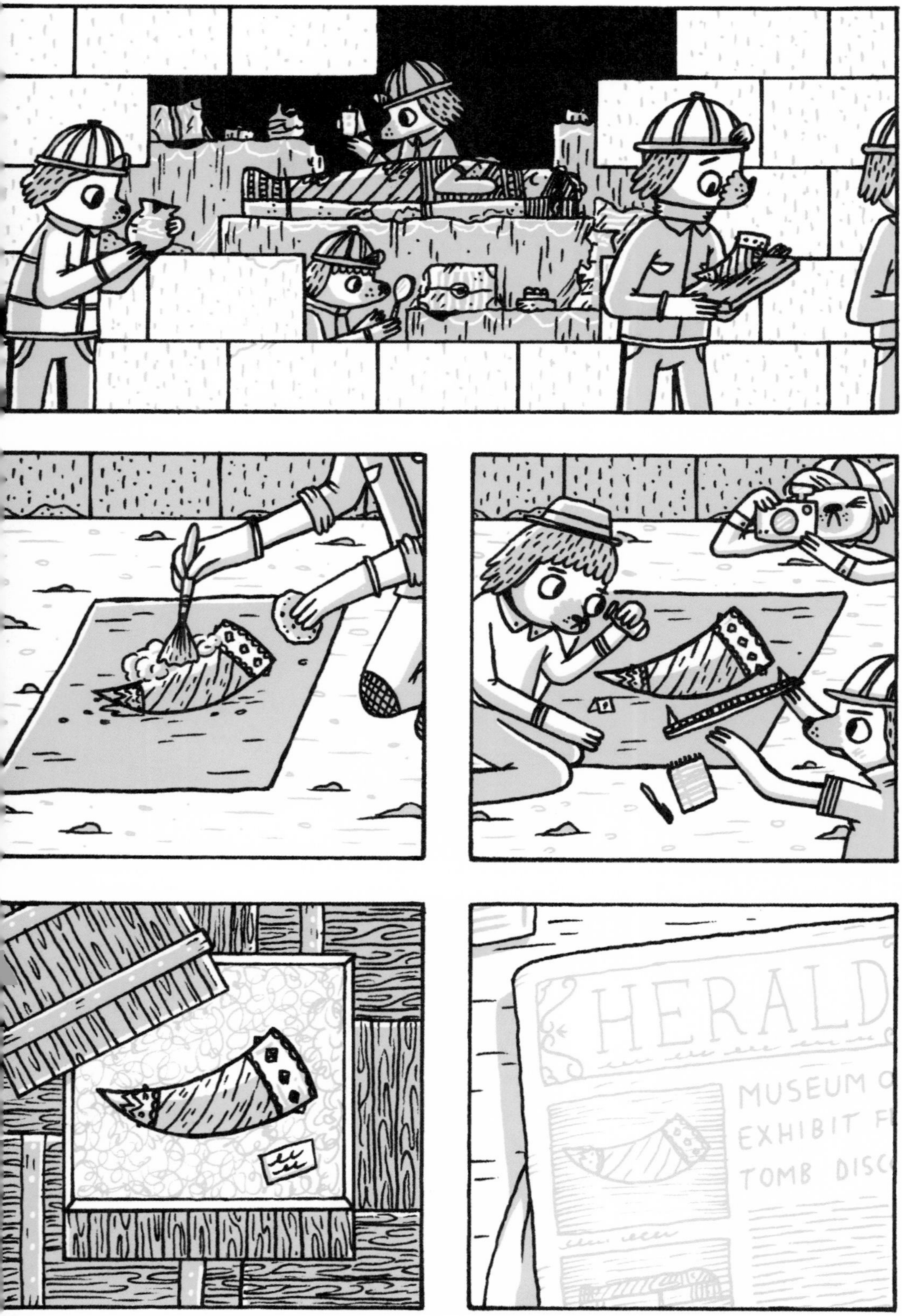
HERALD
MUSEUM O
EXHIBIT F
TOMB DISC

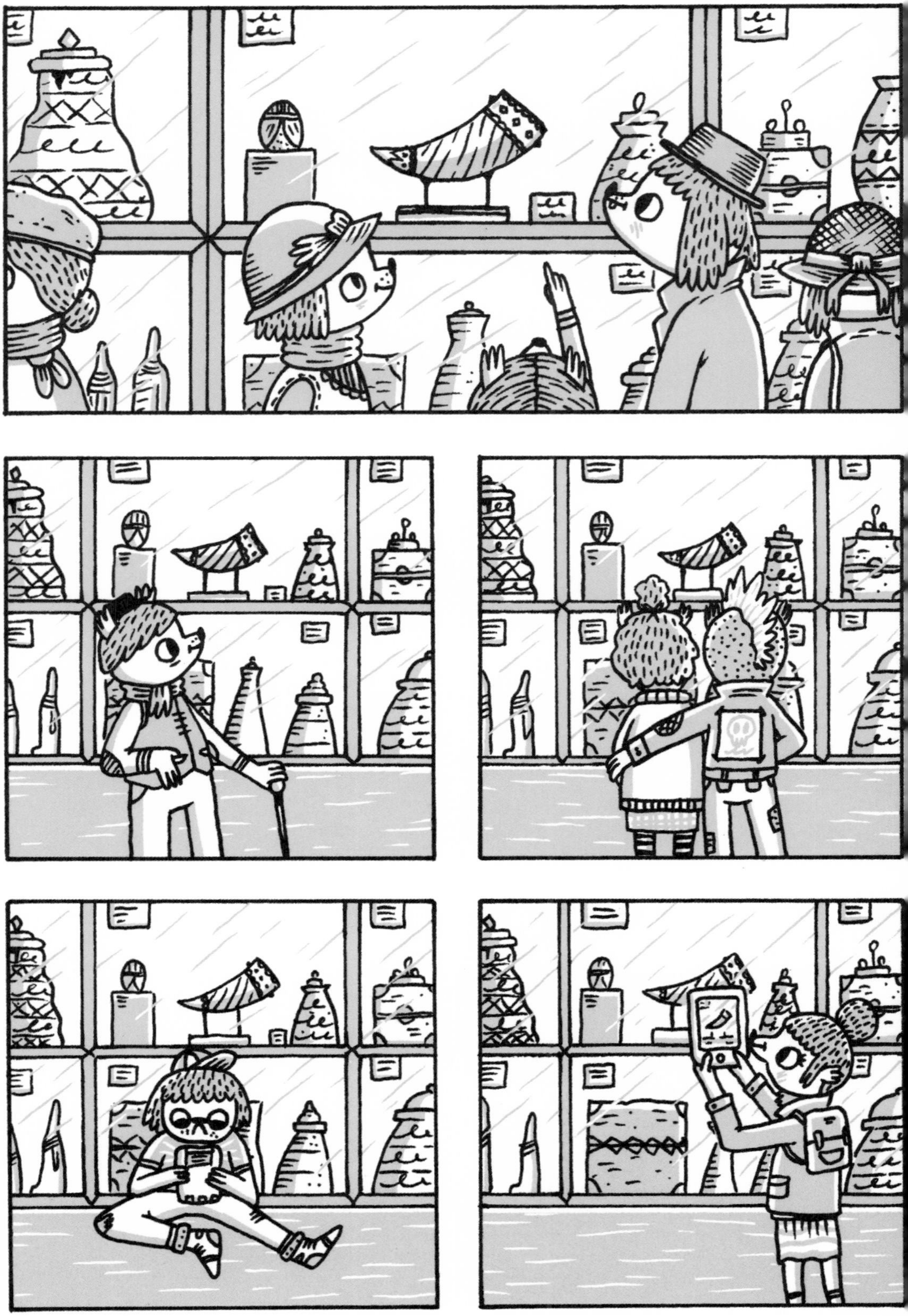

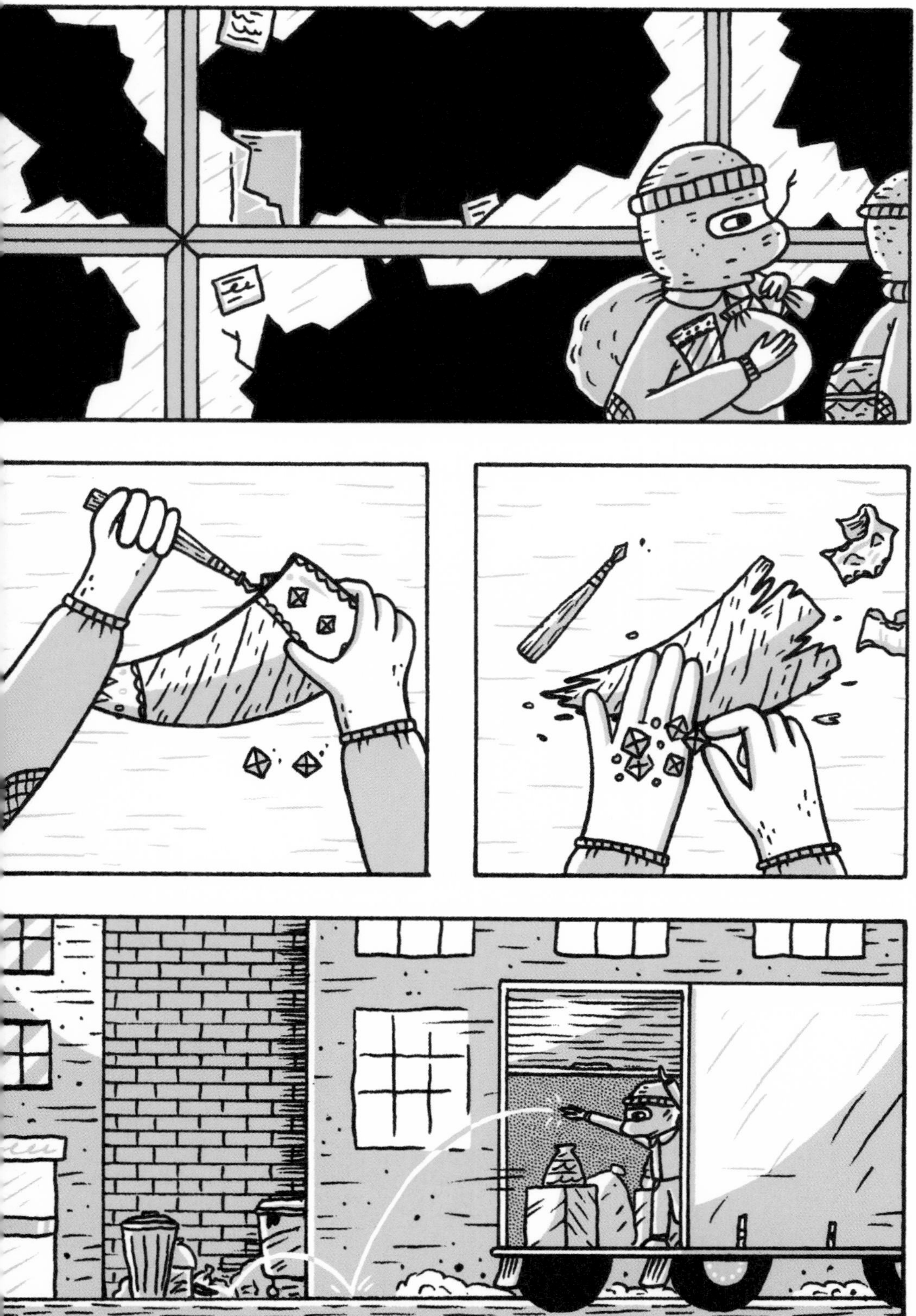

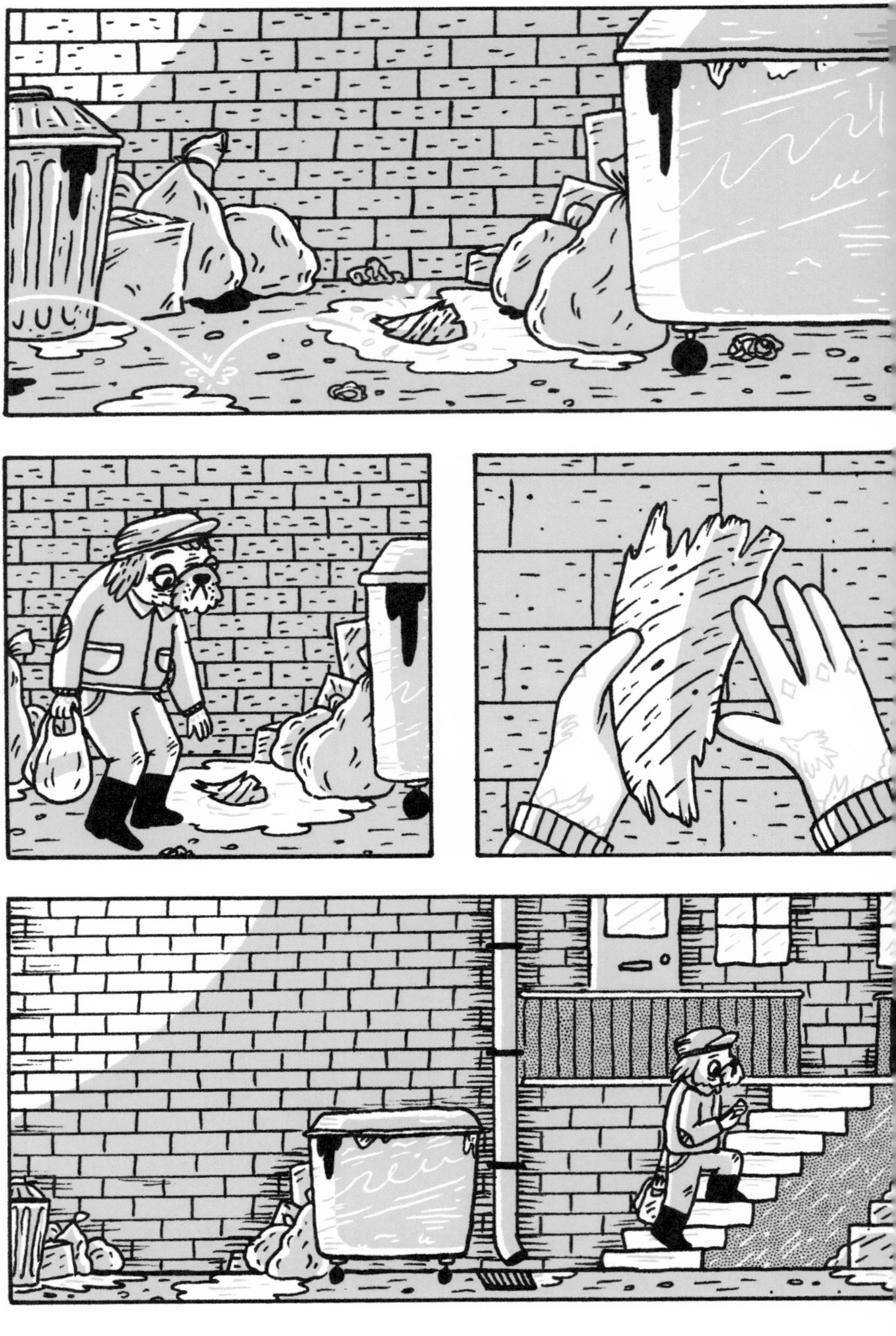

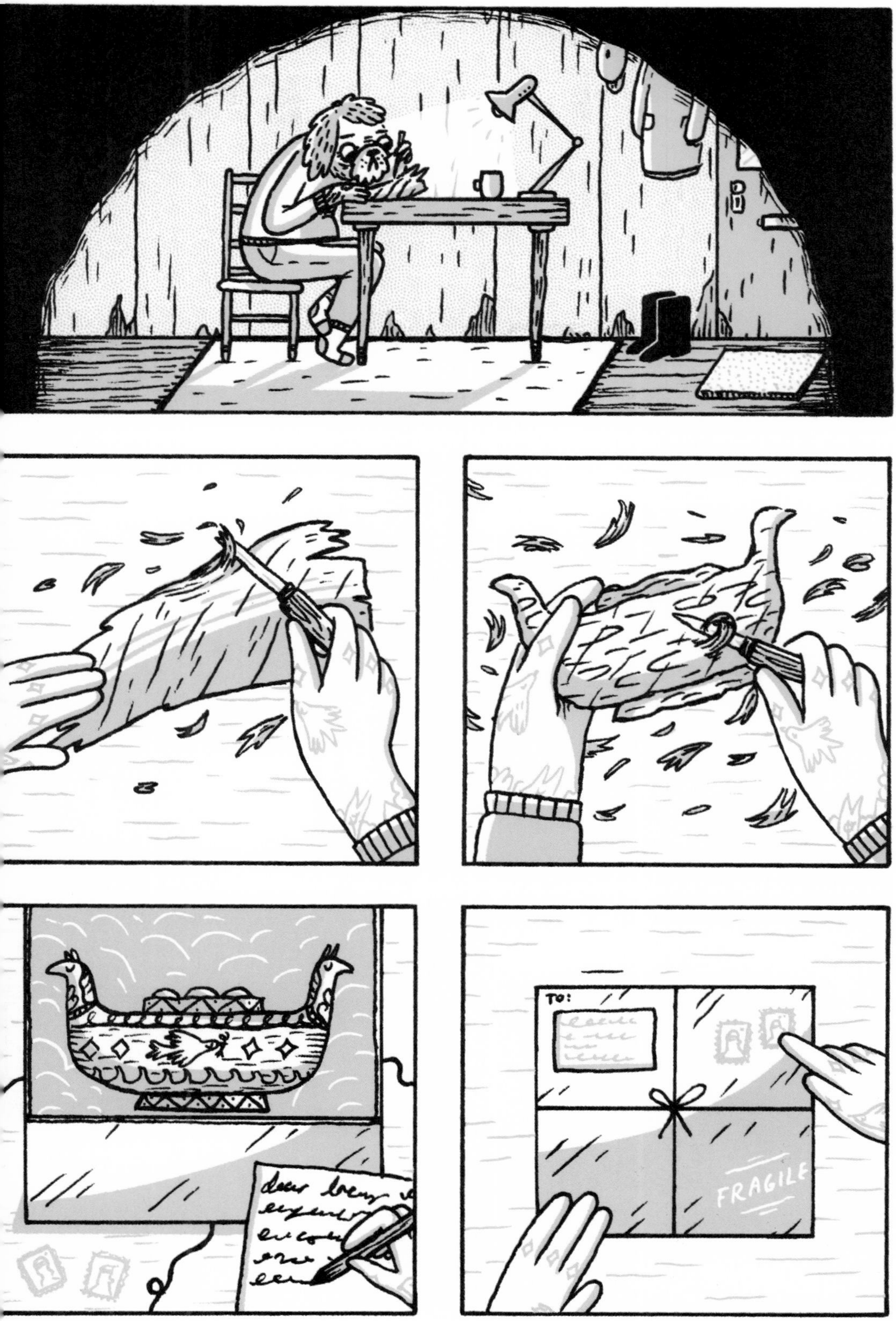
TO:
FRAGILE

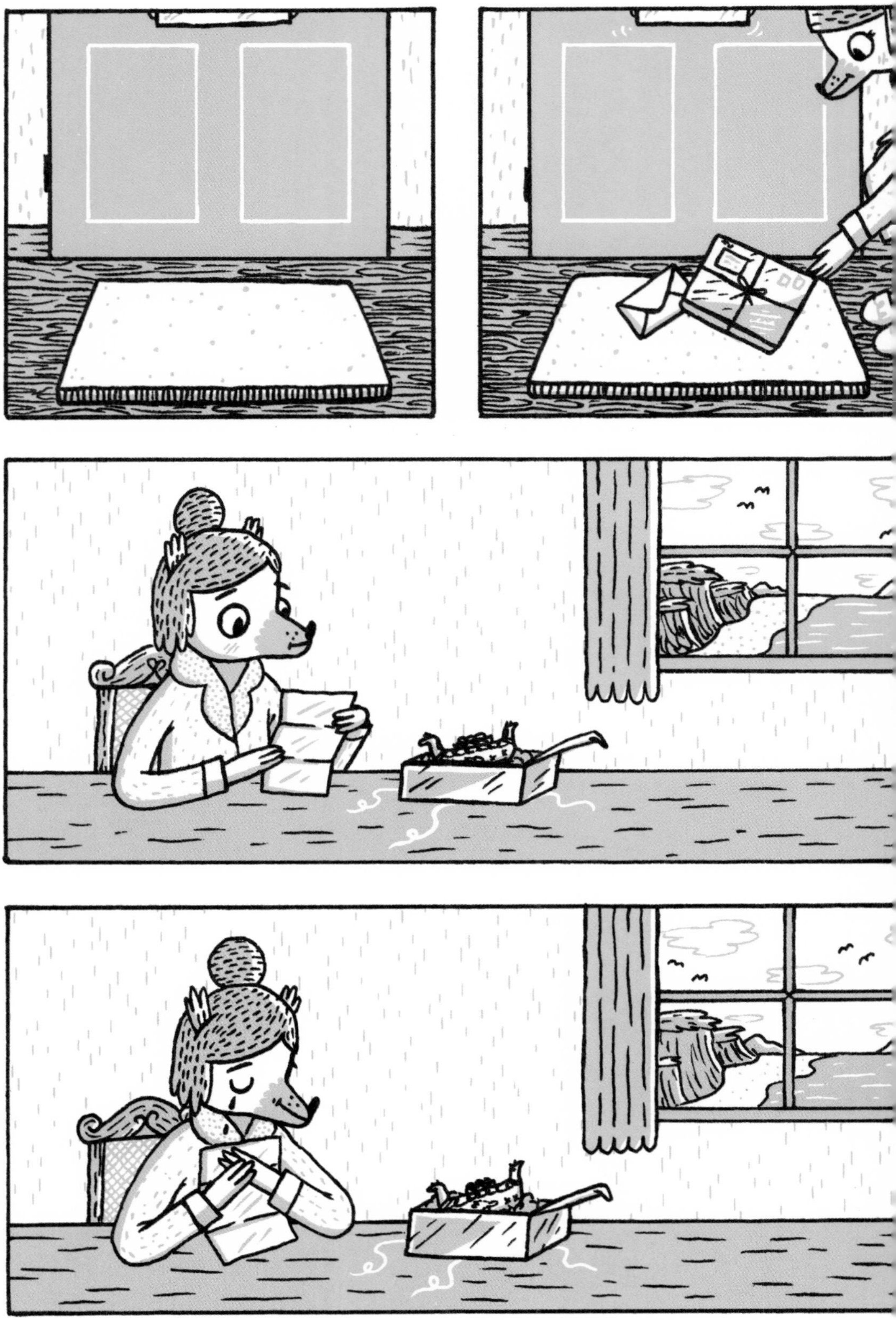

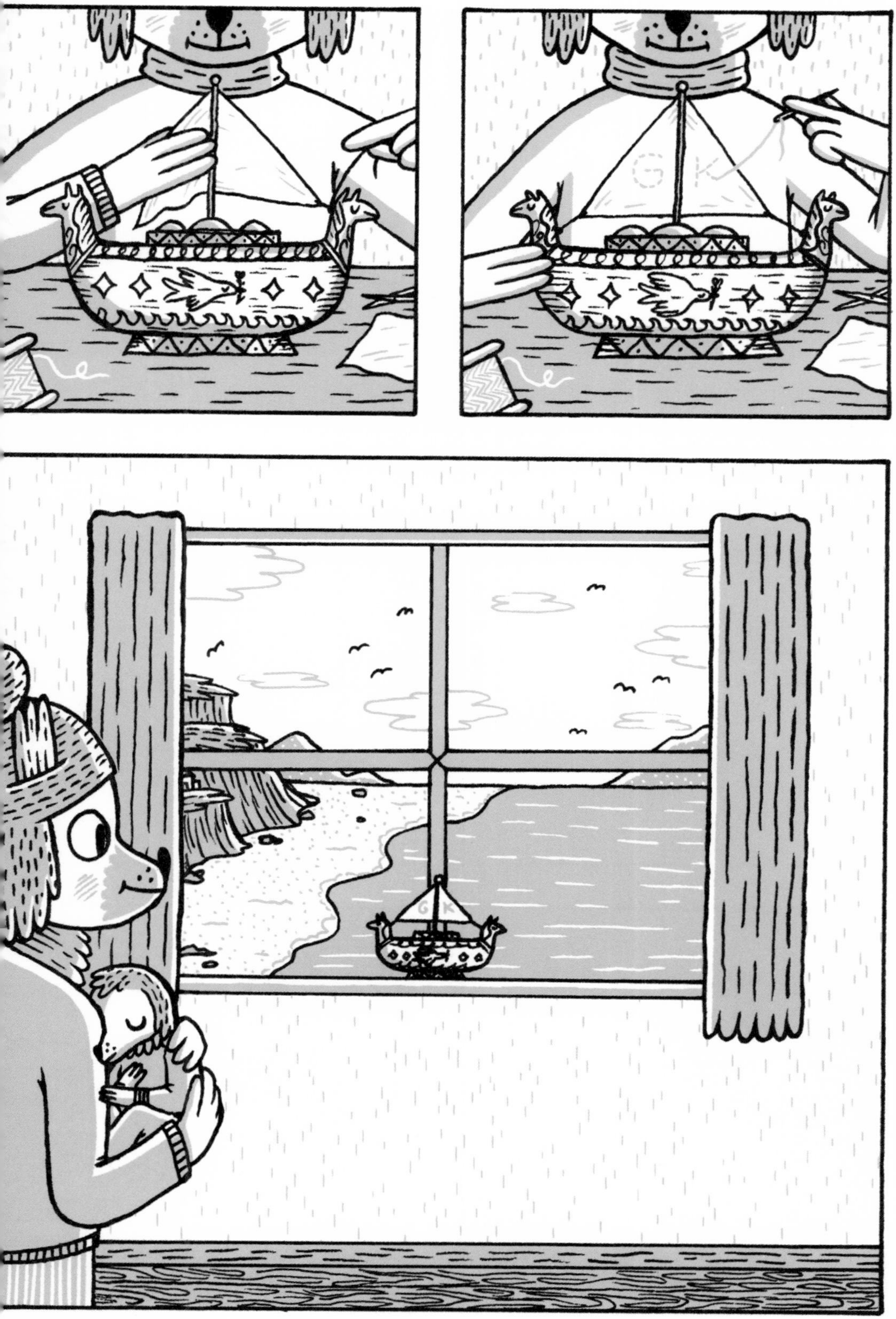

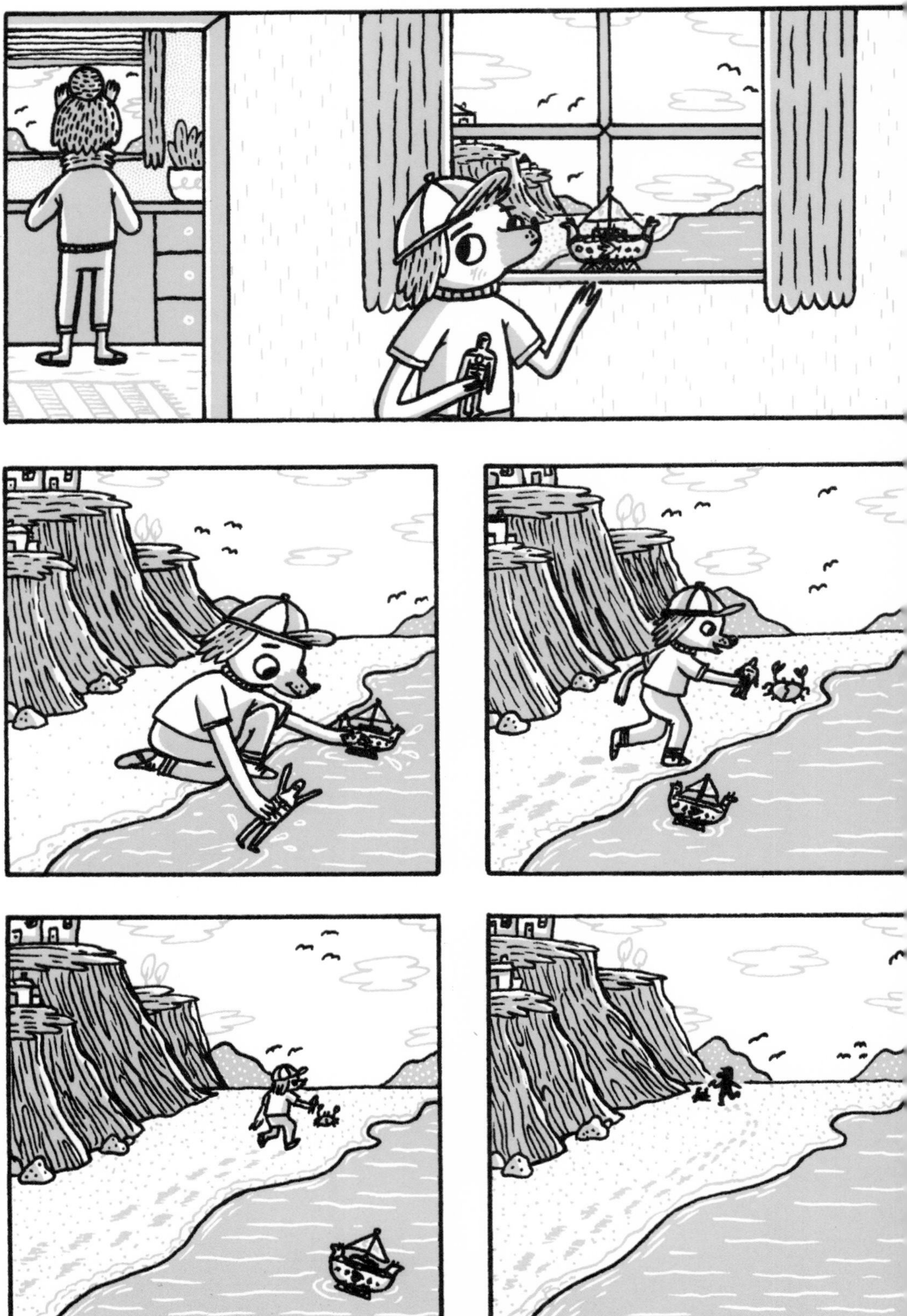

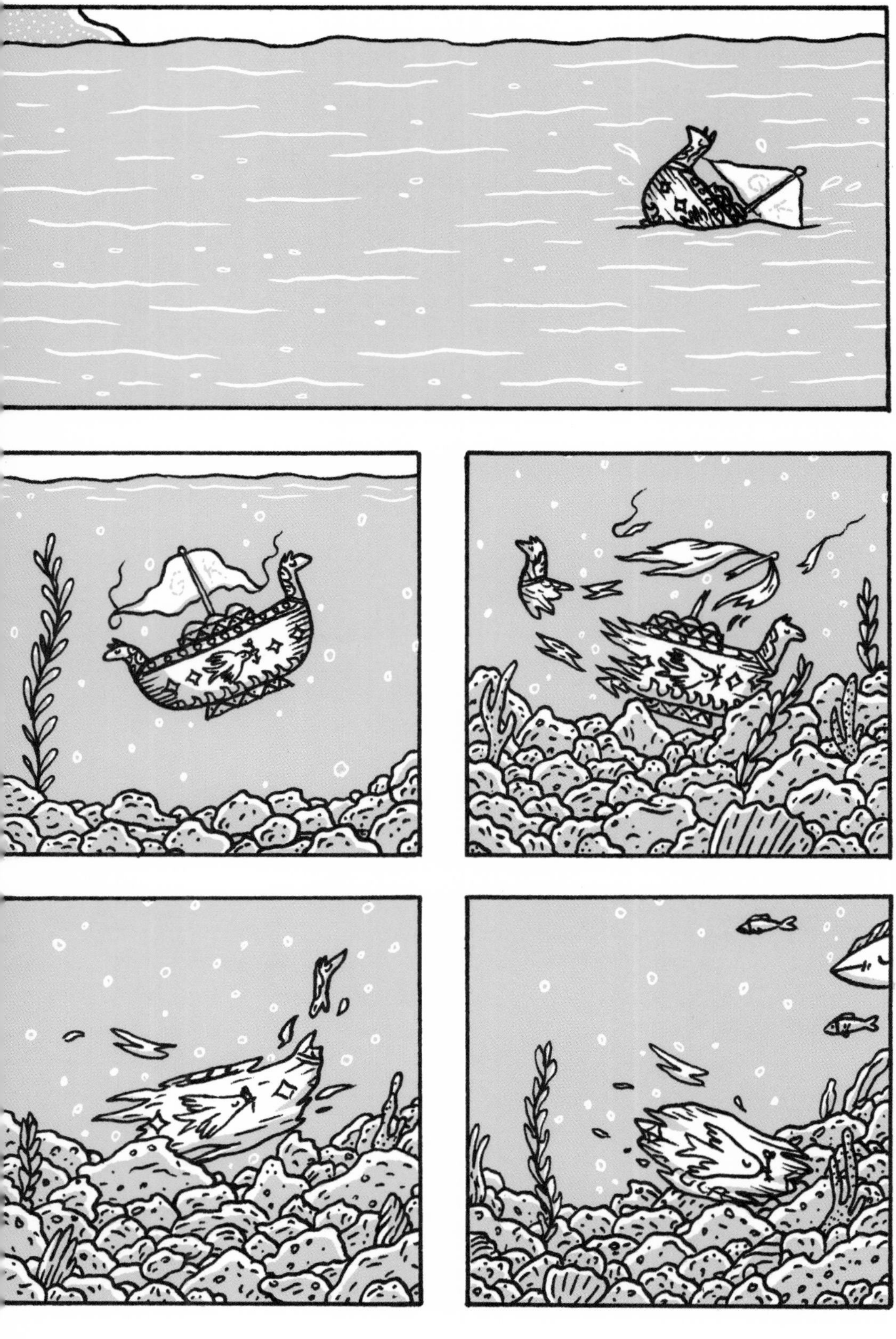

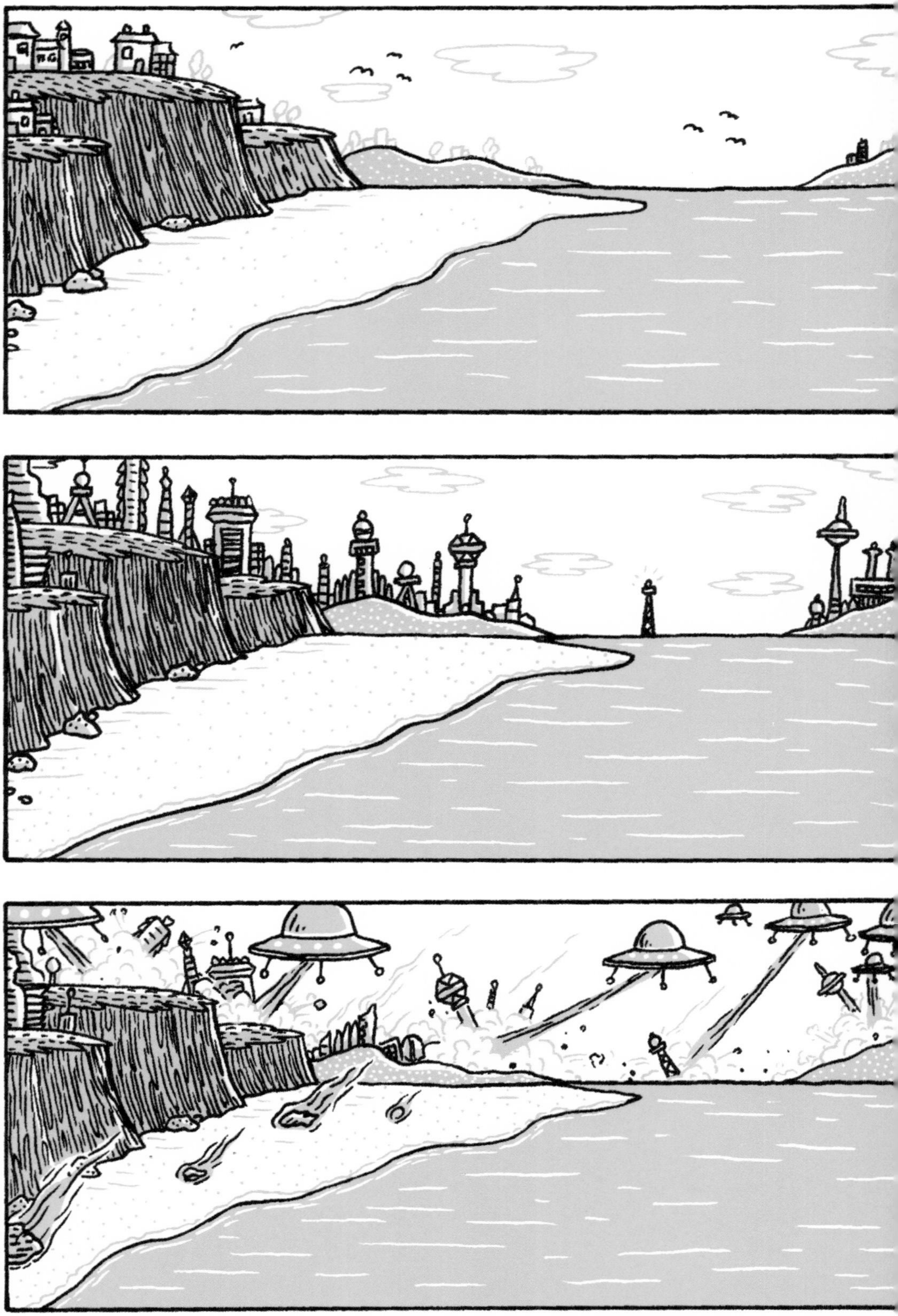

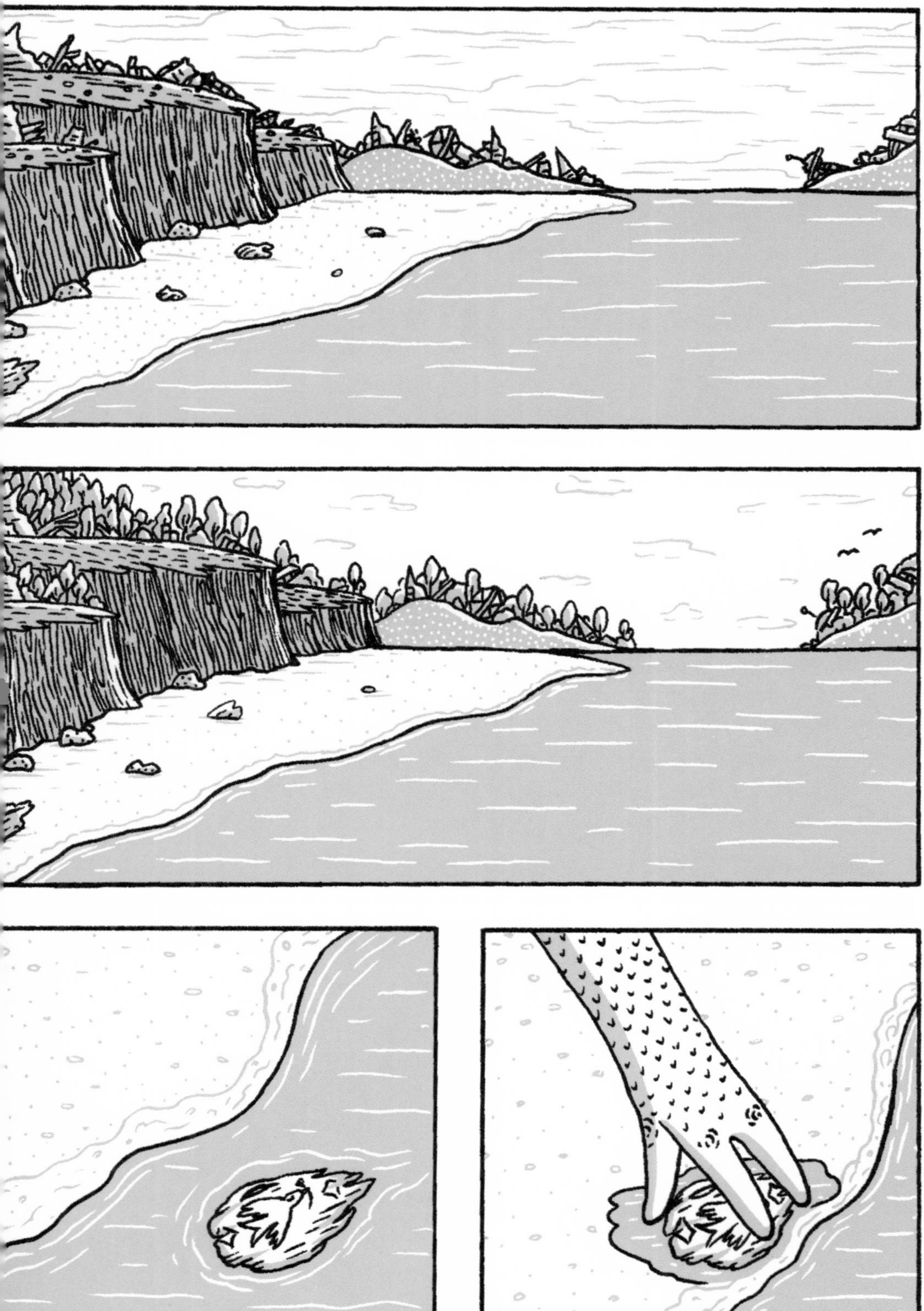

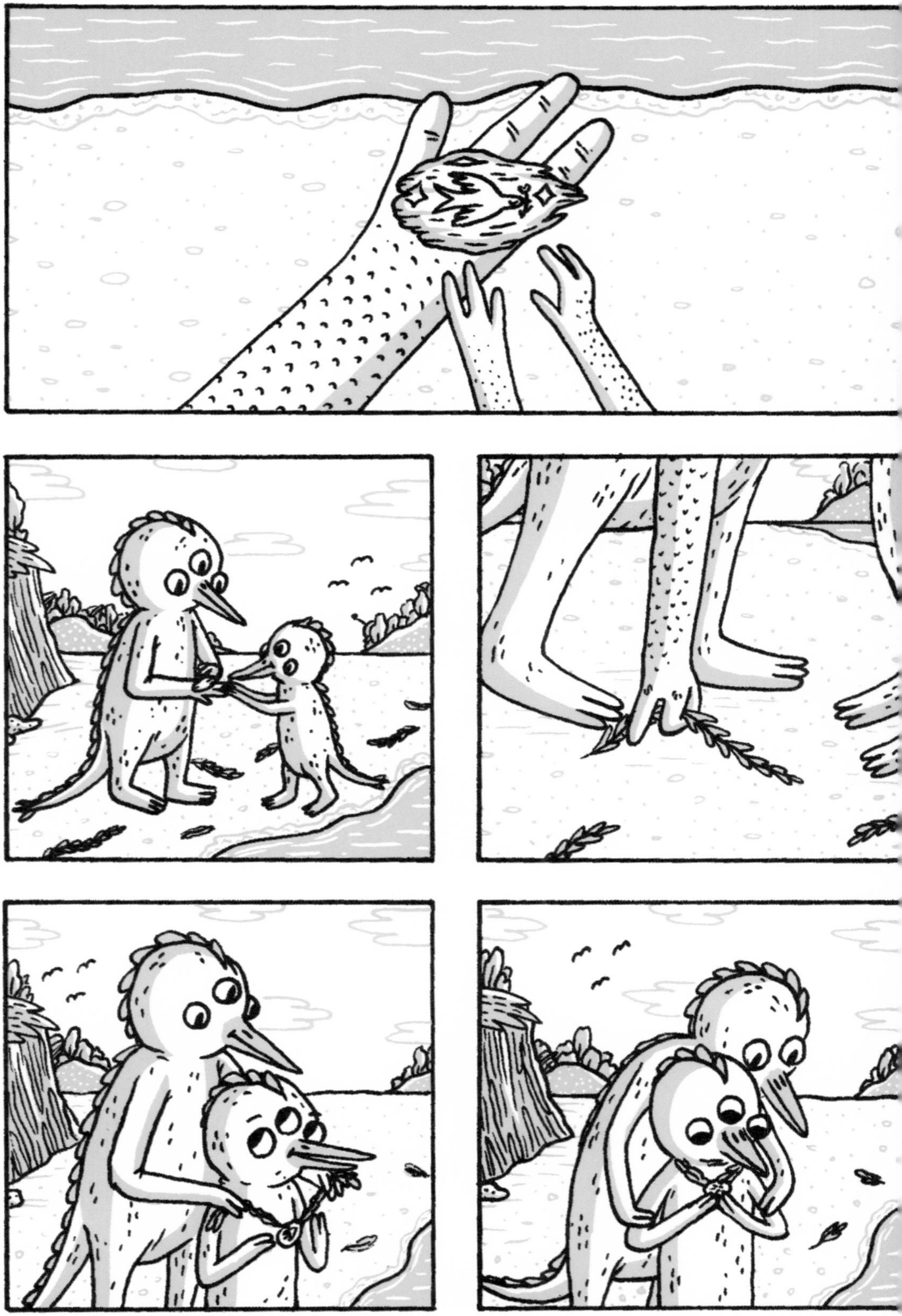

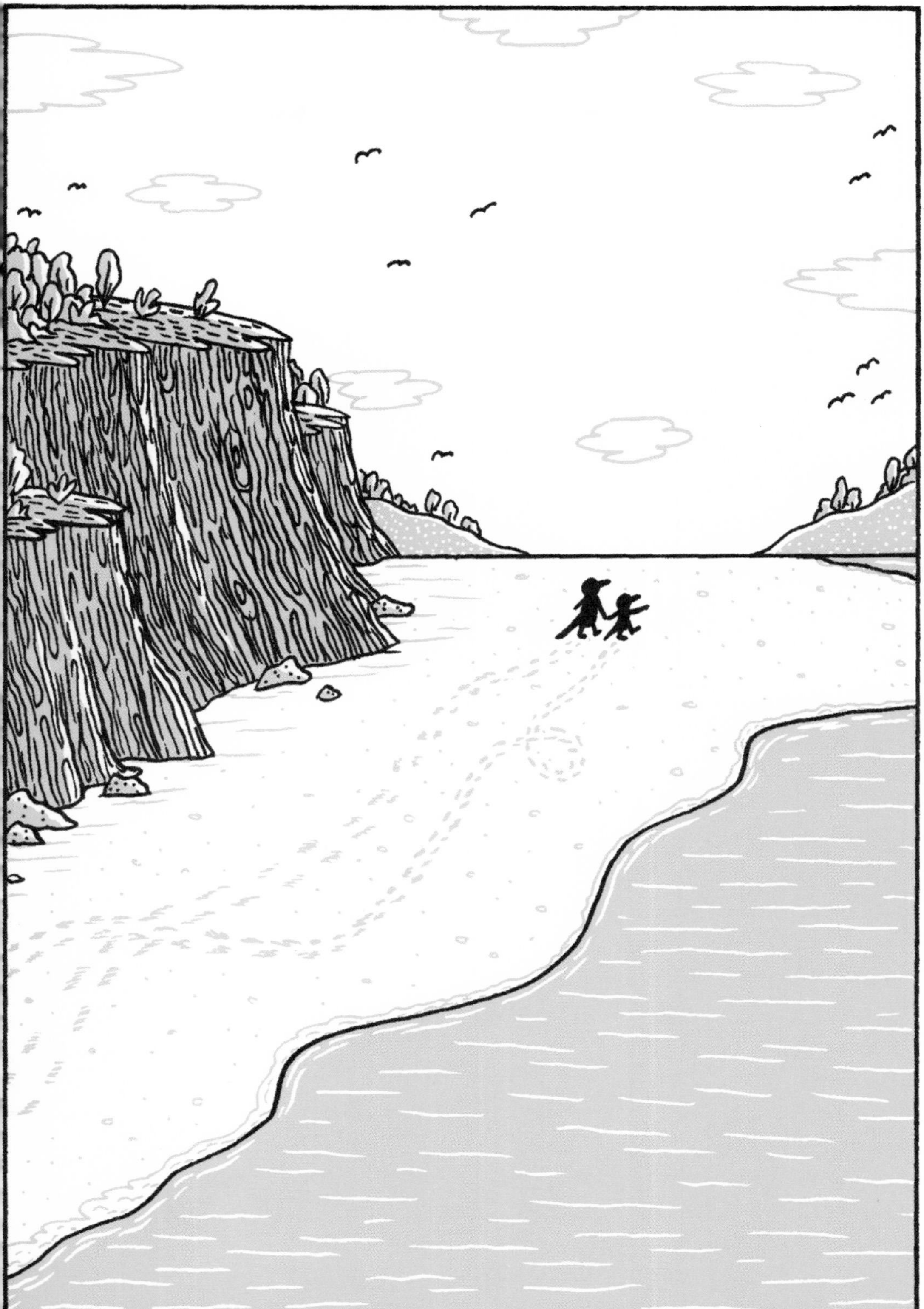

AnYWhere
ROAD
FUMIO OBATA

Fumio Obata

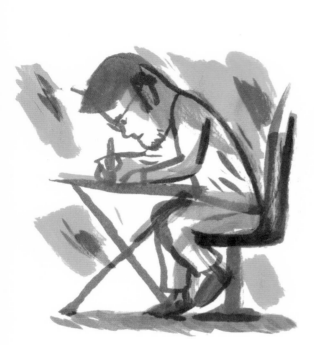

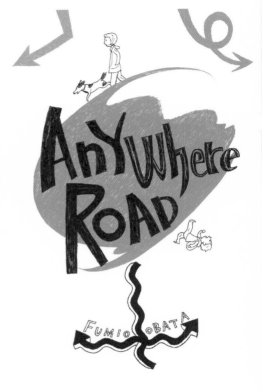

Fumio Obata is a comic artist originally from Tokyo. He ha published two major graphic novels; ***L'Incroyable Histoire de l* *Sauce Soja*** (La Pastèque, 2011) and ***Just So Happens*** (Jonatha Cape, 2014). ***Just So Happens*** has been translated in French Italian, Chinese, and Spanish and will come out in the US i Spring 2015.

He focuses on identity and self-discovery among outsiders. He i a lecturer in BA Illustration at the University of Gloucestershire.

fumioobata.co.uk
@FumioObata

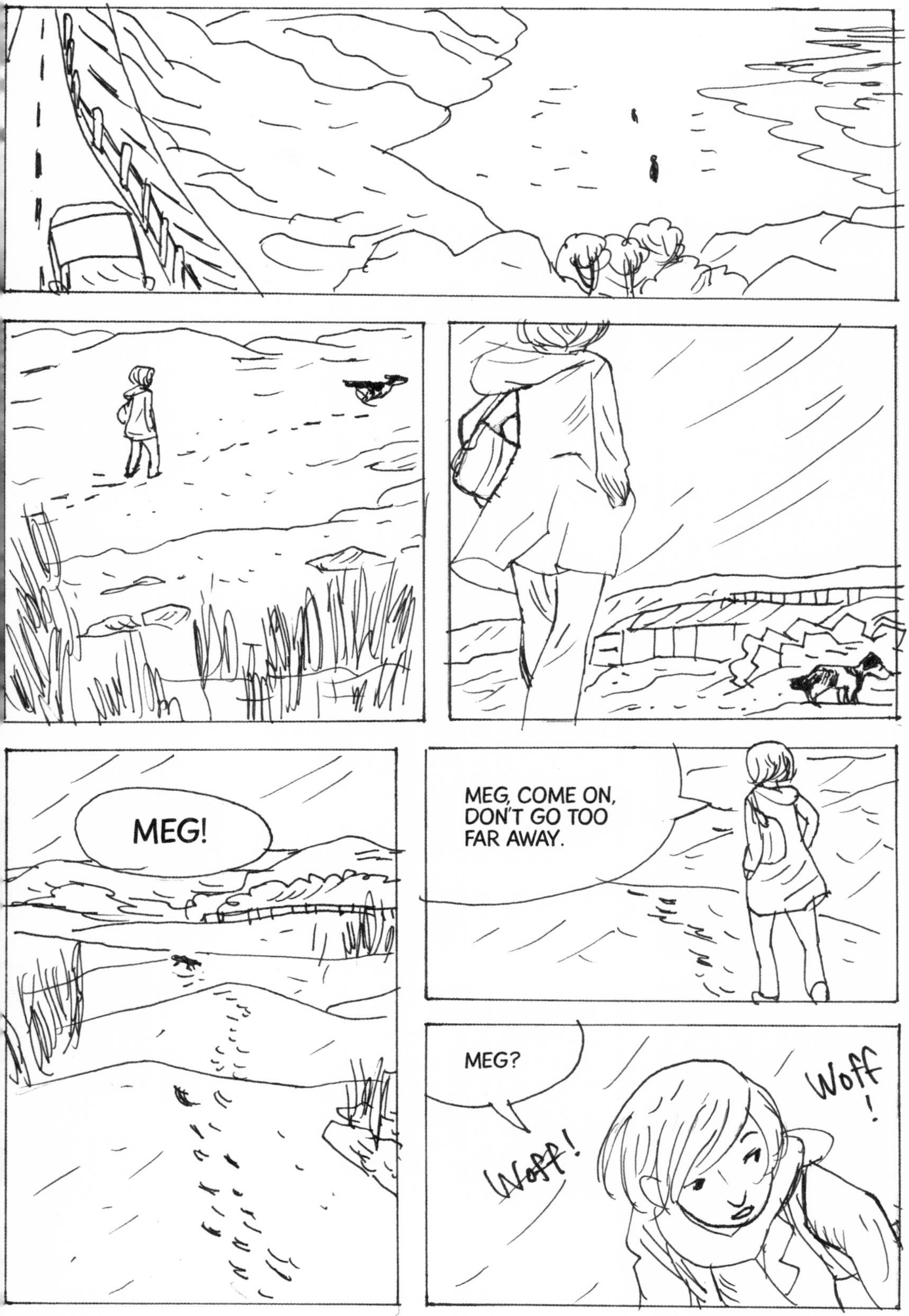
MEG!
MEG, COME ON, DON'T GO TOO FAR AWAY.
MEG?
Woff!
Woff!

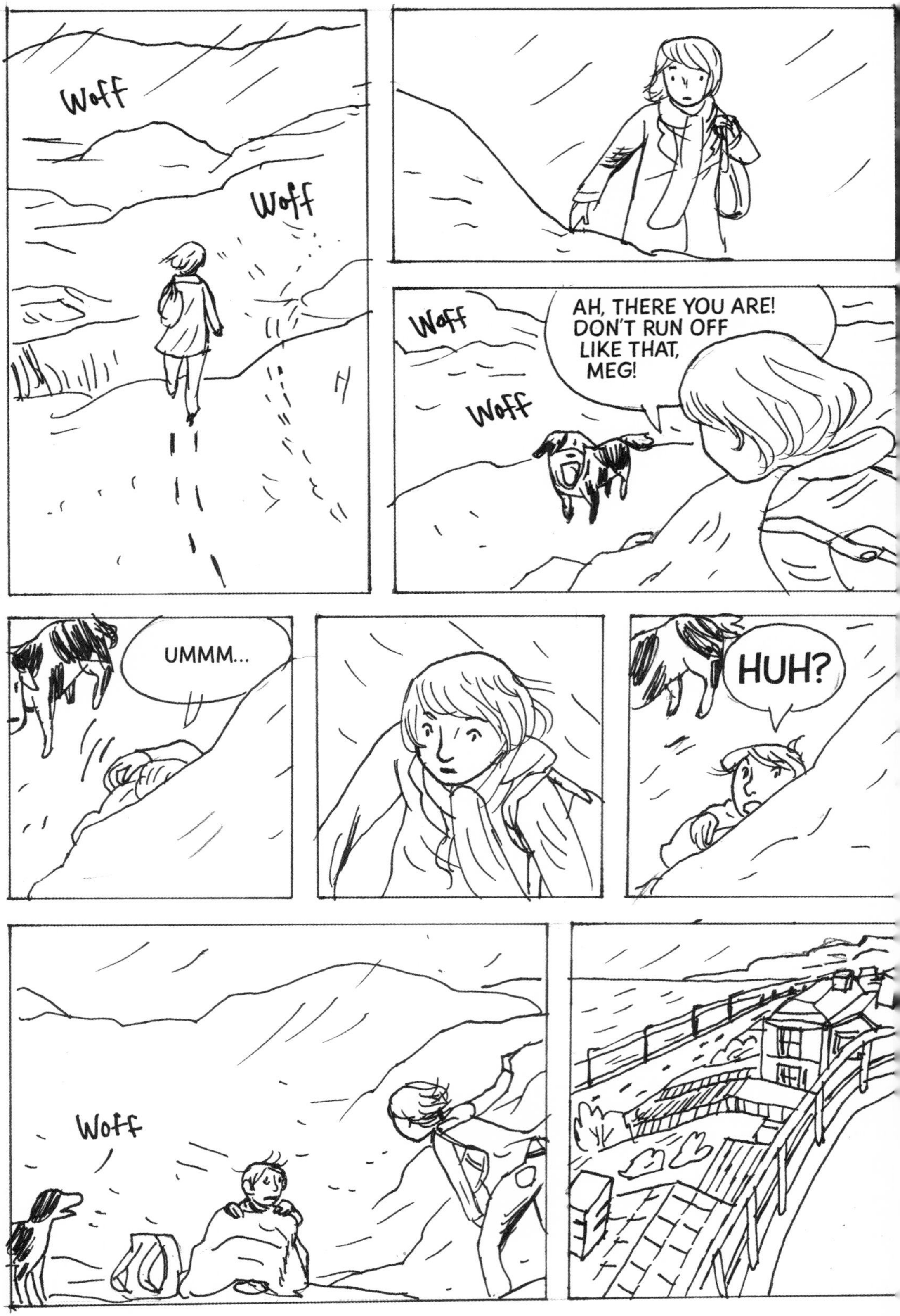
Woff
Woff
Woff
Woff
AH, THERE YOU ARE! DON'T RUN OFF LIKE THAT, MEG!
UMMM...
HUH?
Woff

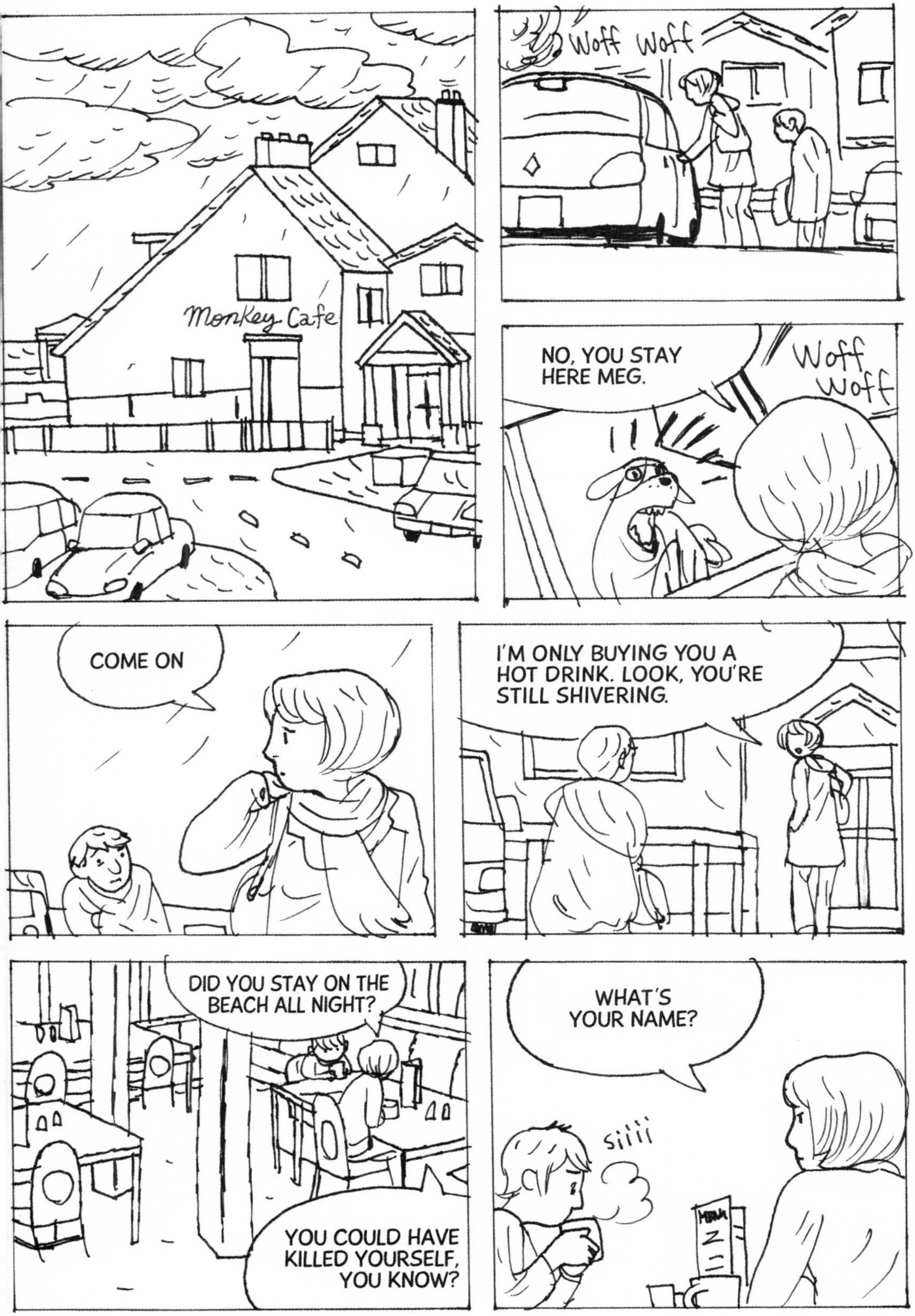
Monkey Cafe
Woff woff
NO, YOU STAY HERE MEG.
Woff woff
COME ON
I'M ONLY BUYING YOU A HOT DRINK. LOOK, YOU'RE STILL SHIVERING.
DID YOU STAY ON THE BEACH ALL NIGHT?
YOU COULD HAVE KILLED YOURSELF, YOU KNOW?
WHAT'S YOUR NAME?
siiii

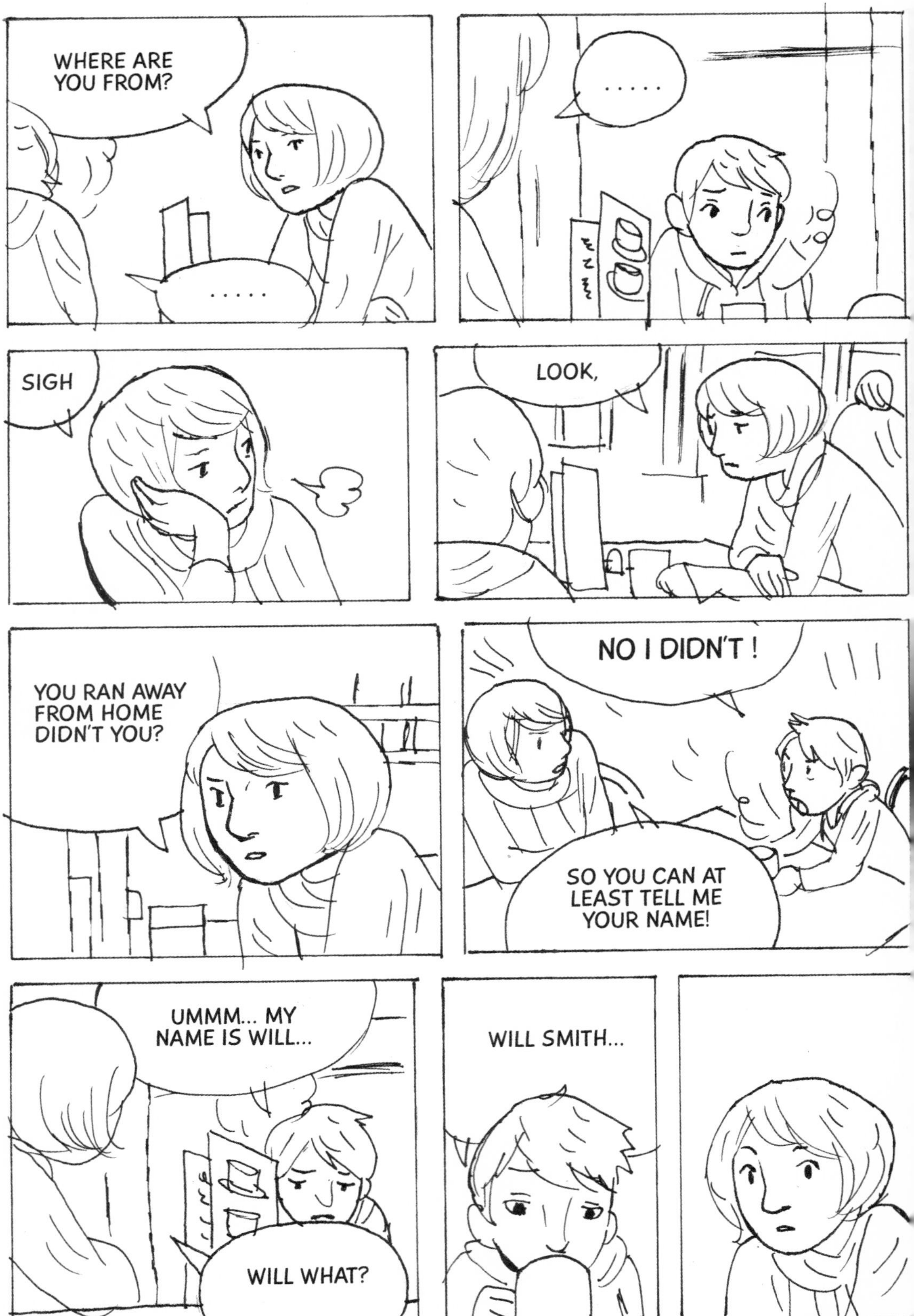
WHERE ARE YOU FROM?
......
......
SIGH
LOOK,
YOU RAN AWAY FROM HOME DIDN'T YOU?
NO I DIDN'T !
SO YOU CAN AT LEAST TELL ME YOUR NAME!
UMMM... MY NAME IS WILL...
WILL WHAT?
WILL SMITH...

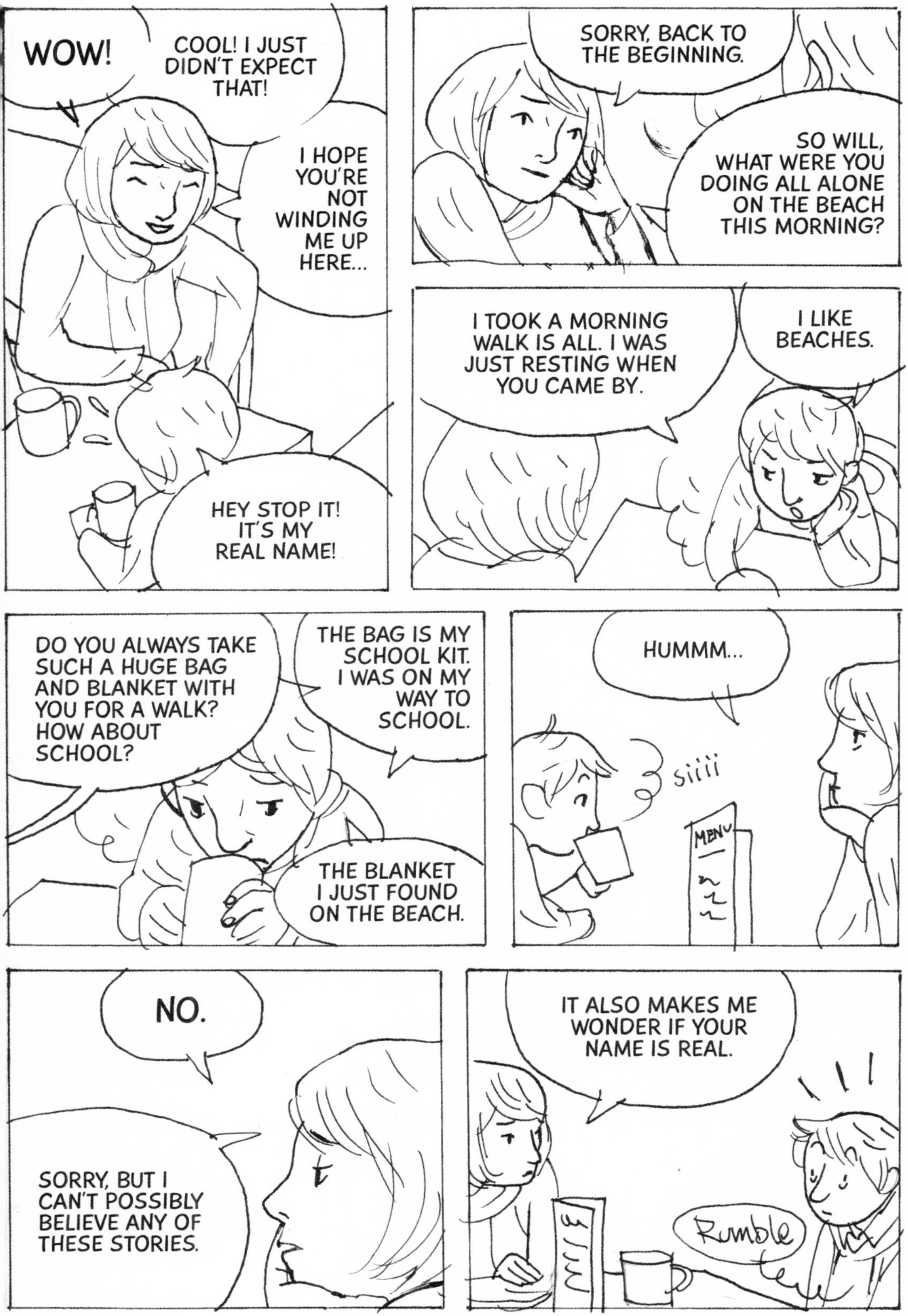
WOW!
COOL! I JUST DIDN'T EXPECT THAT!
I HOPE YOU'RE NOT WINDING ME UP HERE...
HEY STOP IT! IT'S MY REAL NAME!
SORRY, BACK TO THE BEGINNING.
SO WILL, WHAT WERE YOU DOING ALL ALONE ON THE BEACH THIS MORNING?
I TOOK A MORNING WALK IS ALL. I WAS JUST RESTING WHEN YOU CAME BY.
I LIKE BEACHES.
DO YOU ALWAYS TAKE SUCH A HUGE BAG AND BLANKET WITH YOU FOR A WALK? HOW ABOUT SCHOOL?
THE BAG IS MY SCHOOL KIT. I WAS ON MY WAY TO SCHOOL.
THE BLANKET I JUST FOUND ON THE BEACH.
HUMMM...
siiii
MENU
NO.
SORRY, BUT I CAN'T POSSIBLY BELIEVE ANY OF THESE STORIES.
IT ALSO MAKES ME WONDER IF YOUR NAME IS REAL.
Rumble

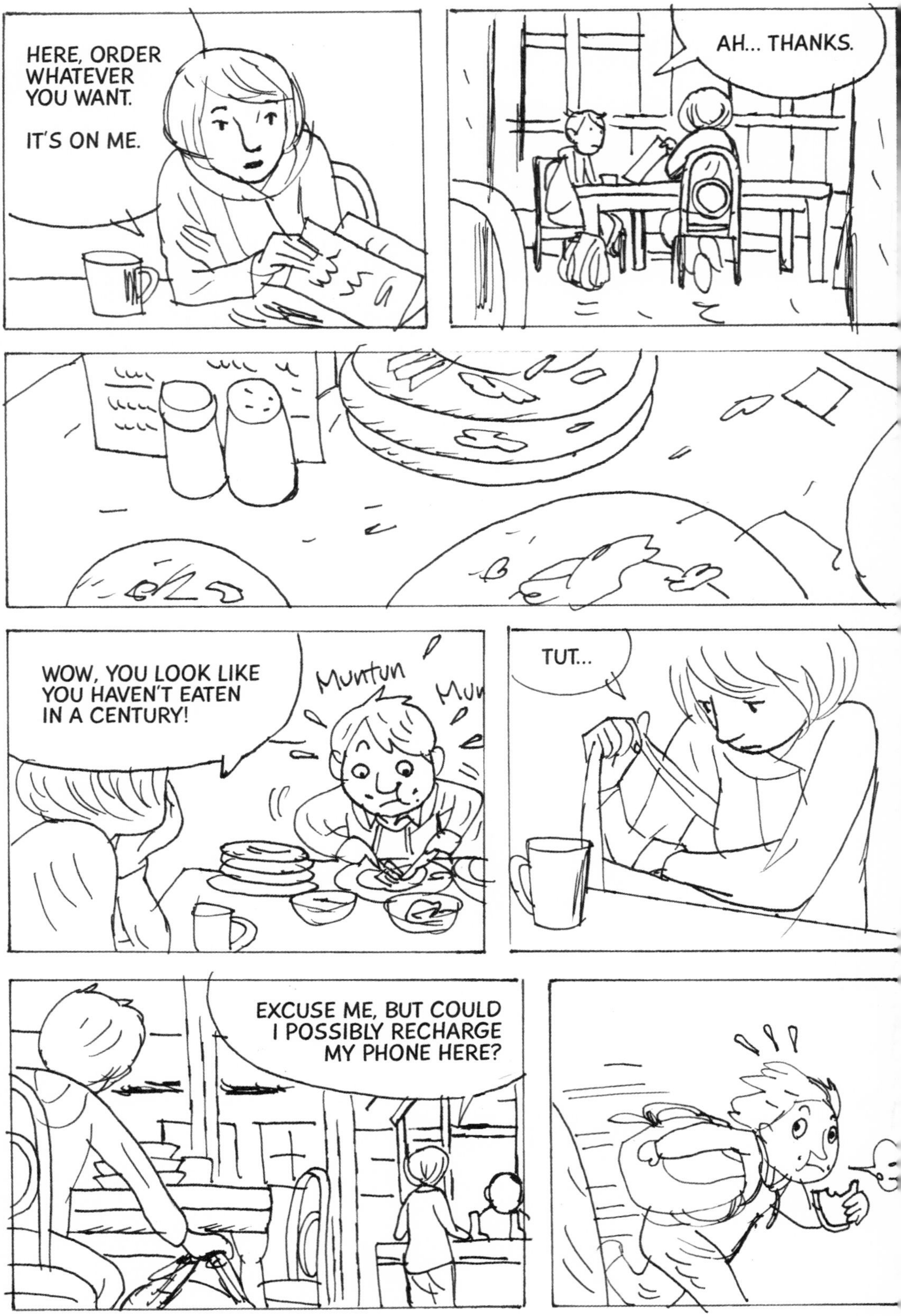
HERE, ORDER WHATEVER YOU WANT.
IT'S ON ME.
AH... THANKS.
WOW, YOU LOOK LIKE YOU HAVEN'T EATEN IN A CENTURY!
Muntun
TUT...
EXCUSE ME, BUT COULD I POSSIBLY RECHARGE MY PHONE HERE?

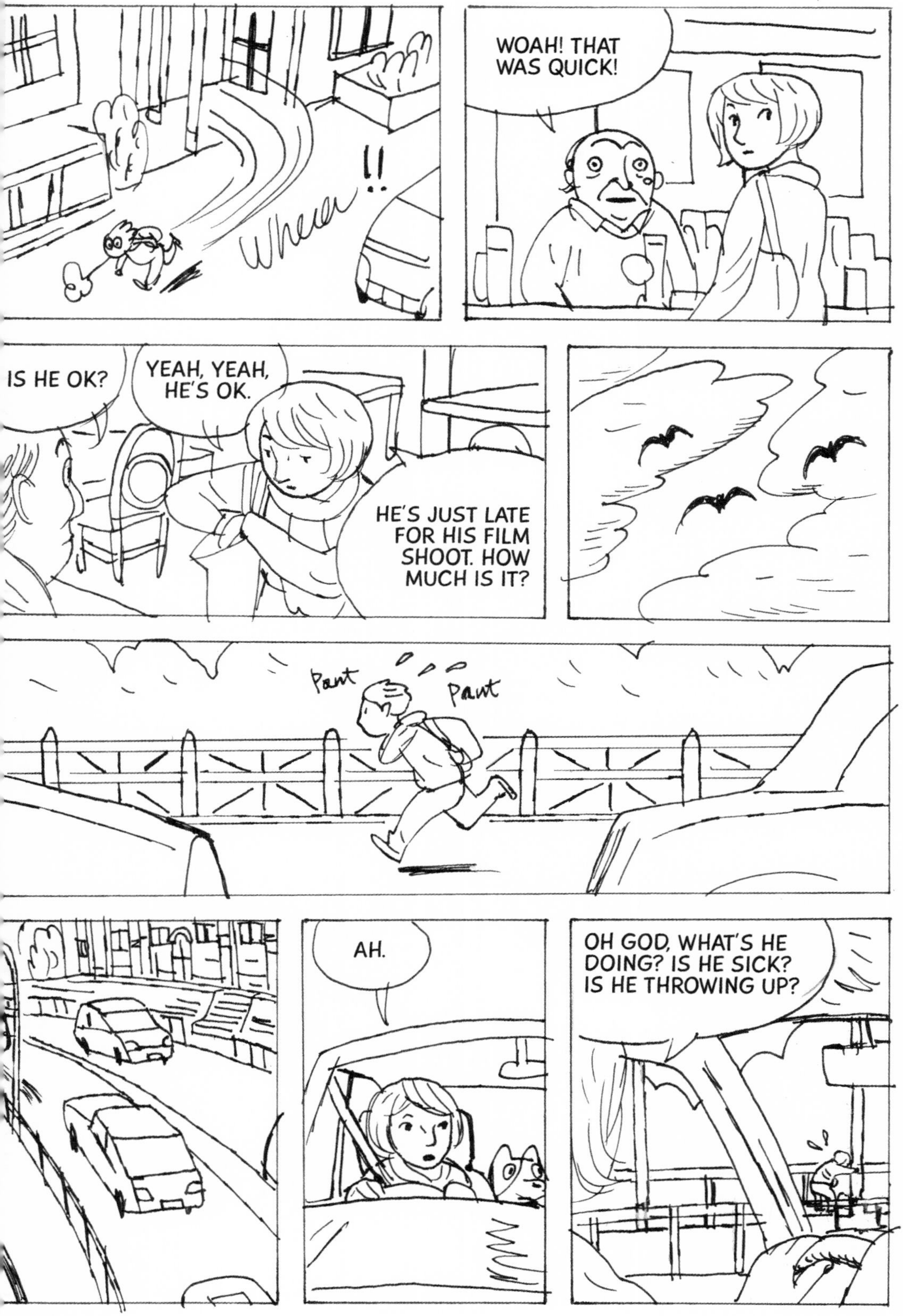

Wheeee
!!
WOAH! THAT WAS QUICK!
IS HE OK?
YEAH, YEAH, HE'S OK.
HE'S JUST LATE FOR HIS FILM SHOOT. HOW MUCH IS IT?
Pant
Pant
AH.
OH GOD, WHAT'S HE DOING? IS HE SICK? IS HE THROWING UP?

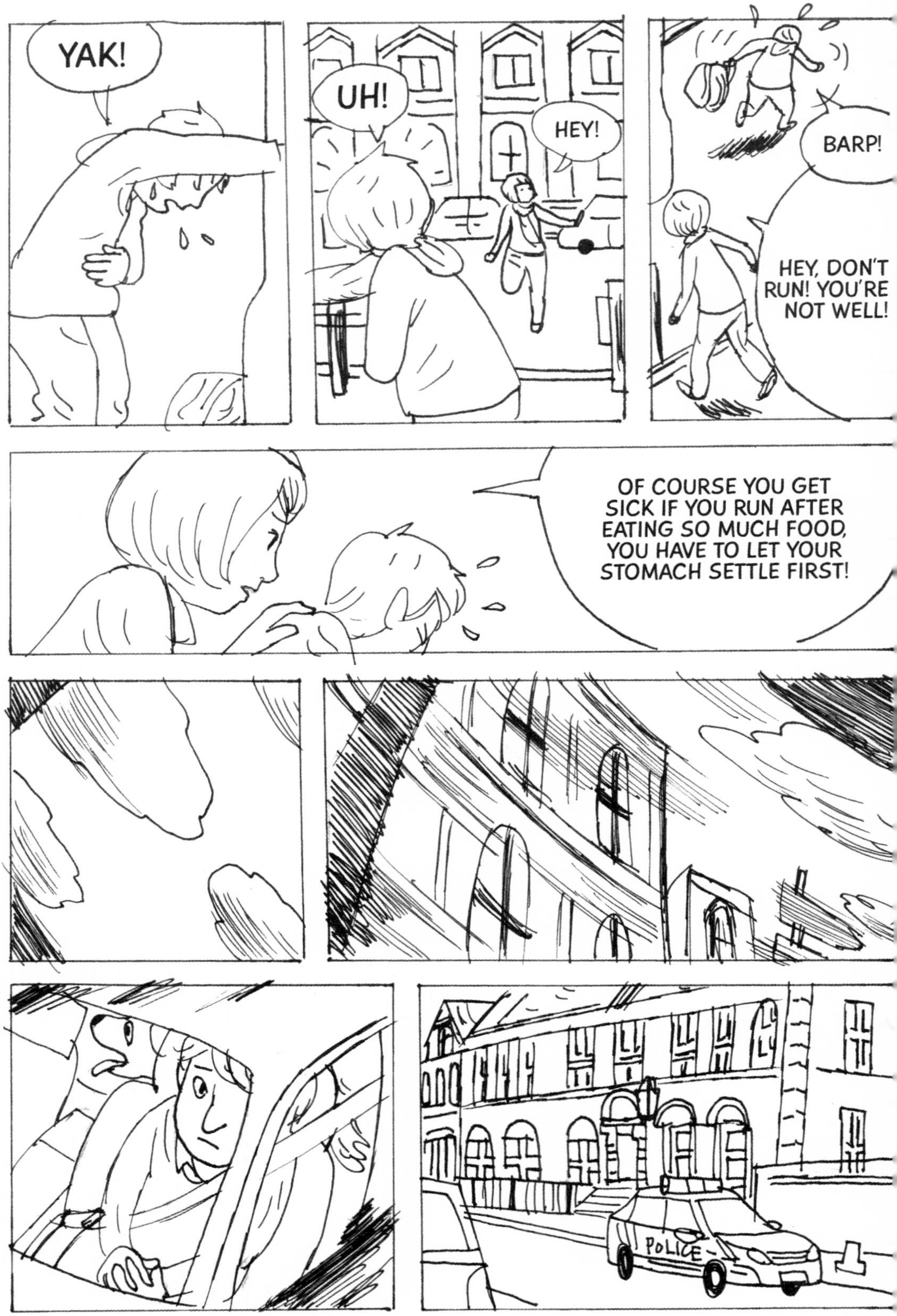
YAK!
UH!
HEY!
BARP!
HEY, DON'T RUN! YOU'RE NOT WELL!
OF COURSE YOU GET SICK IF YOU RUN AFTER EATING SO MUCH FOOD, YOU HAVE TO LET YOUR STOMACH SETTLE FIRST!
POLICE

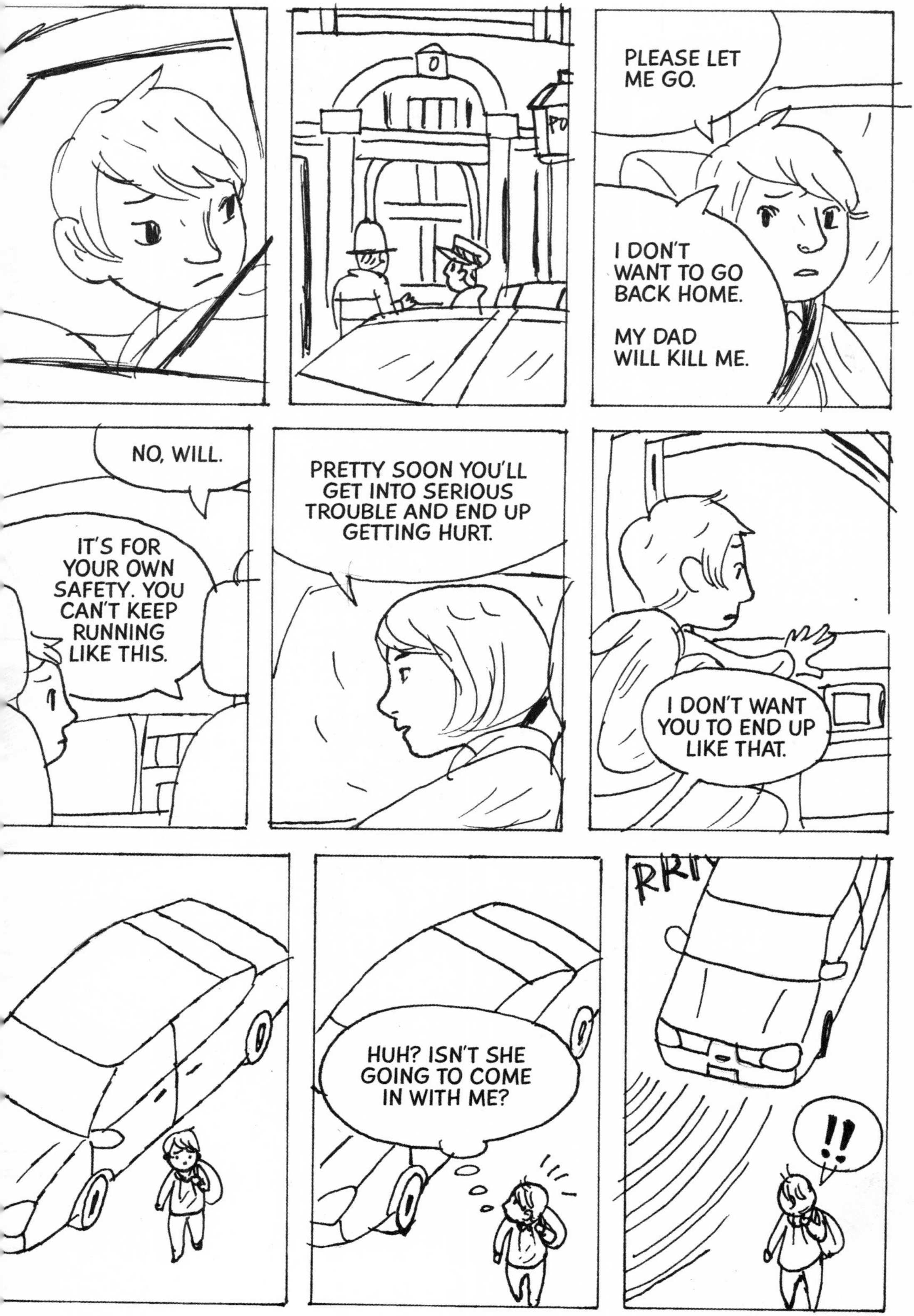
PLEASE LET ME GO.
I DON'T WANT TO GO BACK HOME.
MY DAD WILL KILL ME.
NO, WILL.
IT'S FOR YOUR OWN SAFETY. YOU CAN'T KEEP RUNNING LIKE THIS.
PRETTY SOON YOU'LL GET INTO SERIOUS TROUBLE AND END UP GETTING HURT.
I DON'T WANT YOU TO END UP LIKE THAT.
HUH? ISN'T SHE GOING TO COME IN WITH ME?
RRR
!!

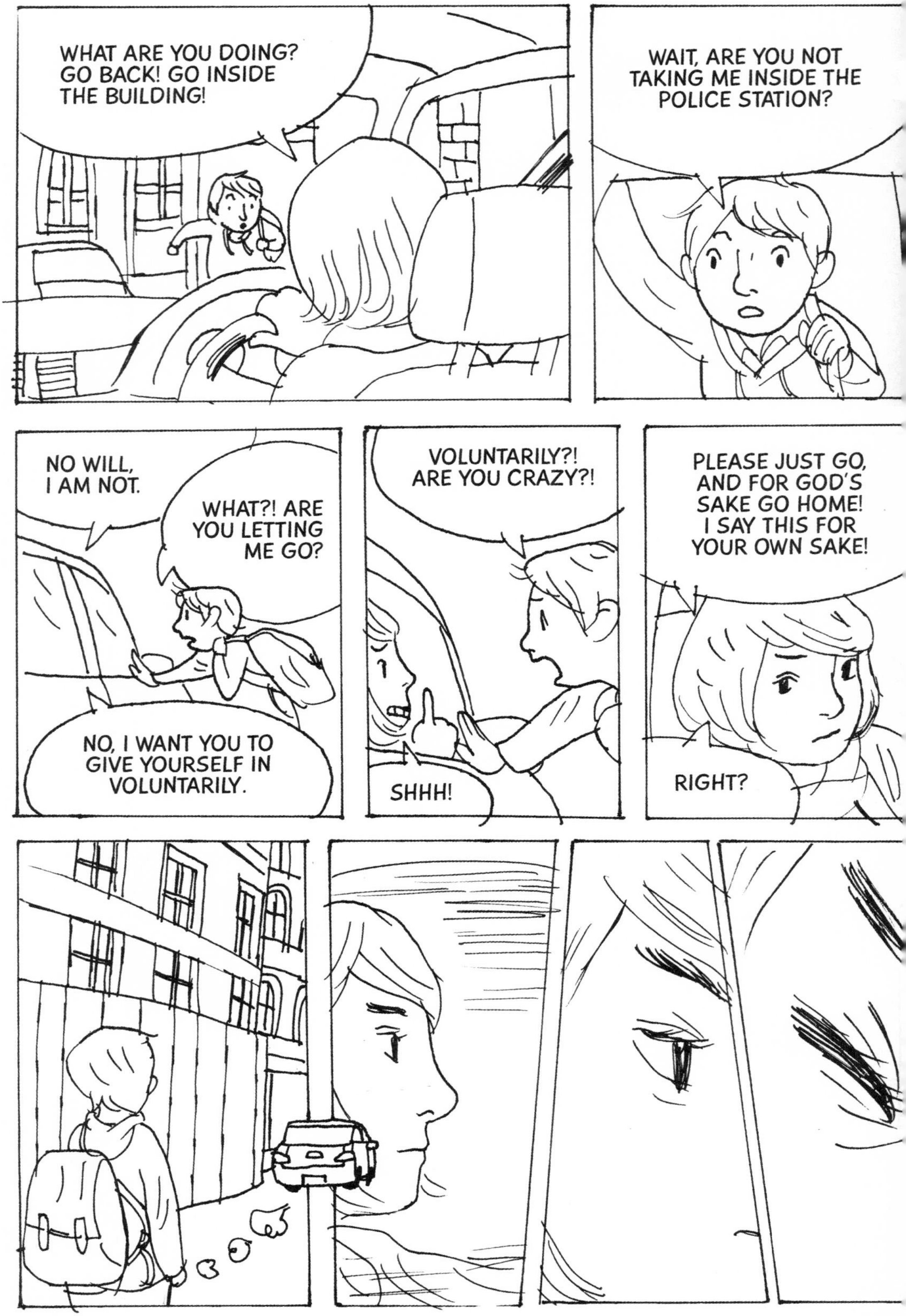
WHAT ARE YOU DOING? GO BACK! GO INSIDE THE BUILDING!
WAIT, ARE YOU NOT TAKING ME INSIDE THE POLICE STATION?
NO WILL, I AM NOT.
WHAT?! ARE YOU LETTING ME GO?
NO, I WANT YOU TO GIVE YOURSELF IN VOLUNTARILY.
VOLUNTARILY?! ARE YOU CRAZY?!
SHHH!
PLEASE JUST GO, AND FOR GOD'S SAKE GO HOME! I SAY THIS FOR YOUR OWN SAKE!
RIGHT?

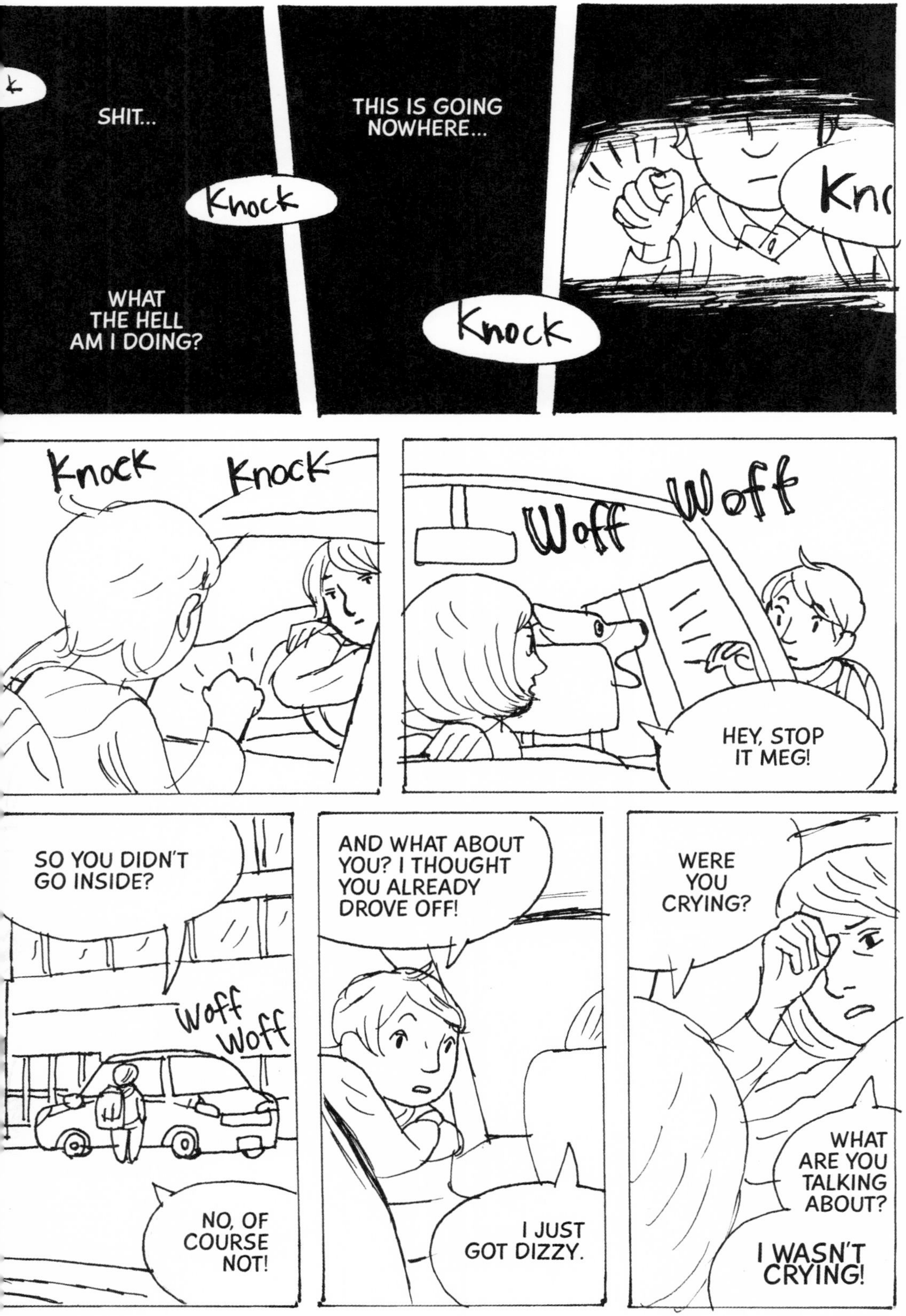

SHIT...
WHAT THE HELL AM I DOING?
Knock
THIS IS GOING NOWHERE...
Knock
Knock
Knock
WOFF
WOFF
HEY, STOP IT MEG!
SO YOU DIDN'T GO INSIDE?
woff woff
NO, OF COURSE NOT!
AND WHAT ABOUT YOU? I THOUGHT YOU ALREADY DROVE OFF!
I JUST GOT DIZZY.
WERE YOU CRYING?
WHAT ARE YOU TALKING ABOUT?
I WASN'T CRYING!

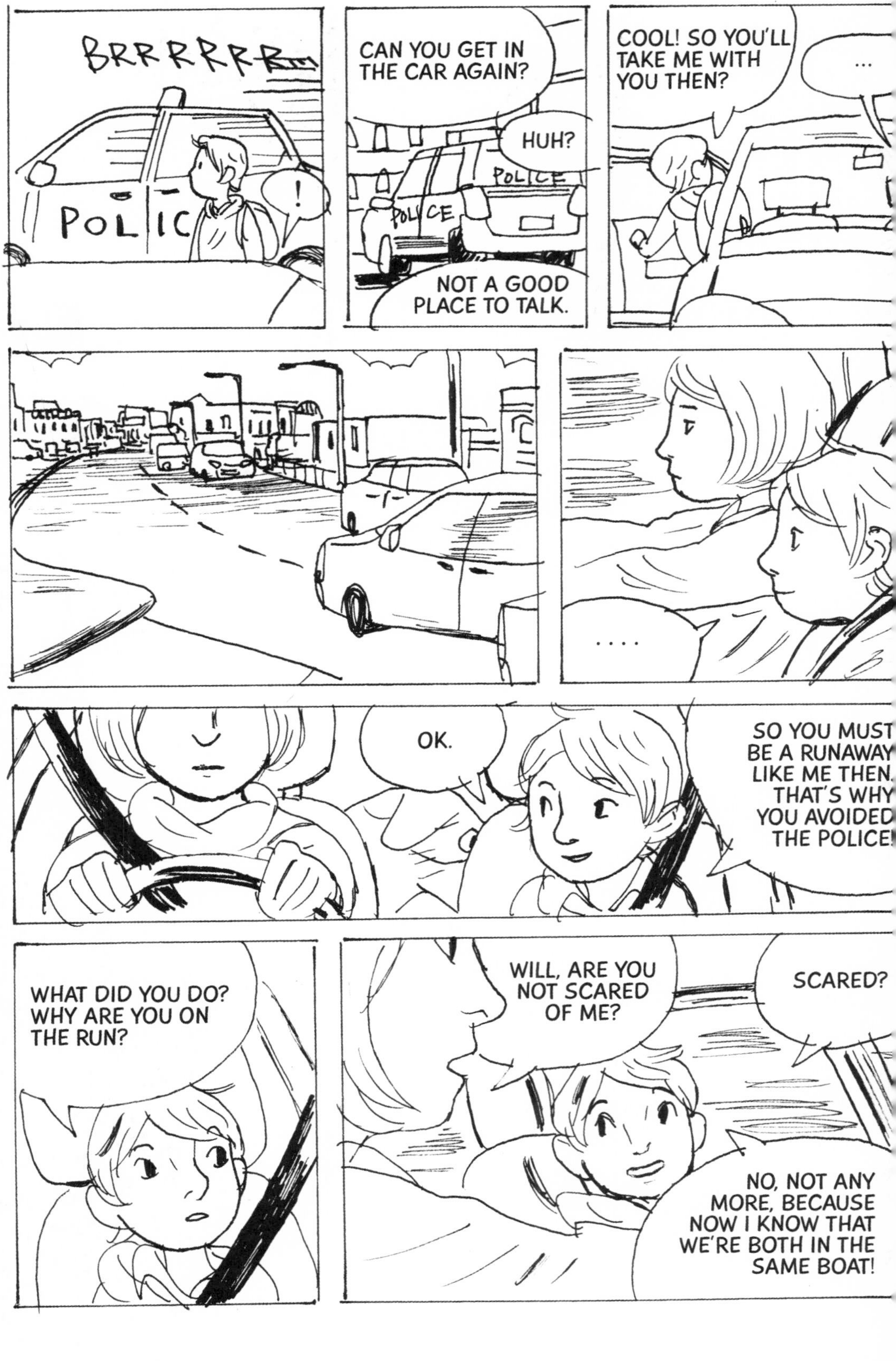
BRRRRRRm
POLIC
!
CAN YOU GET IN THE CAR AGAIN?
HUH?
POLICE
POLICE
NOT A GOOD PLACE TO TALK.
COOL! SO YOU'LL TAKE ME WITH YOU THEN?
...
....
OK.
SO YOU MUST BE A RUNAWAY LIKE ME THEN. THAT'S WHY YOU AVOIDED THE POLICE!
WHAT DID YOU DO? WHY ARE YOU ON THE RUN?
WILL, ARE YOU NOT SCARED OF ME?
SCARED?
NO, NOT ANY MORE, BECAUSE NOW I KNOW THAT WE'RE BOTH IN THE SAME BOAT!

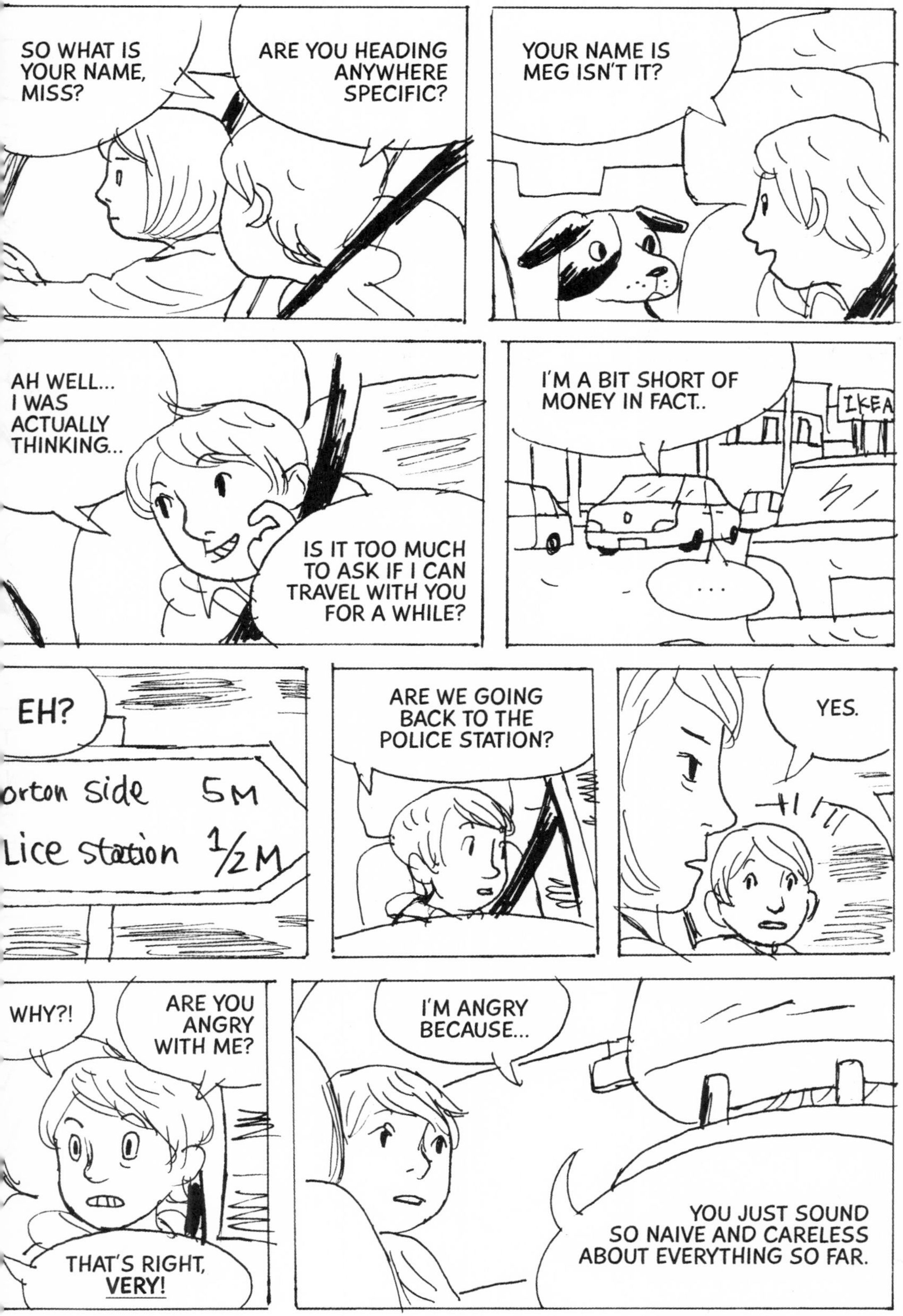

SO WHAT IS YOUR NAME, MISS?
ARE YOU HEADING ANYWHERE SPECIFIC?
YOUR NAME IS MEG ISN'T IT?
AH WELL... I WAS ACTUALLY THINKING...
IS IT TOO MUCH TO ASK IF I CAN TRAVEL WITH YOU FOR A WHILE?
I'M A BIT SHORT OF MONEY IN FACT..
IKEA
...
EH?
orton Side 5M
Lice station 1/2M
ARE WE GOING BACK TO THE POLICE STATION?
YES.
WHY?!
ARE YOU ANGRY WITH ME?
THAT'S RIGHT, VERY!
I'M ANGRY BECAUSE...
YOU JUST SOUND SO NAIVE AND CARELESS ABOUT EVERYTHING SO FAR.

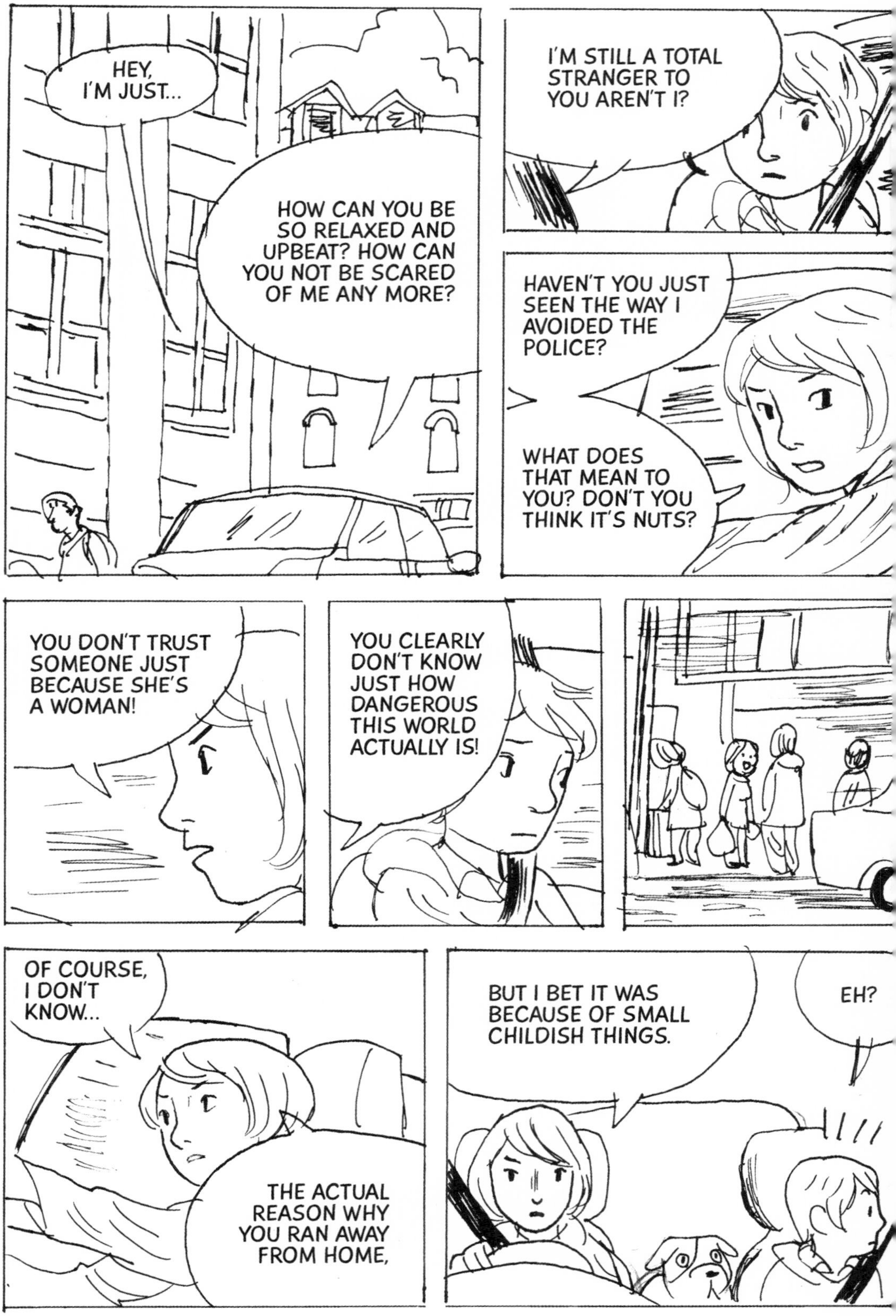
HEY, I'M JUST...
HOW CAN YOU BE SO RELAXED AND UPBEAT? HOW CAN YOU NOT BE SCARED OF ME ANY MORE?
I'M STILL A TOTAL STRANGER TO YOU AREN'T I?
HAVEN'T YOU JUST SEEN THE WAY I AVOIDED THE POLICE?
WHAT DOES THAT MEAN TO YOU? DON'T YOU THINK IT'S NUTS?
YOU DON'T TRUST SOMEONE JUST BECAUSE SHE'S A WOMAN!
YOU CLEARLY DON'T KNOW JUST HOW DANGEROUS THIS WORLD ACTUALLY IS!
OF COURSE, I DON'T KNOW...
THE ACTUAL REASON WHY YOU RAN AWAY FROM HOME,
BUT I BET IT WAS BECAUSE OF SMALL CHILDISH THINGS.
EH?

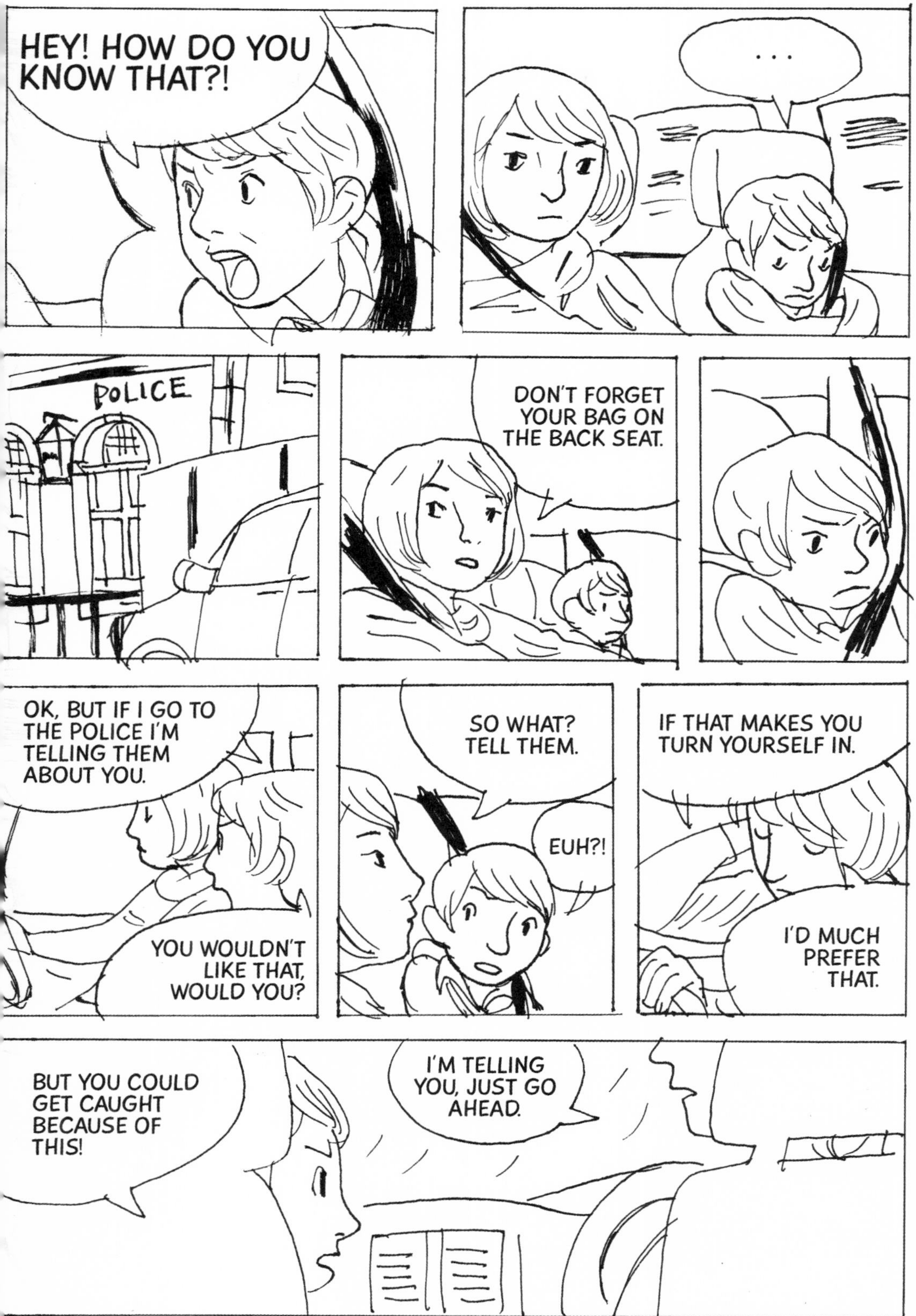
HEY! HOW DO YOU KNOW THAT?!
...
POLICE
DON'T FORGET YOUR BAG ON THE BACK SEAT.
OK, BUT IF I GO TO THE POLICE I'M TELLING THEM ABOUT YOU.
YOU WOULDN'T LIKE THAT, WOULD YOU?
SO WHAT? TELL THEM.
EUH?!
IF THAT MAKES YOU TURN YOURSELF IN.
I'D MUCH PREFER THAT.
BUT YOU COULD GET CAUGHT BECAUSE OF THIS!
I'M TELLING YOU, JUST GO AHEAD.

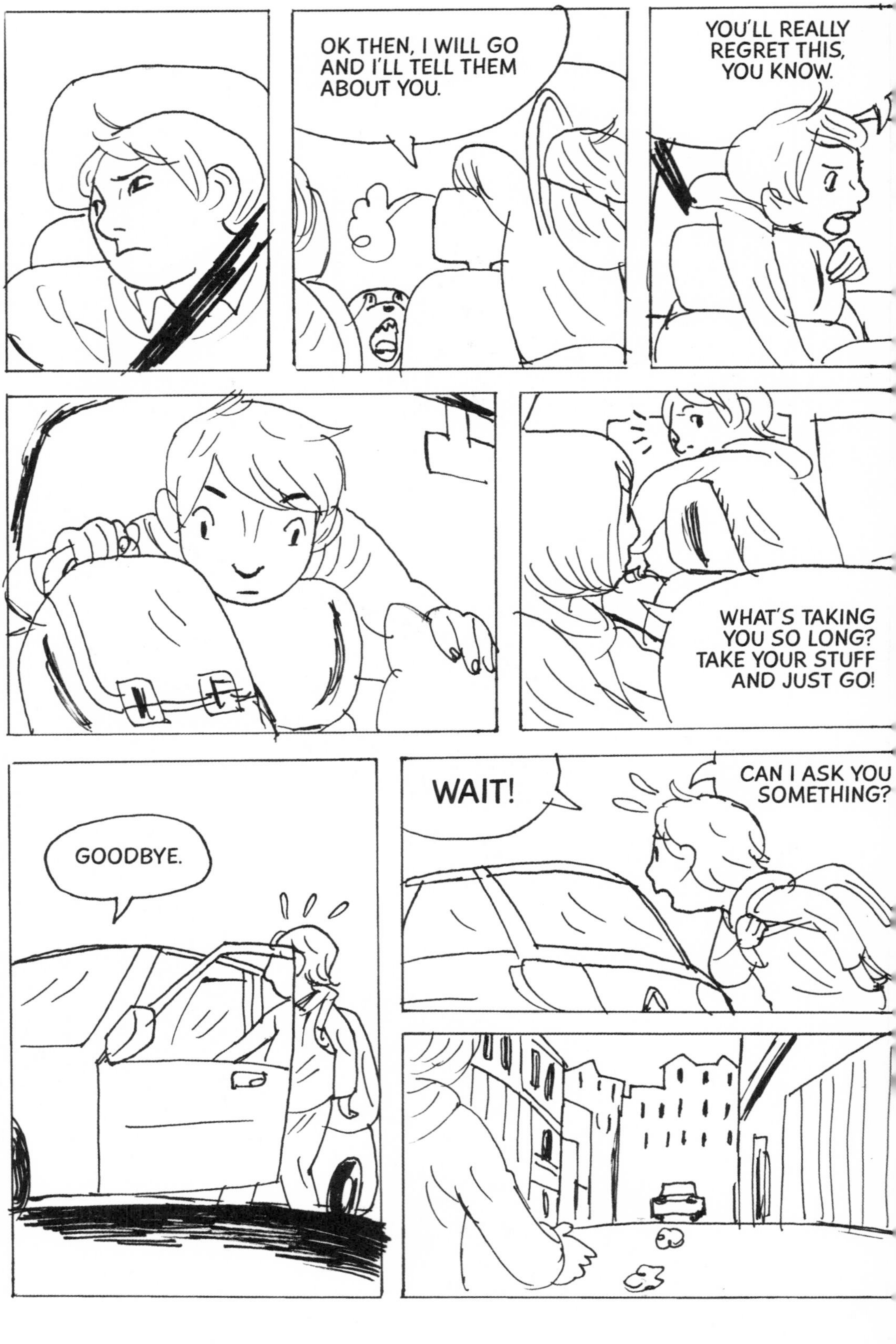

OK THEN, I WILL GO AND I'LL TELL THEM ABOUT YOU.
YOU'LL REALLY REGRET THIS, YOU KNOW.
WHAT'S TAKING YOU SO LONG? TAKE YOUR STUFF AND JUST GO!
GOODBYE.
WAIT!
CAN I ASK YOU SOMETHING?

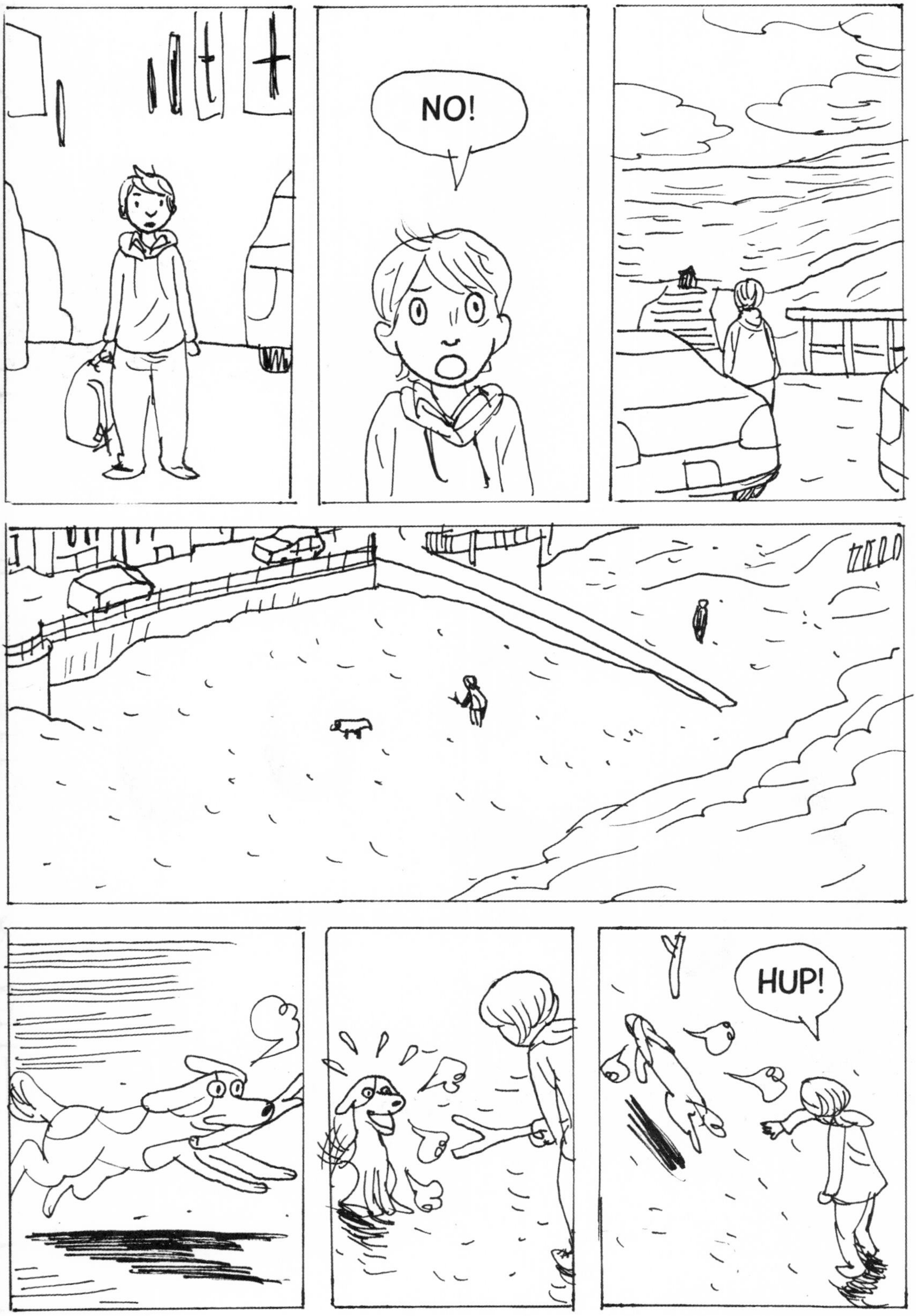
NO!
HUP!

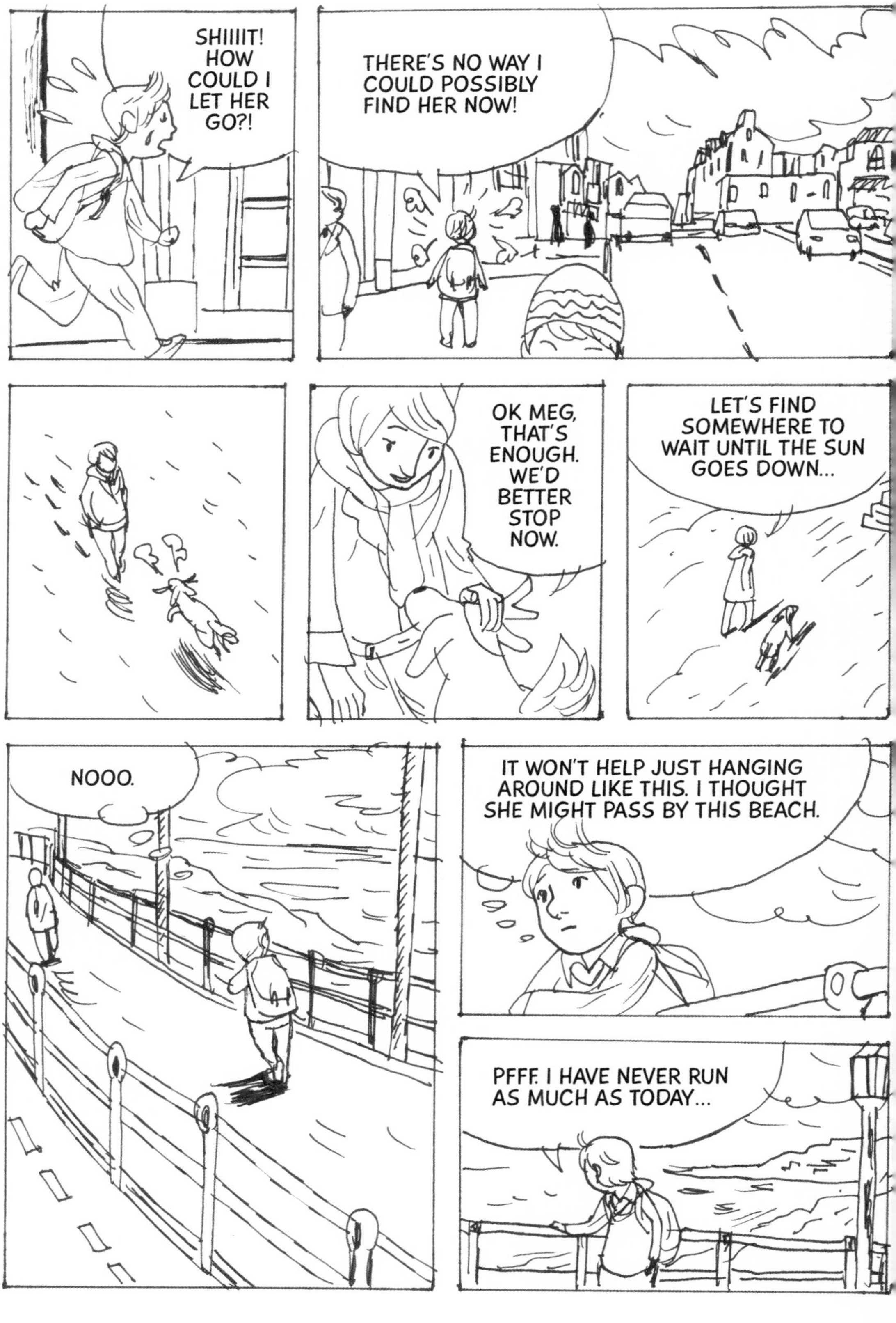
SHIIIIT! HOW COULD I LET HER GO?!
THERE'S NO WAY I COULD POSSIBLY FIND HER NOW!
OK MEG, THAT'S ENOUGH. WE'D BETTER STOP NOW.
LET'S FIND SOMEWHERE TO WAIT UNTIL THE SUN GOES DOWN...
NOOO.
IT WON'T HELP JUST HANGING AROUND LIKE THIS. I THOUGHT SHE MIGHT PASS BY THIS BEACH.
PFFF. I HAVE NEVER RUN AS MUCH AS TODAY...

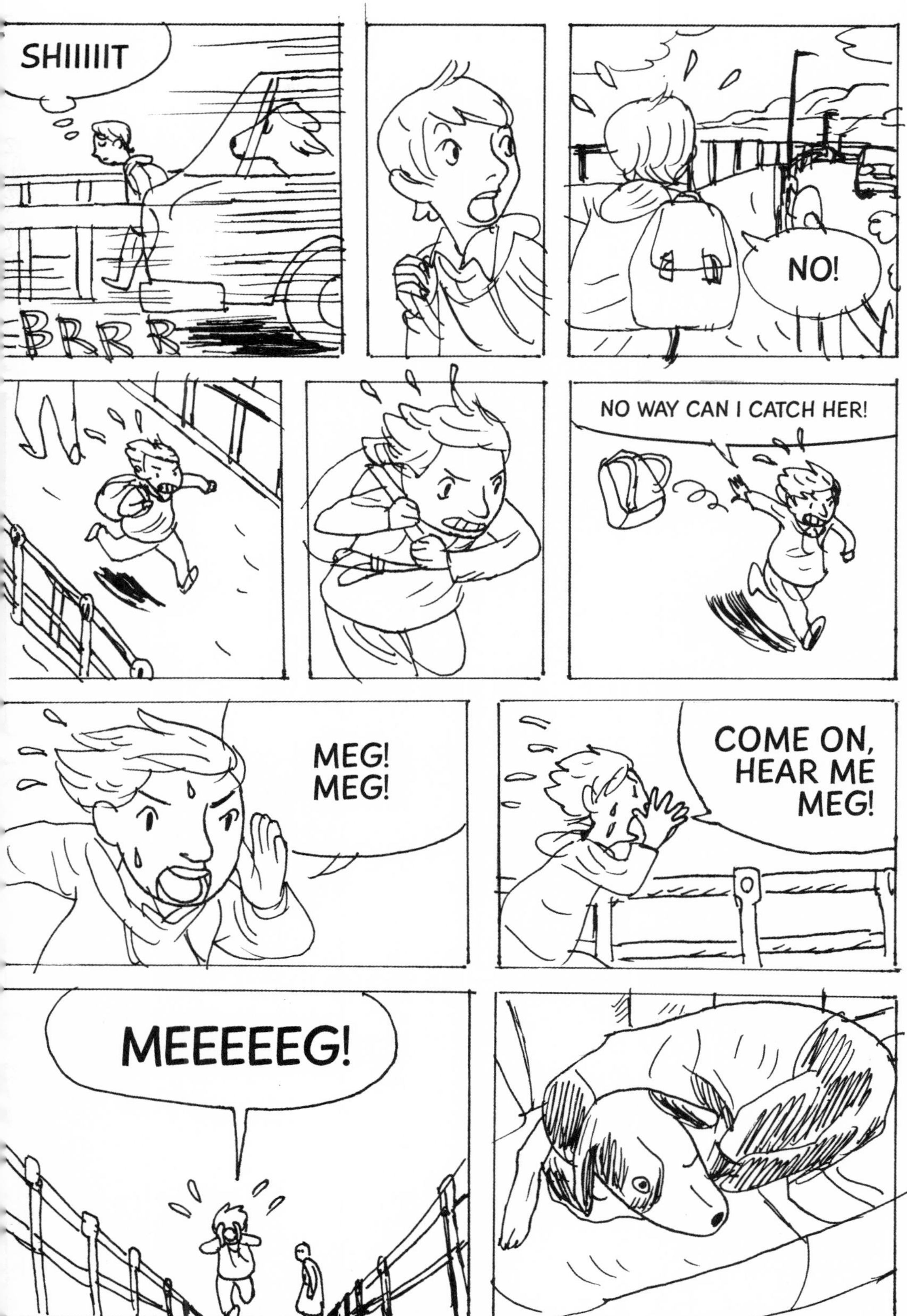
SHIIIIIT
BRRR
NO!
NO WAY CAN I CATCH HER!
MEG! MEG!
COME ON, HEAR ME MEG!
MEEEEEG!

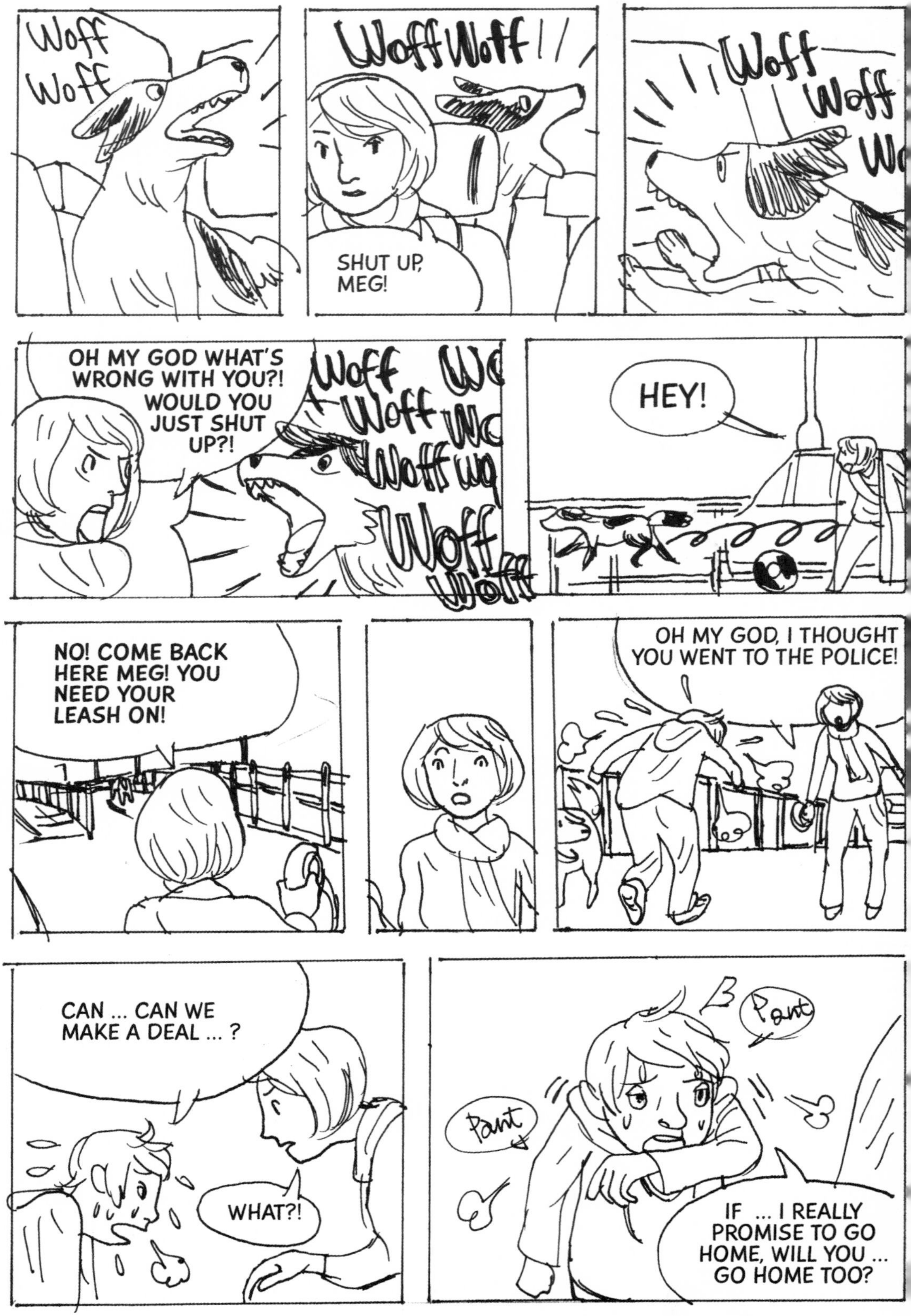
Woff Woff
Woff Woff
SHUT UP, MEG!
Woff Woff
OH MY GOD WHAT'S WRONG WITH YOU?! WOULD YOU JUST SHUT UP?!
Woff Woff Woff Woff Woff
HEY!
NO! COME BACK HERE MEG! YOU NEED YOUR LEASH ON!
OH MY GOD, I THOUGHT YOU WENT TO THE POLICE!
CAN ... CAN WE MAKE A DEAL ... ?
WHAT?!
Pant
Pant
IF ... I REALLY PROMISE TO GO HOME, WILL YOU ... GO HOME TOO?

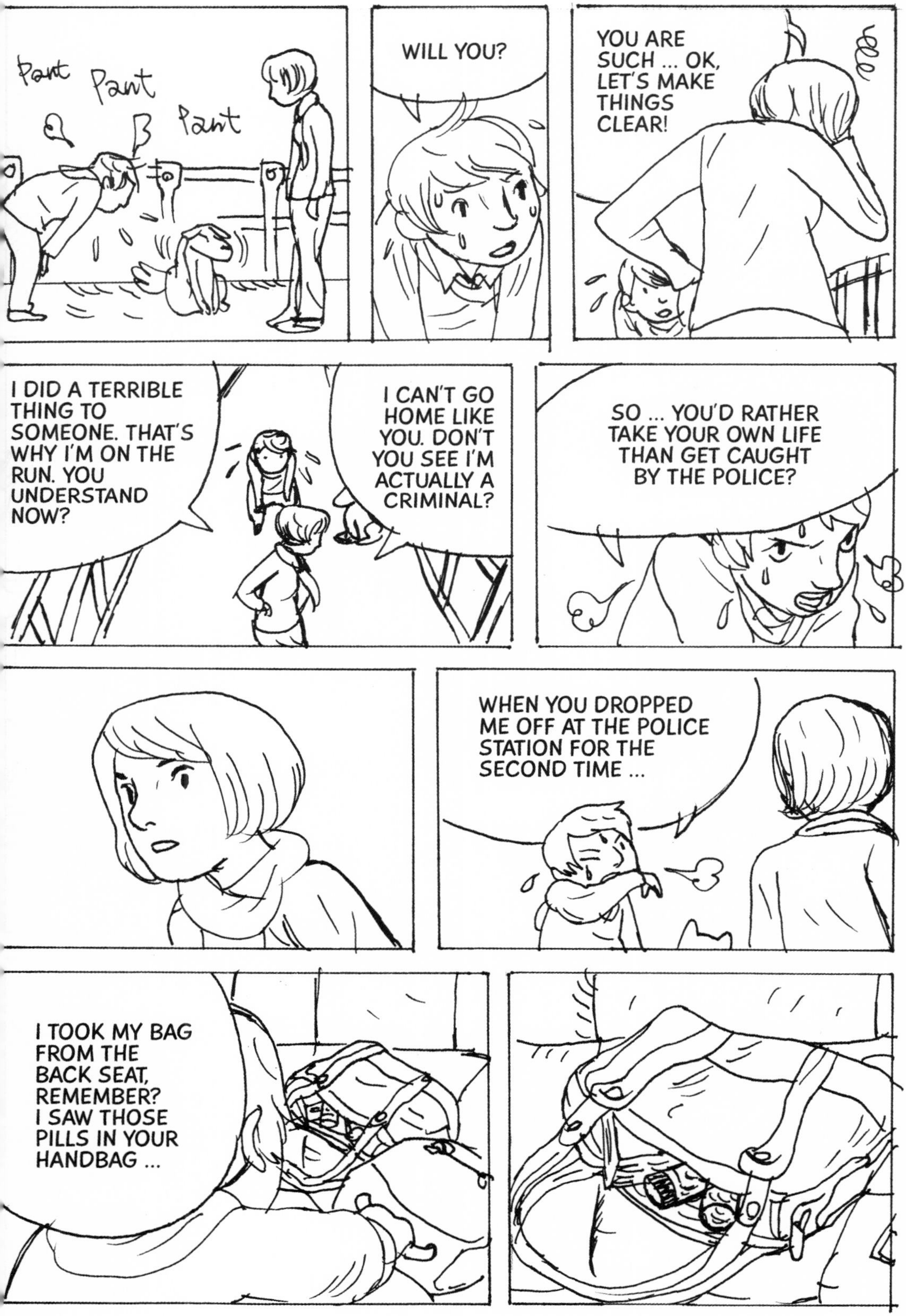
Pant
Pant
Pant
WILL YOU?
YOU ARE SUCH ... OK, LET'S MAKE THINGS CLEAR!
I DID A TERRIBLE THING TO SOMEONE. THAT'S WHY I'M ON THE RUN. YOU UNDERSTAND NOW?
I CAN'T GO HOME LIKE YOU. DON'T YOU SEE I'M ACTUALLY A CRIMINAL?
SO ... YOU'D RATHER TAKE YOUR OWN LIFE THAN GET CAUGHT BY THE POLICE?
WHEN YOU DROPPED ME OFF AT THE POLICE STATION FOR THE SECOND TIME ...
I TOOK MY BAG FROM THE BACK SEAT, REMEMBER? I SAW THOSE PILLS IN YOUR HANDBAG ...

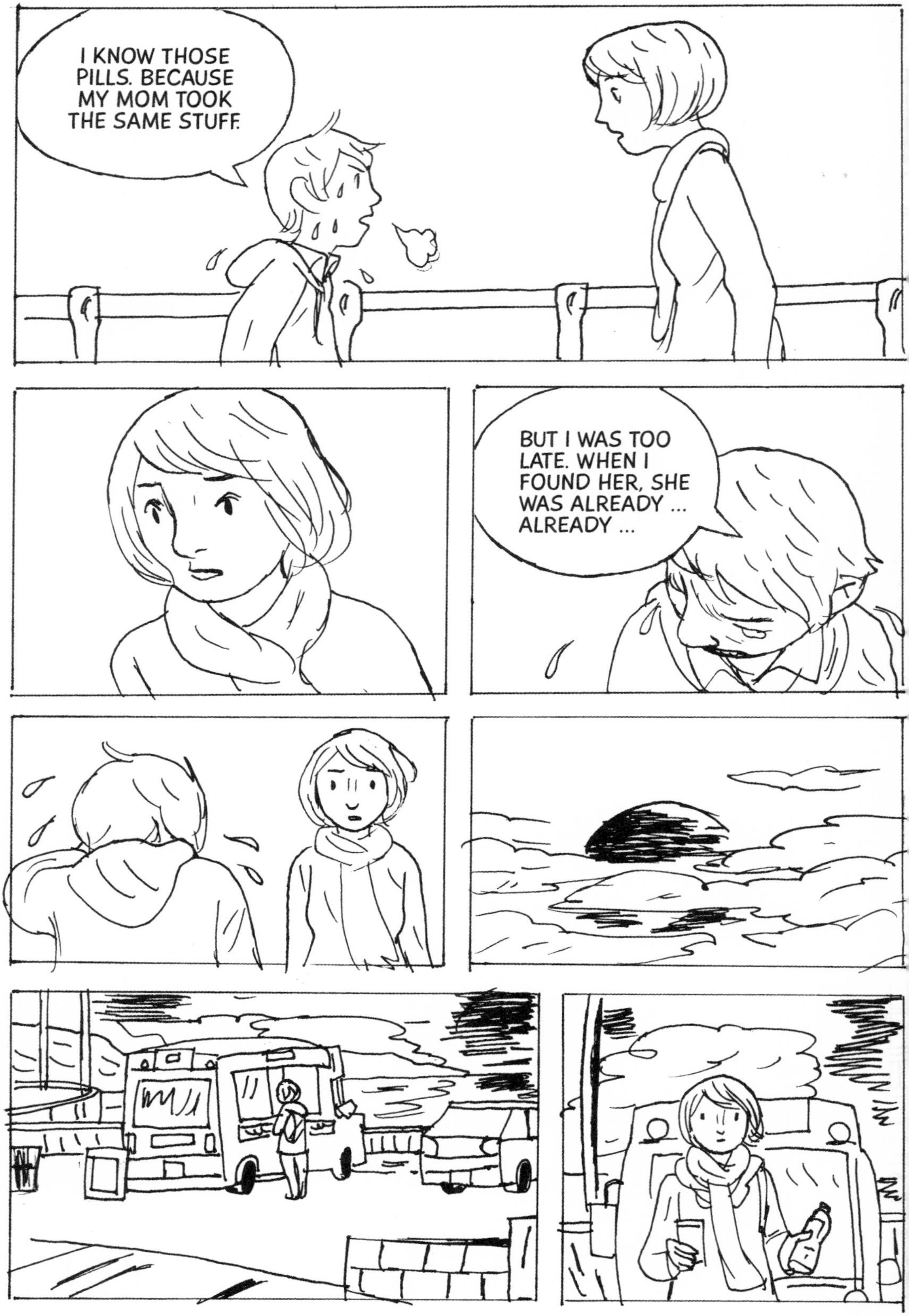
I KNOW THOSE PILLS. BECAUSE MY MOM TOOK THE SAME STUFF.
BUT I WAS TOO LATE. WHEN I FOUND HER, SHE WAS ALREADY ... ALREADY ...

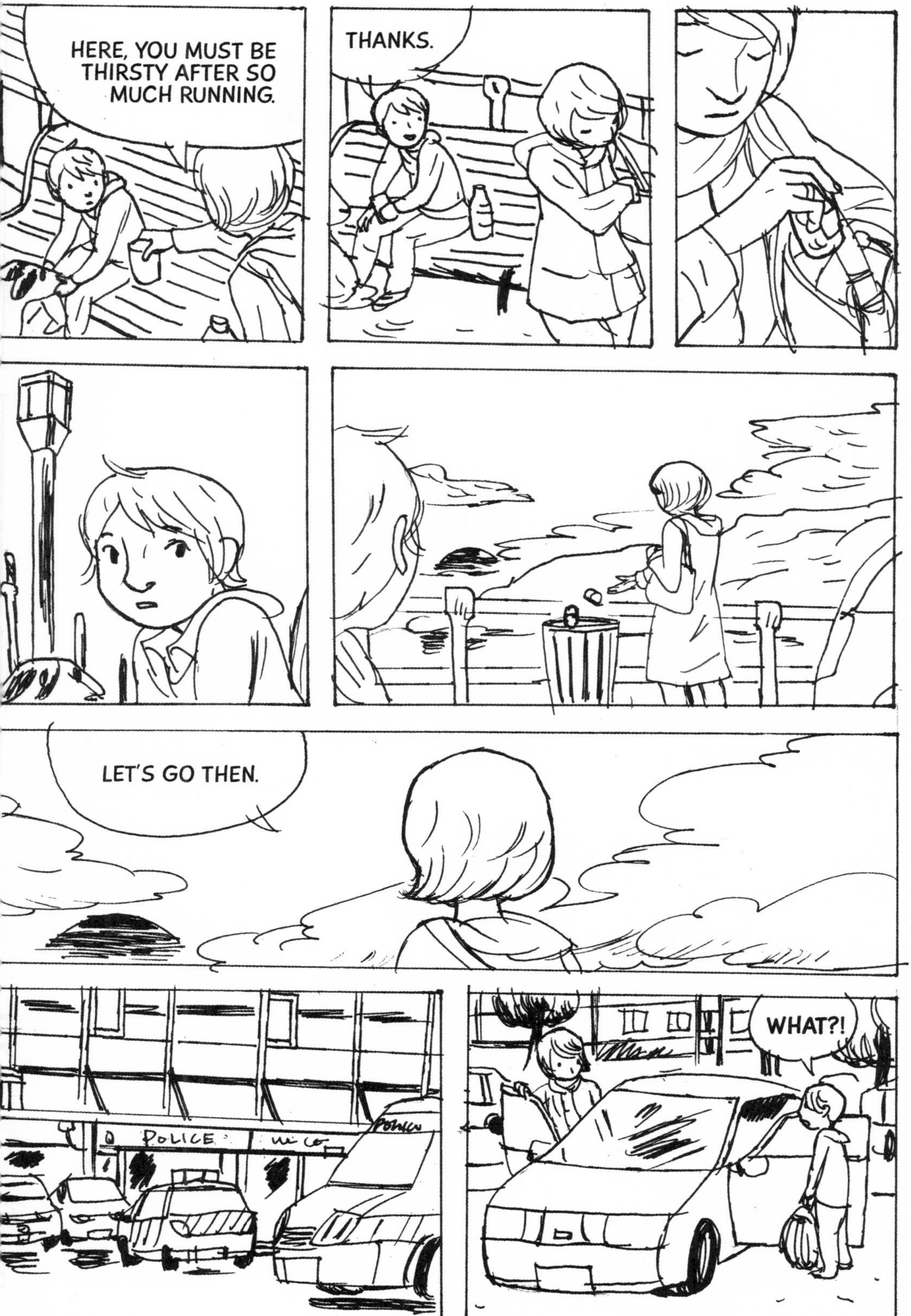
HERE, YOU MUST BE THIRSTY AFTER SO MUCH RUNNING.
THANKS.
LET'S GO THEN.
POLICE
WHAT?!

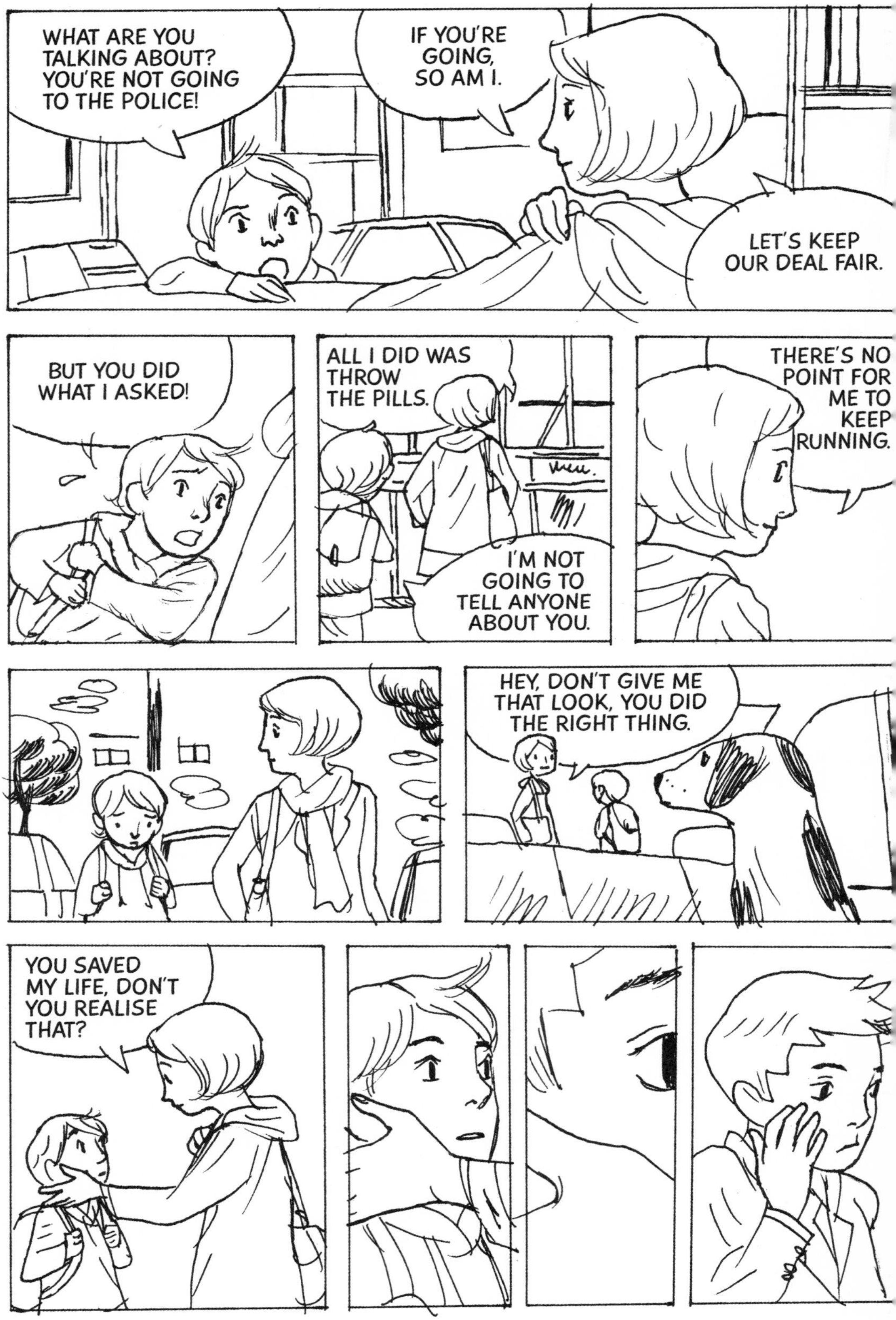
WHAT ARE YOU TALKING ABOUT? YOU'RE NOT GOING TO THE POLICE!
IF YOU'RE GOING, SO AM I.
LET'S KEEP OUR DEAL FAIR.
BUT YOU DID WHAT I ASKED!
ALL I DID WAS THROW THE PILLS.
I'M NOT GOING TO TELL ANYONE ABOUT YOU.
THERE'S NO POINT FOR ME TO KEEP RUNNING.
HEY, DON'T GIVE ME THAT LOOK, YOU DID THE RIGHT THING.
YOU SAVED MY LIFE, DON'T YOU REALISE THAT?

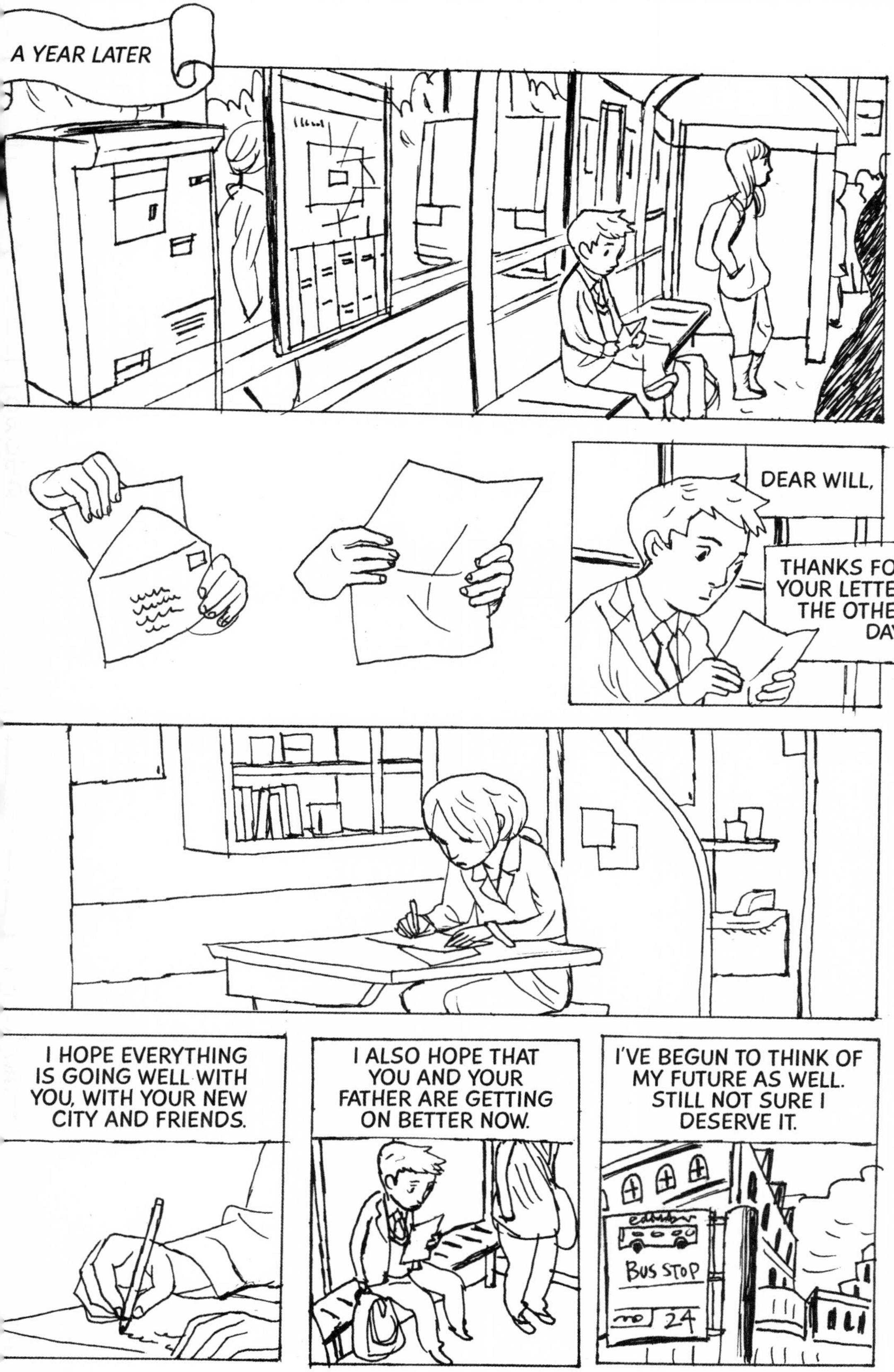
A YEAR LATER
DEAR WILL,
THANKS FOR YOUR LETTER THE OTHER DAY.
I HOPE EVERYTHING IS GOING WELL WITH YOU, WITH YOUR NEW CITY AND FRIENDS.
I ALSO HOPE THAT YOU AND YOUR FATHER ARE GETTING ON BETTER NOW.
I'VE BEGUN TO THINK OF MY FUTURE AS WELL. STILL NOT SURE I DESERVE IT.
BUS STOP
24

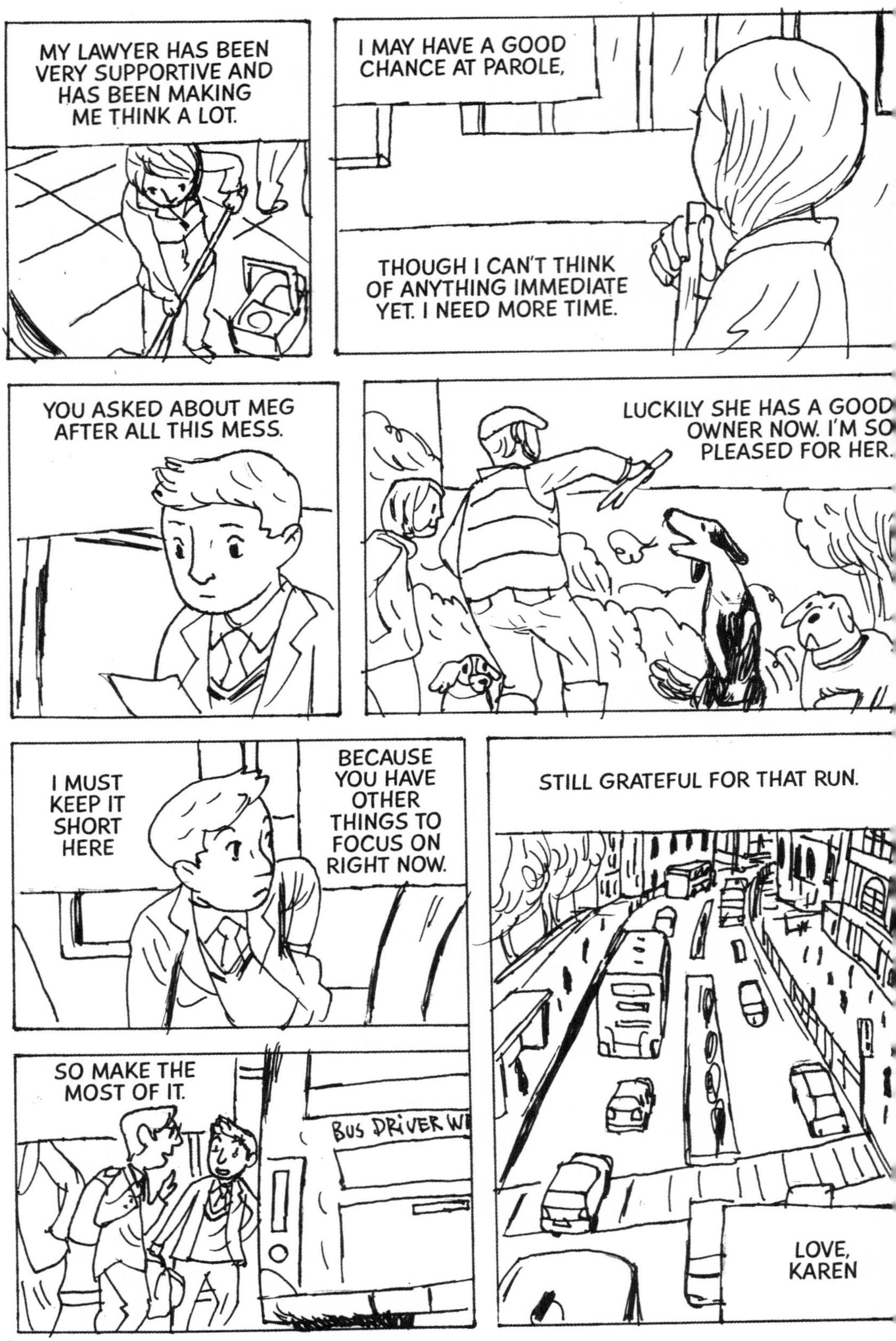
MY LAWYER HAS BEEN VERY SUPPORTIVE AND HAS BEEN MAKING ME THINK A LOT.
I MAY HAVE A GOOD CHANCE AT PAROLE,
THOUGH I CAN'T THINK OF ANYTHING IMMEDIATE YET. I NEED MORE TIME.
YOU ASKED ABOUT MEG AFTER ALL THIS MESS.
LUCKILY SHE HAS A GOOD OWNER NOW. I'M SO PLEASED FOR HER.
I MUST KEEP IT SHORT HERE
BECAUSE YOU HAVE OTHER THINGS TO FOCUS ON RIGHT NOW.
SO MAKE THE MOST OF IT.
BUS DRIVER W
STILL GRATEFUL FOR THAT RUN.
LOVE, KAREN

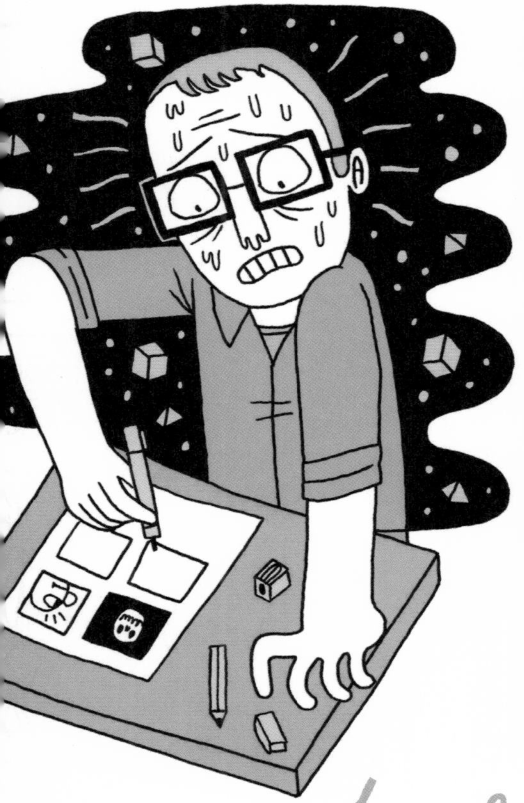

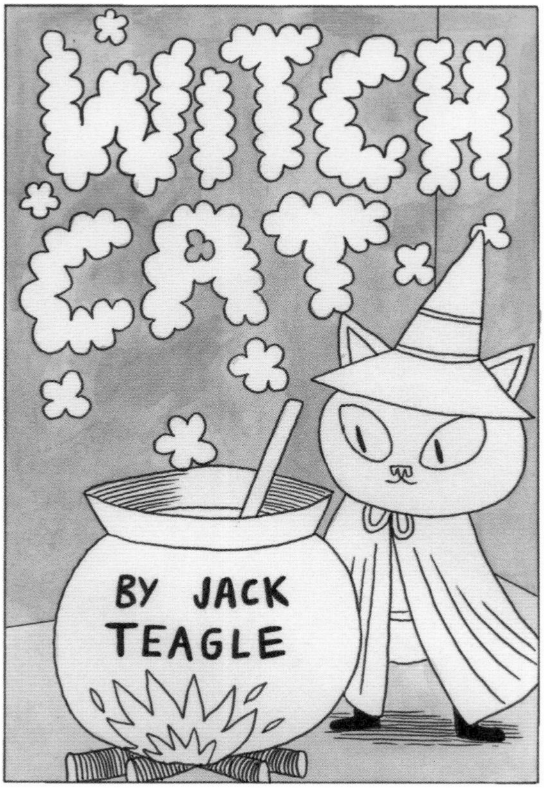
WITCH CAT
BY JACK TEAGLE

Jack Teagle

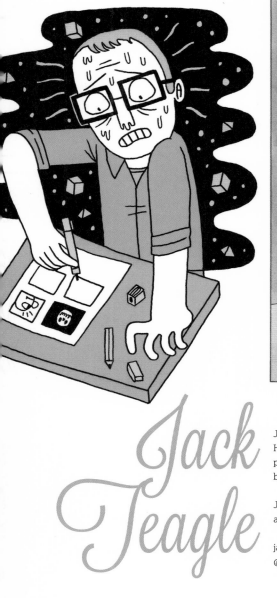

Jack is a freelance illustrator based in South West England. He keeps many sketchbooks and goes through many tubes of paint. His books ***Fight #2*** and ***Jeff Job Hunter*** been published by Nobrow.

Jack loves collecting action figures, reading badly written silver age comics and watching classic horror films.

jackteagle.co.uk
@jackteagle

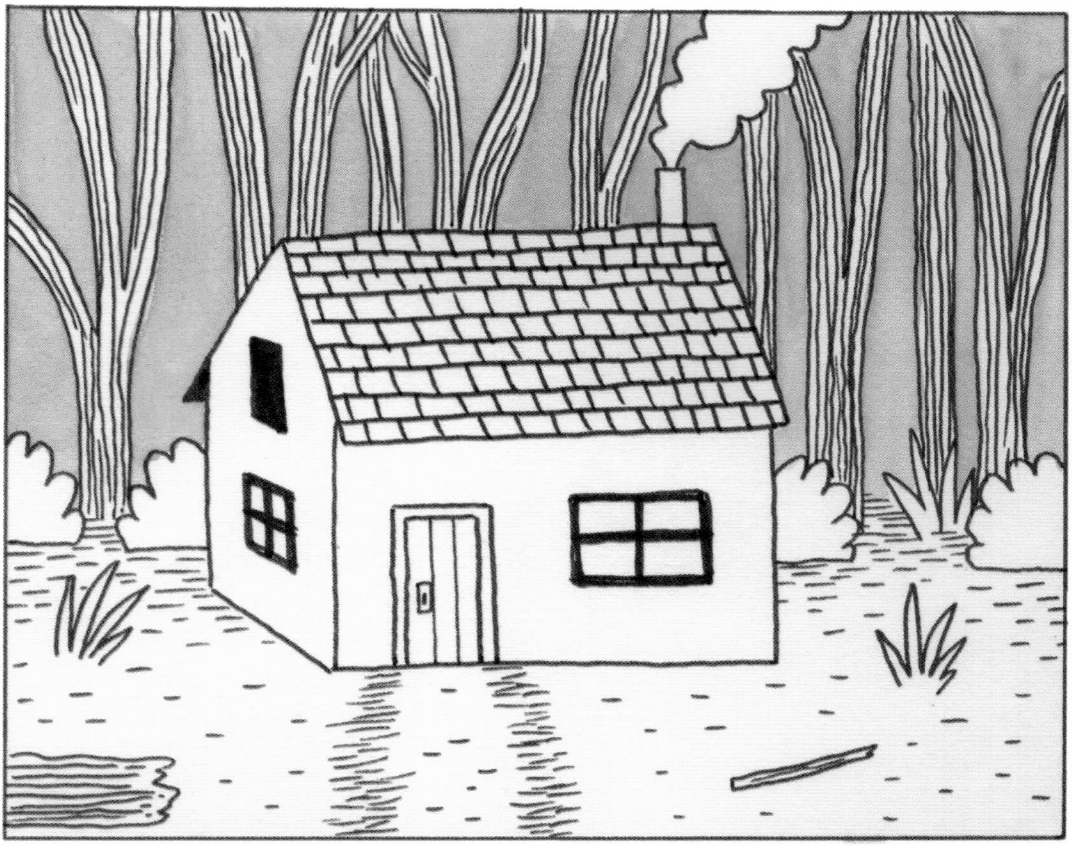

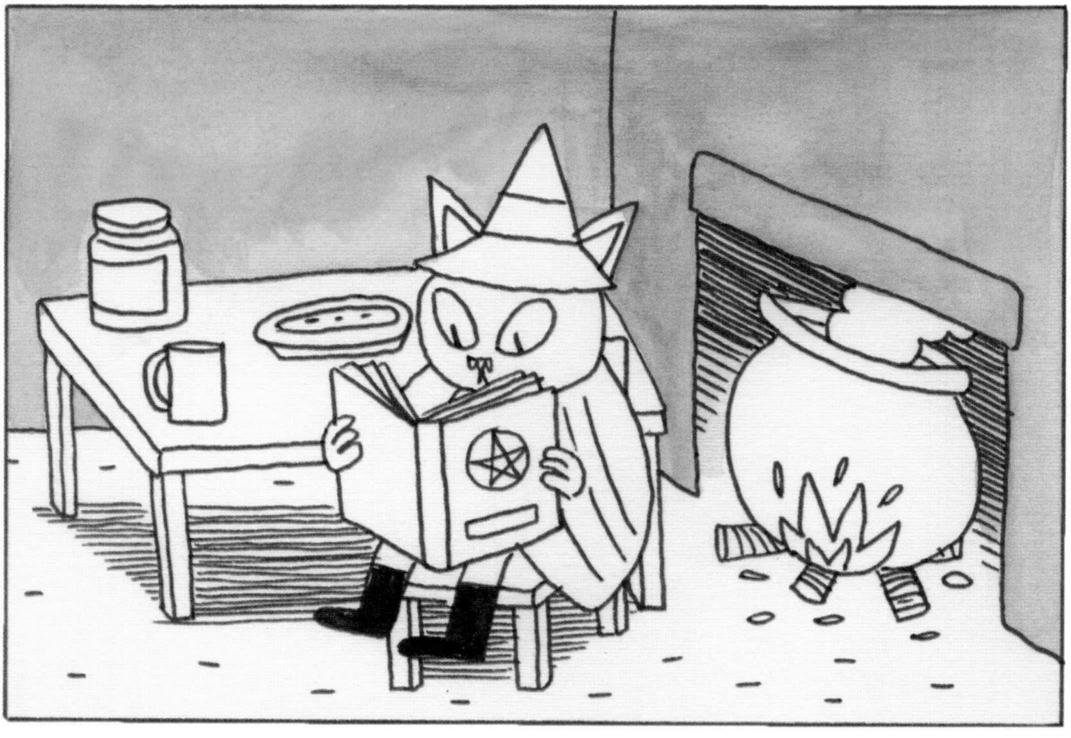

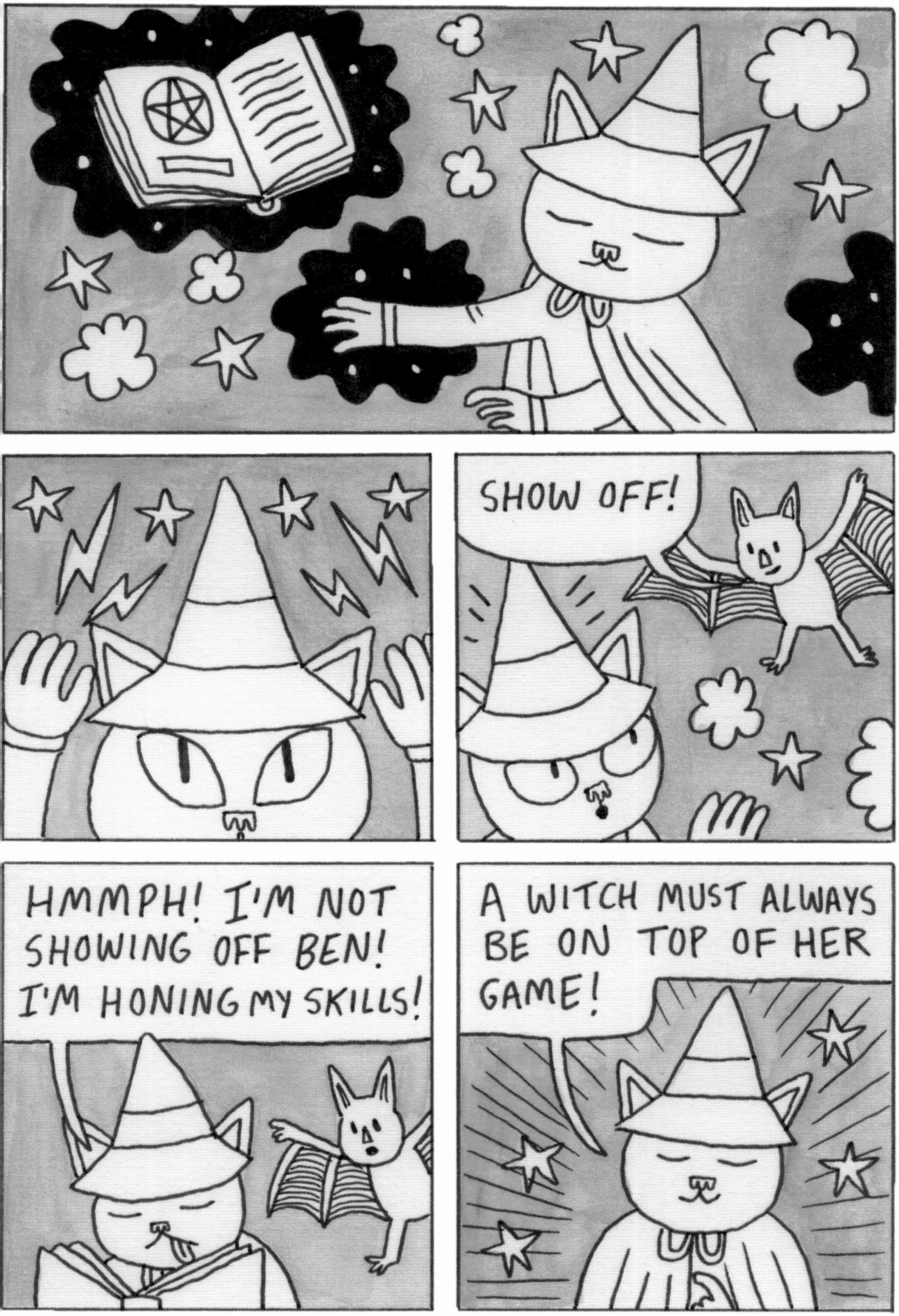
SHOW OFF!
HMMPH! I'M NOT SHOWING OFF BEN! I'M HONING MY SKILLS!
A WITCH MUST ALWAYS BE ON TOP OF HER GAME!

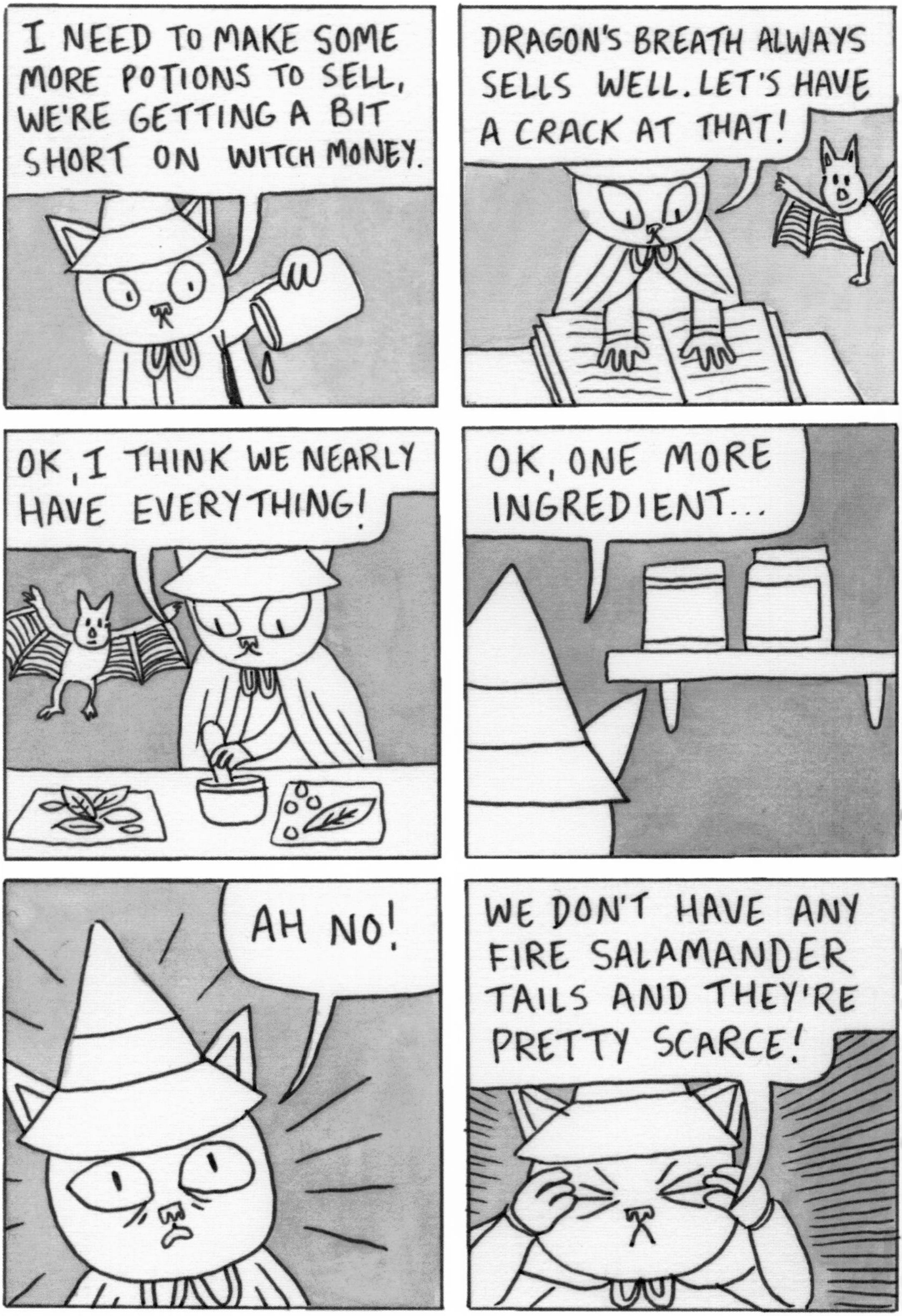
I NEED TO MAKE SOME MORE POTIONS TO SELL, WE'RE GETTING A BIT SHORT ON WITCH MONEY.
DRAGON'S BREATH ALWAYS SELLS WELL. LET'S HAVE A CRACK AT THAT!
OK, I THINK WE NEARLY HAVE EVERYTHING!
OK, ONE MORE INGREDIENT...
AH NO!
WE DON'T HAVE ANY FIRE SALAMANDER TAILS AND THEY'RE PRETTY SCARCE!

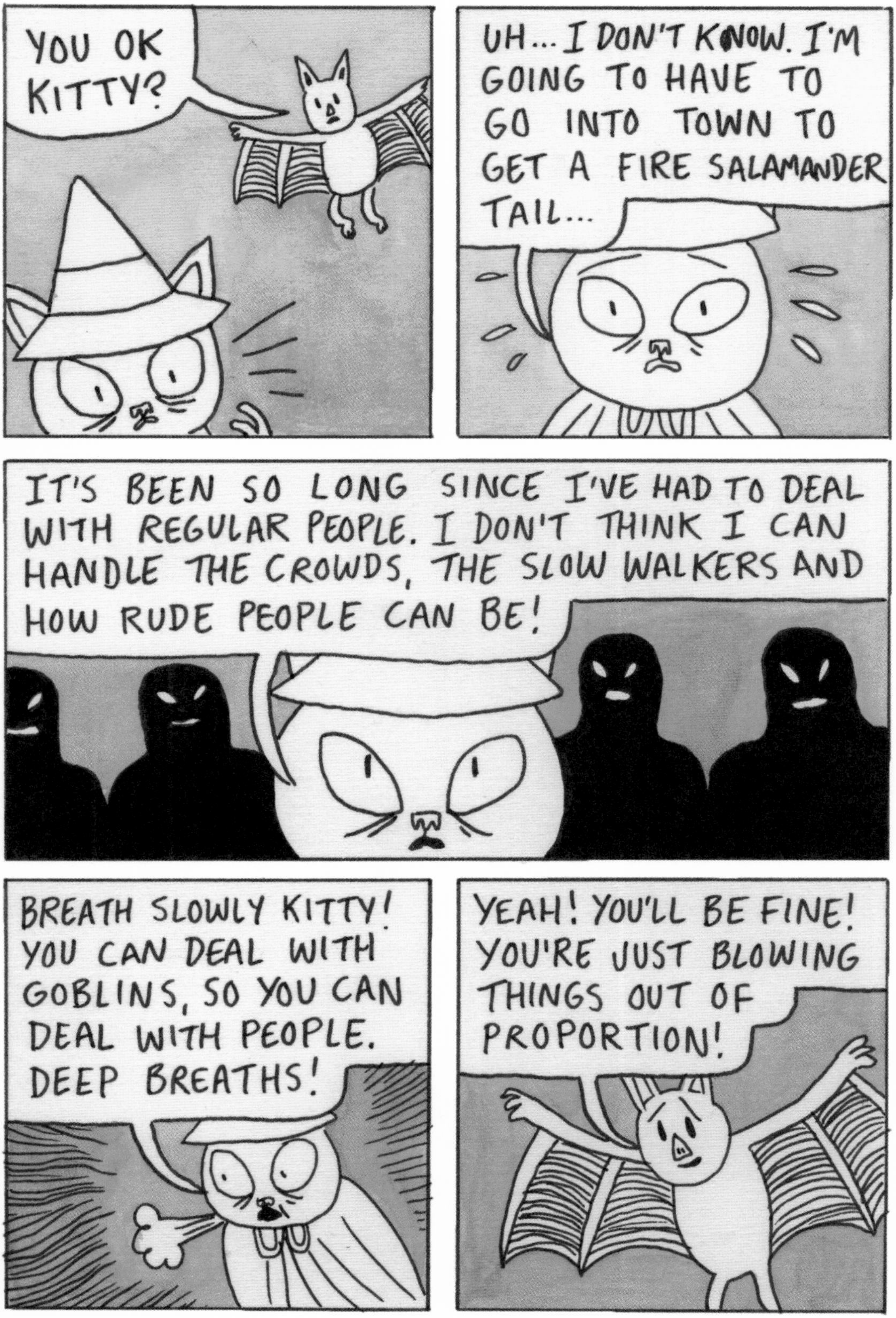
YOU OK KITTY?
UH... I DON'T KNOW. I'M GOING TO HAVE TO GO INTO TOWN TO GET A FIRE SALAMANDER TAIL...
IT'S BEEN SO LONG SINCE I'VE HAD TO DEAL WITH REGULAR PEOPLE. I DON'T THINK I CAN HANDLE THE CROWDS, THE SLOW WALKERS AND HOW RUDE PEOPLE CAN BE!
BREATH SLOWLY KITTY! YOU CAN DEAL WITH GOBLINS, SO YOU CAN DEAL WITH PEOPLE. DEEP BREATHS!
YEAH! YOU'LL BE FINE! YOU'RE JUST BLOWING THINGS OUT OF PROPORTION!

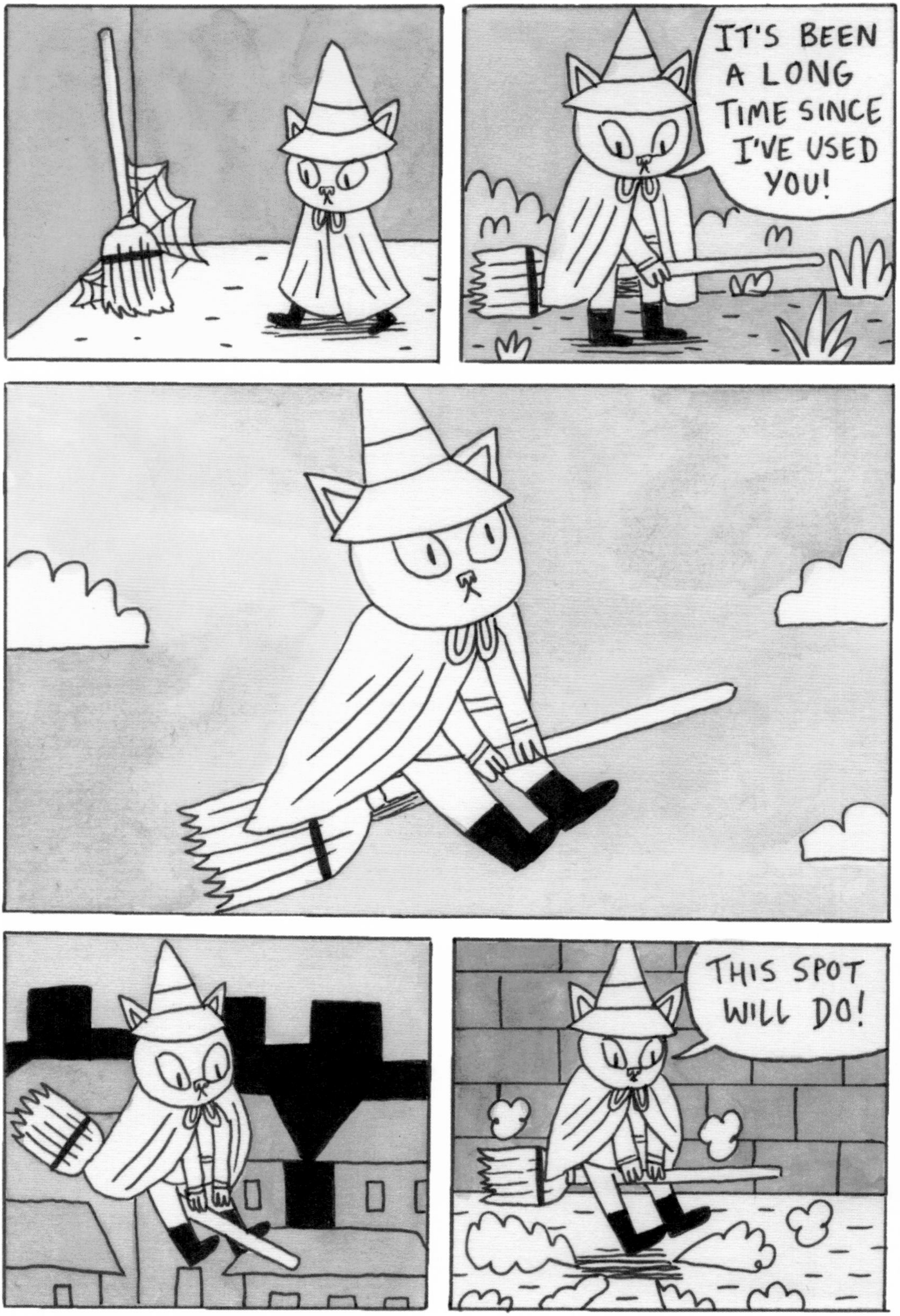
IT'S BEEN A LONG TIME SINCE I'VE USED YOU!
THIS SPOT WILL DO!

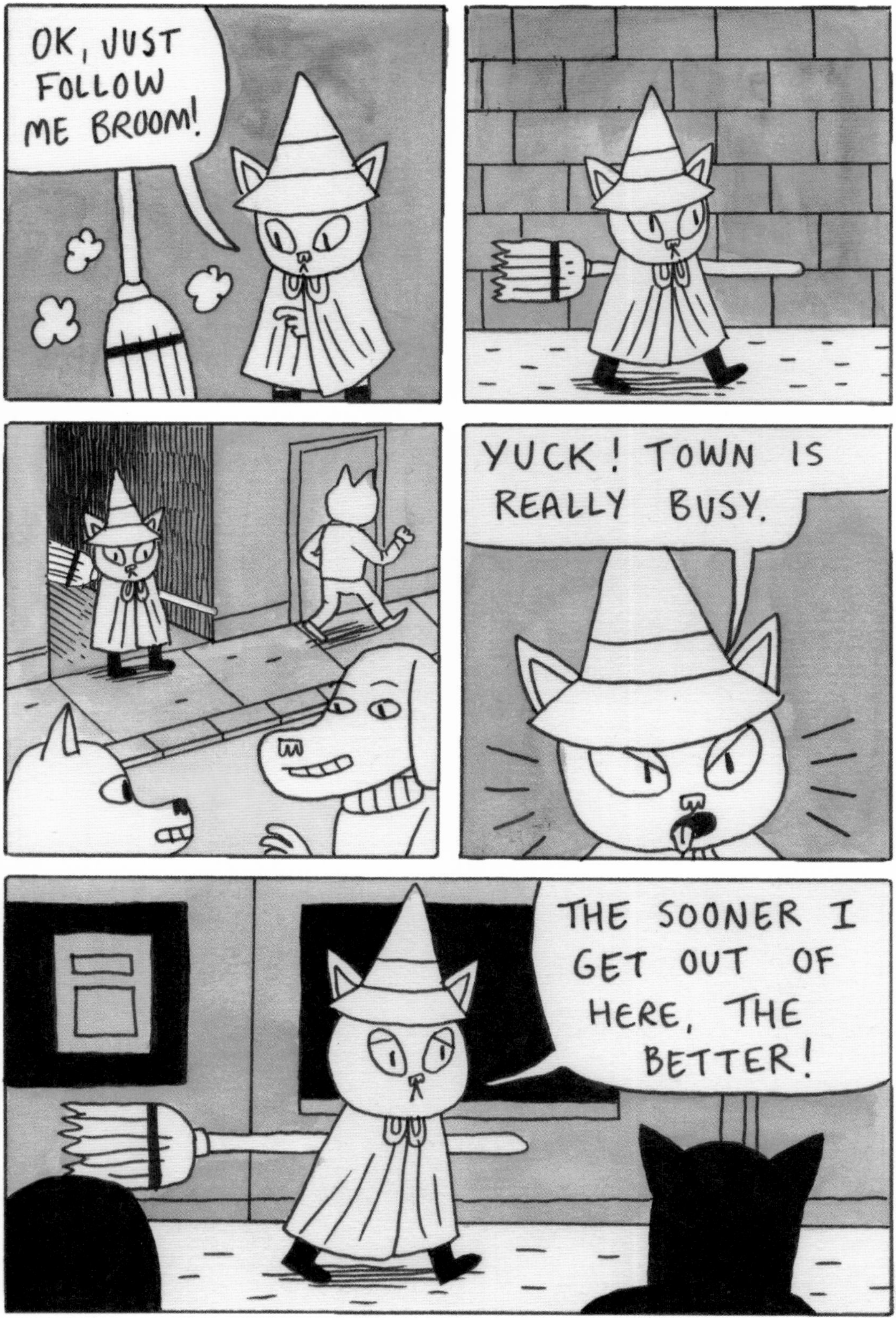
OK, JUST FOLLOW ME BROOM!
YUCK! TOWN IS REALLY BUSY.
THE SOONER I GET OUT OF HERE, THE BETTER!

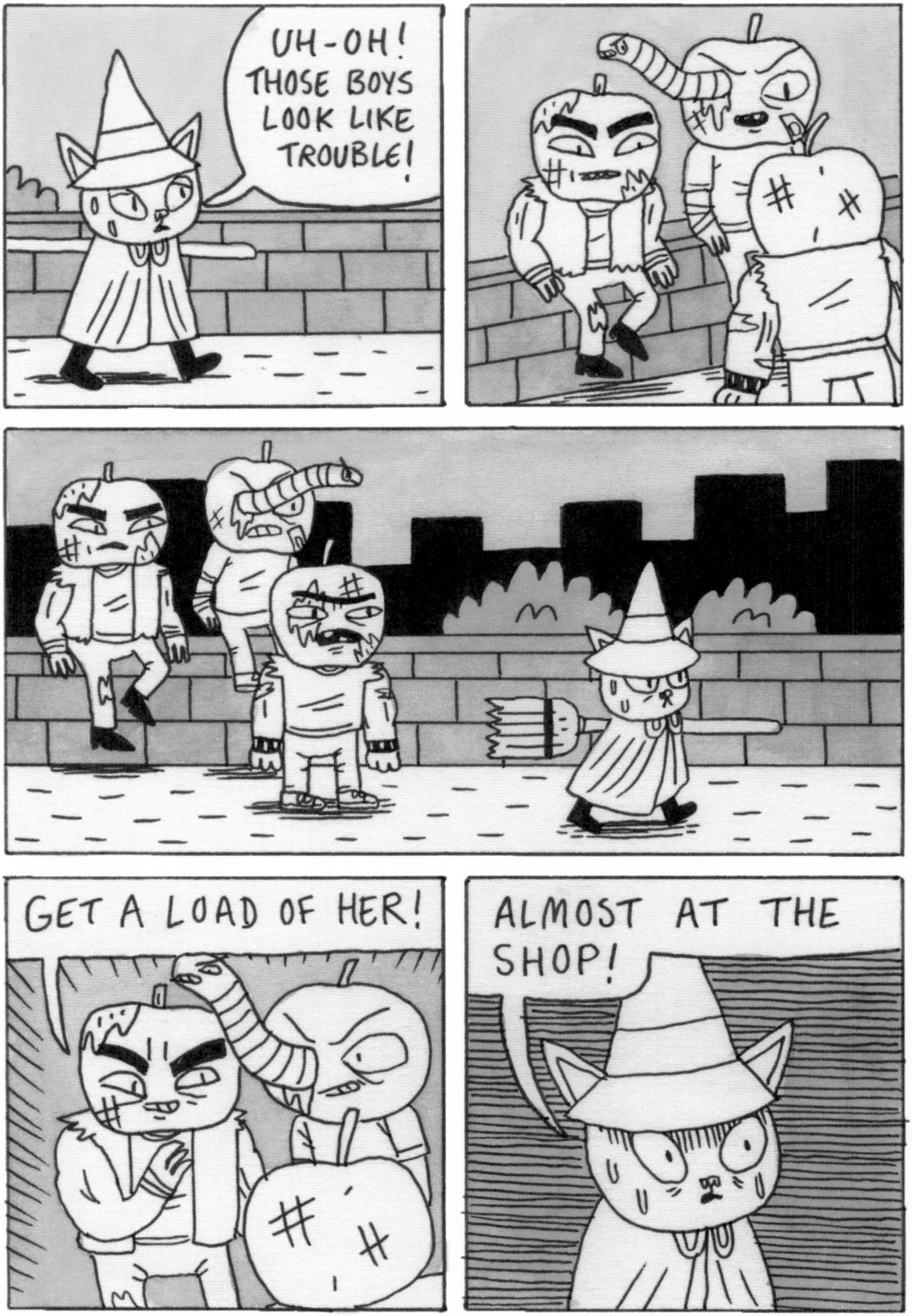
UH-OH! THOSE BOYS LOOK LIKE TROUBLE!
GET A LOAD OF HER!
ALMOST AT THE SHOP!

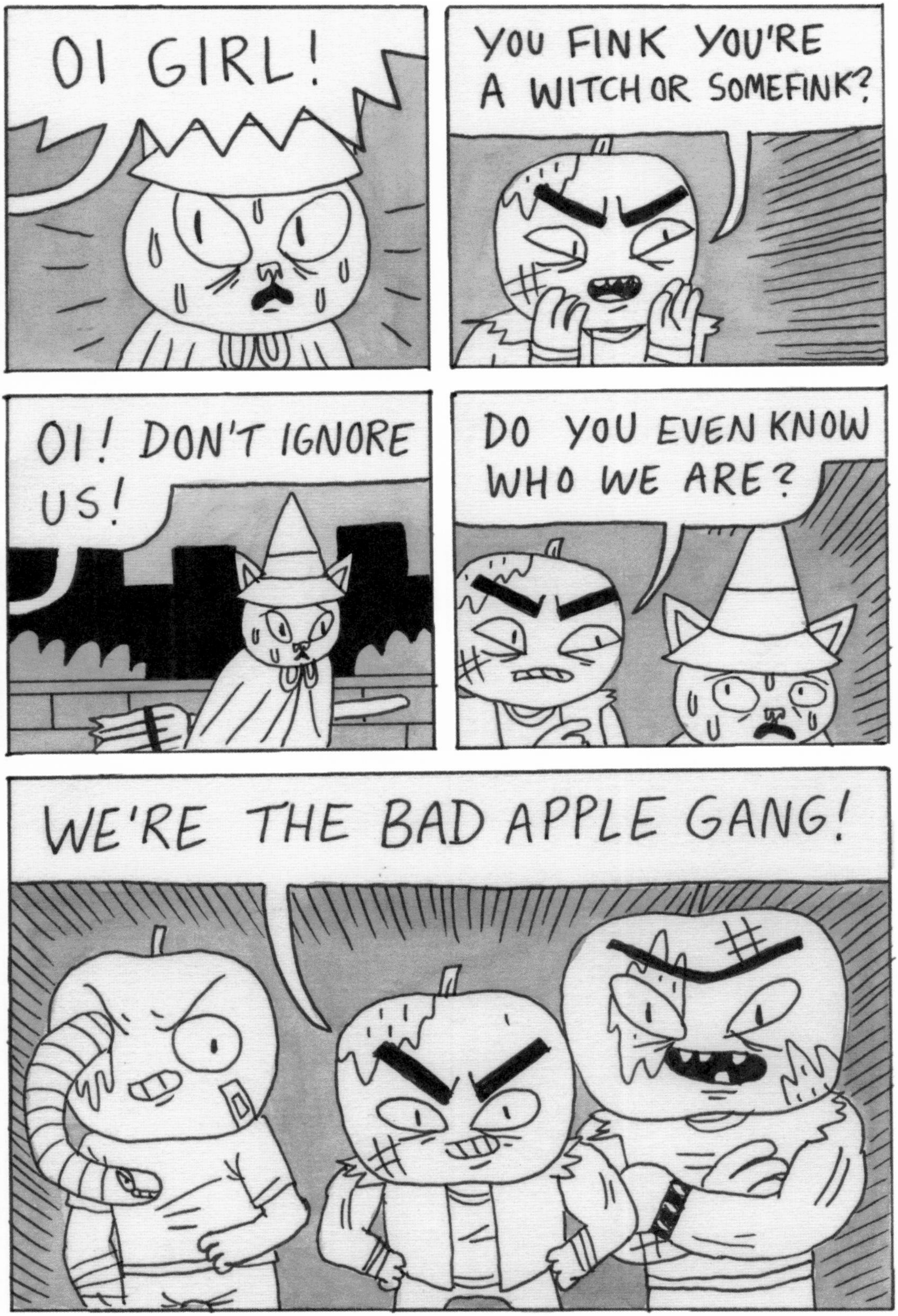
OI GIRL!
YOU FINK YOU'RE A WITCH OR SOMEFINK?
OI! DON'T IGNORE US!
DO YOU EVEN KNOW WHO WE ARE?
WE'RE THE BAD APPLE GANG!

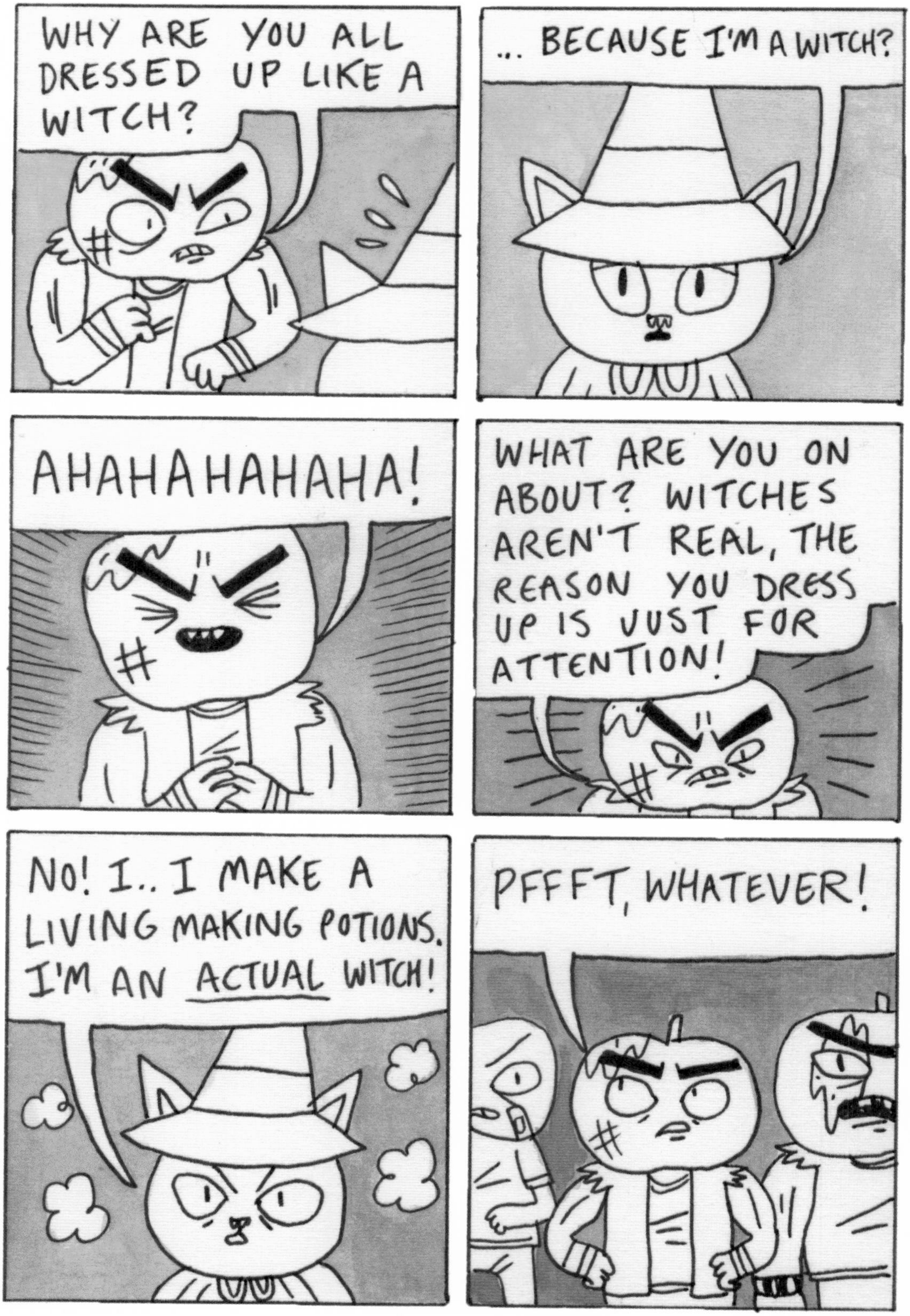
WHY ARE YOU ALL DRESSED UP LIKE A WITCH?
... BECAUSE I'M A WITCH?
AHAHAHAHAHAHA!
WHAT ARE YOU ON ABOUT? WITCHES AREN'T REAL, THE REASON YOU DRESS UP IS JUST FOR ATTENTION!
NO! I.. I MAKE A LIVING MAKING POTIONS. I'M AN ACTUAL WITCH!
PFFFT, WHATEVER!

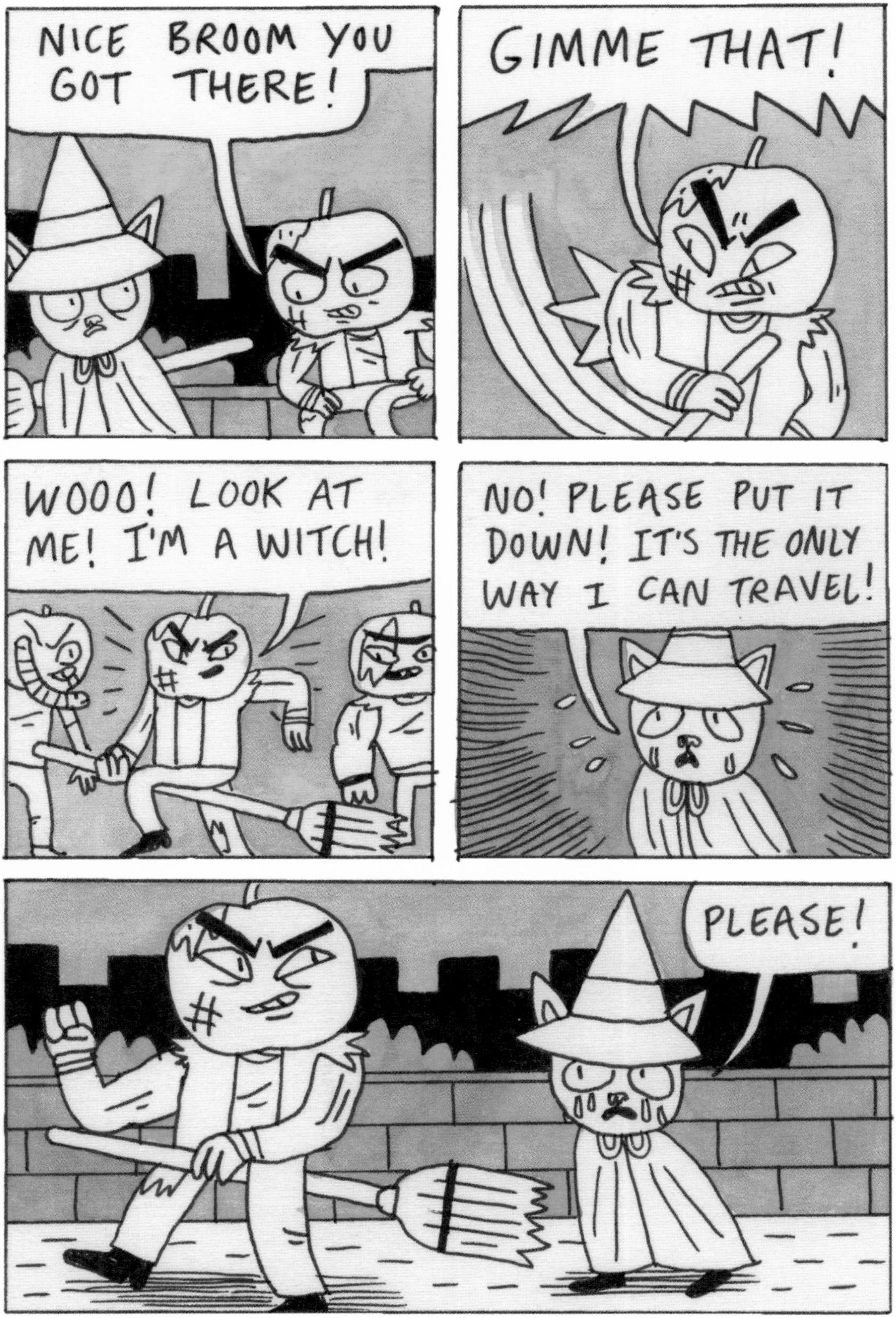
NICE BROOM YOU GOT THERE!
GIMME THAT!
WOOO! LOOK AT ME! I'M A WITCH!
NO! PLEASE PUT IT DOWN! IT'S THE ONLY WAY I CAN TRAVEL!
PLEASE!

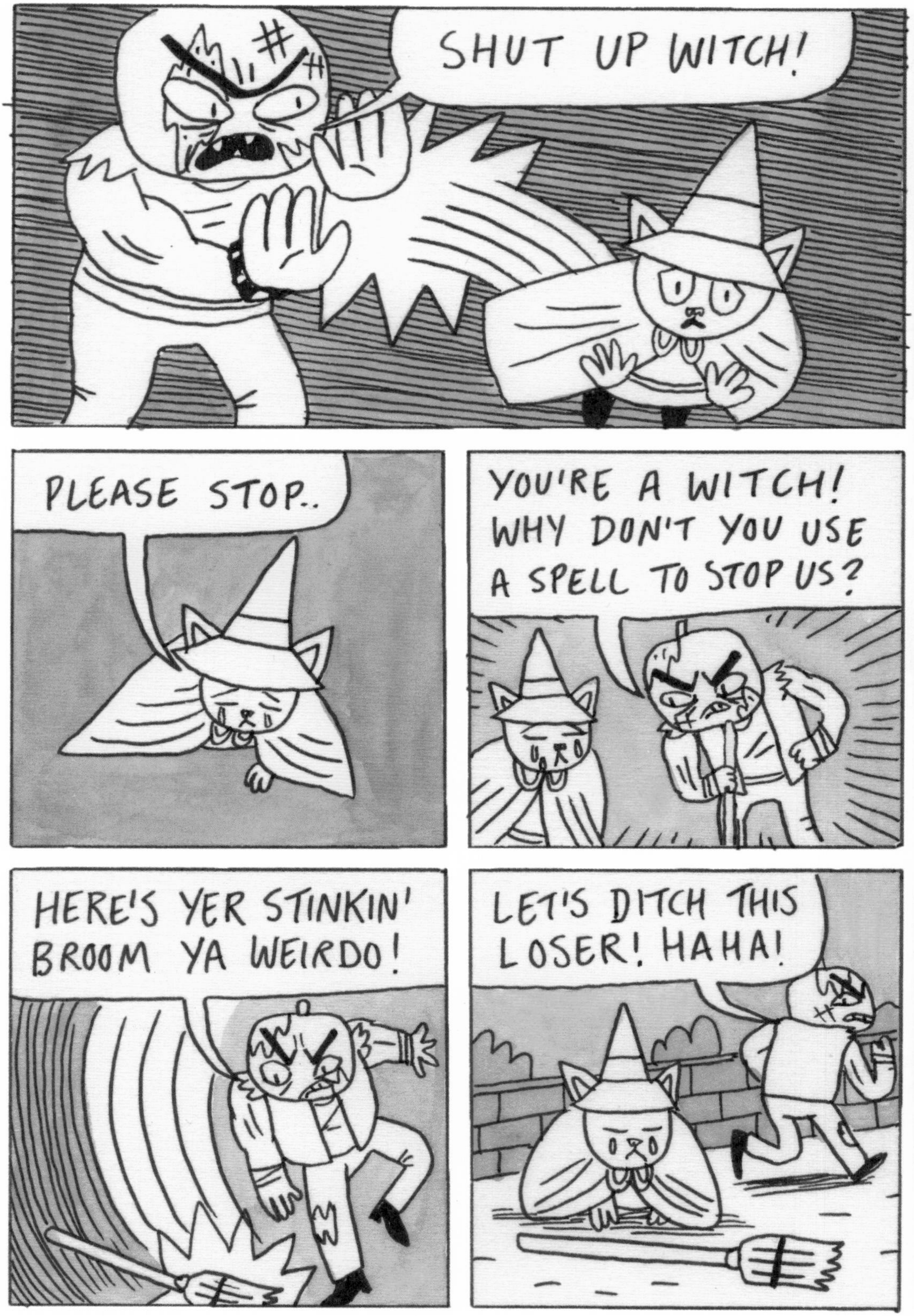
SHUT UP WITCH!
PLEASE STOP..
YOU'RE A WITCH! WHY DON'T YOU USE A SPELL TO STOP US?
HERE'S YER STINKIN' BROOM YA WEIRDO!
LET'S DITCH THIS LOSER! HAHA!

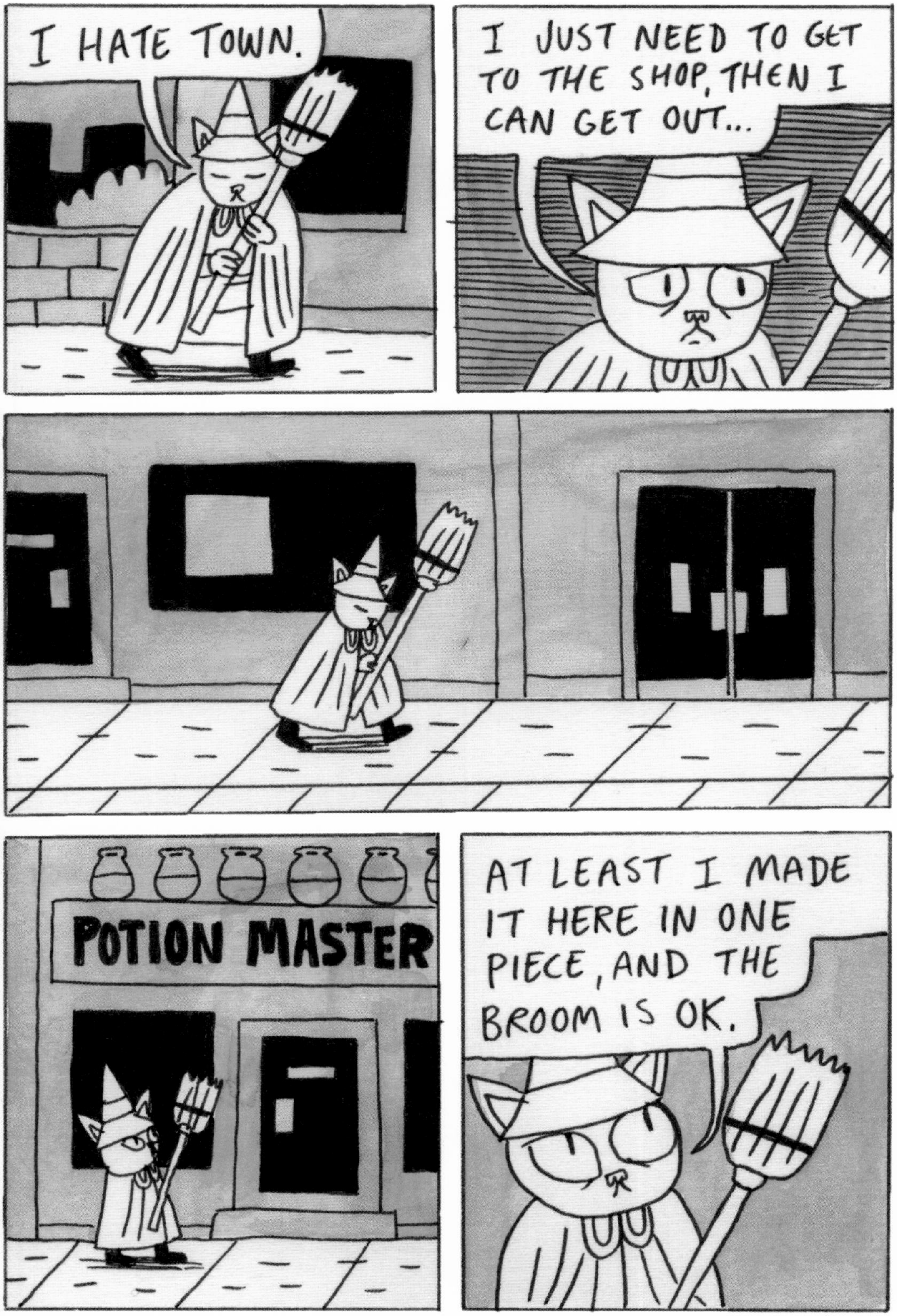
I HATE TOWN.
I JUST NEED TO GET TO THE SHOP, THEN I CAN GET OUT...
POTION MASTER
AT LEAST I MADE IT HERE IN ONE PIECE, AND THE BROOM IS OK.

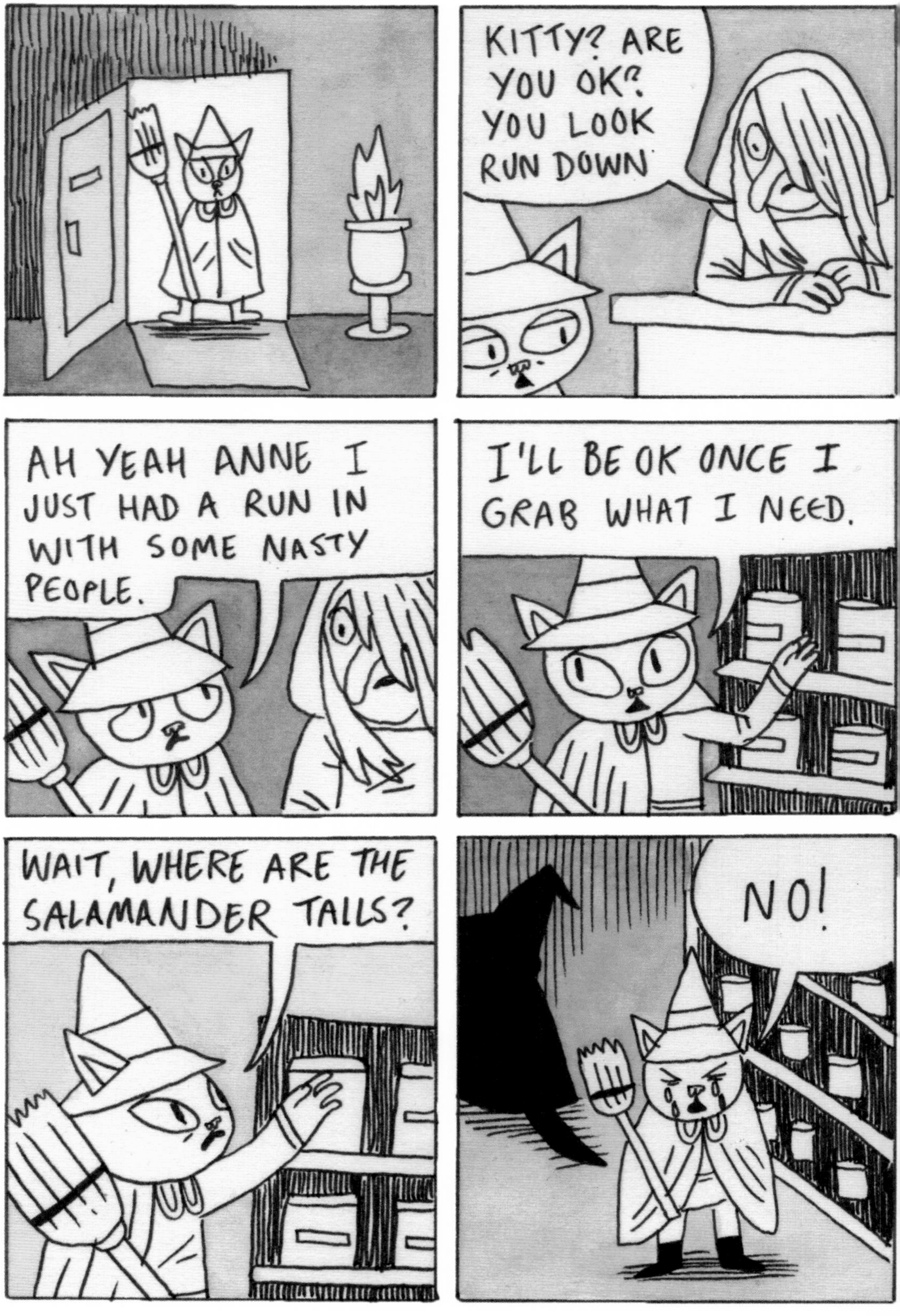

KITTY? ARE YOU OK? YOU LOOK RUN DOWN
AH YEAH ANNE I JUST HAD A RUN IN WITH SOME NASTY PEOPLE.
I'LL BE OK ONCE I GRAB WHAT I NEED.
WAIT, WHERE ARE THE SALAMANDER TAILS?
NO!

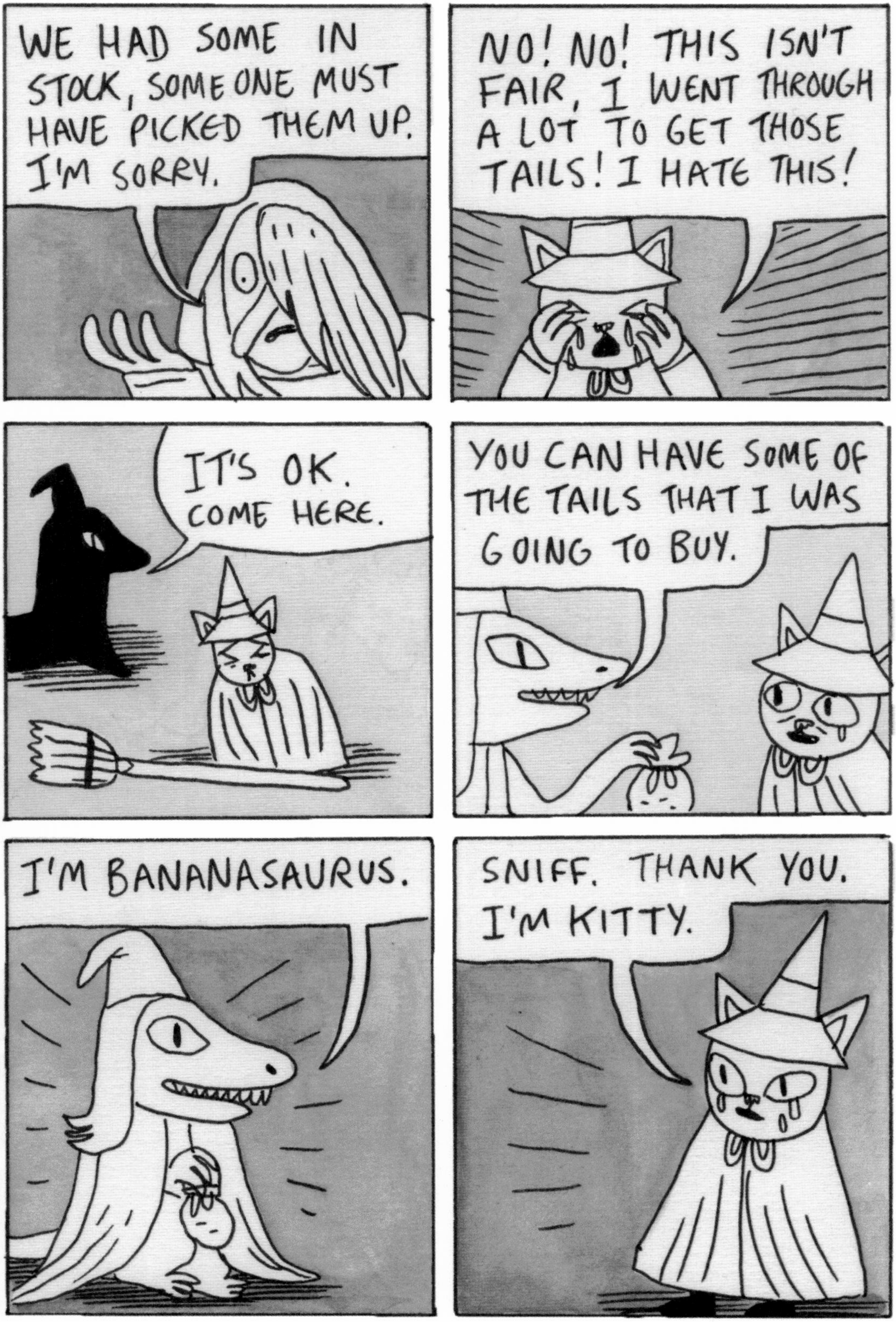
WE HAD SOME IN STOCK, SOMEONE MUST HAVE PICKED THEM UP. I'M SORRY.
NO! NO! THIS ISN'T FAIR, I WENT THROUGH A LOT TO GET THOSE TAILS! I HATE THIS!
IT'S OK. COME HERE.
YOU CAN HAVE SOME OF THE TAILS THAT I WAS GOING TO BUY.
I'M BANANASAURUS.
SNIFF. THANK YOU. I'M KITTY.

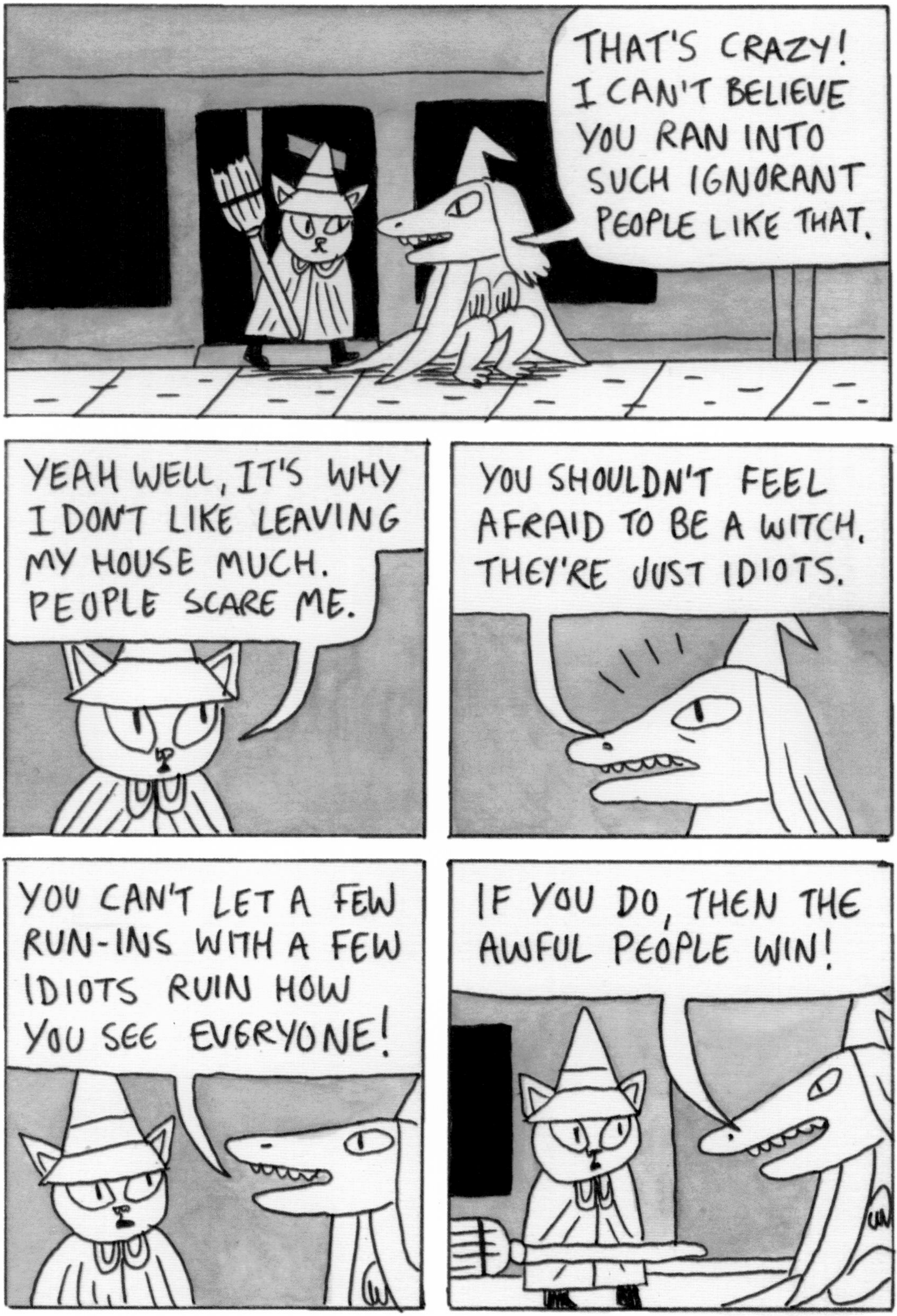
THAT'S CRAZY! I CAN'T BELIEVE YOU RAN INTO SUCH IGNORANT PEOPLE LIKE THAT.
YEAH WELL, IT'S WHY I DON'T LIKE LEAVING MY HOUSE MUCH. PEOPLE SCARE ME.
YOU SHOULDN'T FEEL AFRAID TO BE A WITCH. THEY'RE JUST IDIOTS.
YOU CAN'T LET A FEW RUN-INS WITH A FEW IDIOTS RUIN HOW YOU SEE EVERYONE!
IF YOU DO, THEN THE AWFUL PEOPLE WIN!

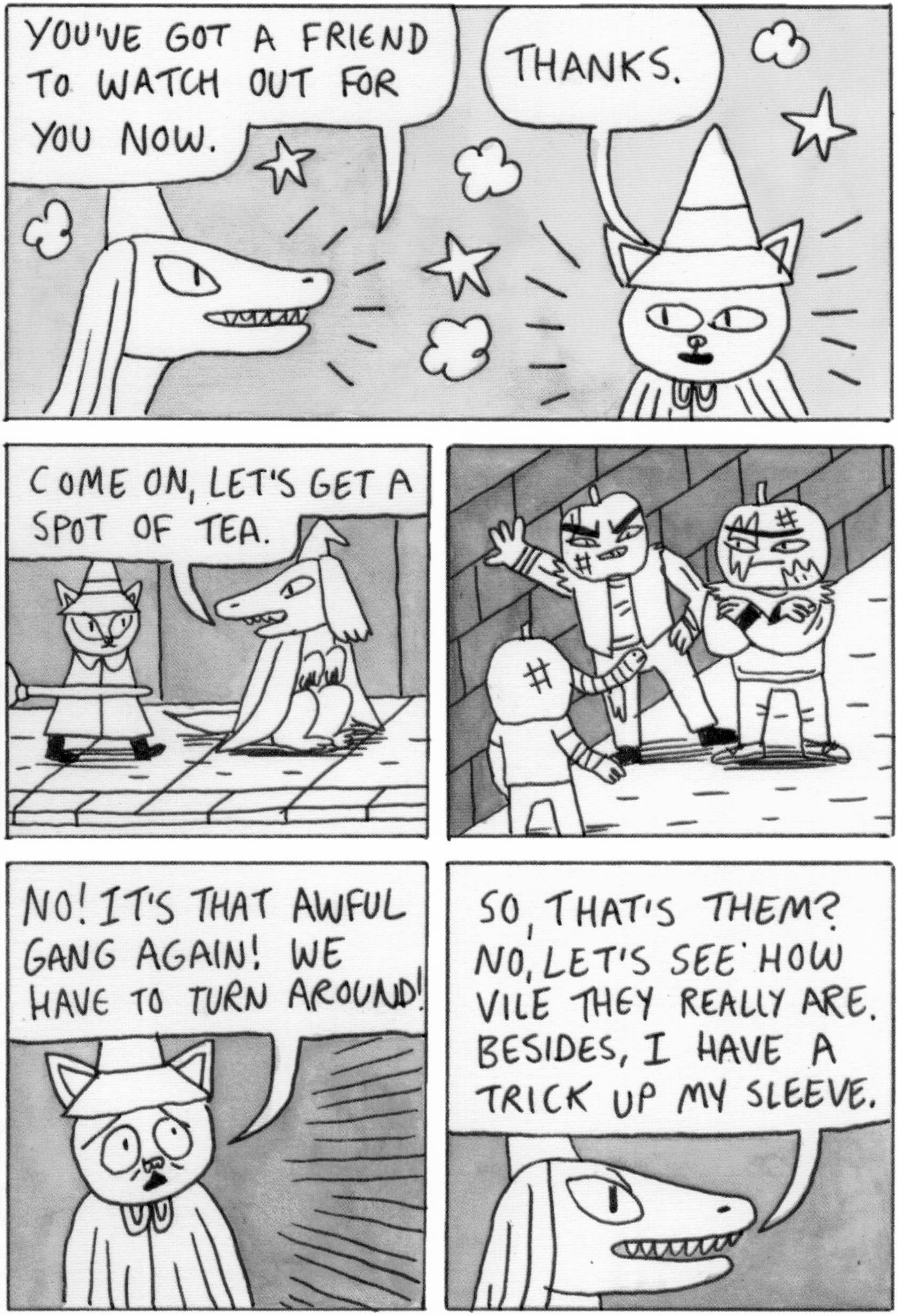
YOU'VE GOT A FRIEND TO WATCH OUT FOR YOU NOW.
THANKS.
COME ON, LET'S GET A SPOT OF TEA.
NO! IT'S THAT AWFUL GANG AGAIN! WE HAVE TO TURN AROUND!
SO, THAT'S THEM? NO, LET'S SEE HOW VILE THEY REALLY ARE. BESIDES, I HAVE A TRICK UP MY SLEEVE.

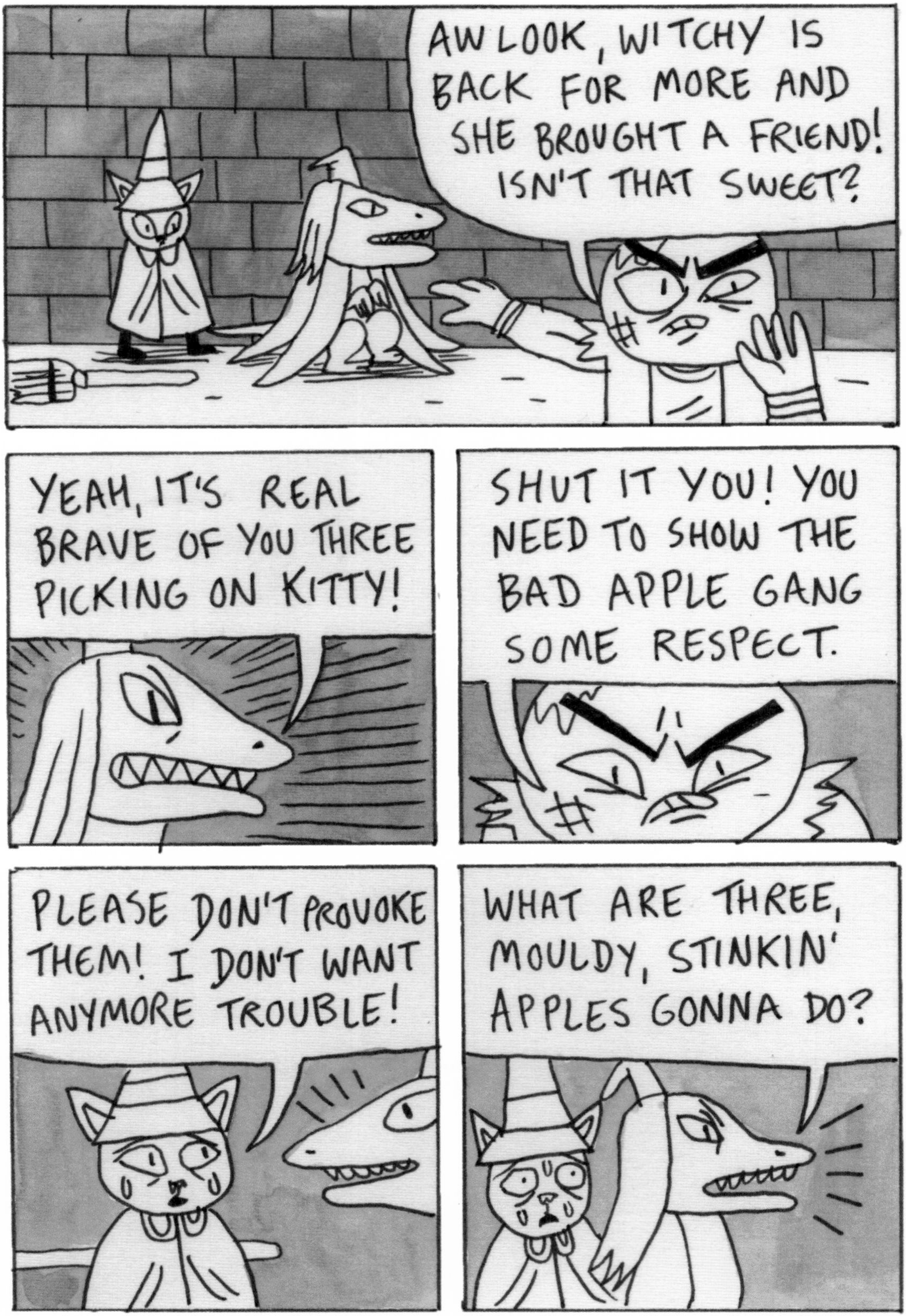

AW LOOK, WITCHY IS BACK FOR MORE AND SHE BROUGHT A FRIEND! ISN'T THAT SWEET?
YEAH, IT'S REAL BRAVE OF YOU THREE PICKING ON KITTY!
SHUT IT YOU! YOU NEED TO SHOW THE BAD APPLE GANG SOME RESPECT.
PLEASE DON'T PROVOKE THEM! I DON'T WANT ANYMORE TROUBLE!
WHAT ARE THREE, MOULDY, STINKIN' APPLES GONNA DO?

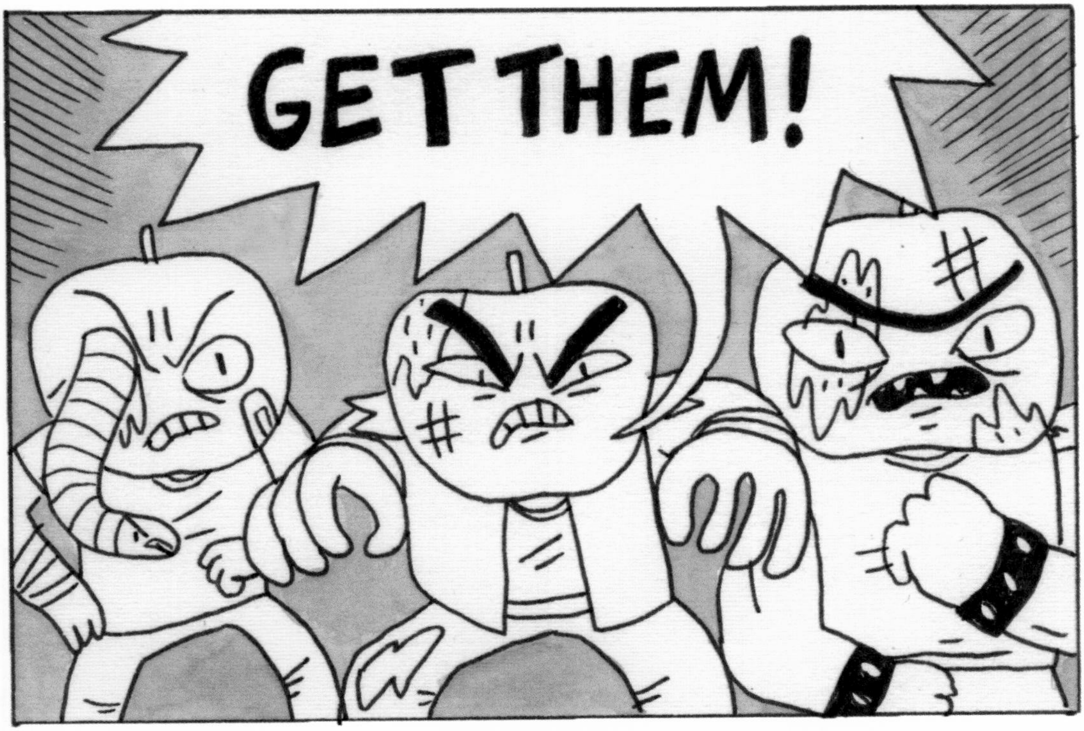
GET THEM!

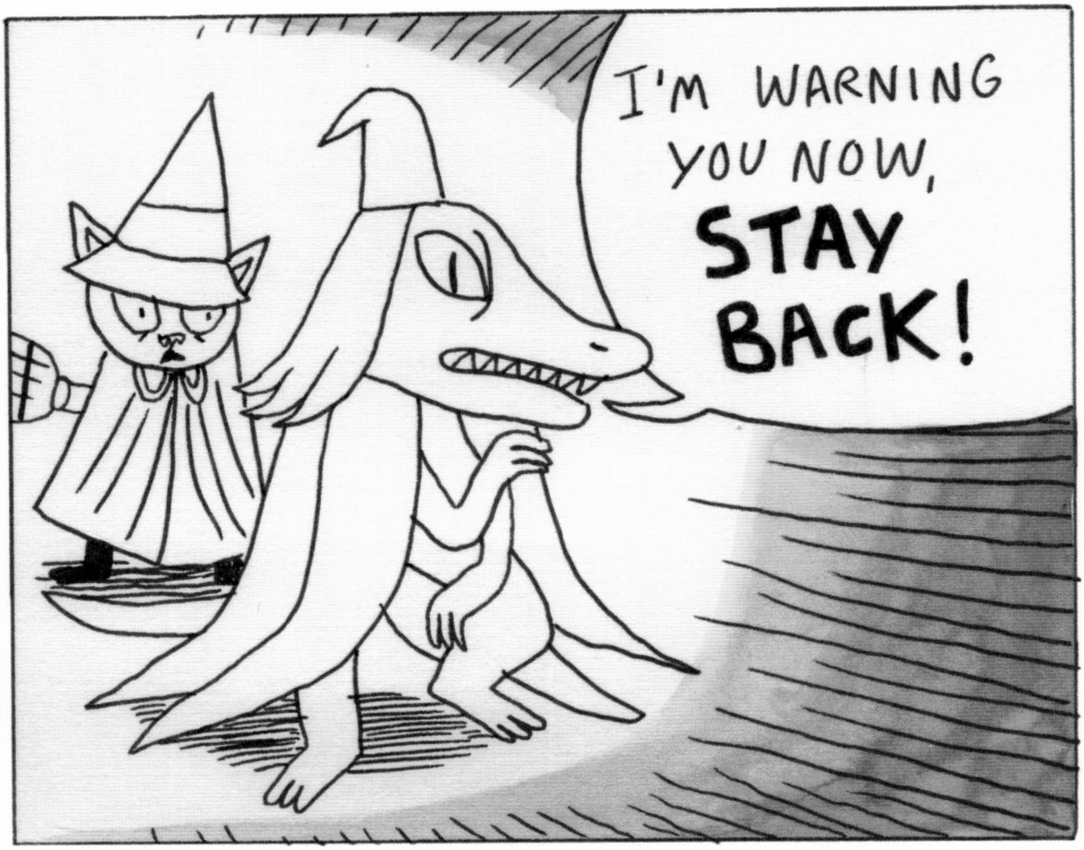
I'M WARNING YOU NOW, STAY BACK!

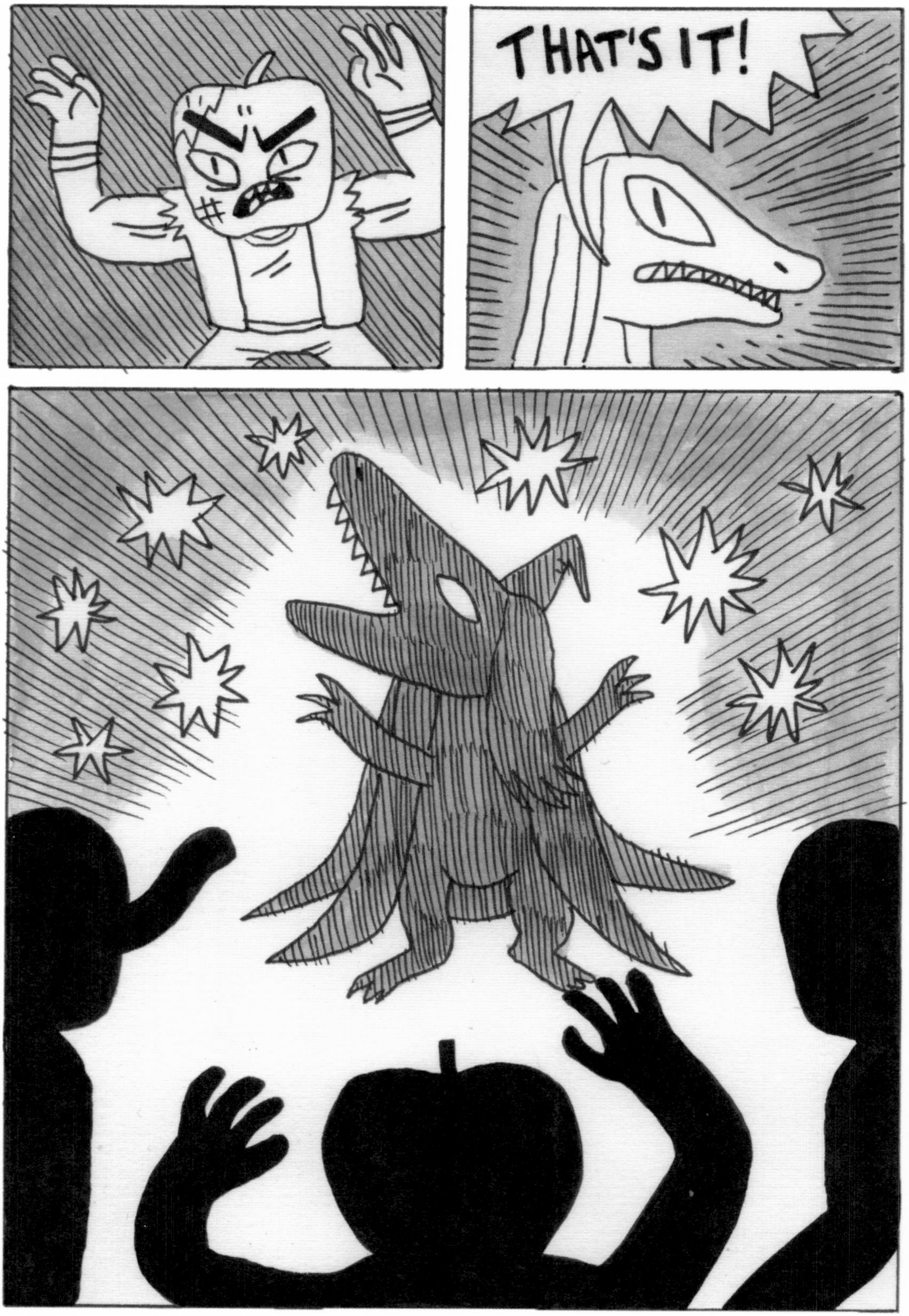
THAT'S IT!

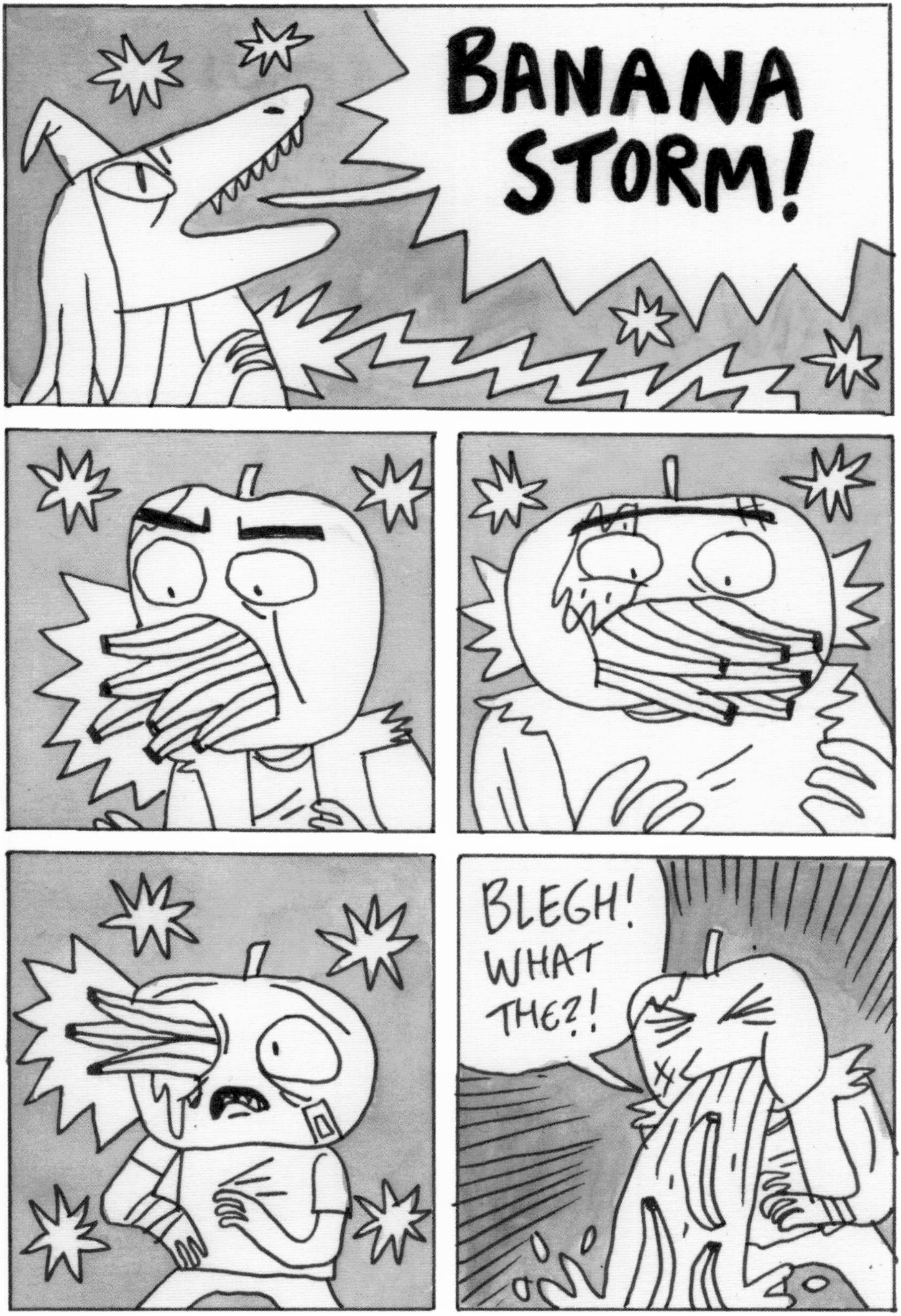
BANANA STORM!
BLEGH! WHAT THE?!

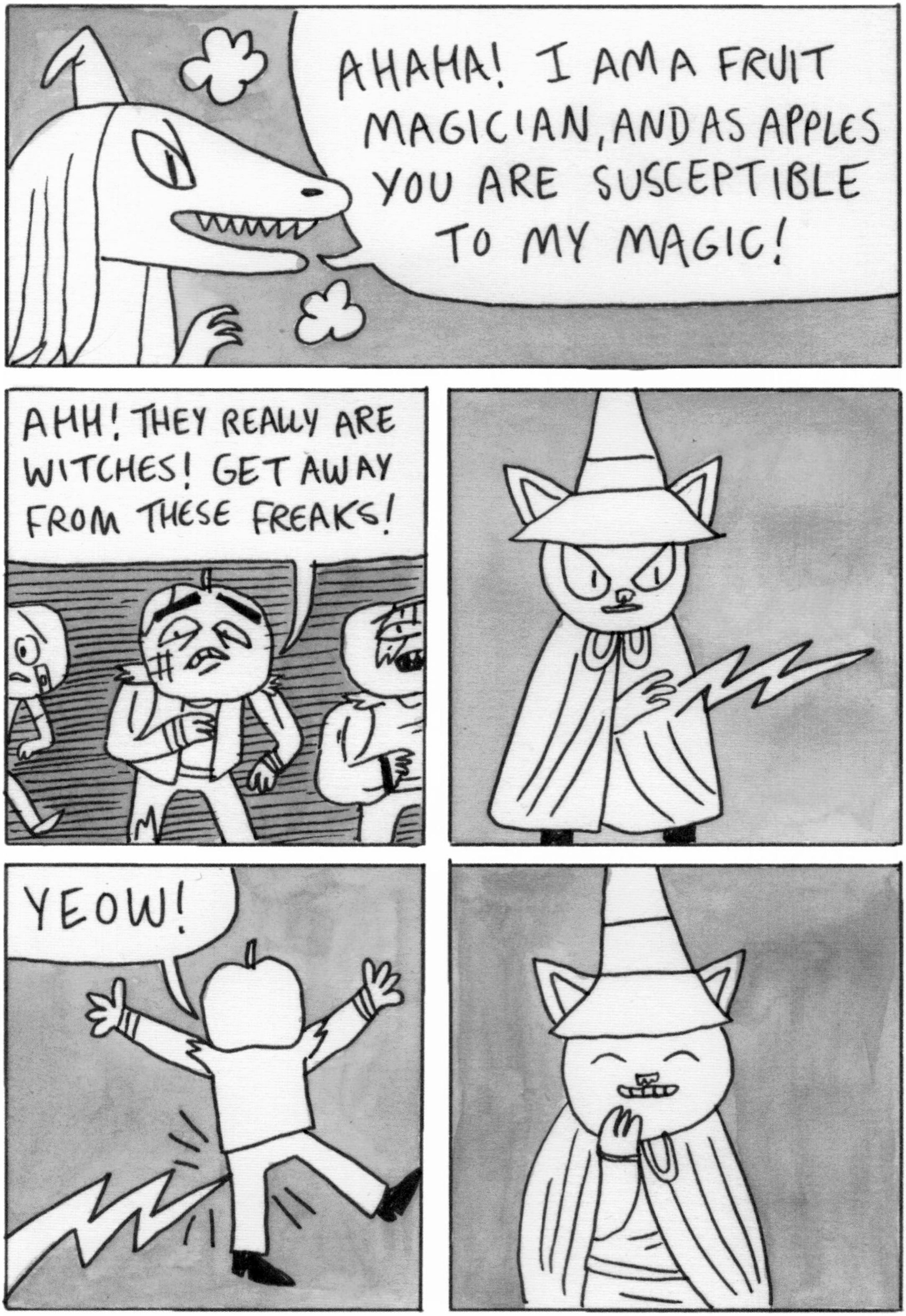
AHAHA! I AM A FRUIT MAGICIAN, AND AS APPLES YOU ARE SUSCEPTIBLE TO MY MAGIC!
AHH! THEY REALLY ARE WITCHES! GET AWAY FROM THESE FREAKS!
YEOW!

HAHA, NICE ONE KITTY! YEAH, YOU SHOW 'EM WHO'S BOSS!
WITCHES ALWAYS STICK TOGETHER!

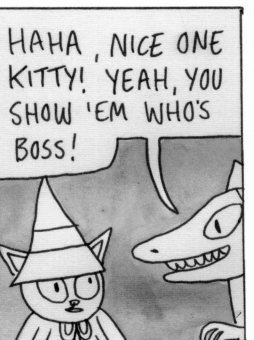

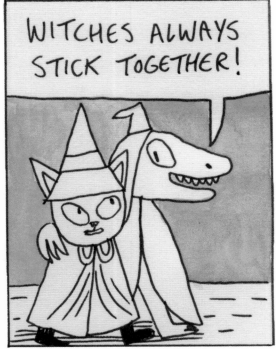

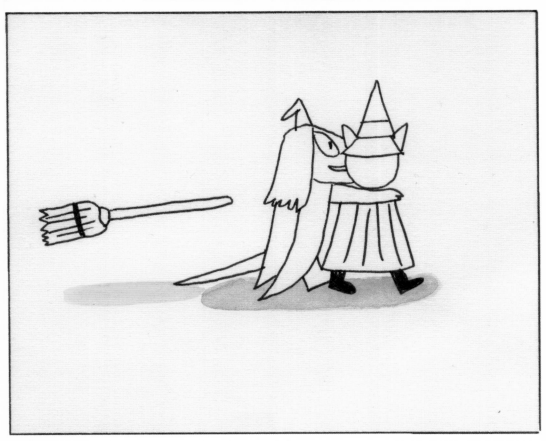

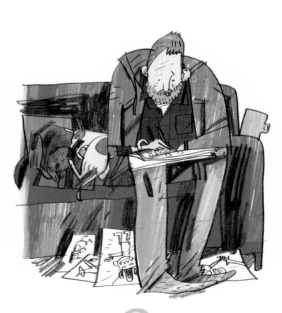

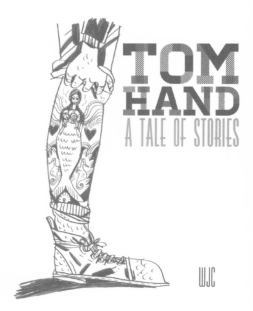

TOM
HAND
A TALE OF STORIES
WJC

Warwick Johnson Cadwell

Warwick Johnson-Cadwell is an artist and comic maker Illustrating for newspapers, childrens books and comic publications including Walker Books, *Tank Girl*, *Moose Kid Comics* and *The Phoenix*. Also creating *Dangeritis*, in partnership with Robert Ball which was self published and nominated for a British Comic Award in the category Best Comic in 2014.

He is continually trying to complete his book *Gungle* for Blank Slate Books.

warwickjohnsoncadwell.blogspot.co.uk
@WarwickJC

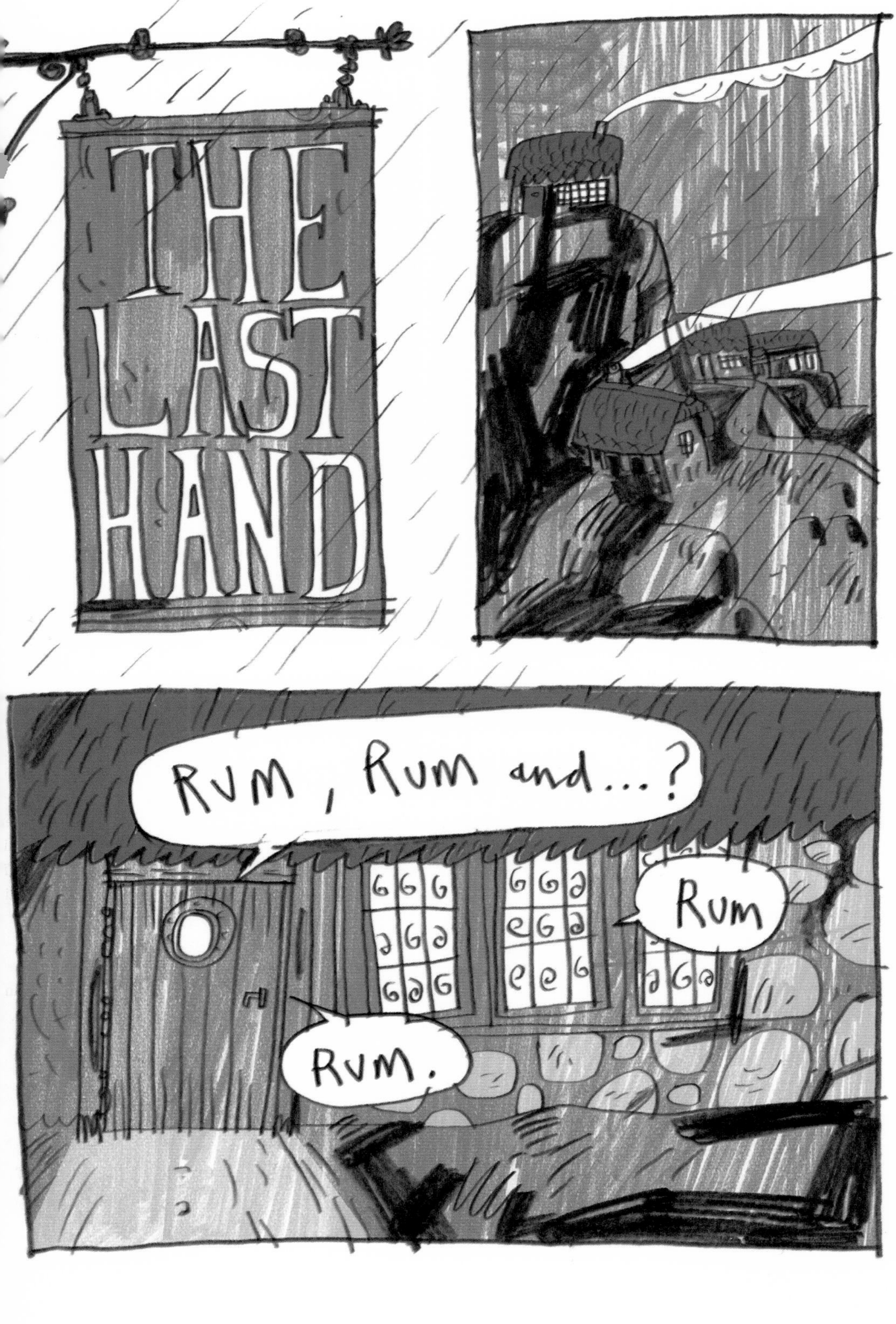
THE LAST HAND
RUM, Rum and...?
Rum
RUM.

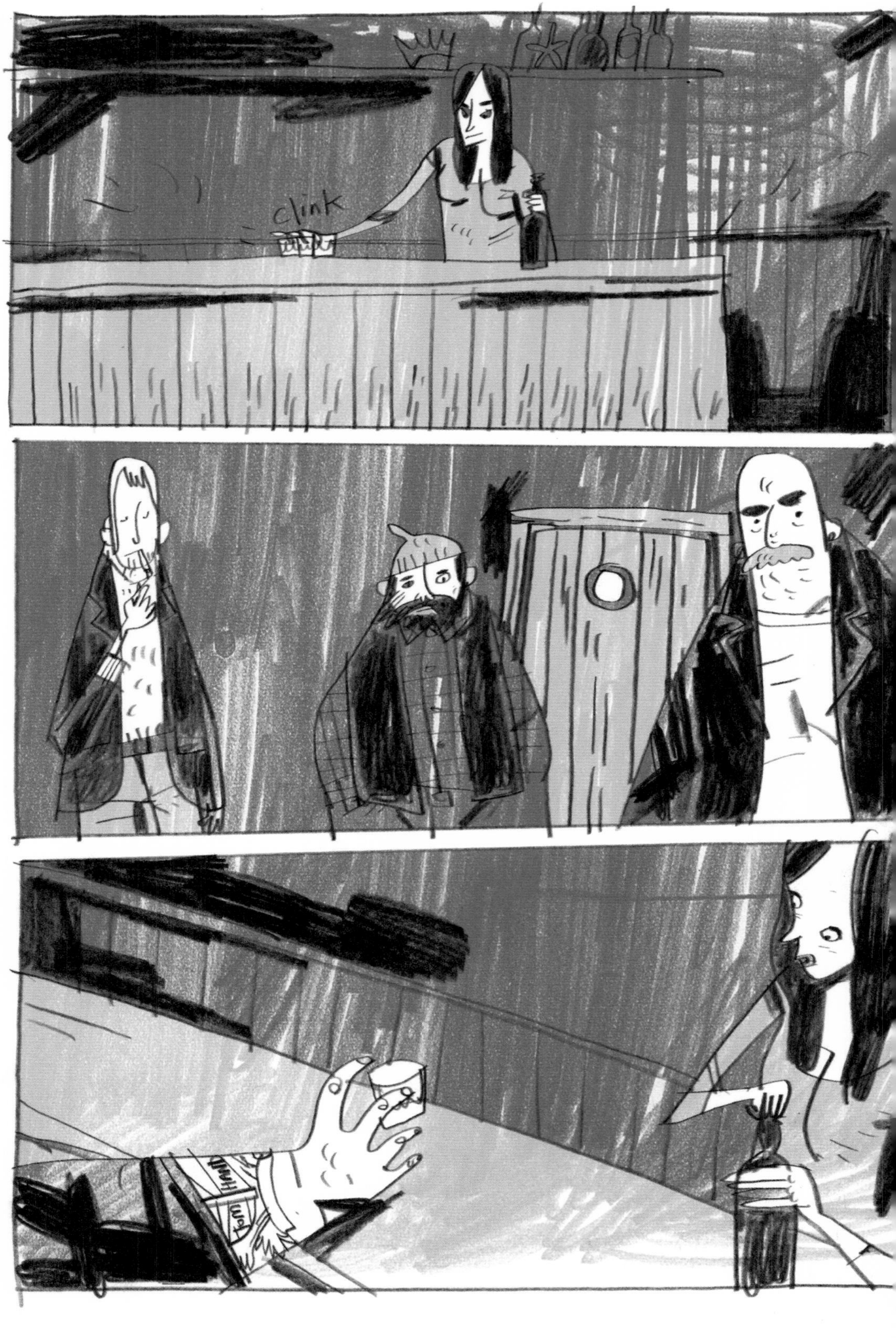
clink

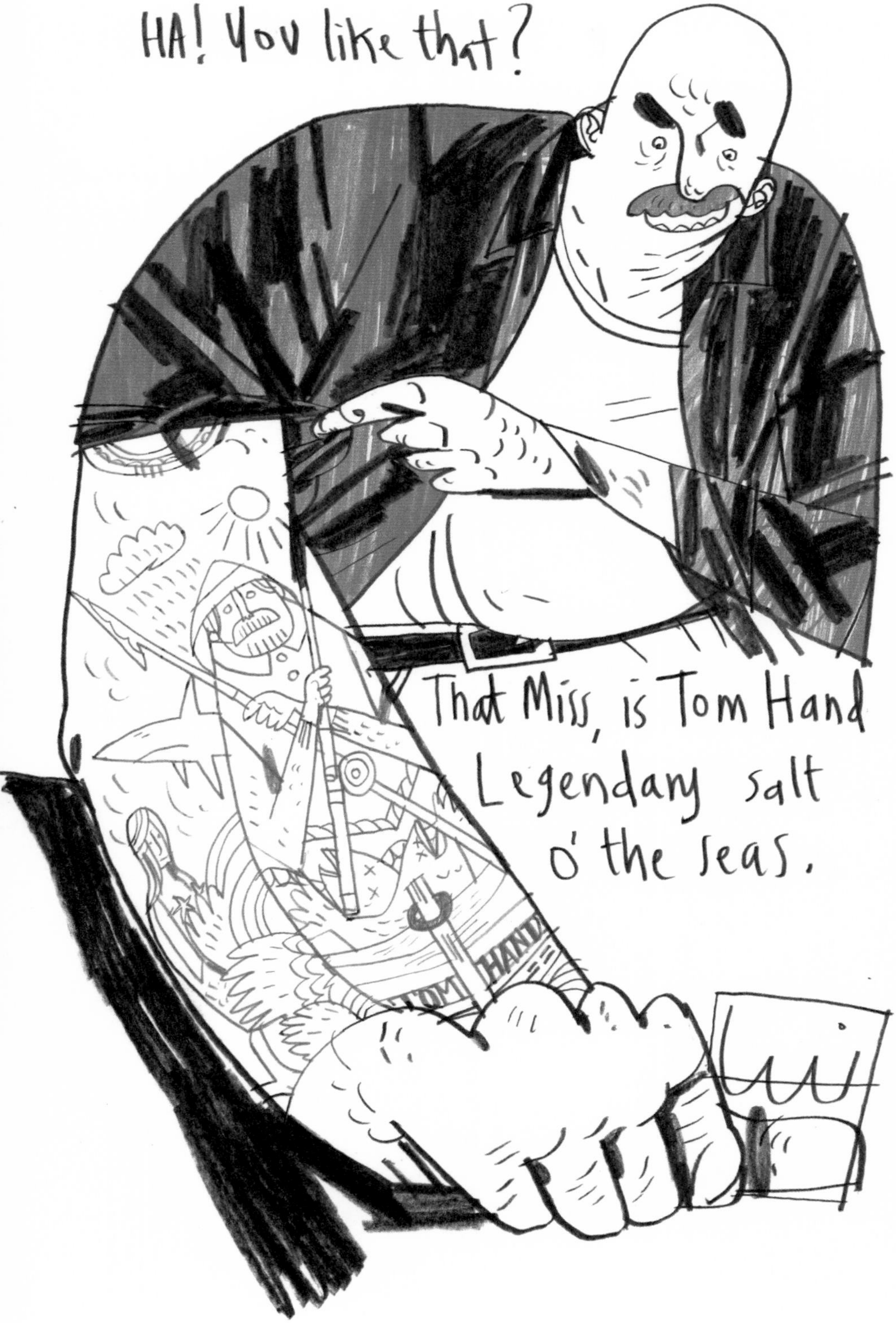
HA! You like that?
That Miss, is Tom Hand
Legendary salt
o' the seas.
TOM HAND

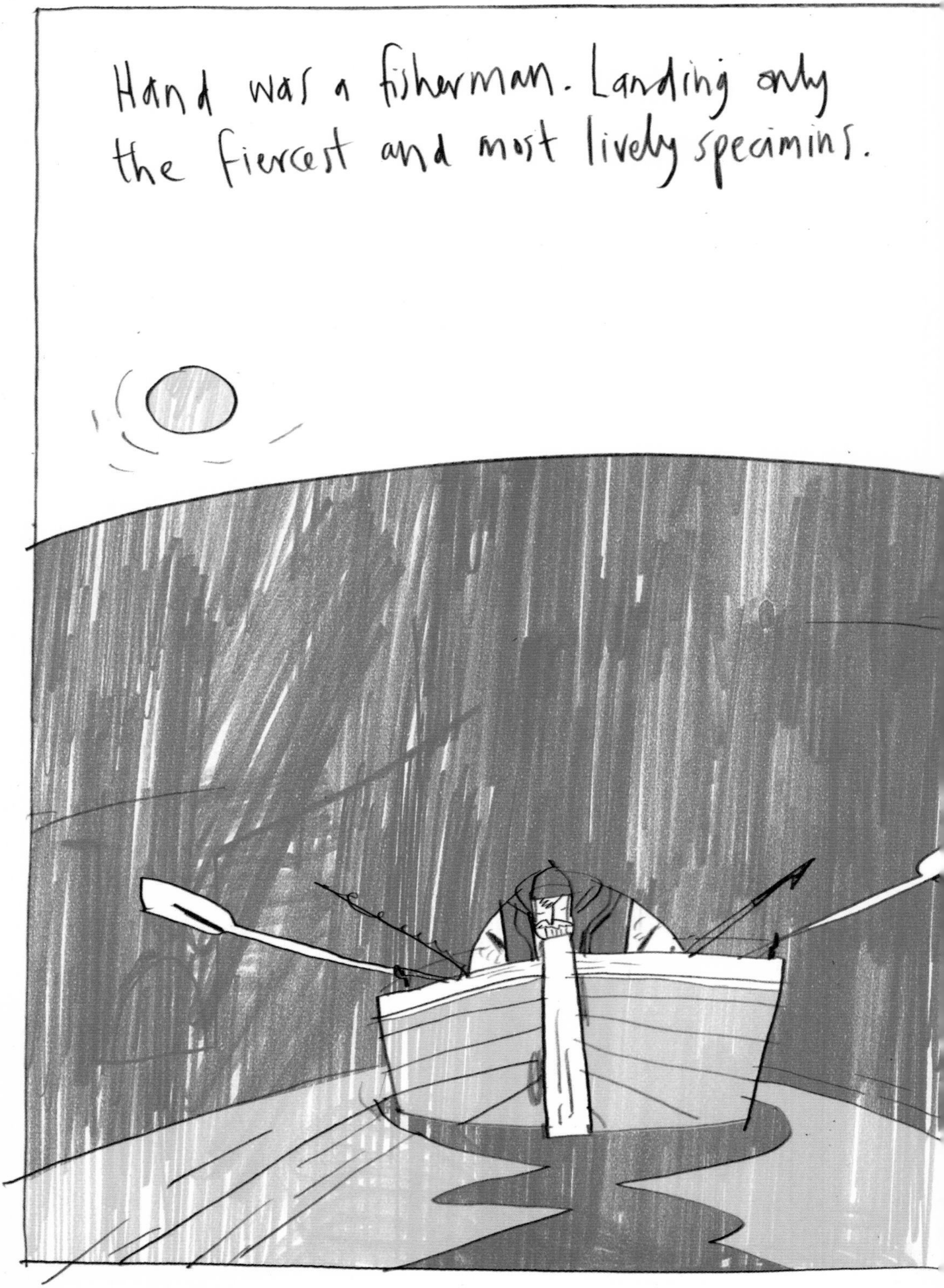
Hand was a fisherman. Landing only the fiercest and most lively specimins.

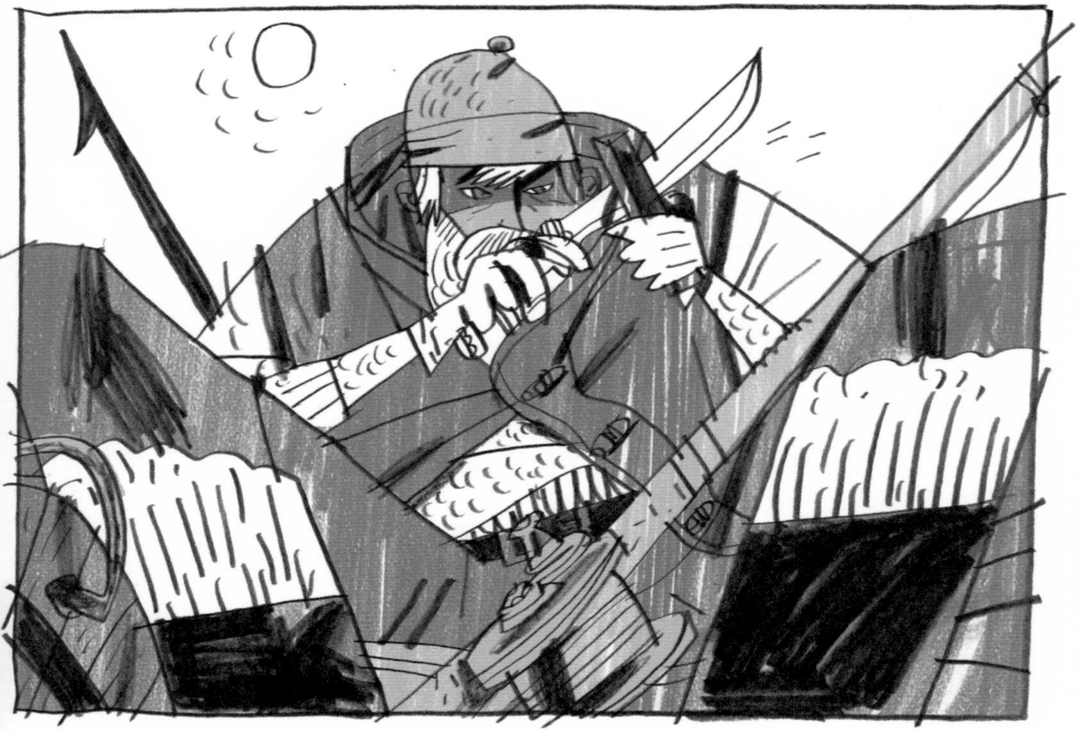

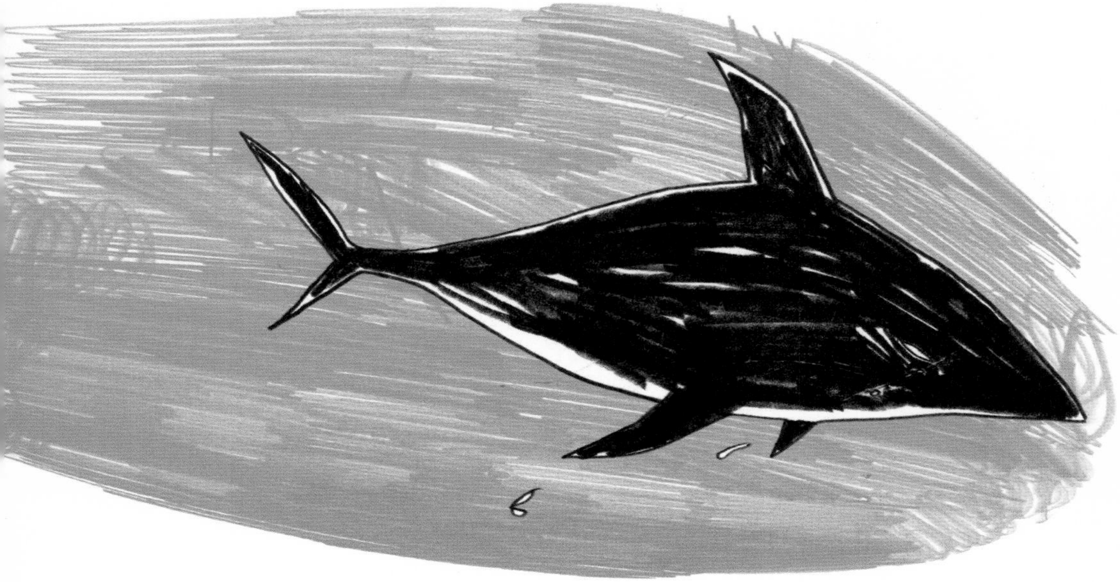

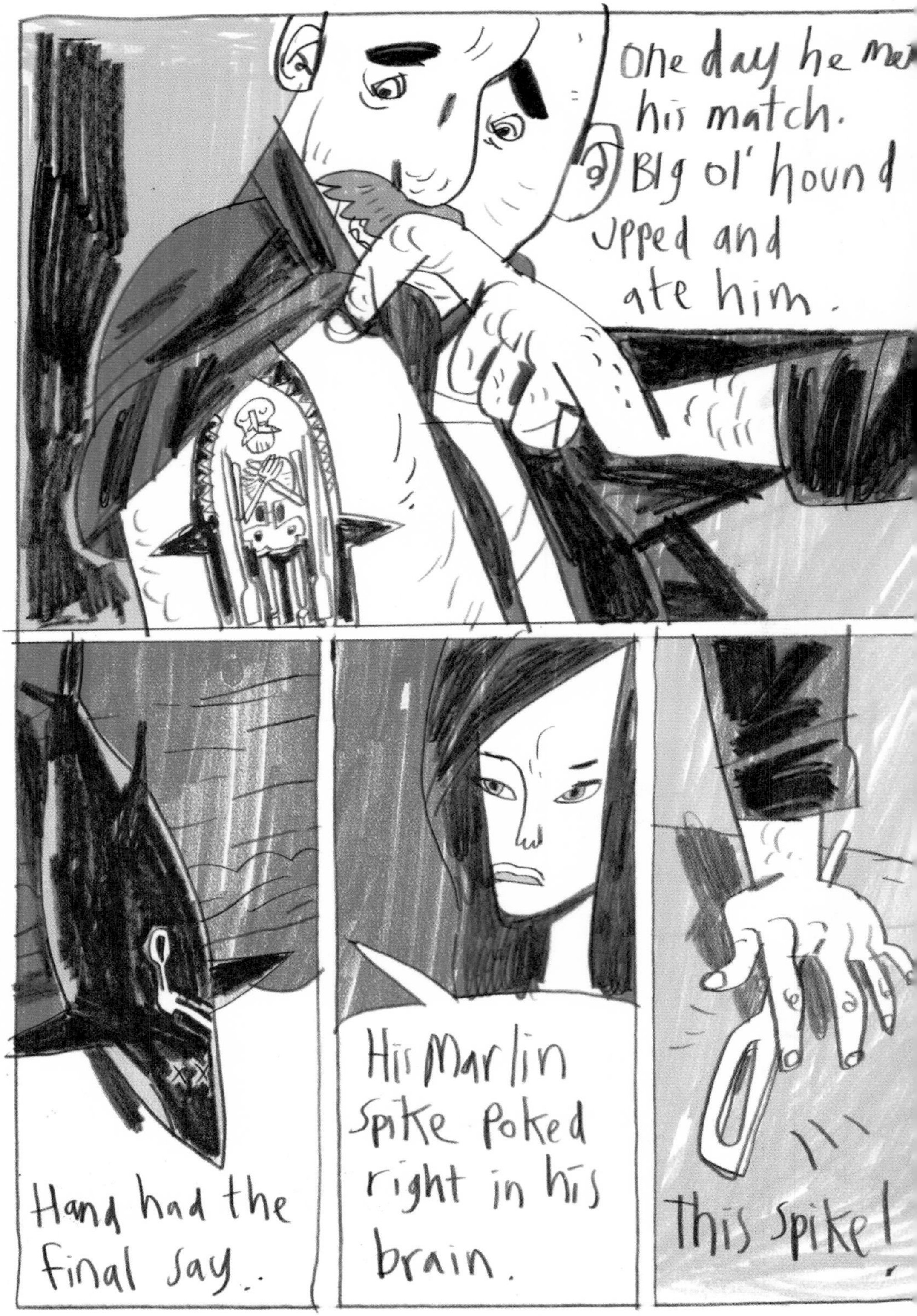
One day he met his match. Big ol' hound upped and ate him.
Hand had the final say..
His Marlin Spike poked right in his brain.
This spike!

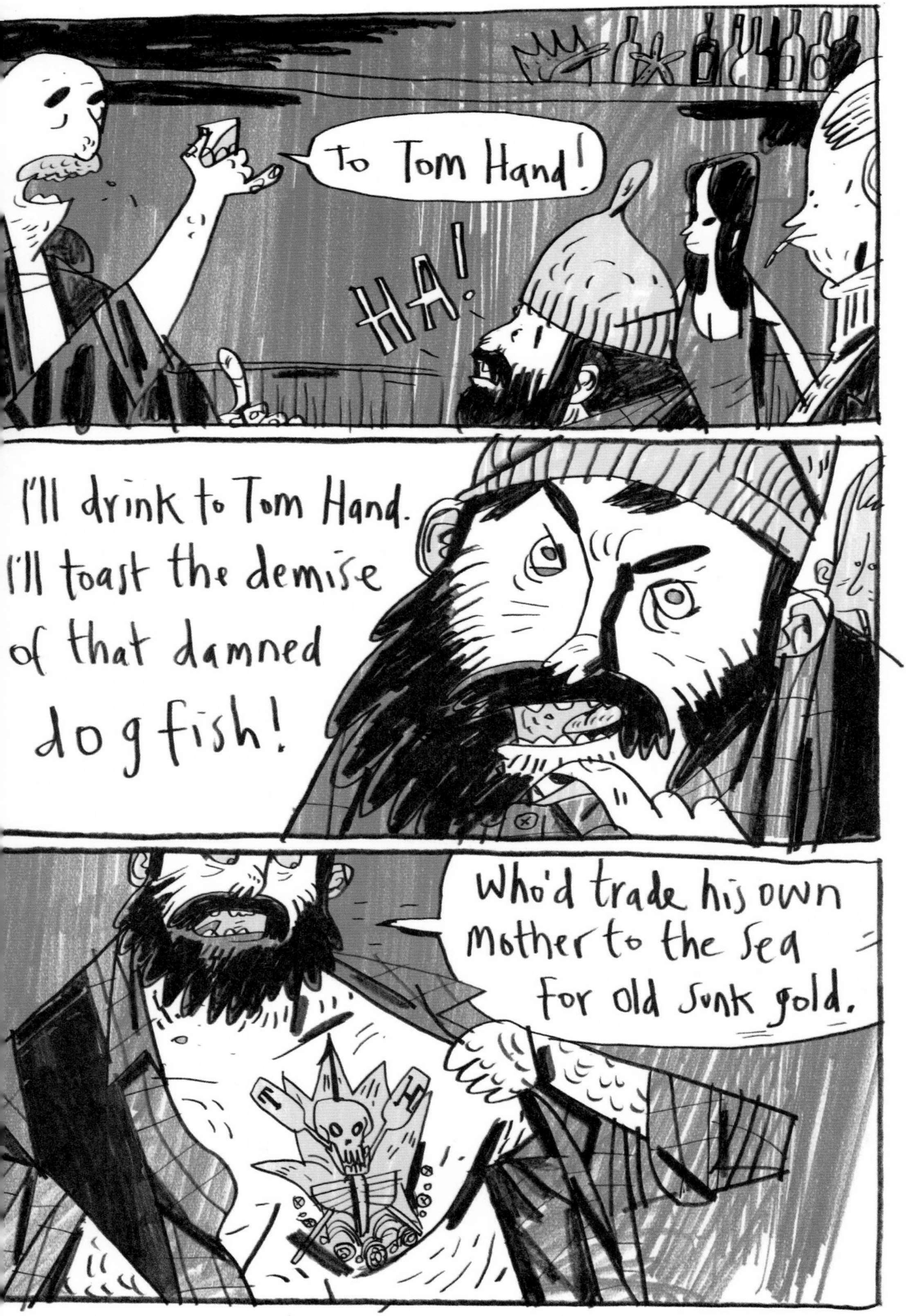
To Tom Hand!
HA!
I'll drink to Tom Hand. I'll toast the demise of that damned dogfish!
Who'd trade his own mother to the sea for old sunk gold.
T
H

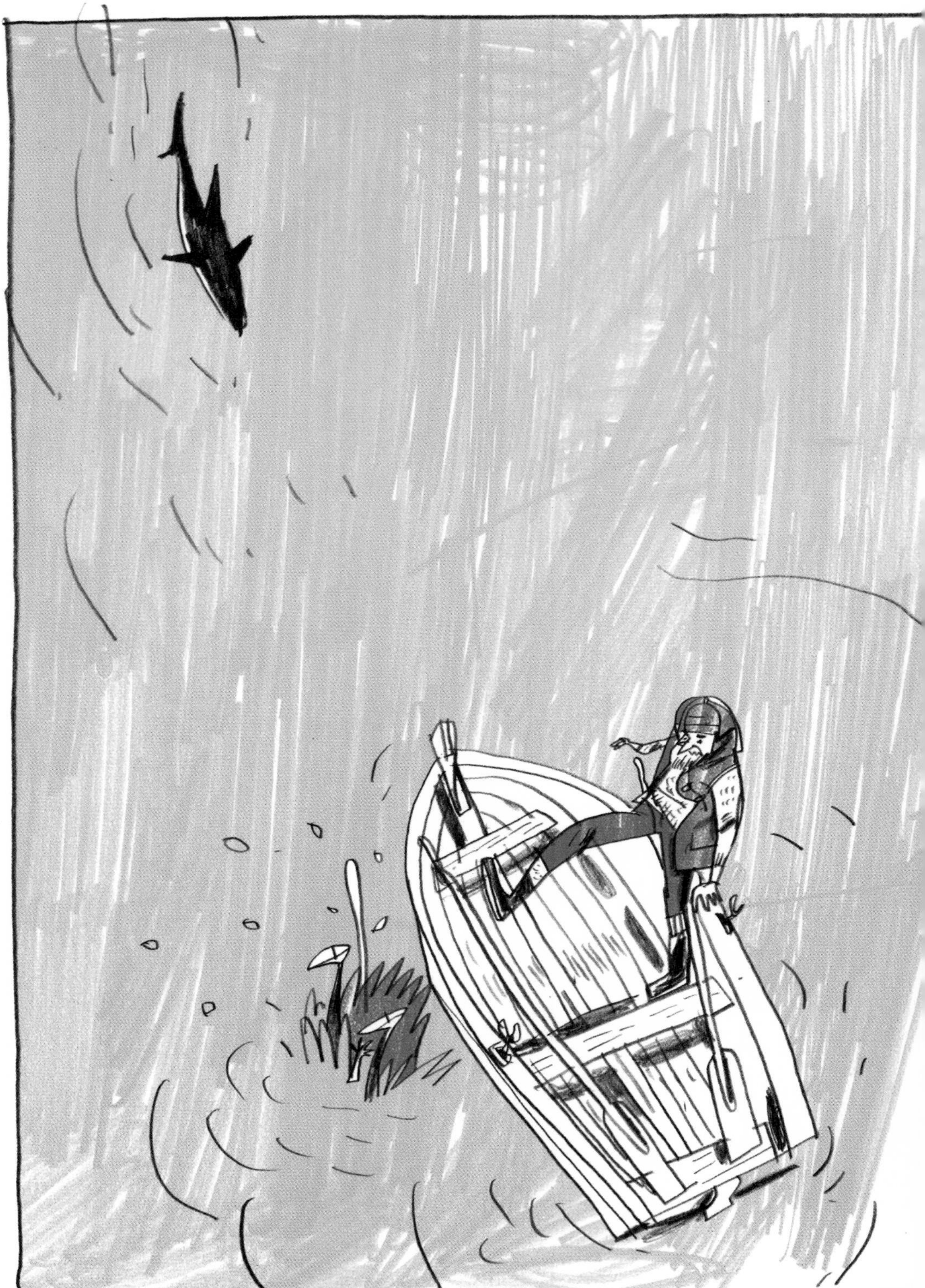

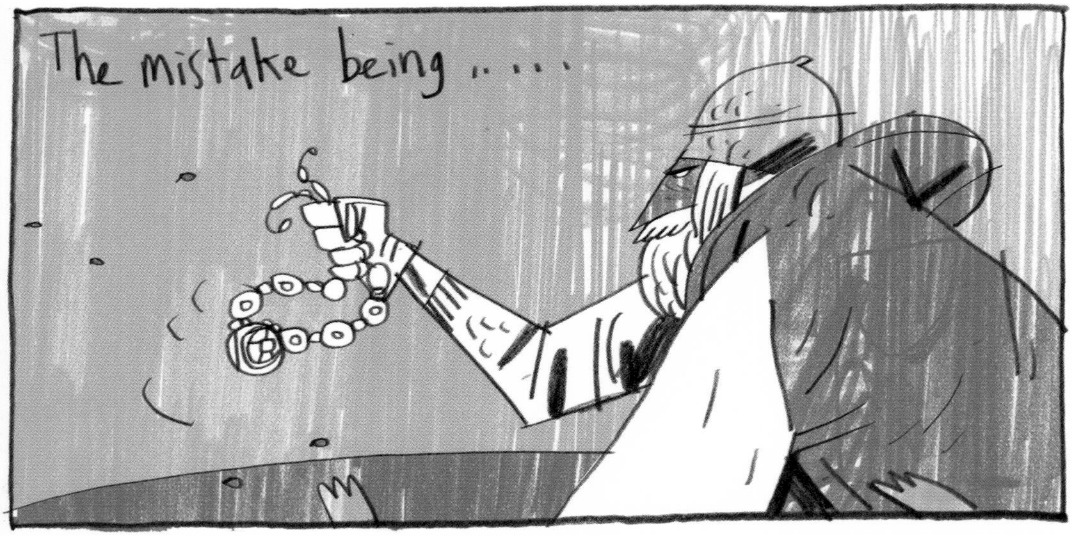
The mistake being . . . .

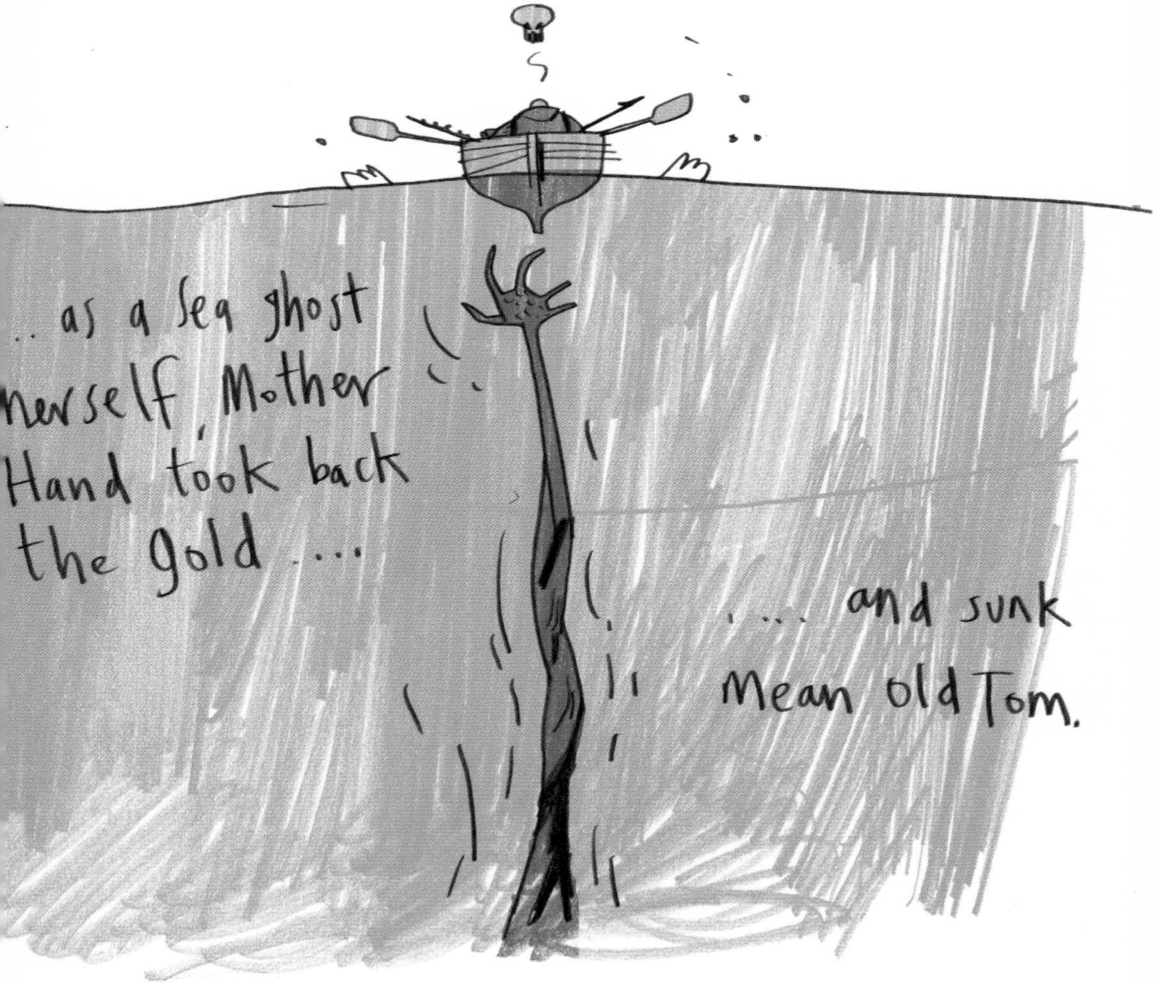
.. as a sea ghost
herself, Mother
Hand took back
the gold ...
. ... and sunk
Mean old Tom.

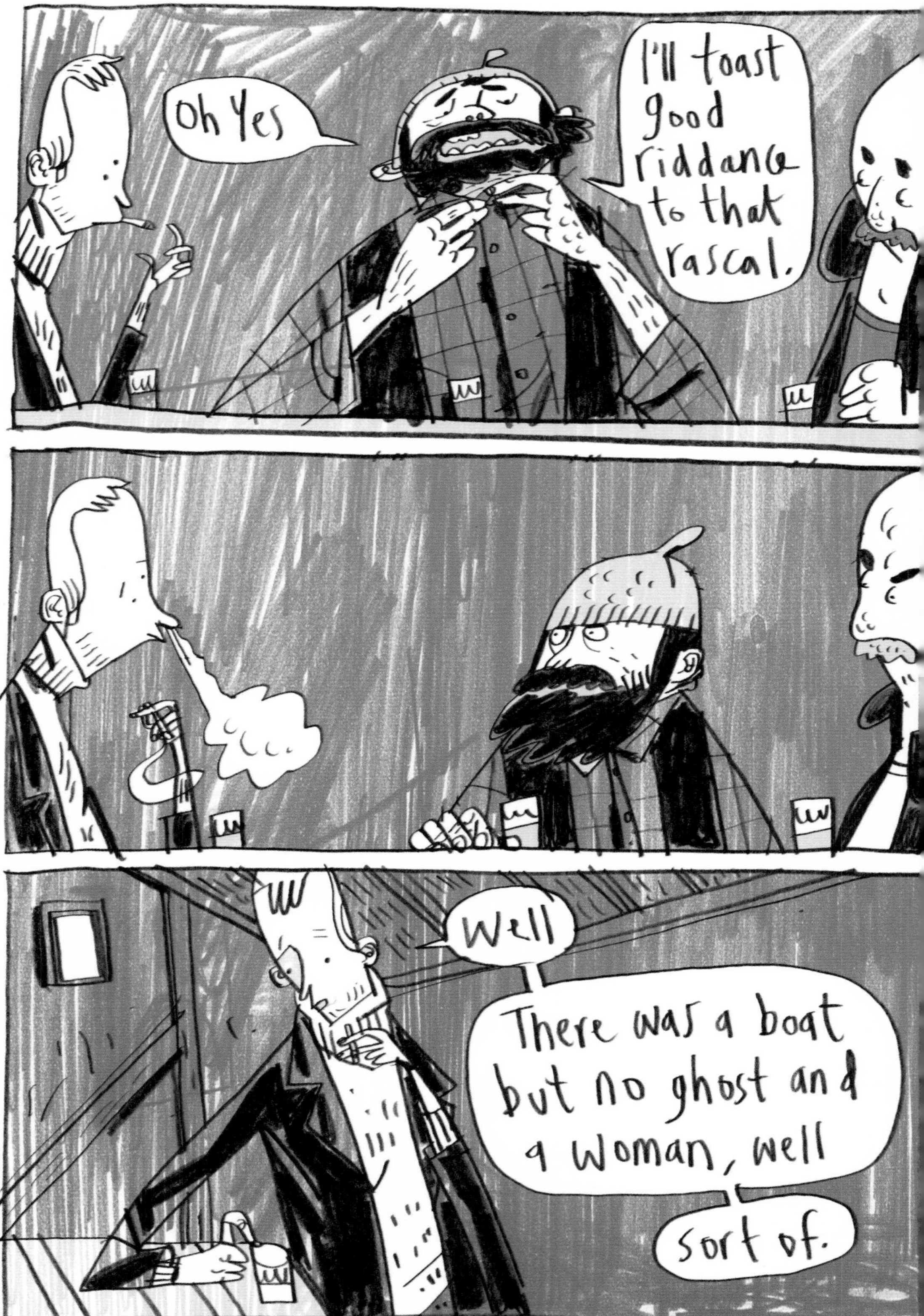
Oh Yes
I'll toast good riddance to that rascal.
Well
There was a boat but no ghost and a woman, well
sort of.

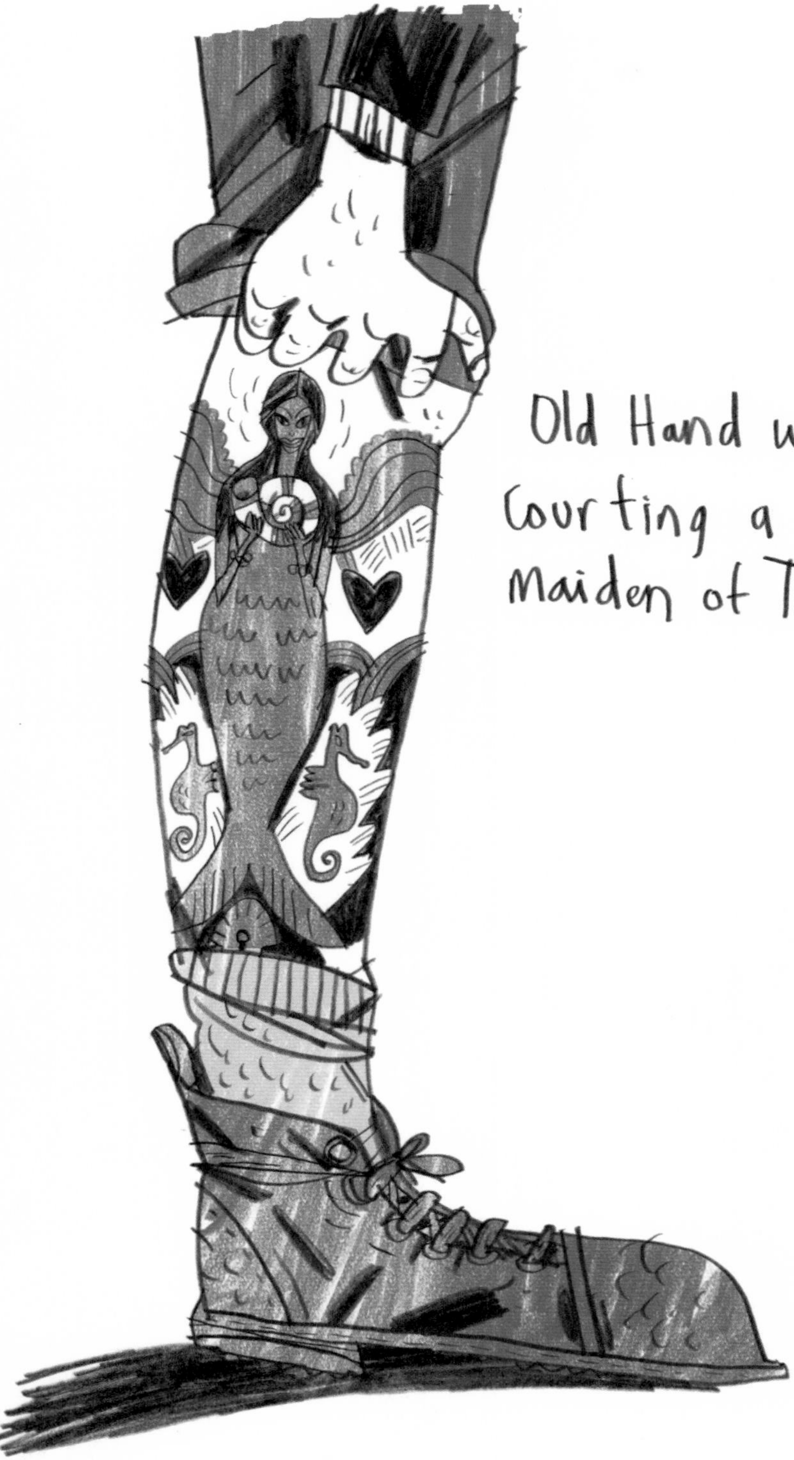

Old Hand was courting a maiden of The Deep.

A right romance they had too.

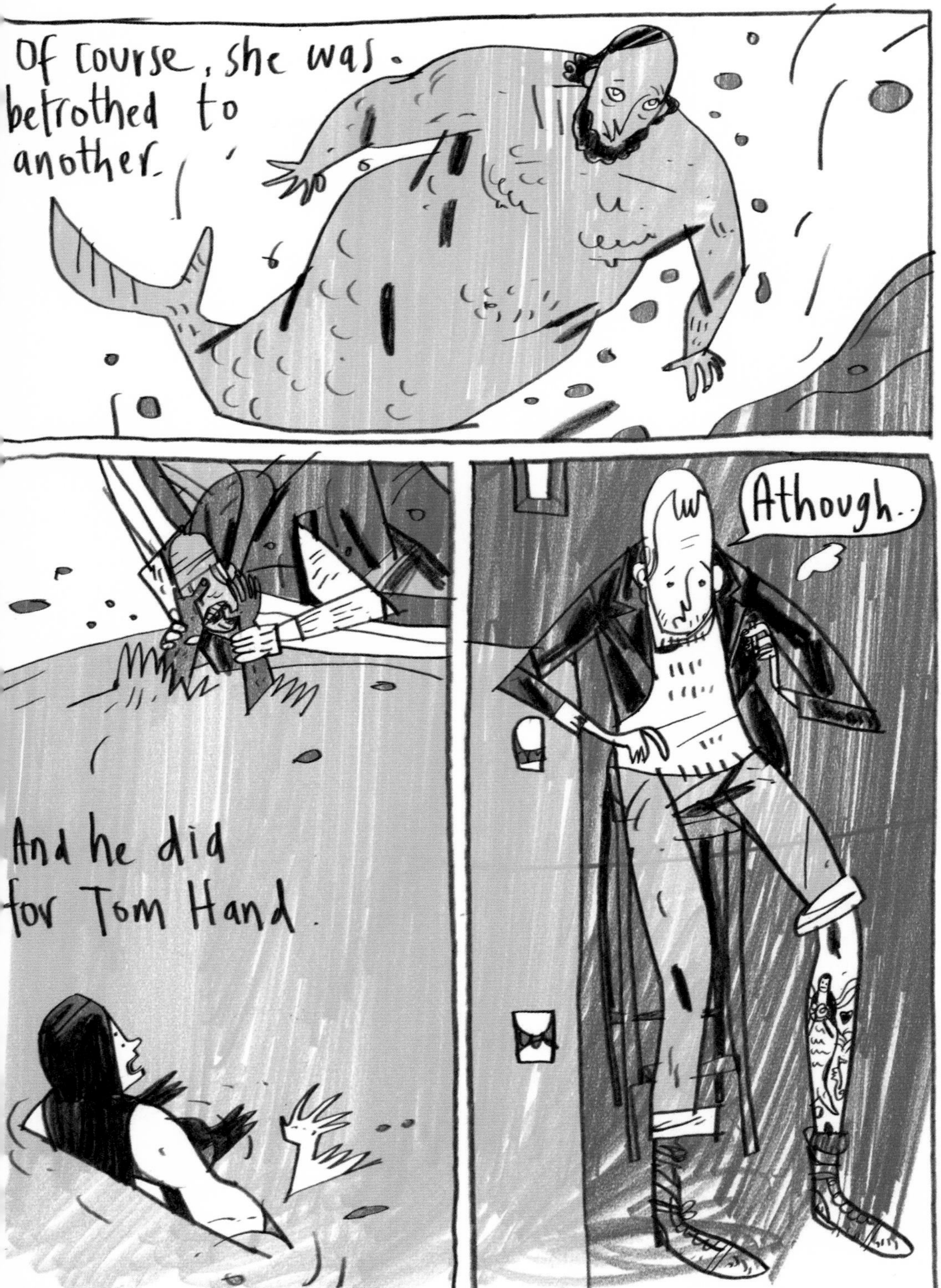
Of course, she was betrothed to another.
And he did for Tom Hand.
Athough..

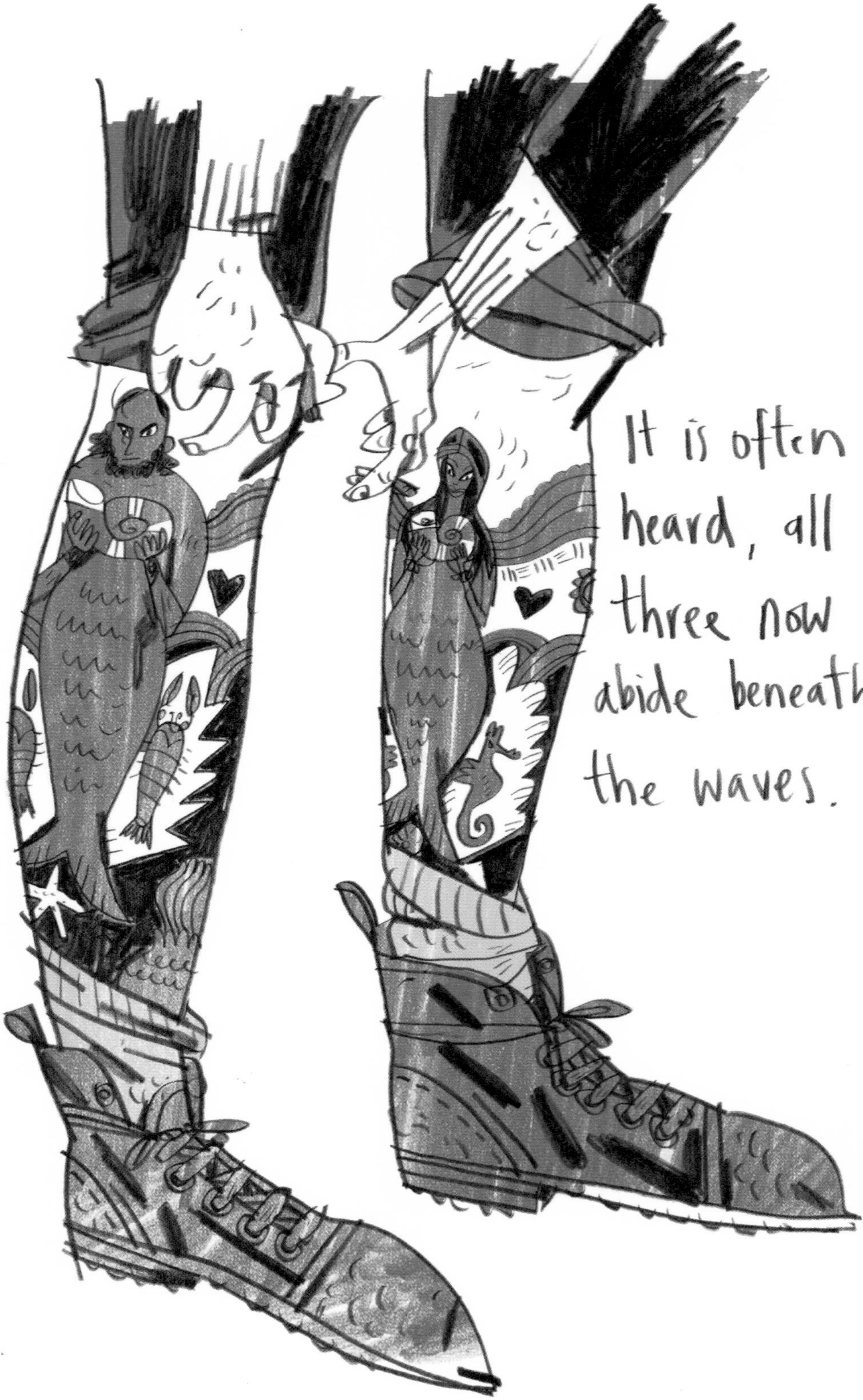

It is often heard, all three now abide beneath the waves.

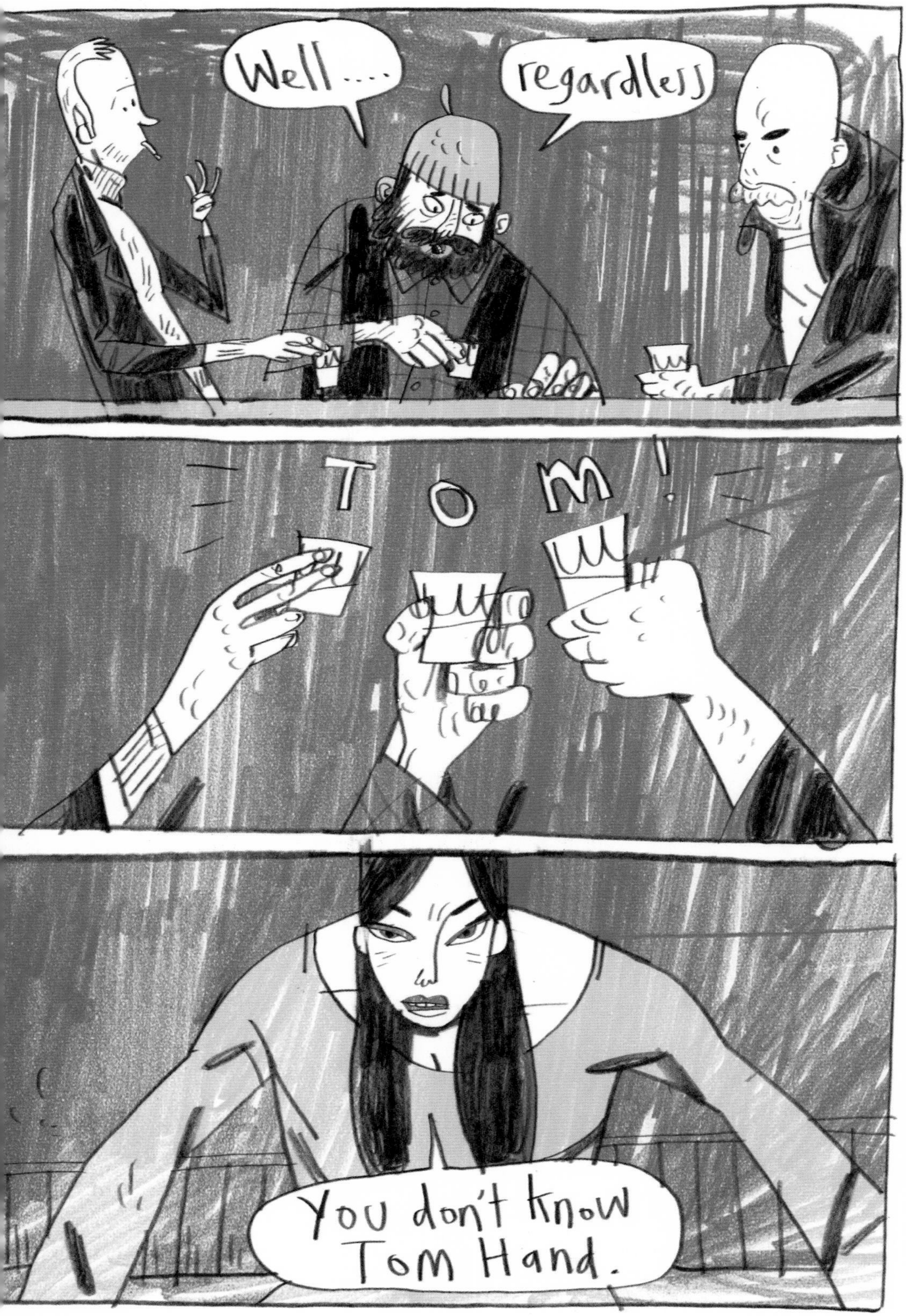
Well....
regardless
TOM!
You don't know Tom Hand.

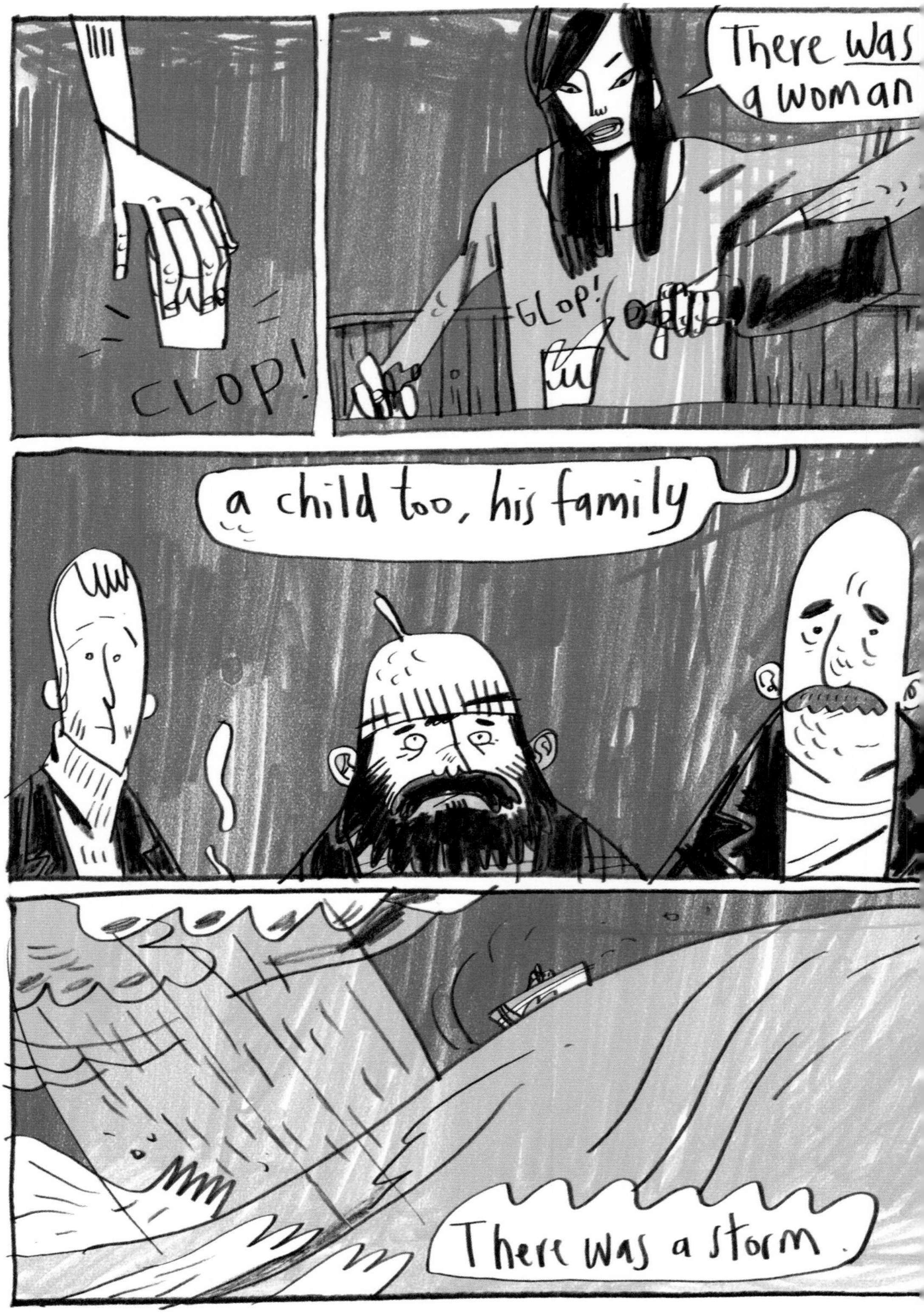
CLOP!
There was a woman
GLOP!
a child too, his family
There was a storm.

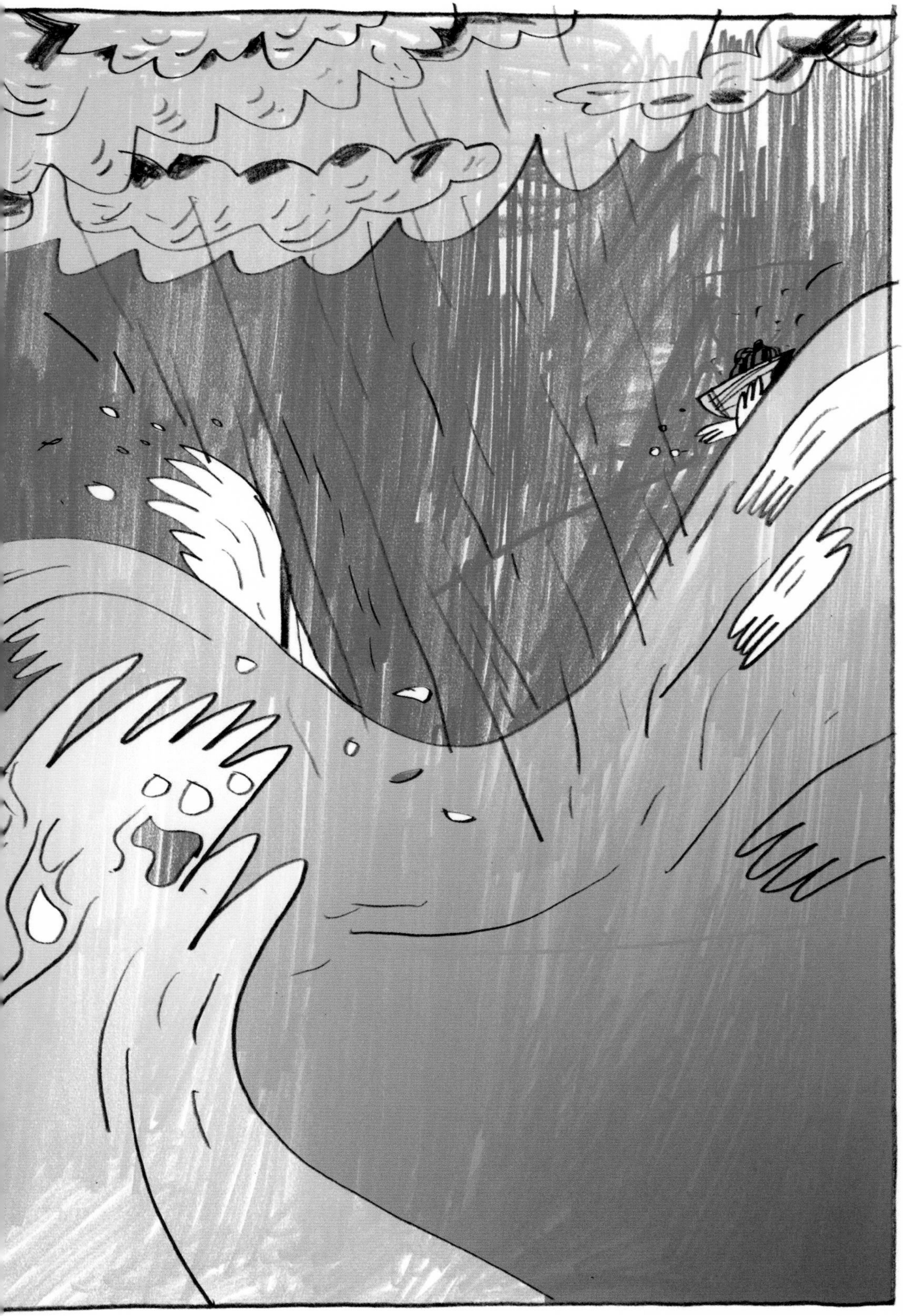

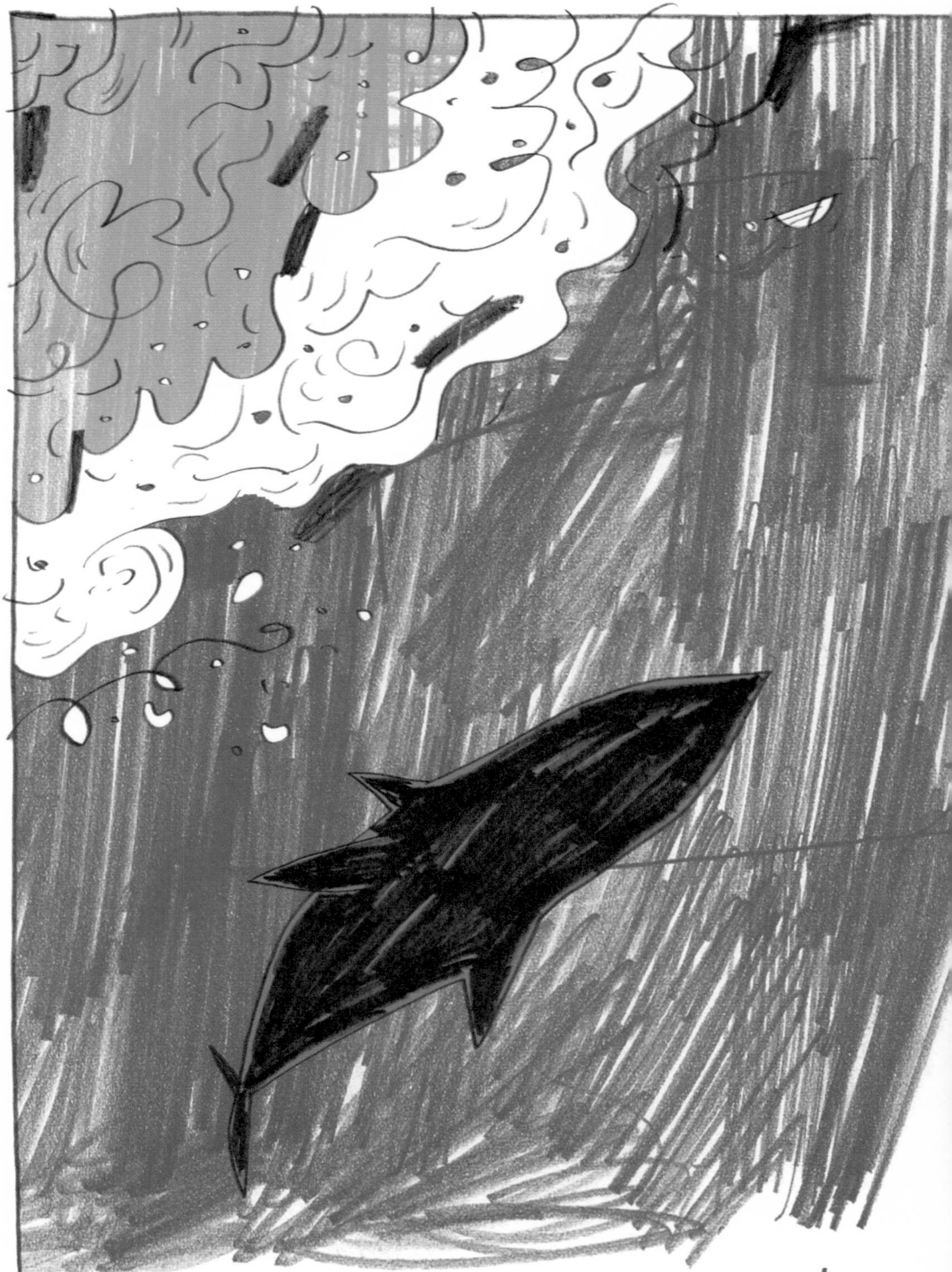
and there was a Monster.

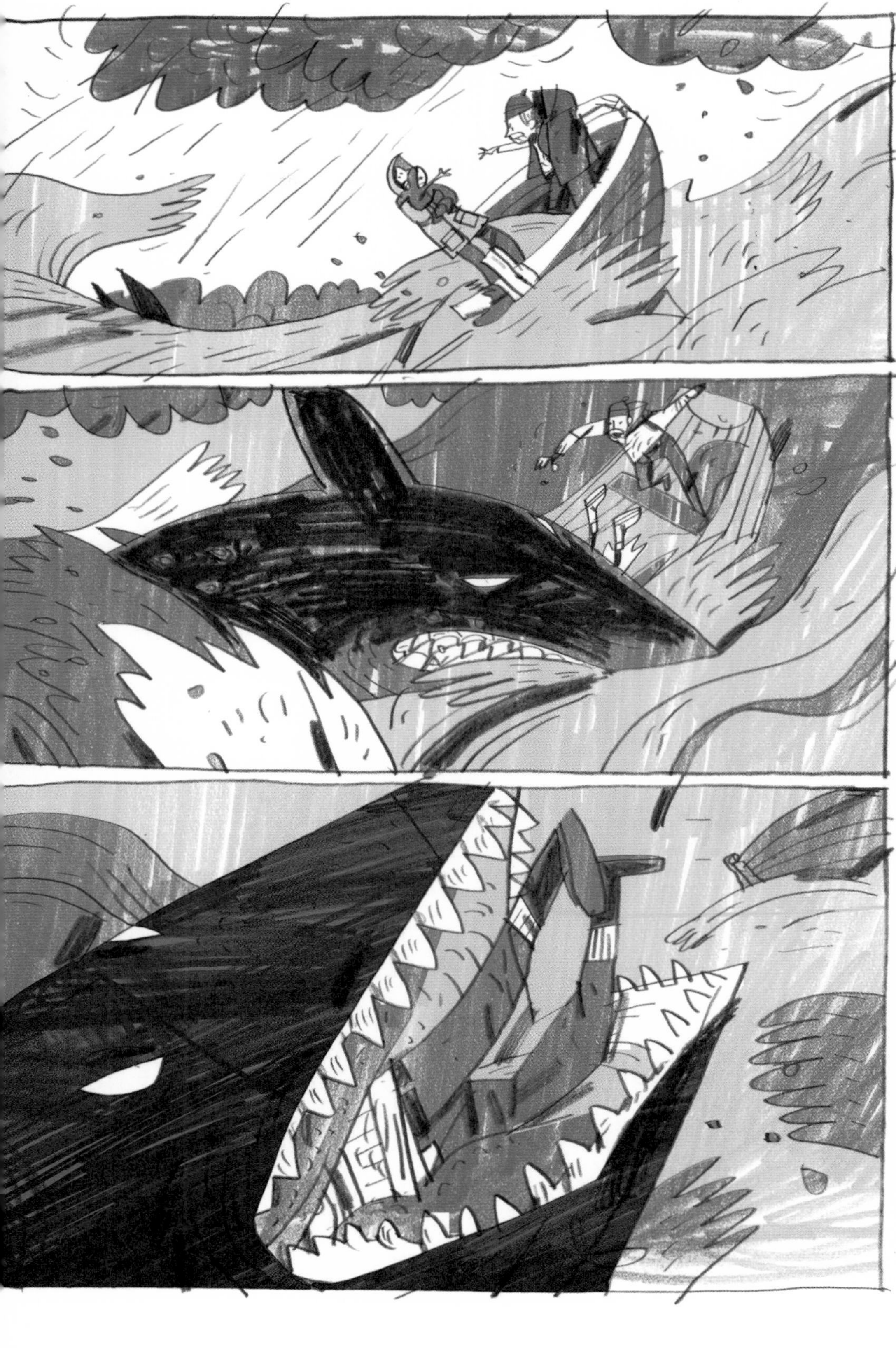

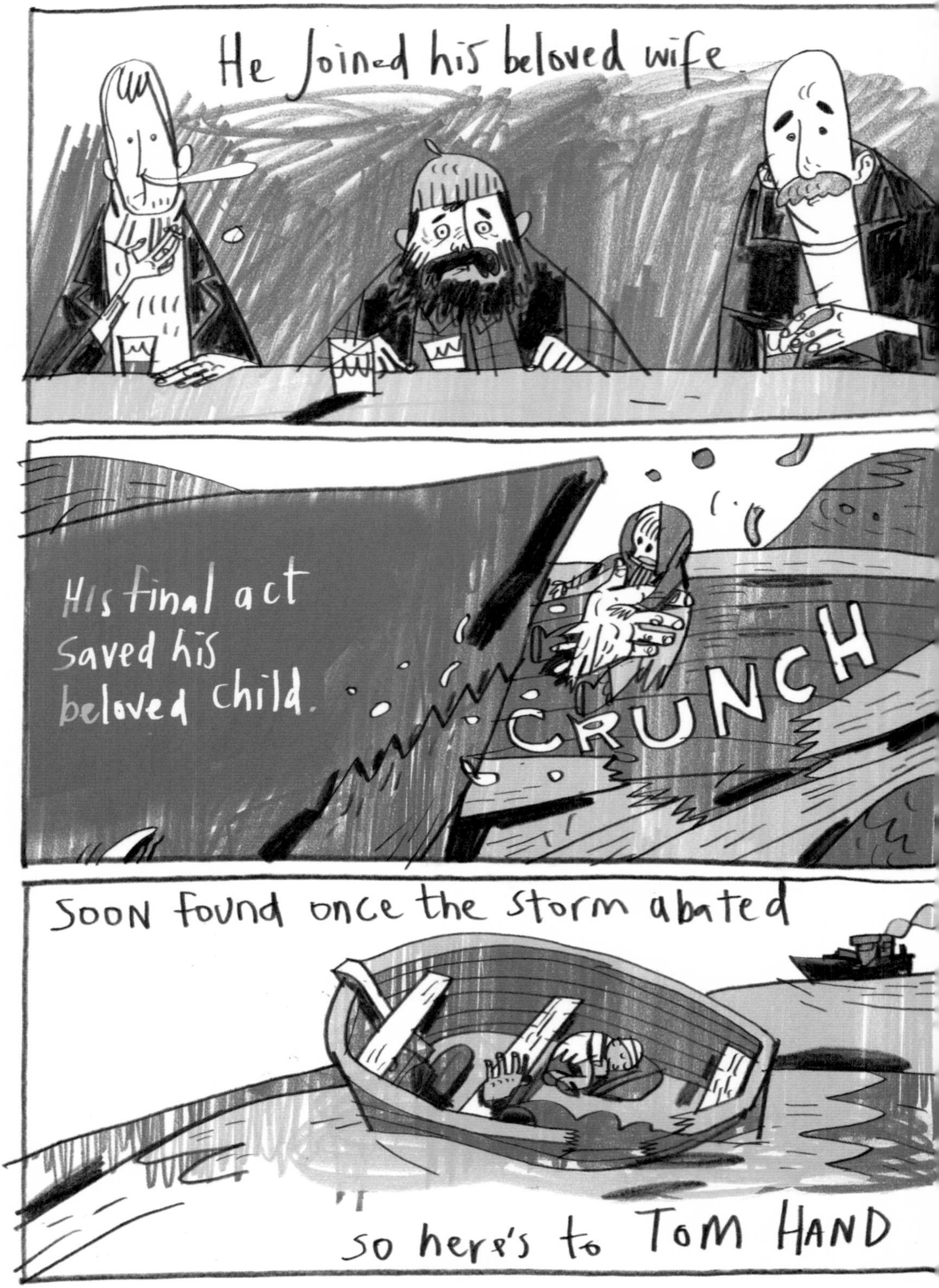
He joined his beloved wife.
His final act saved his beloved child.
CRUNCH
Soon found once the storm abated
so here's to TOM HAND

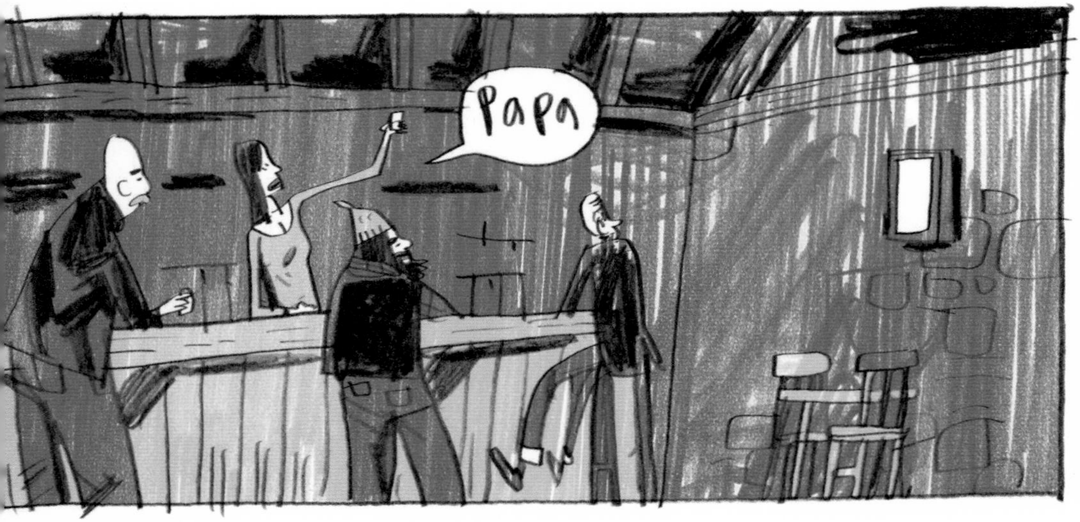
Papa

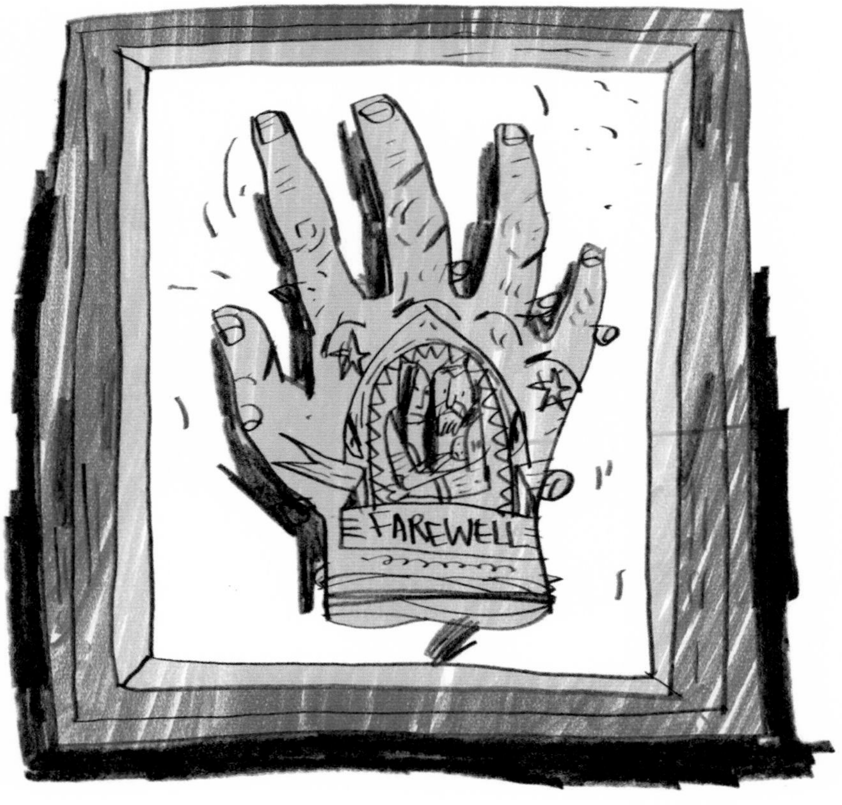
FAREWELL

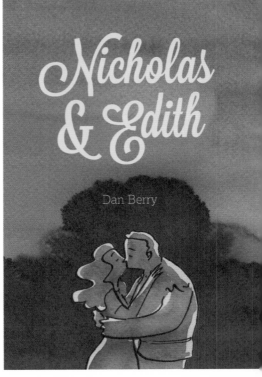

Dan Berry

Dan is a cartoonist, lecturer and podcaster. He is the author and artist of The Suitcase published by Blank Slate Books and has self published a number of books including The End, Carry Me, Throw Your Keys Away and Hey You! He lectures in comics and illustration at the North Wales School of Art & Design at Glyndwr University.

He is the host of the interview podcast Make It Then Tell Everybody.

thingsbydan.co.uk
@thingsbydan

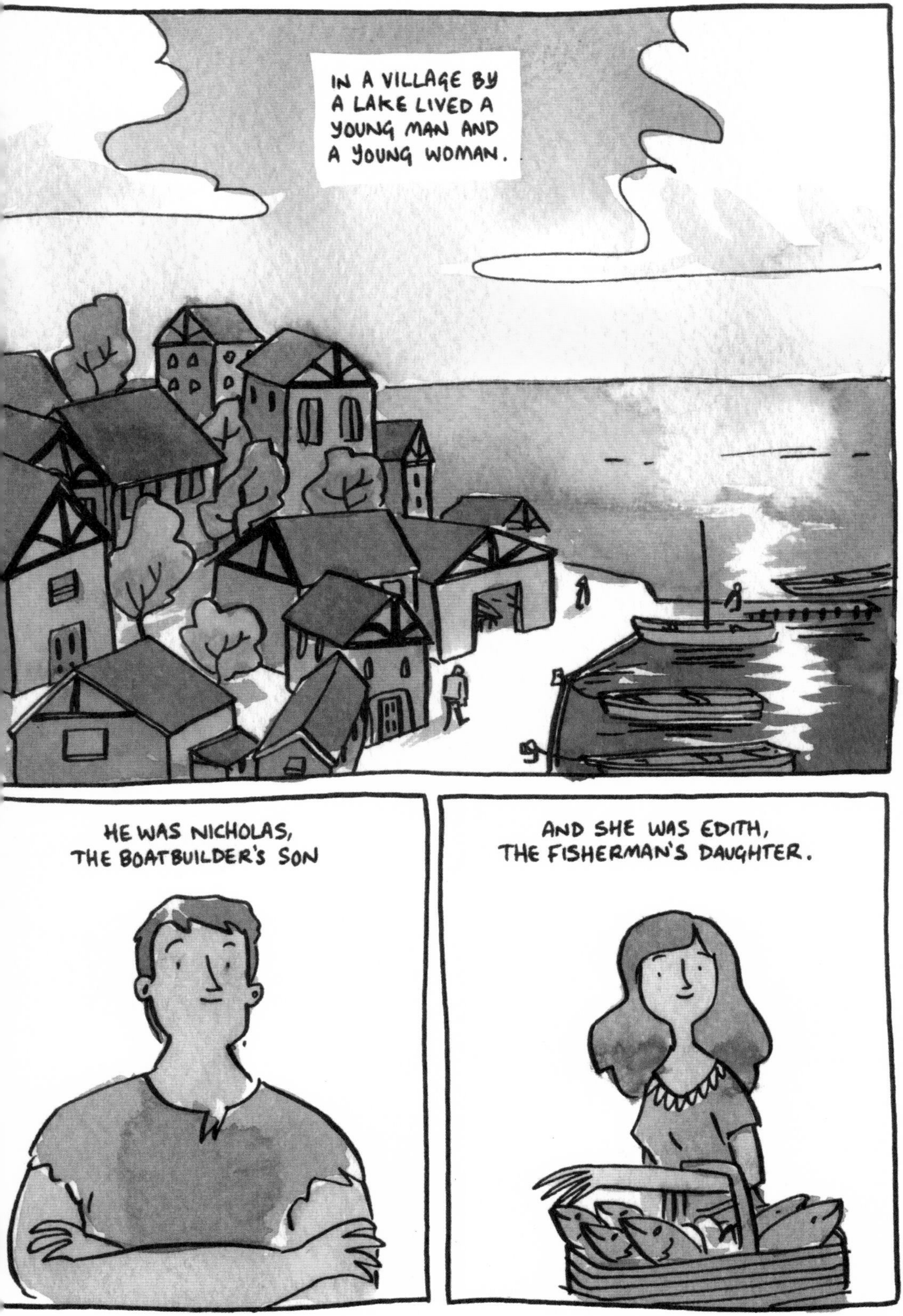
IN A VILLAGE BY A LAKE LIVED A YOUNG MAN AND A YOUNG WOMAN.
HE WAS NICHOLAS, THE BOATBUILDER'S SON
AND SHE WAS EDITH, THE FISHERMAN'S DAUGHTER.

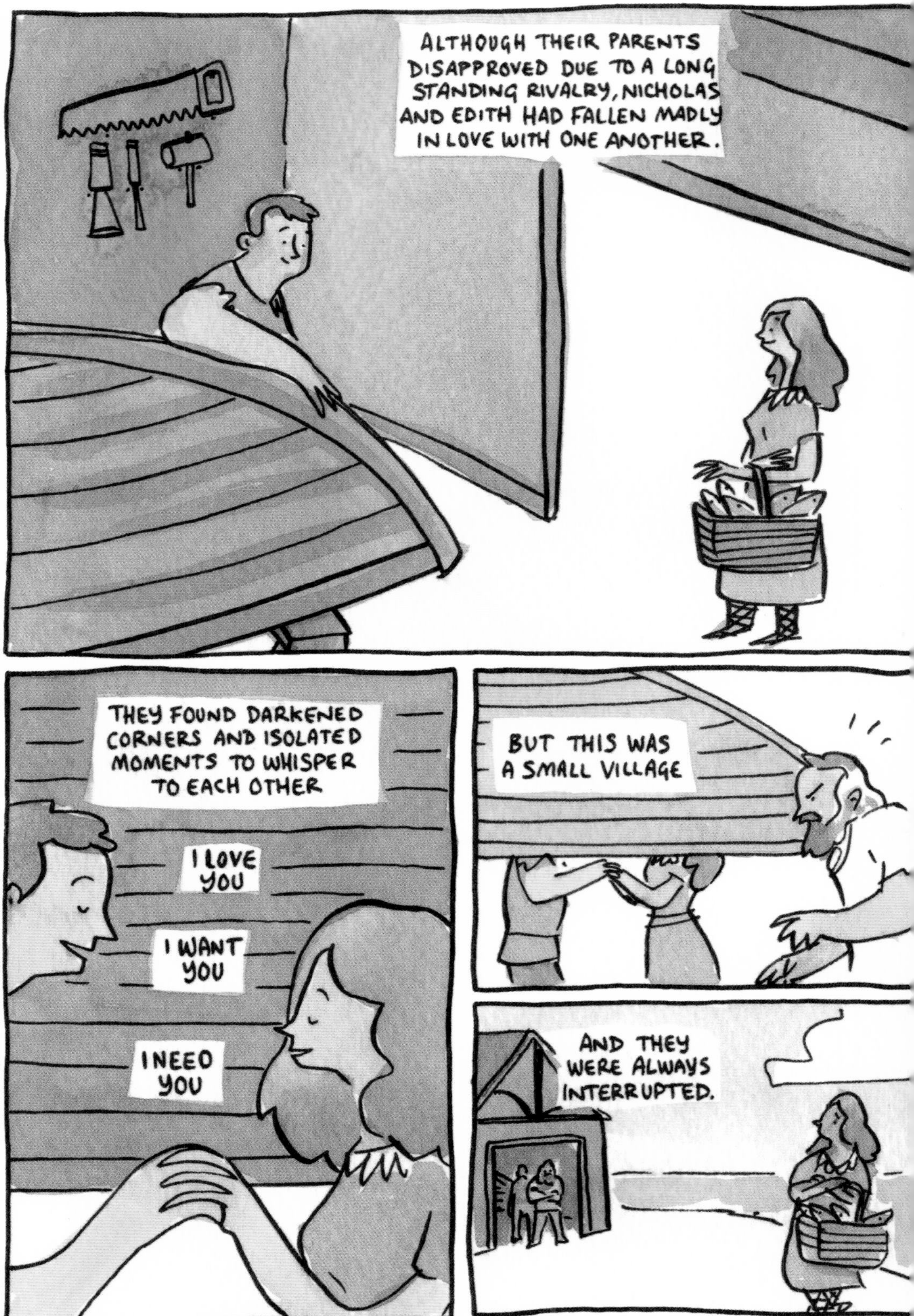
ALTHOUGH THEIR PARENTS DISAPPROVED DUE TO A LONG STANDING RIVALRY, NICHOLAS AND EDITH HAD FALLEN MADLY IN LOVE WITH ONE ANOTHER.
THEY FOUND DARKENED CORNERS AND ISOLATED MOMENTS TO WHISPER TO EACH OTHER
I LOVE YOU
I WANT YOU
I NEED YOU
BUT THIS WAS A SMALL VILLAGE
AND THEY WERE ALWAYS INTERRUPTED.

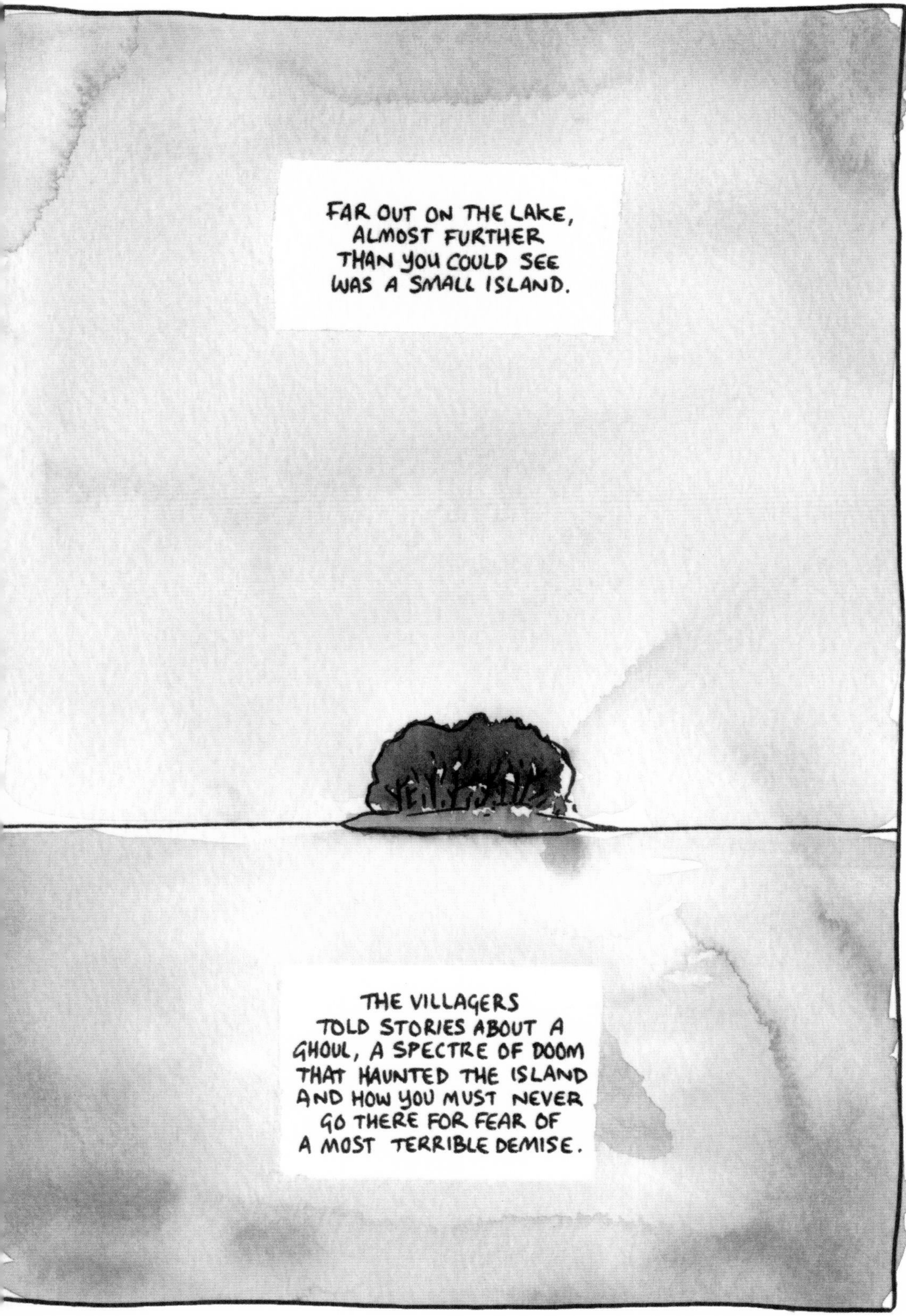
FAR OUT ON THE LAKE, ALMOST FURTHER THAN YOU COULD SEE WAS A SMALL ISLAND.
THE VILLAGERS TOLD STORIES ABOUT A GHOUL, A SPECTRE OF DOOM THAT HAUNTED THE ISLAND AND HOW YOU MUST NEVER GO THERE FOR FEAR OF A MOST TERRIBLE DEMISE.

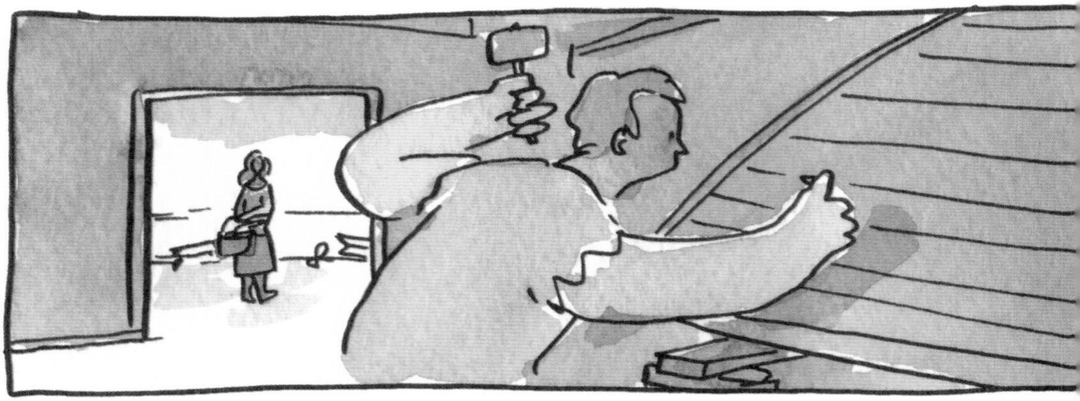

EAGER TO FIND TIME ALONE WITH EDITH AND DISMISSING THE STORIES OF THE ISLAND AS CAUTIONARY TALES FOR STUPID CHILDREN, EACH DAY WHEN SHE CAME TO DELIVER THE FISH, NICHOLAS WOULD WHISPER TO HER:

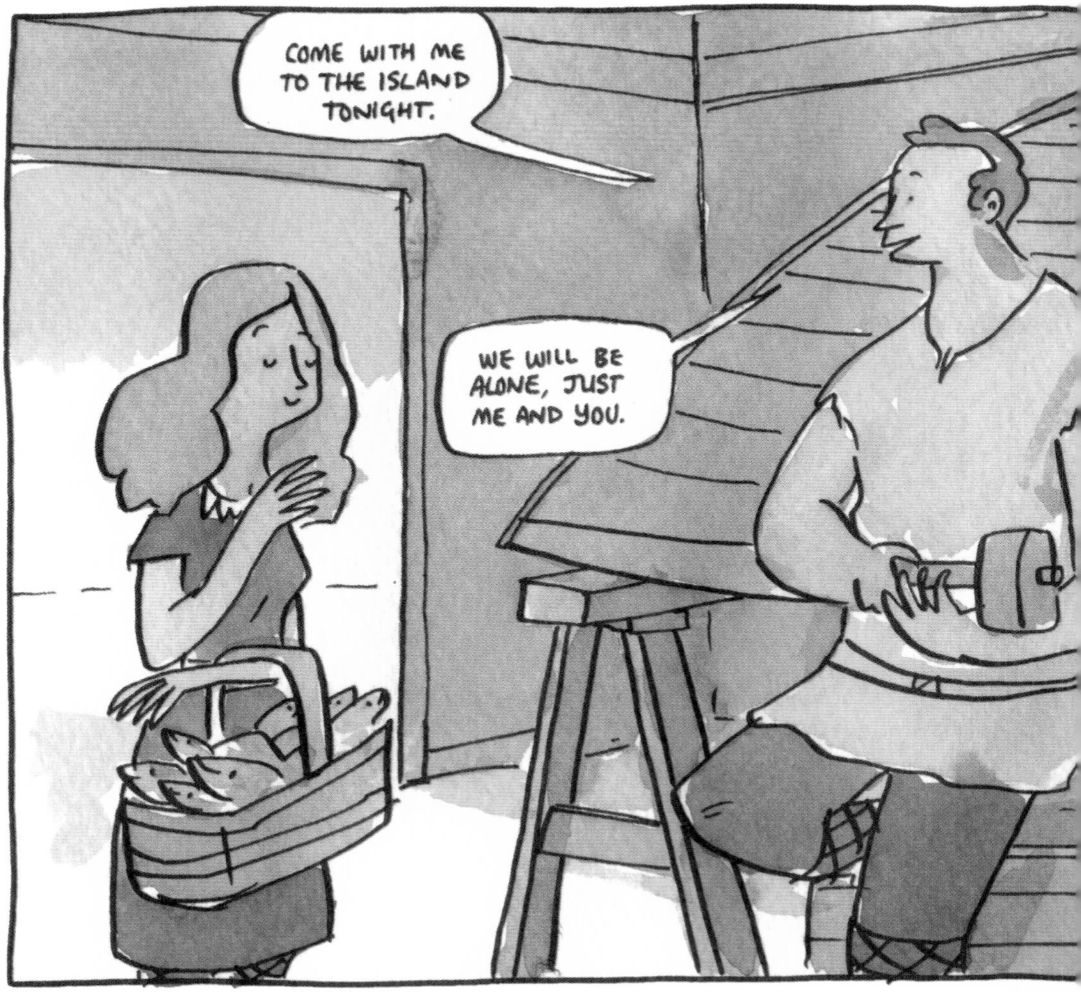
COME WITH ME TO THE ISLAND TONIGHT.
WE WILL BE ALONE, JUST ME AND YOU.

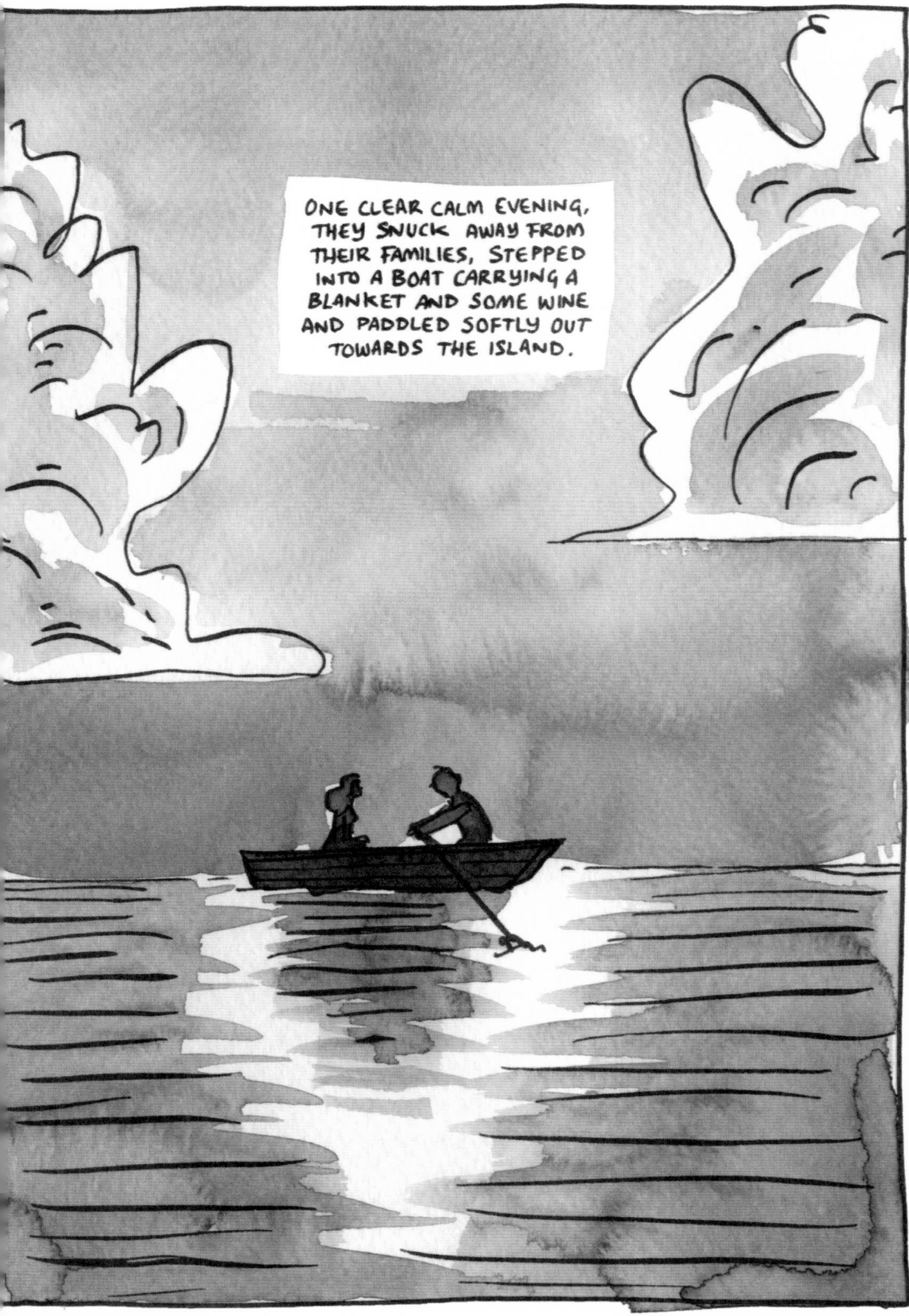
ONE CLEAR CALM EVENING, THEY SNUCK AWAY FROM THEIR FAMILIES, STEPPED INTO A BOAT CARRYING A BLANKET AND SOME WINE AND PADDLED SOFTLY OUT TOWARDS THE ISLAND.

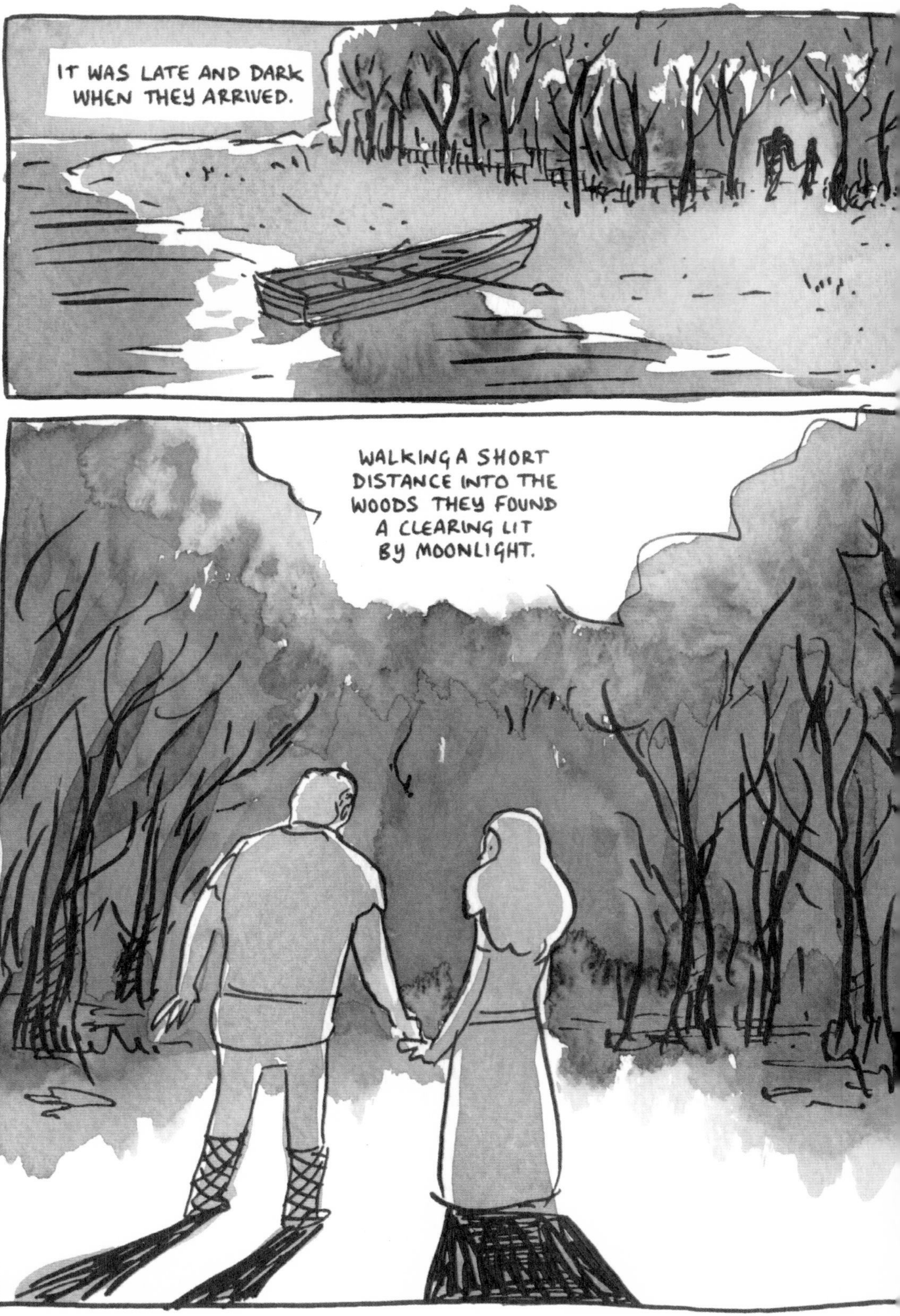
IT WAS LATE AND DARK WHEN THEY ARRIVED.
WALKING A SHORT DISTANCE INTO THE WOODS THEY FOUND A CLEARING LIT BY MOONLIGHT.

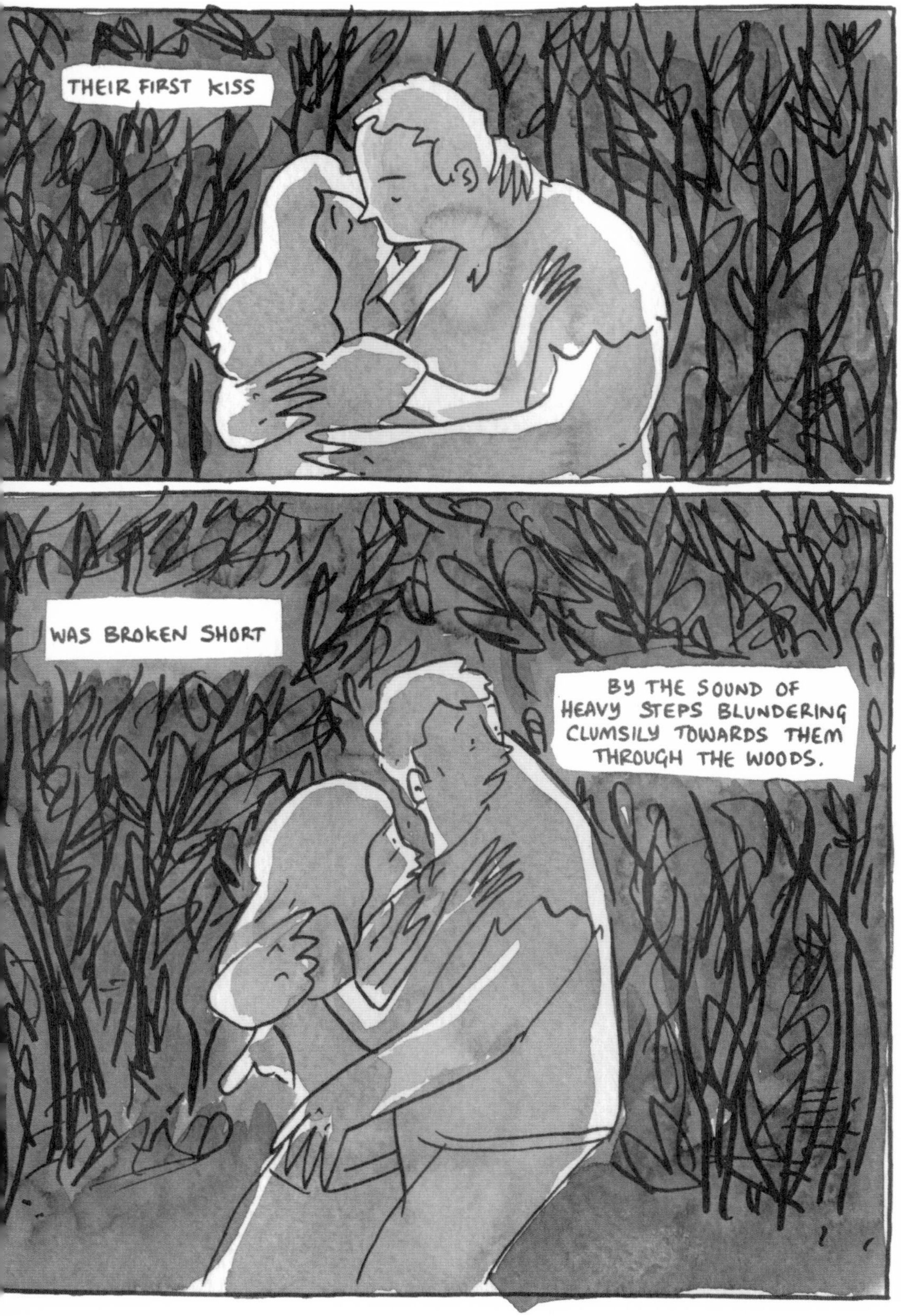
THEIR FIRST KISS
WAS BROKEN SHORT
BY THE SOUND OF HEAVY STEPS BLUNDERING CLUMSILY TOWARDS THEM THROUGH THE WOODS.

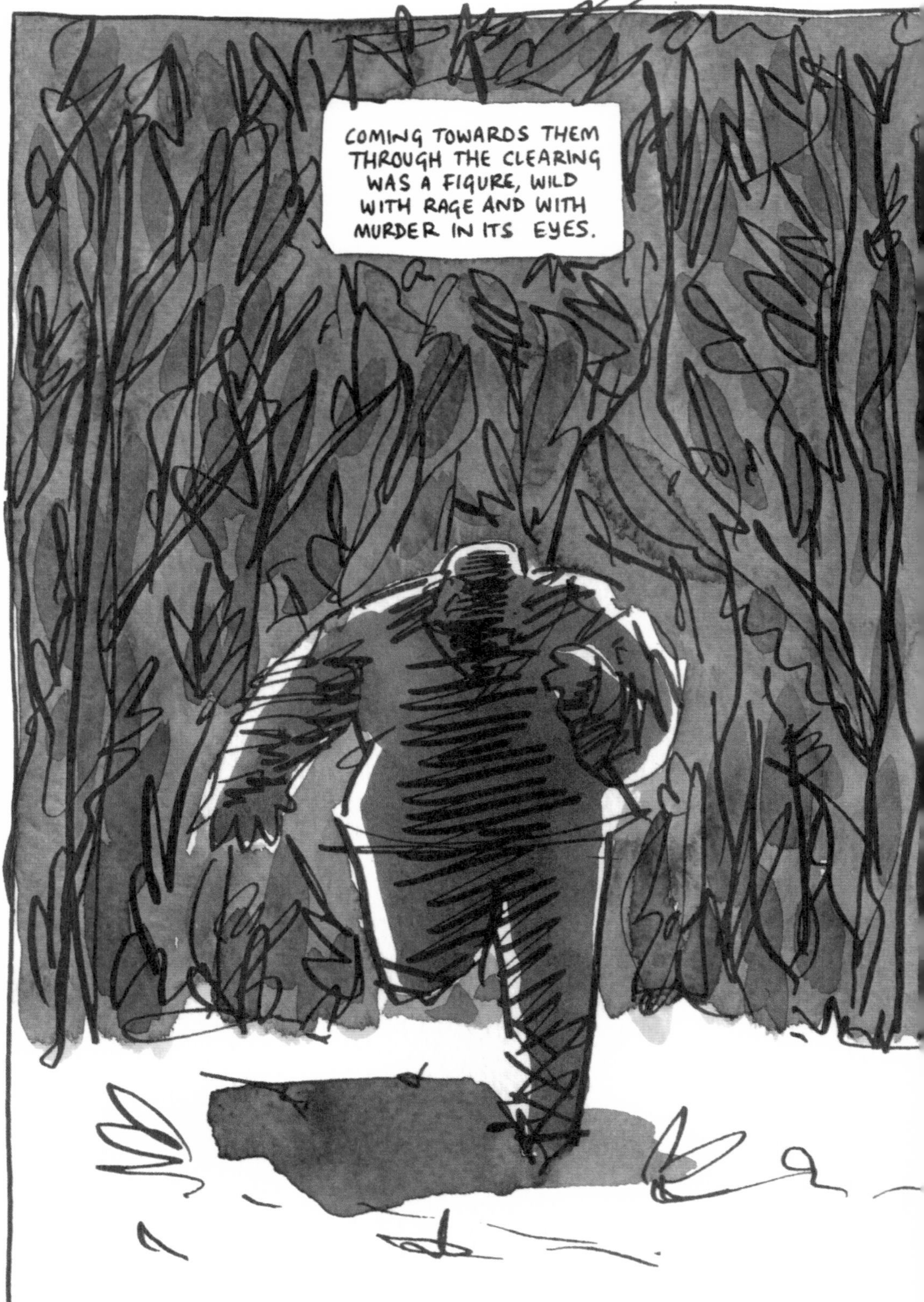
COMING TOWARDS THEM THROUGH THE CLEARING WAS A FIGURE, WILD WITH RAGE AND WITH MURDER IN ITS EYES.

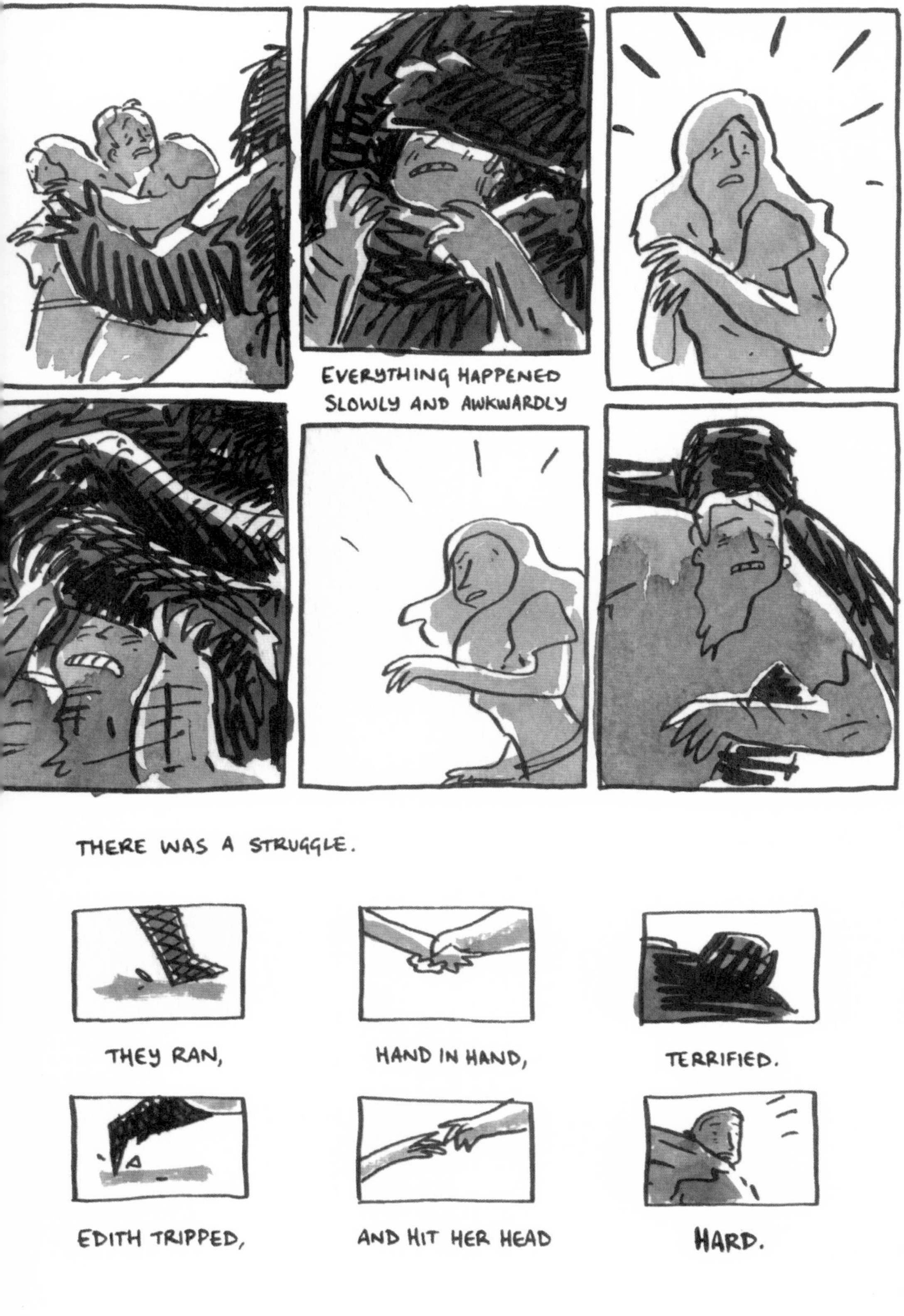
EVERYTHING HAPPENED SLOWLY AND AWKWARDLY
THERE WAS A STRUGGLE.
THEY RAN,
HAND IN HAND,
TERRIFIED.
EDITH TRIPPED,
AND HIT HER HEAD
HARD.

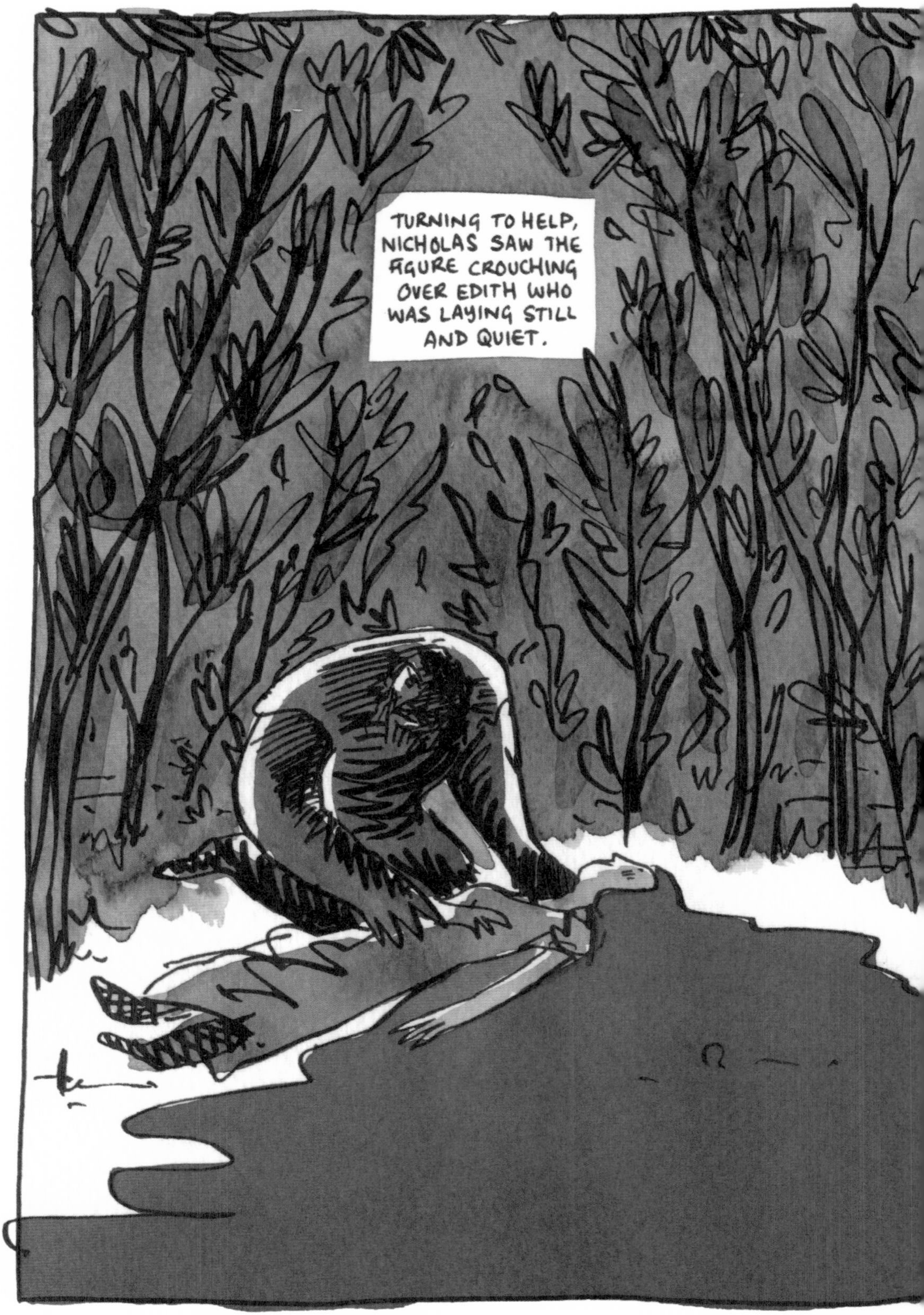
TURNING TO HELP, NICHOLAS SAW THE FIGURE CROUCHING OVER EDITH WHO WAS LAYING STILL AND QUIET.

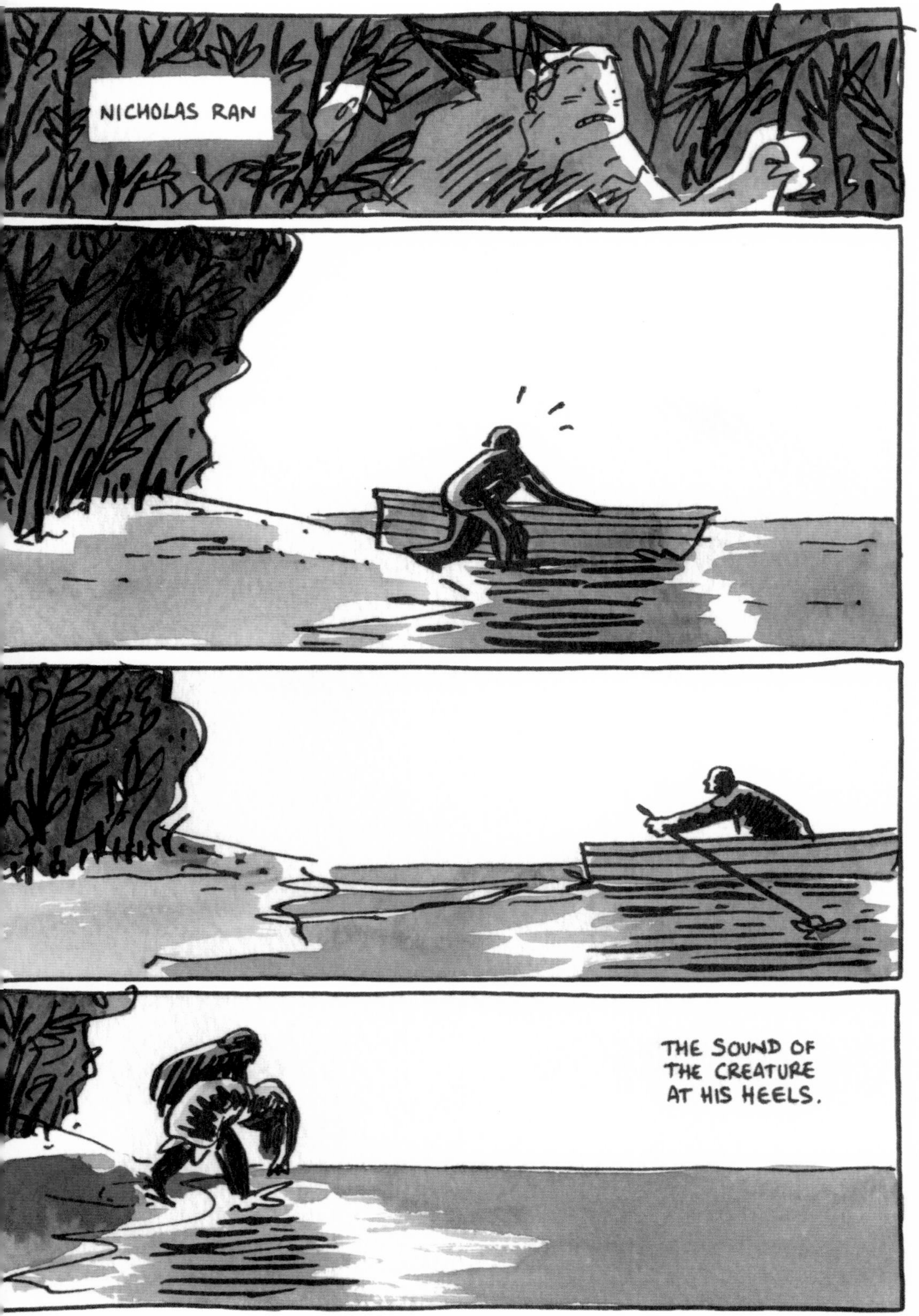
NICHOLAS RAN
THE SOUND OF THE CREATURE AT HIS HEELS.

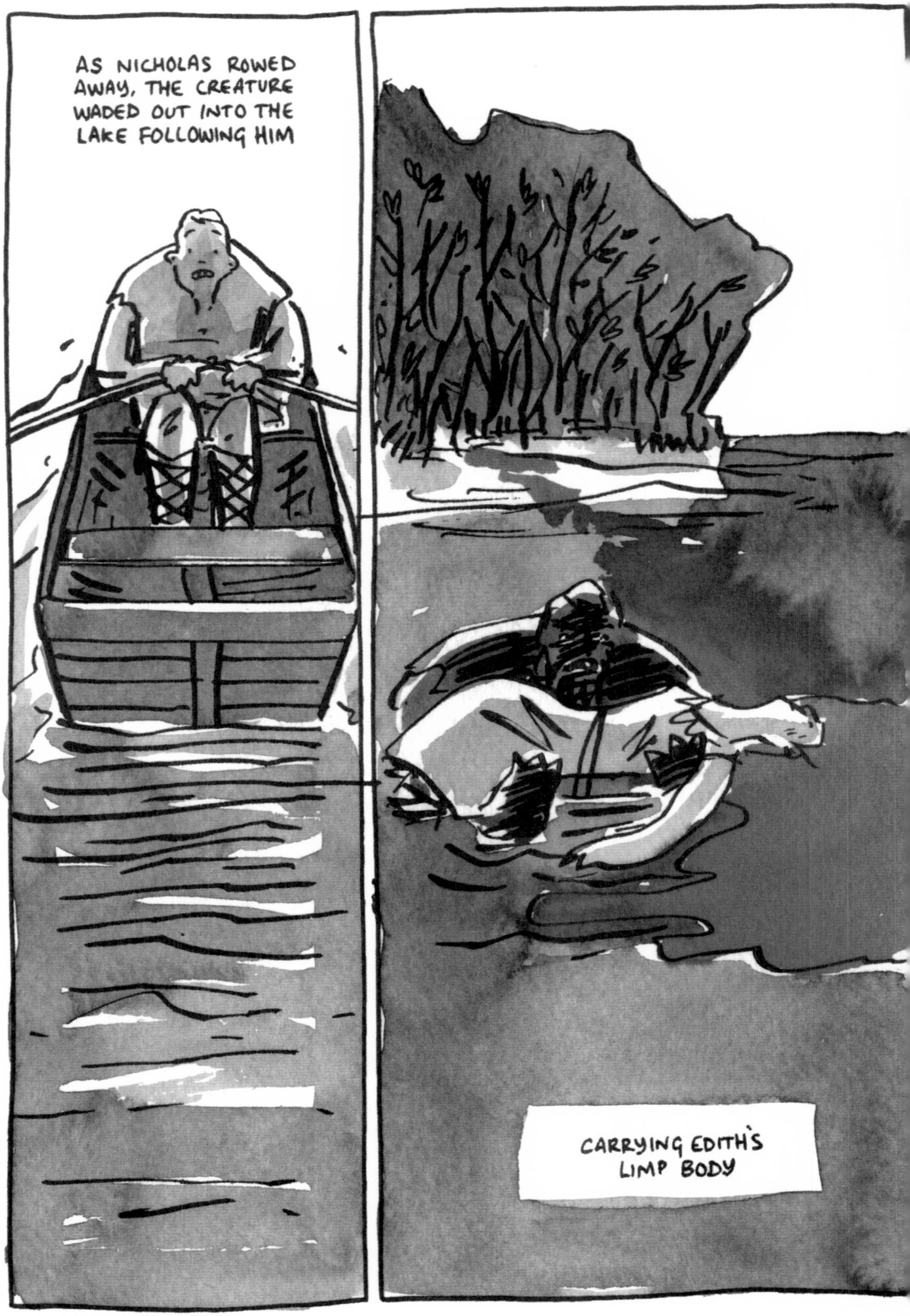
AS NICHOLAS ROWED AWAY, THE CREATURE WADED OUT INTO THE LAKE FOLLOWING HIM
CARRYING EDITH'S LIMP BODY

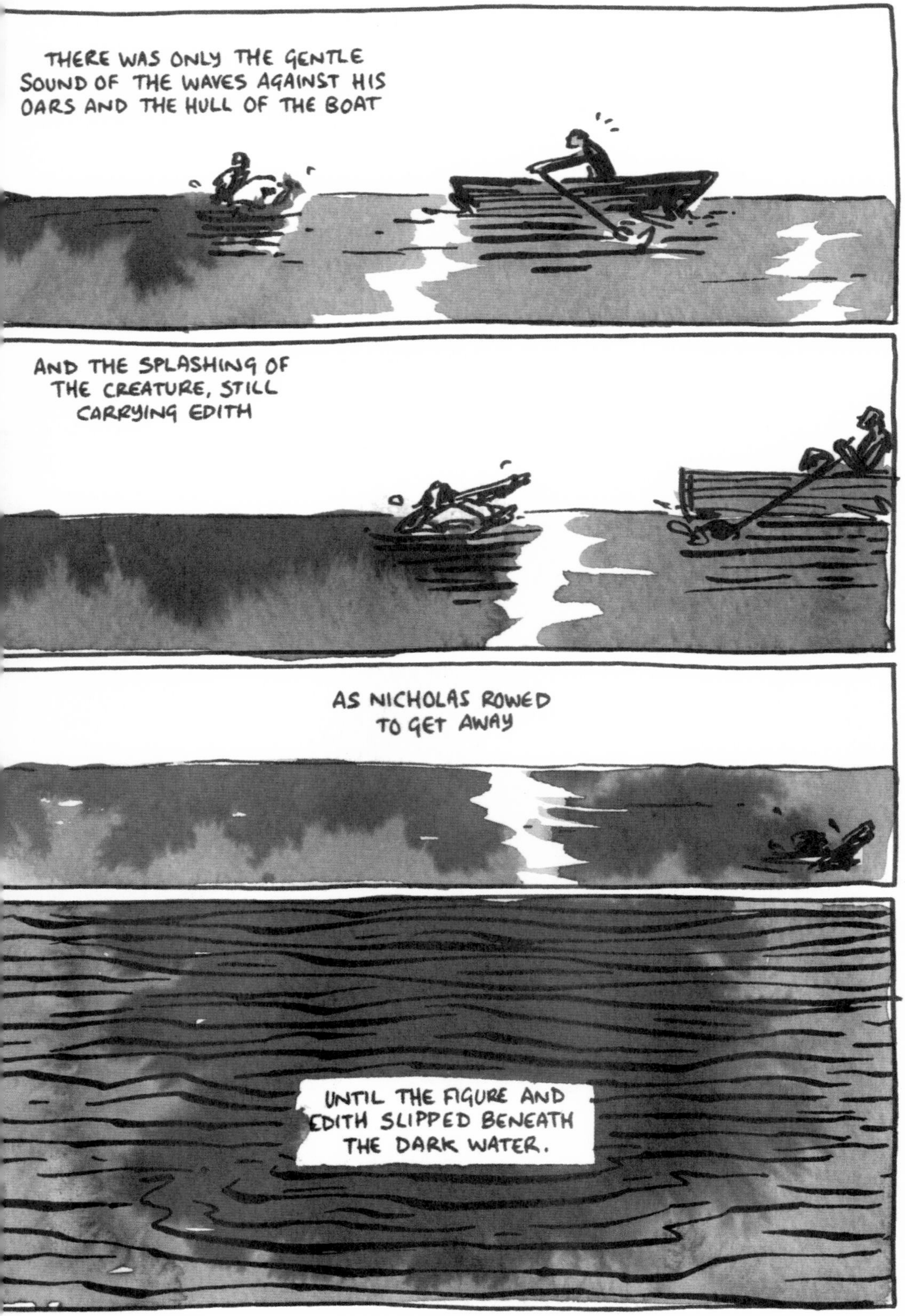
THERE WAS ONLY THE GENTLE SOUND OF THE WAVES AGAINST HIS OARS AND THE HULL OF THE BOAT
AND THE SPLASHING OF THE CREATURE, STILL CARRYING EDITH
AS NICHOLAS ROWED TO GET AWAY
UNTIL THE FIGURE AND EDITH SLIPPED BENEATH THE DARK WATER.

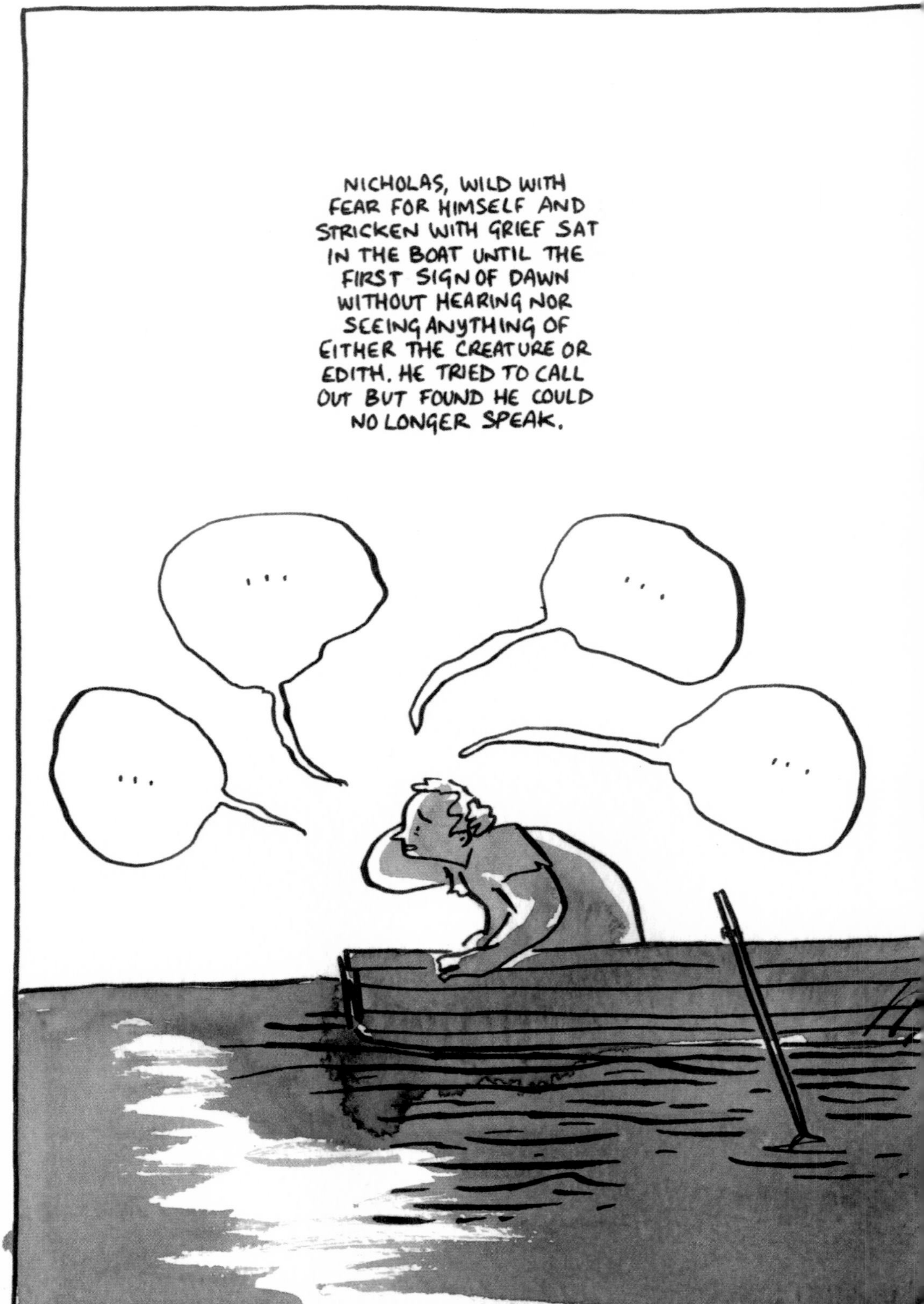
NICHOLAS, WILD WITH FEAR FOR HIMSELF AND STRICKEN WITH GRIEF SAT IN THE BOAT UNTIL THE FIRST SIGN OF DAWN WITHOUT HEARING NOR SEEING ANYTHING OF EITHER THE CREATURE OR EDITH. HE TRIED TO CALL OUT BUT FOUND HE COULD NO LONGER SPEAK.
...
...
...
...

RETURNING TO THE VILLAGE
WAS HARD FOR NICHOLAS.
THEIR ABSENCE HAD BEEN
NOTICED. VOICELESS,
NICHOLAS WAS UNABLE TO
EXPLAIN WHAT HAD HAPPENED.
A SEARCH WAS MOUNTED
BUT NOTHING WAS FOUND.

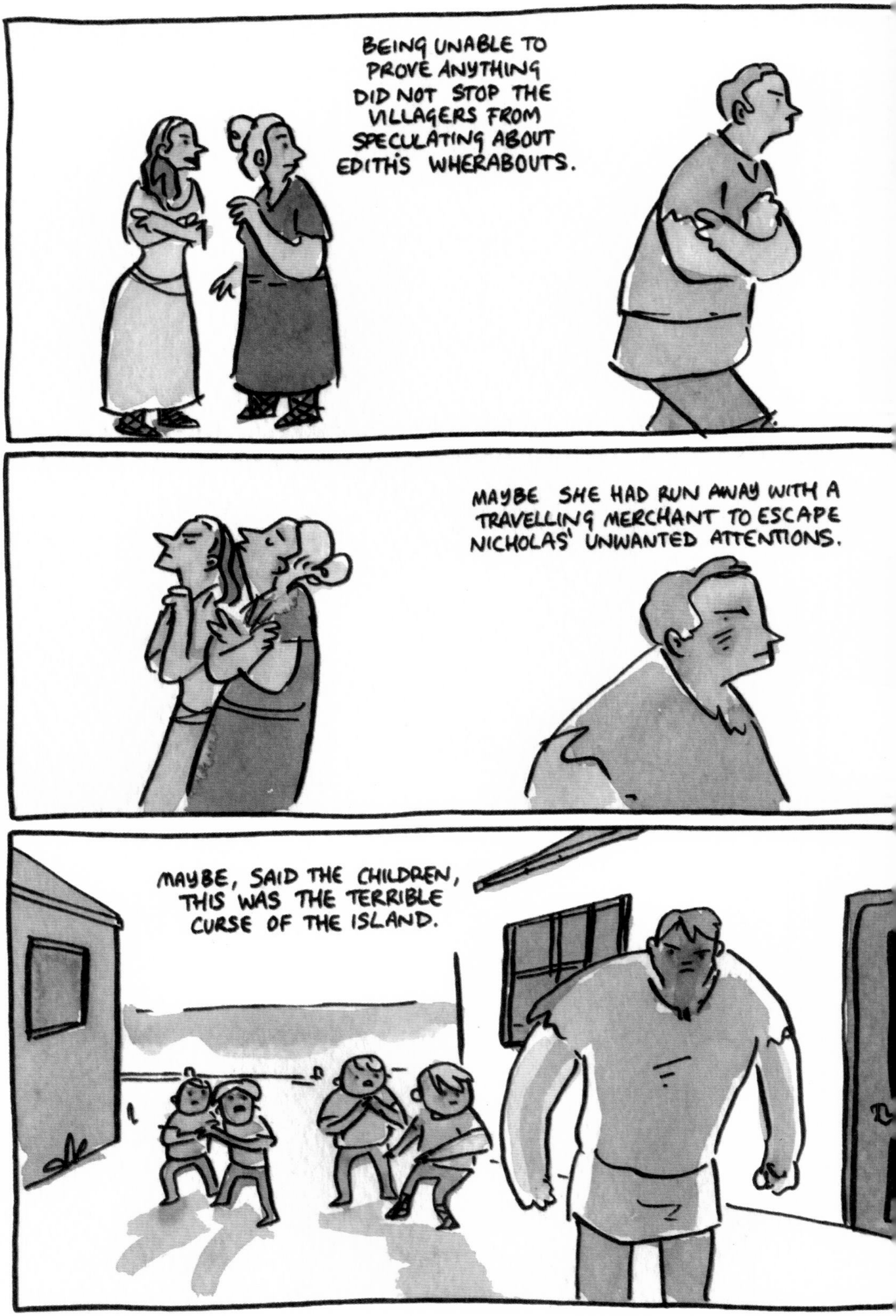
BEING UNABLE TO PROVE ANYTHING DID NOT STOP THE VILLAGERS FROM SPECULATING ABOUT EDITH'S WHERABOUTS.
MAYBE SHE HAD RUN AWAY WITH A TRAVELLING MERCHANT TO ESCAPE NICHOLAS' UNWANTED ATTENTIONS.
MAYBE, SAID THE CHILDREN, THIS WAS THE TERRIBLE CURSE OF THE ISLAND.

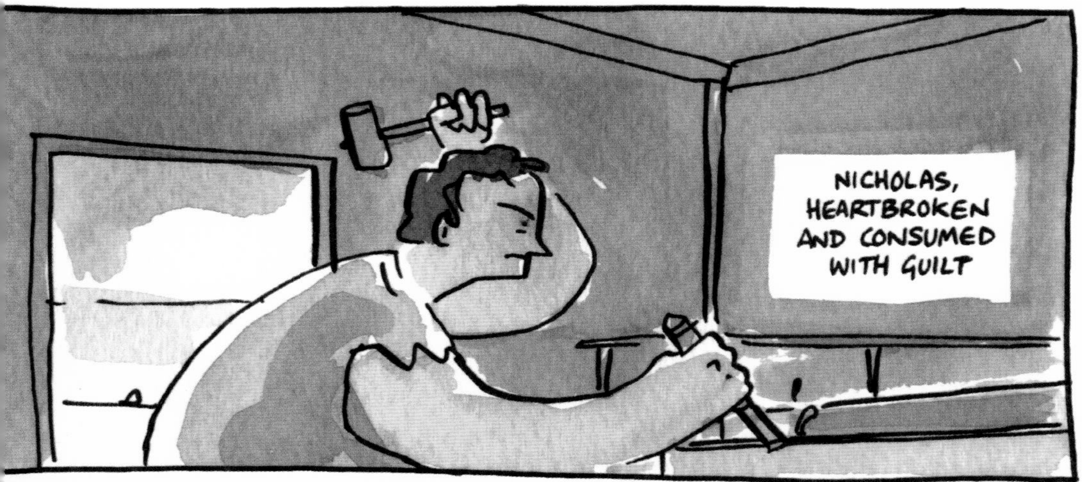
NICHOLAS, HEARTBROKEN AND CONSUMED WITH GUILT

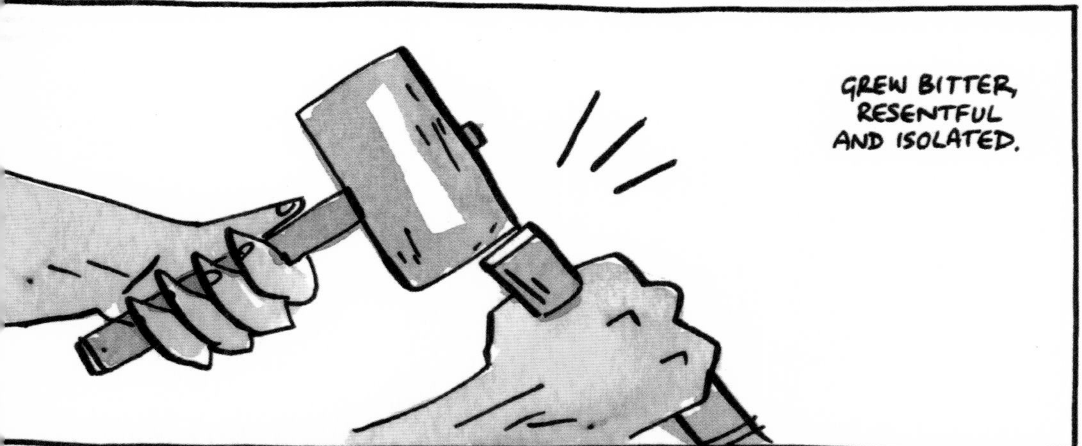
GREW BITTER, RESENTFUL AND ISOLATED.

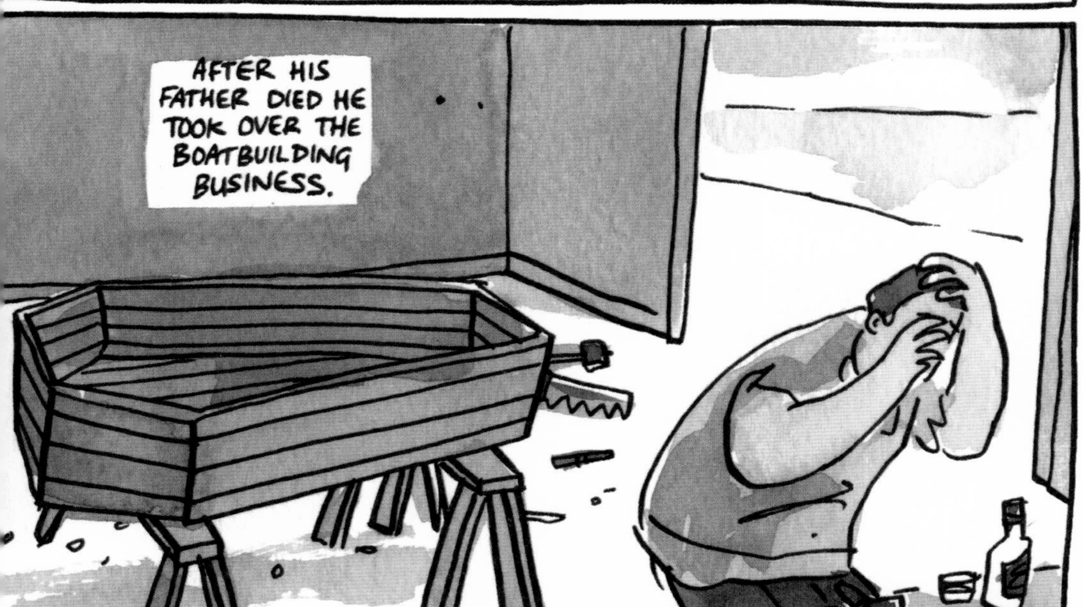
AFTER HIS FATHER DIED HE TOOK OVER THE BOATBUILDING BUSINESS.

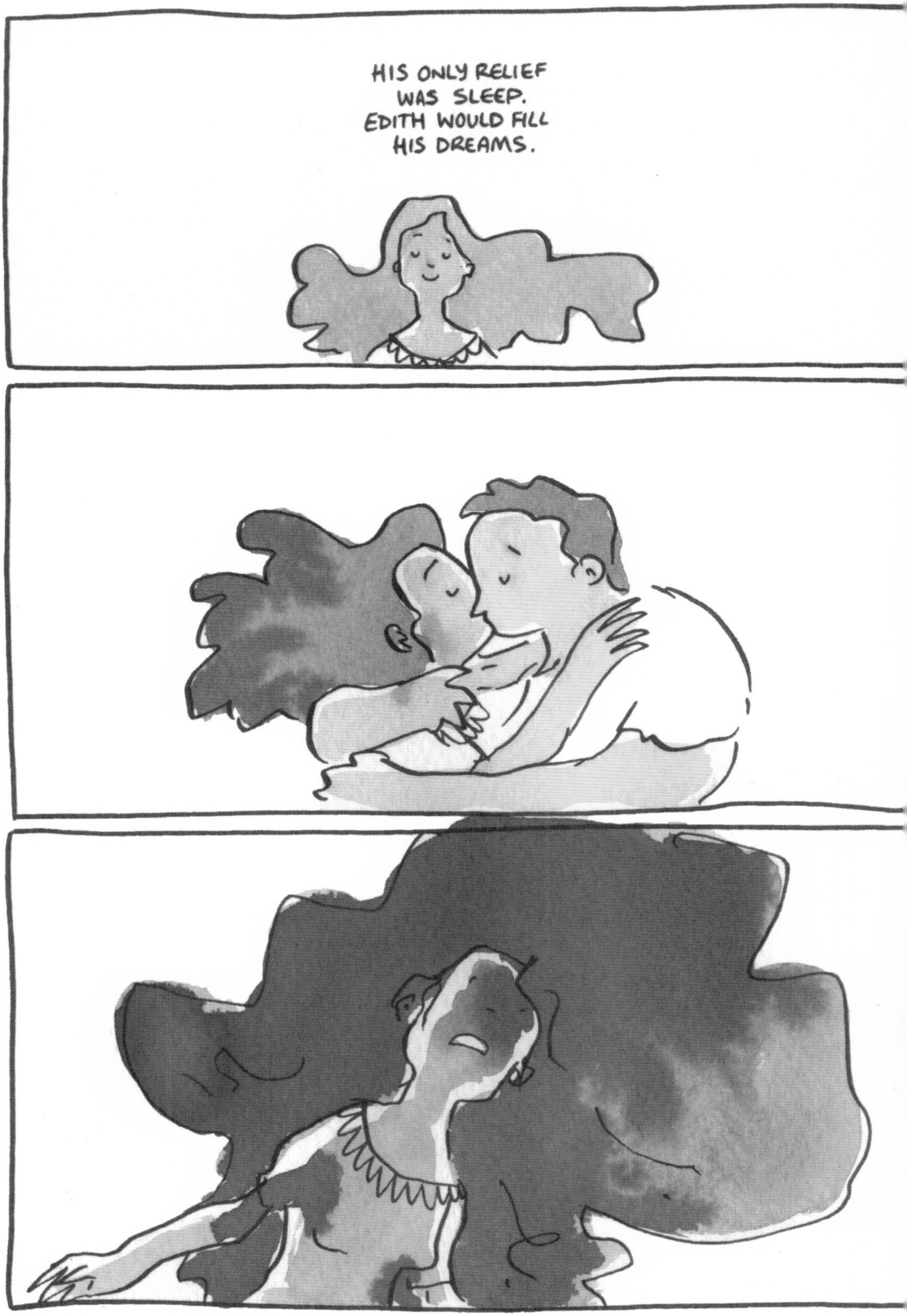
HIS ONLY RELIEF
WAS SLEEP.
EDITH WOULD FILL
HIS DREAMS.

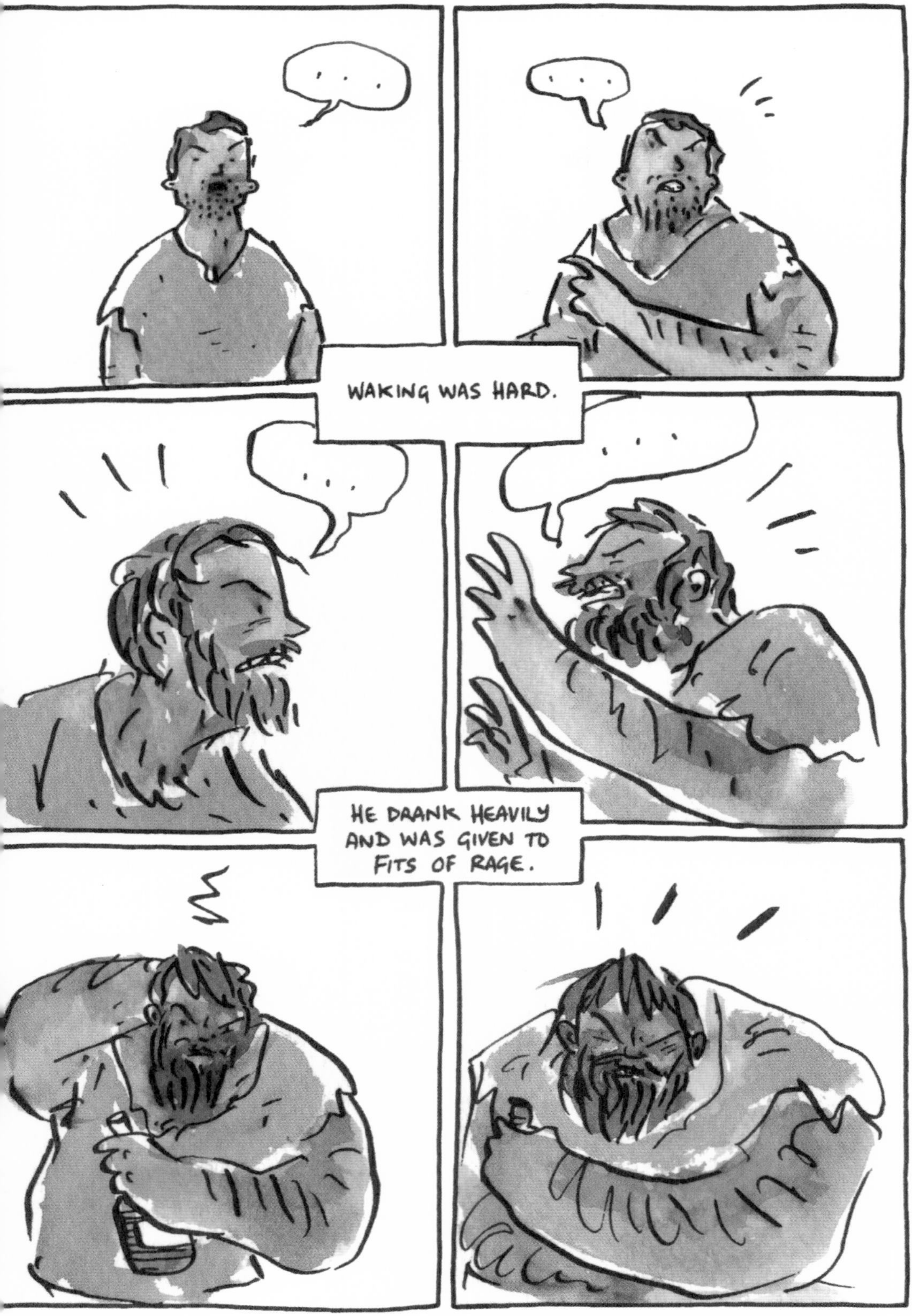
. . .
. . .
WAKING WAS HARD.
. . .
. . .
HE DRANK HEAVILY AND WAS GIVEN TO FITS OF RAGE.

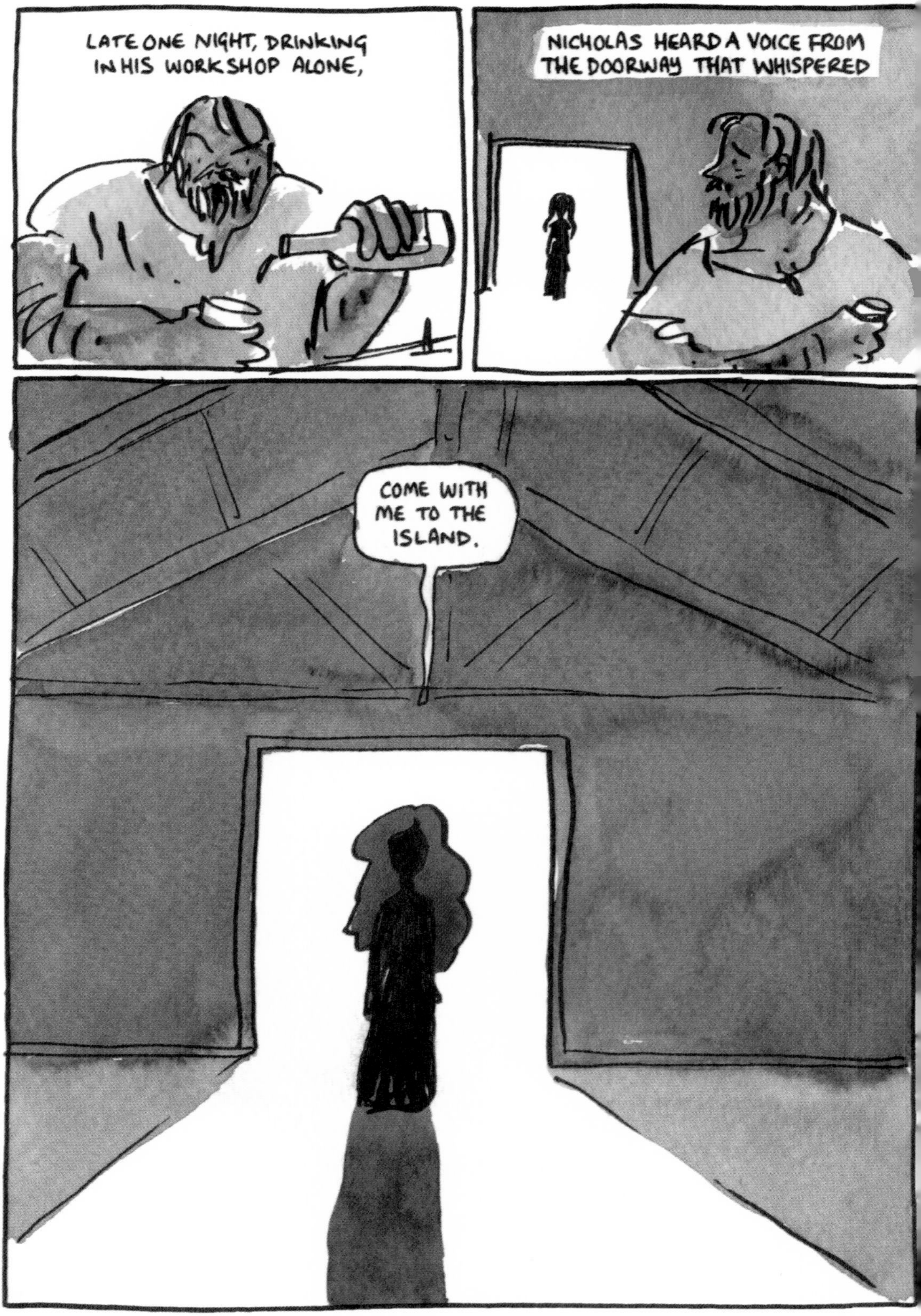
LATE ONE NIGHT, DRINKING IN HIS WORKSHOP ALONE,
NICHOLAS HEARD A VOICE FROM THE DOORWAY THAT WHISPERED
COME WITH ME TO THE ISLAND.

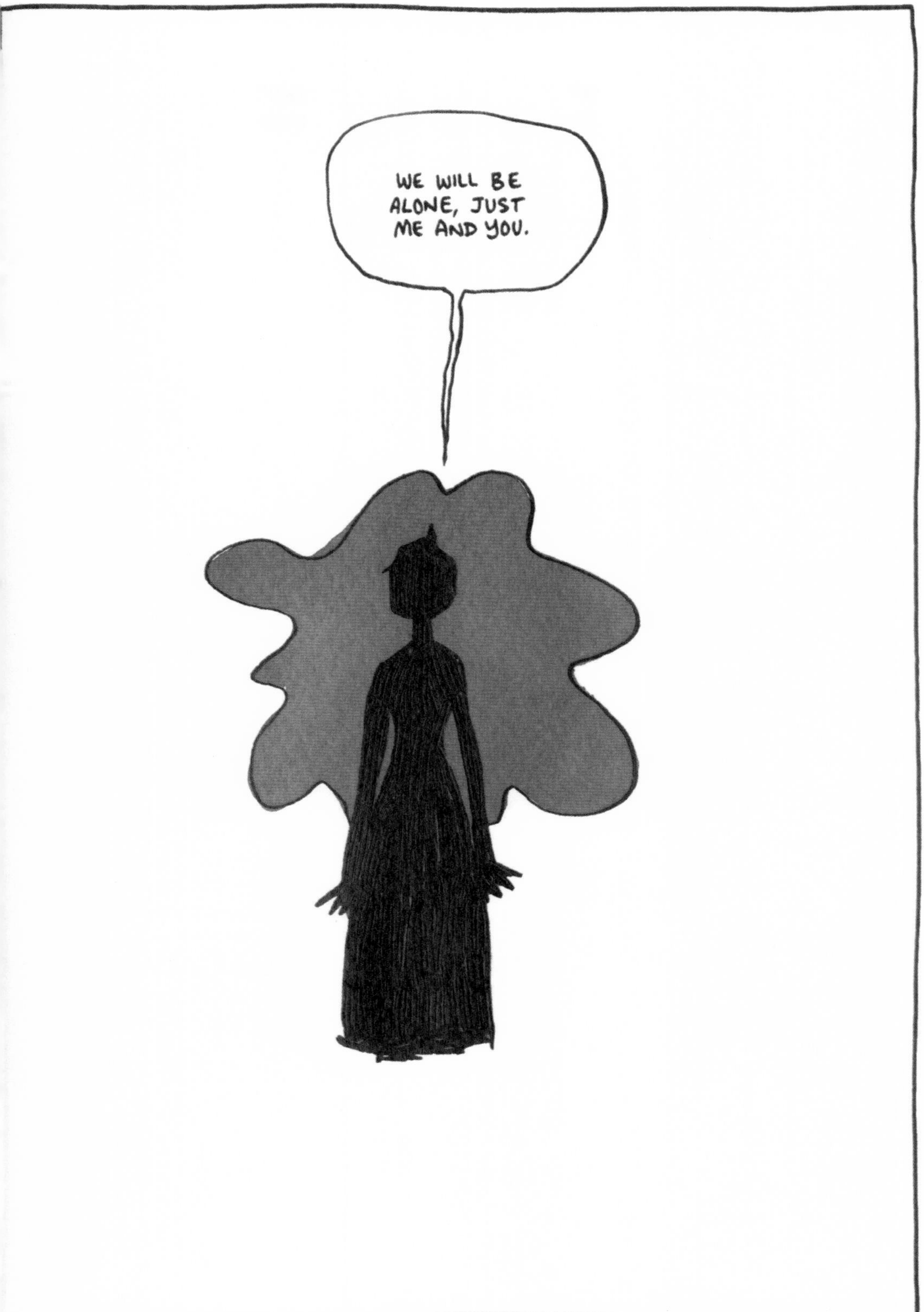
WE WILL BE ALONE, JUST ME AND YOU.

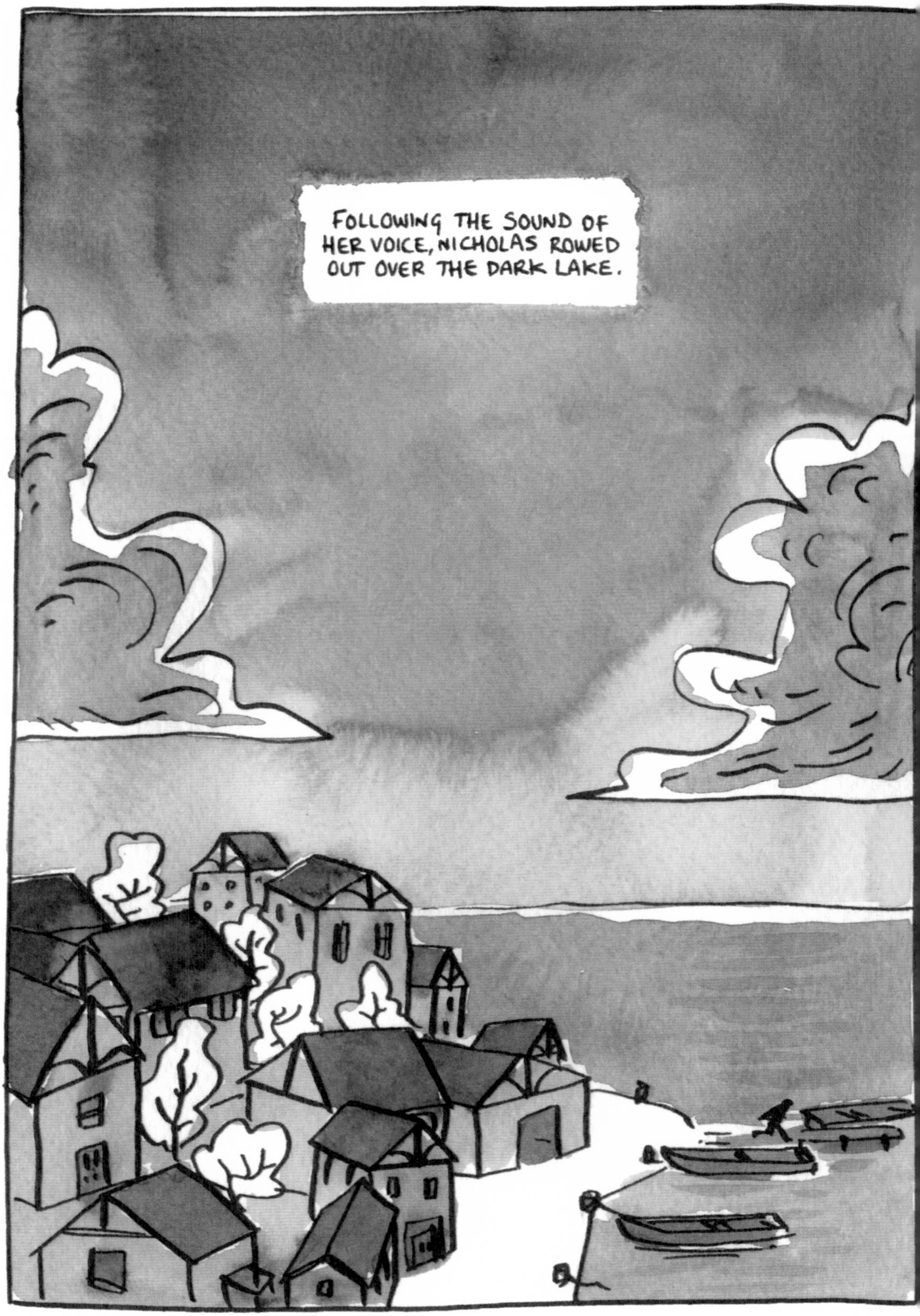
FOLLOWING THE SOUND OF HER VOICE, NICHOLAS ROWED OUT OVER THE DARK LAKE.

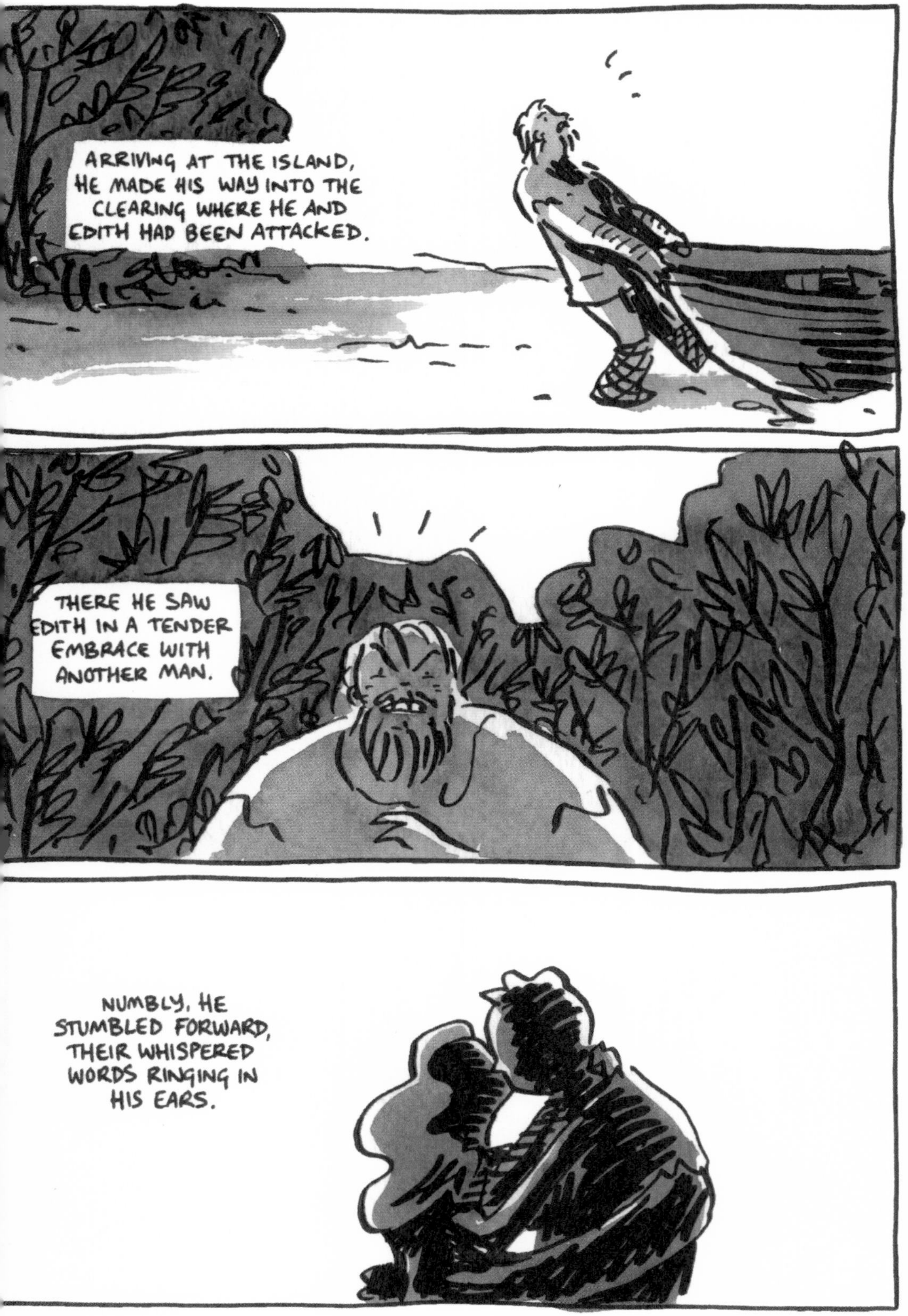
ARRIVING AT THE ISLAND, HE MADE HIS WAY INTO THE CLEARING WHERE HE AND EDITH HAD BEEN ATTACKED.
THERE HE SAW EDITH IN A TENDER EMBRACE WITH ANOTHER MAN.
NUMBLY, HE STUMBLED FORWARD, THEIR WHISPERED WORDS RINGING IN HIS EARS.

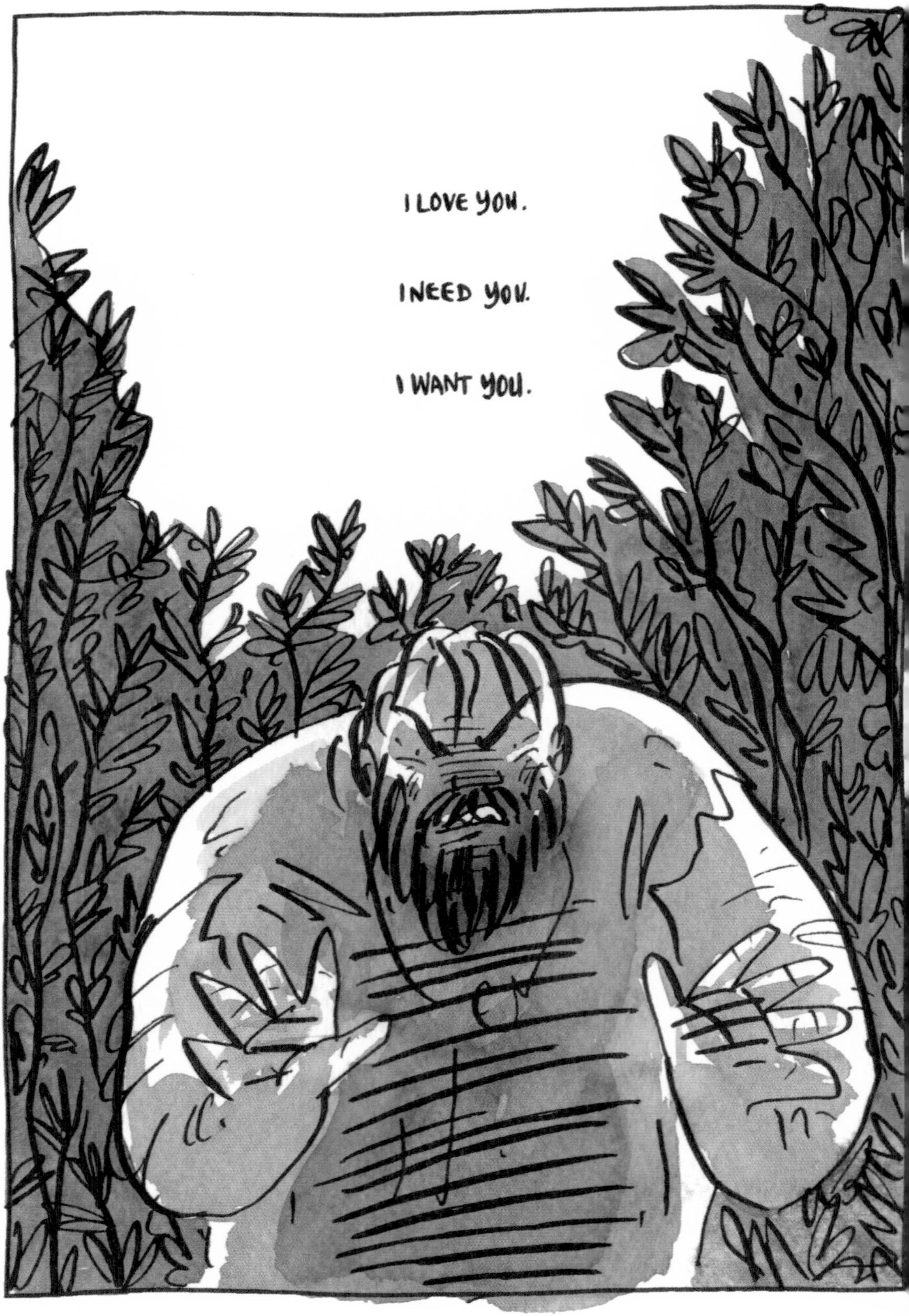
I LOVE YOU.
I NEED YOU.
I WANT YOU.

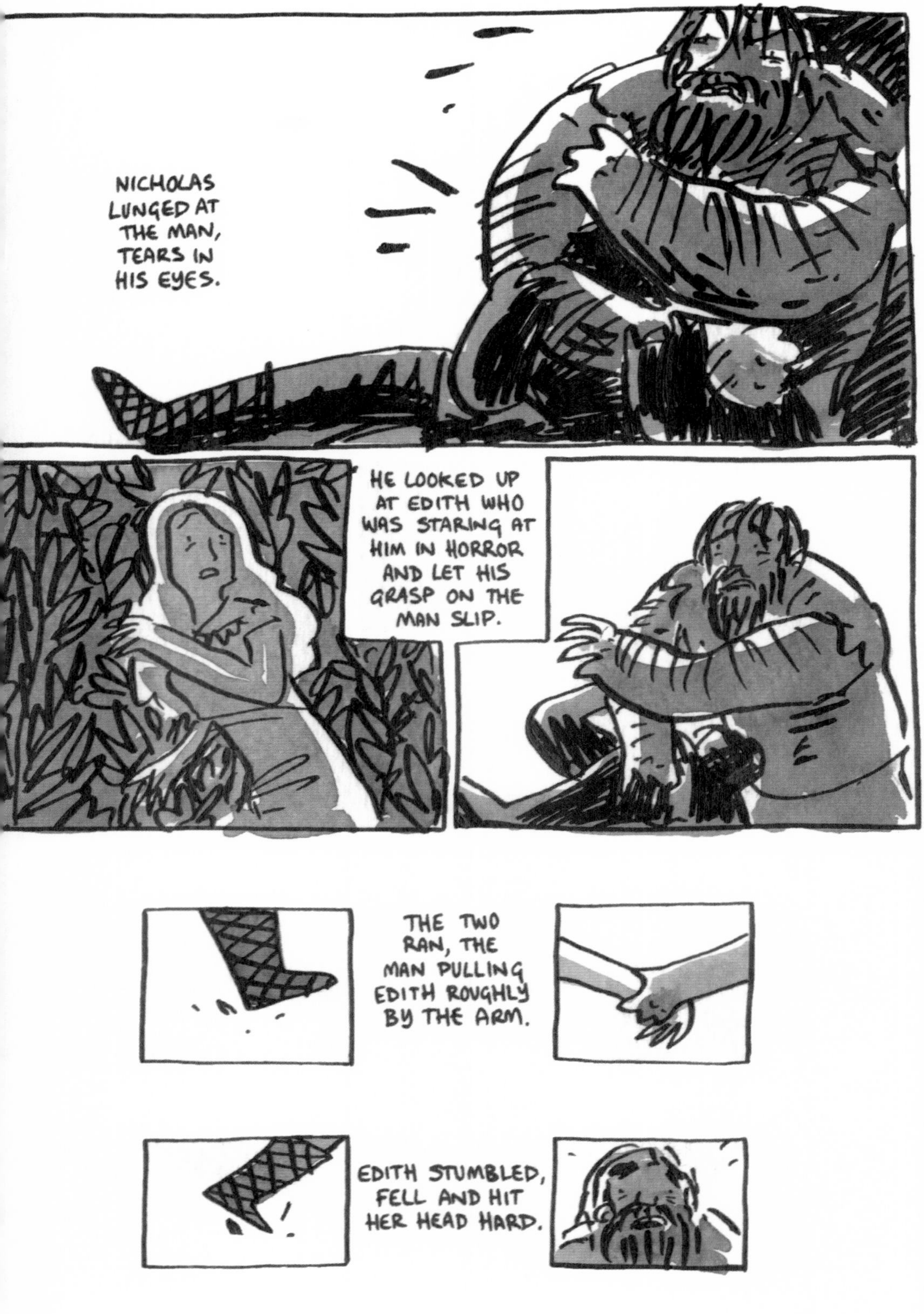
NICHOLAS LUNGED AT THE MAN, TEARS IN HIS EYES.
HE LOOKED UP AT EDITH WHO WAS STARING AT HIM IN HORROR AND LET HIS GRASP ON THE MAN SLIP.
THE TWO RAN, THE MAN PULLING EDITH ROUGHLY BY THE ARM.
EDITH STUMBLED, FELL AND HIT HER HEAD HARD.

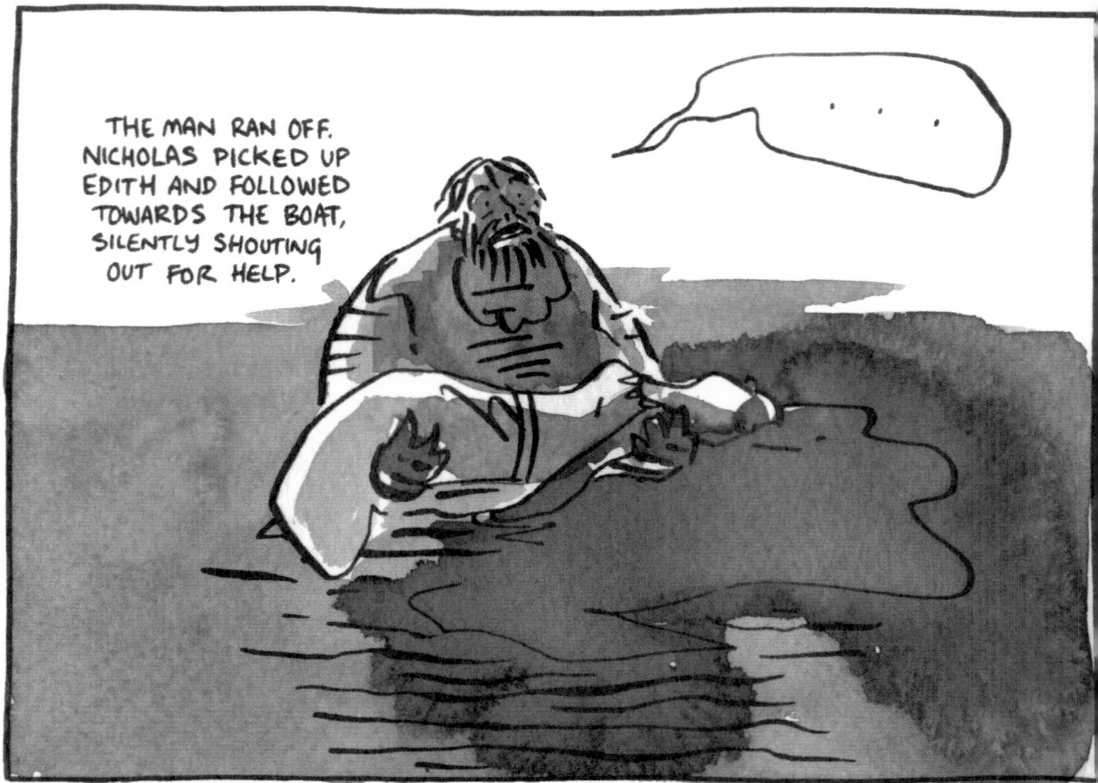
THE MAN RAN OFF. NICHOLAS PICKED UP EDITH AND FOLLOWED TOWARDS THE BOAT, SILENTLY SHOUTING OUT FOR HELP.
. . .

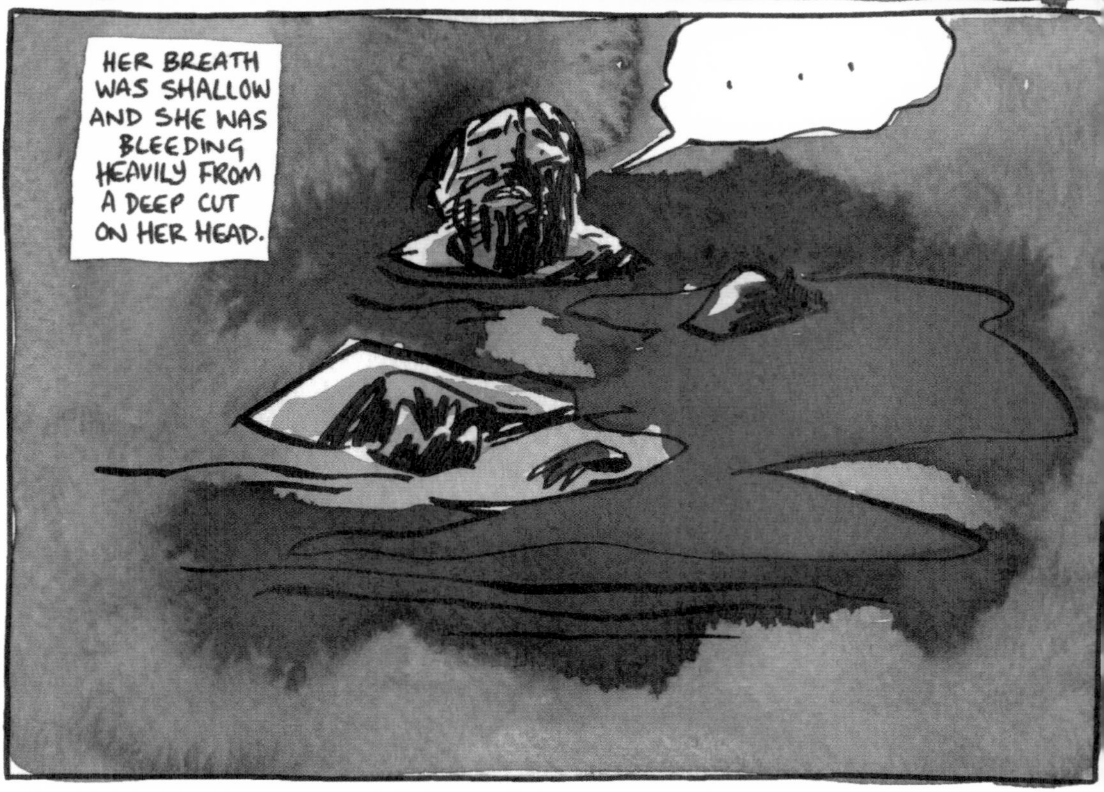
HER BREATH WAS SHALLOW AND SHE WAS BLEEDING HEAVILY FROM A DEEP CUT ON HER HEAD.
. . .

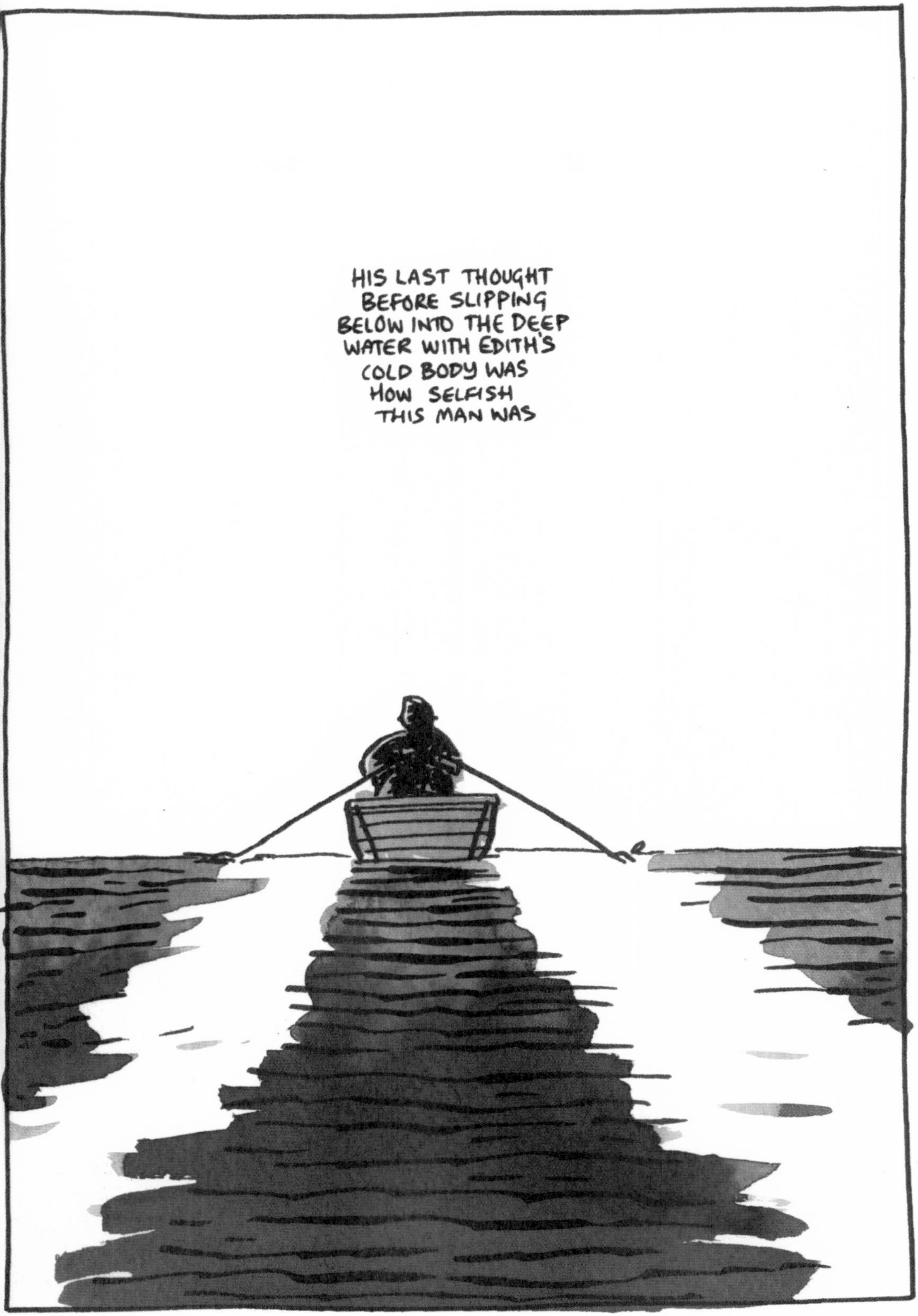
HIS LAST THOUGHT BEFORE SLIPPING BELOW INTO THE DEEP WATER WITH EDITH'S COLD BODY WAS HOW SELFISH THIS MAN WAS

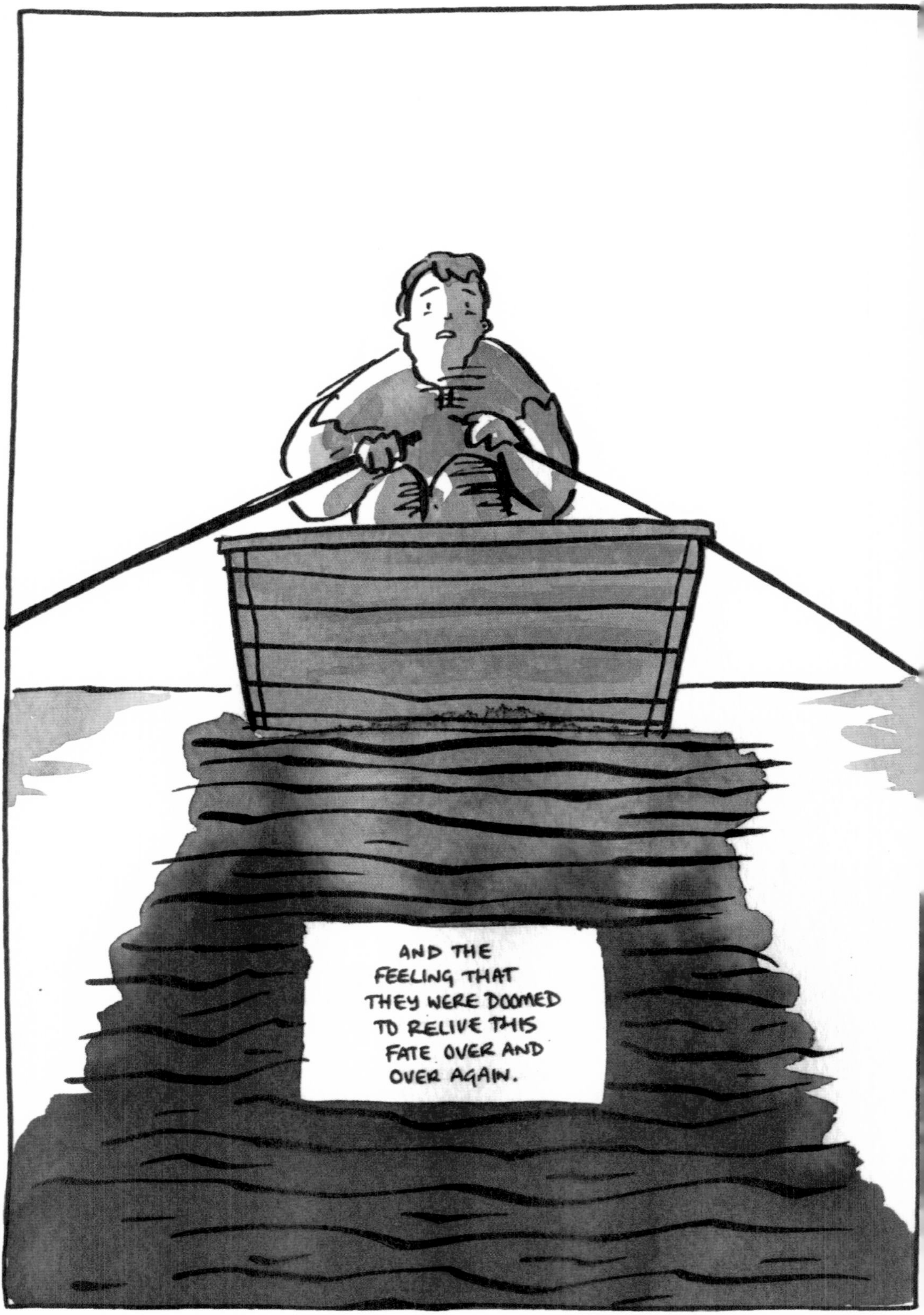
AND THE FEELING THAT THEY WERE DOOMED TO RELIVE THIS FATE OVER AND OVER AGAIN.

LAKES INTERNATIONAL
COMIC ART FESTIVAL

24

[HCM]

TWENTY FOUR HOUR
COMICS MARATHON

Start drawing - 3pm, 16 October
Collect books from printers - 9pm, 17 October
On sale at Lakes International Comic Art Festival - 10am, 18 October

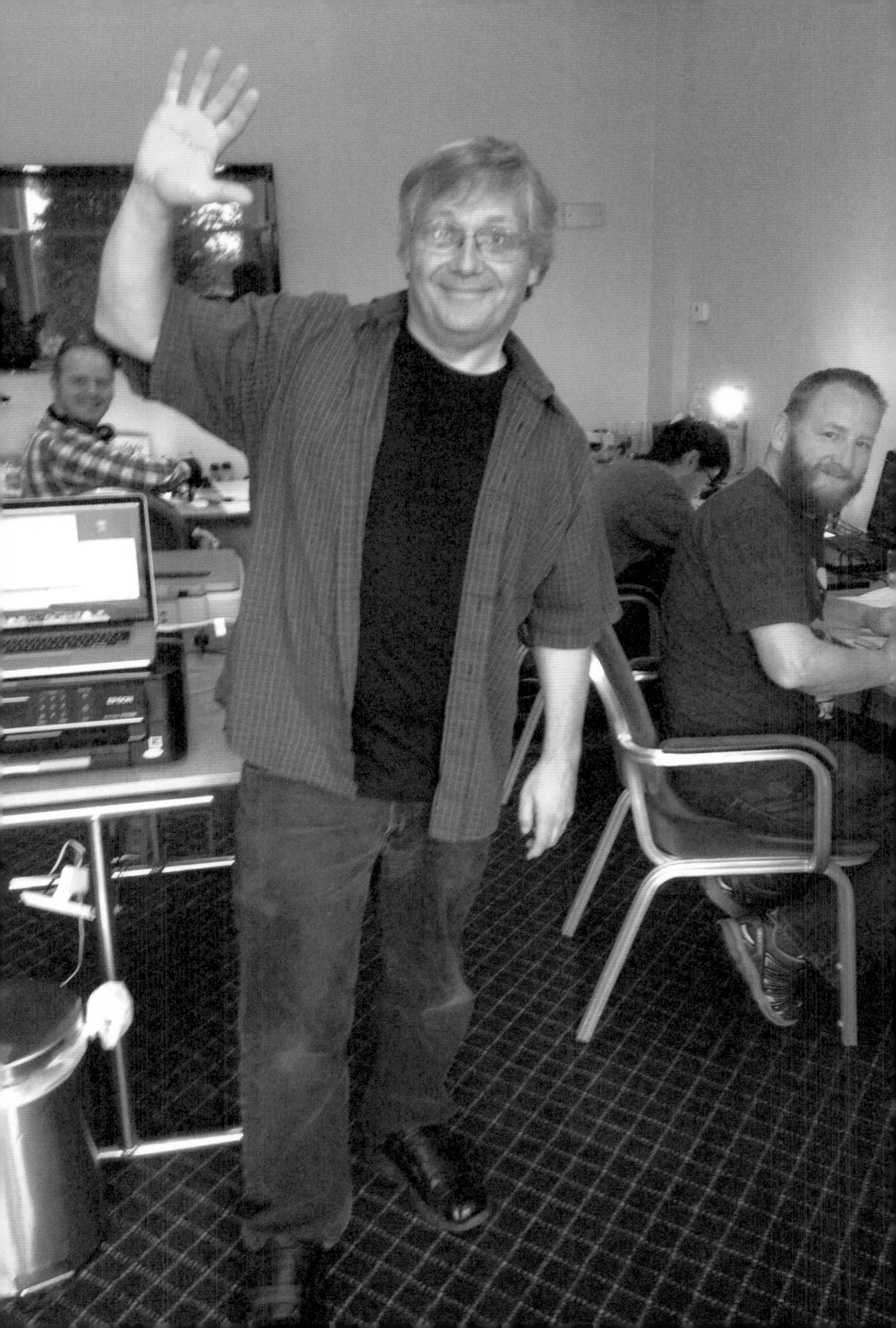

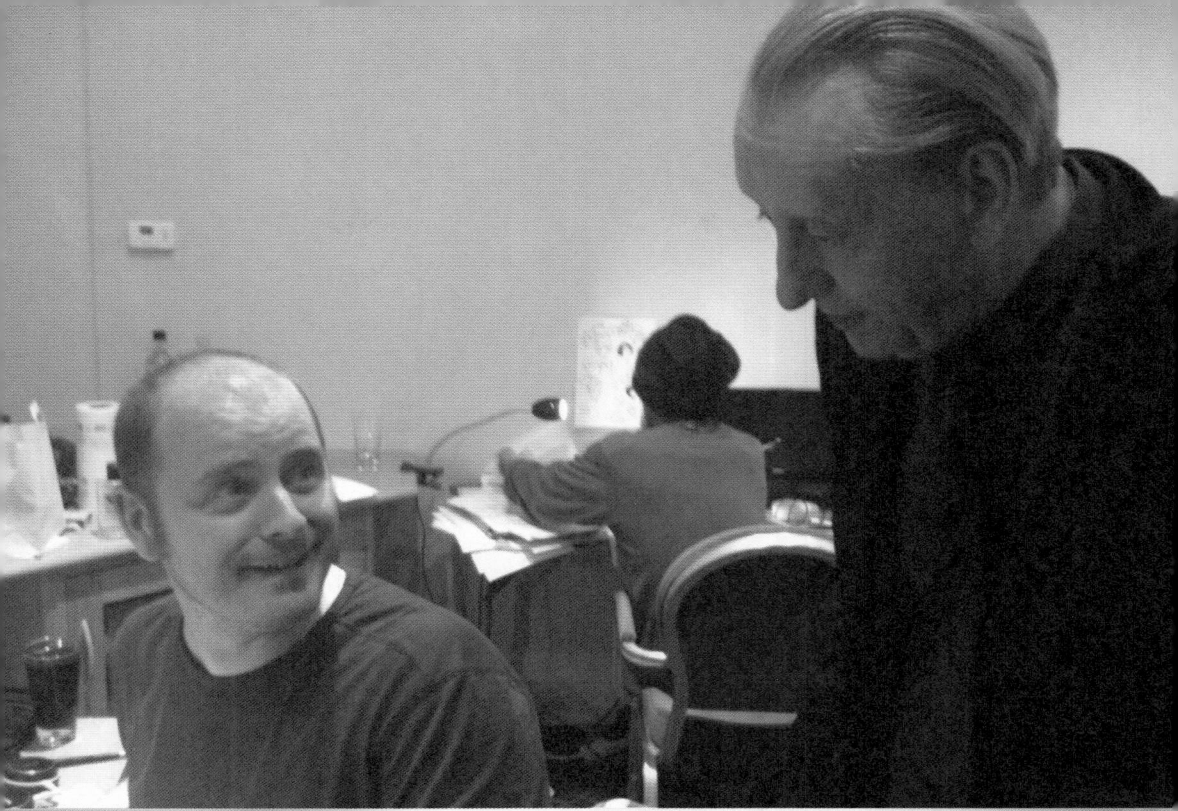

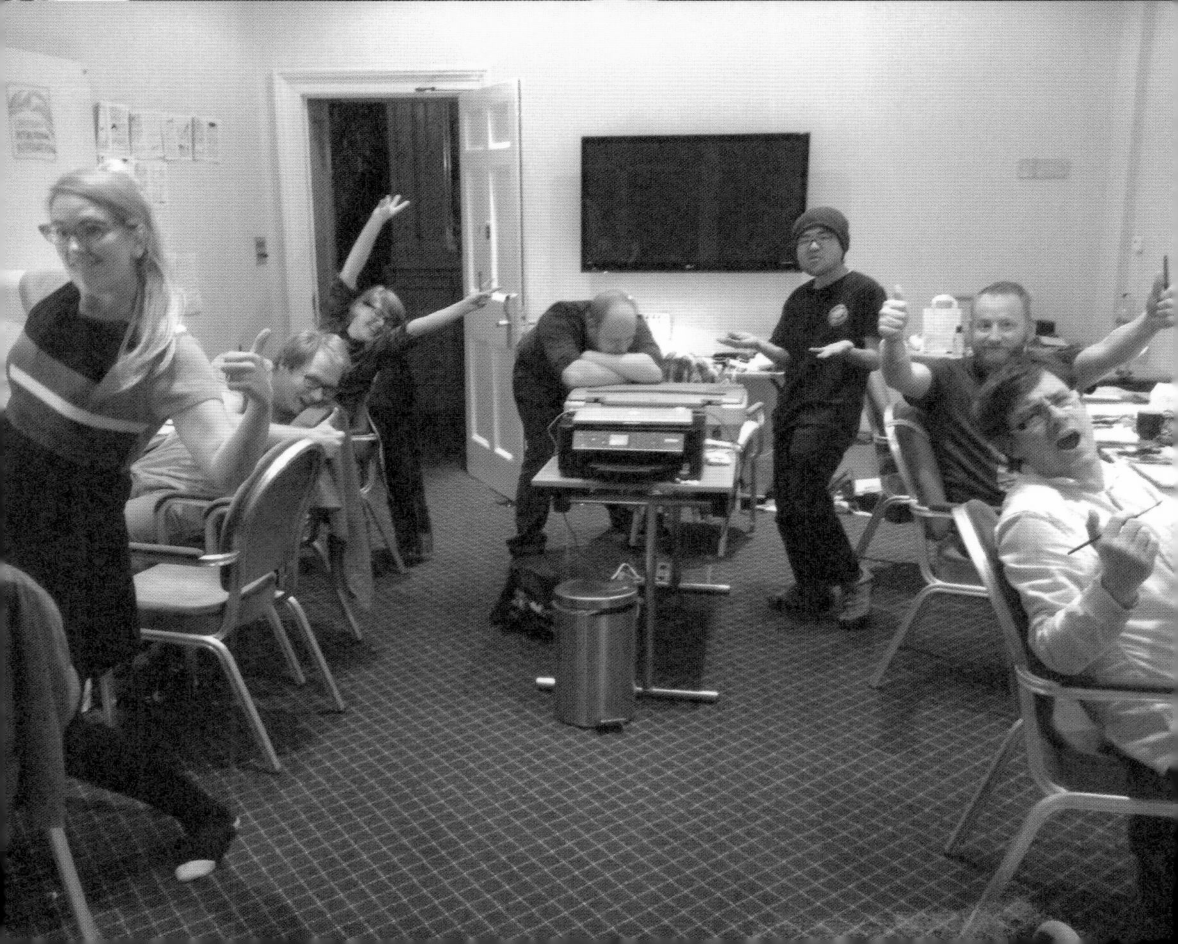

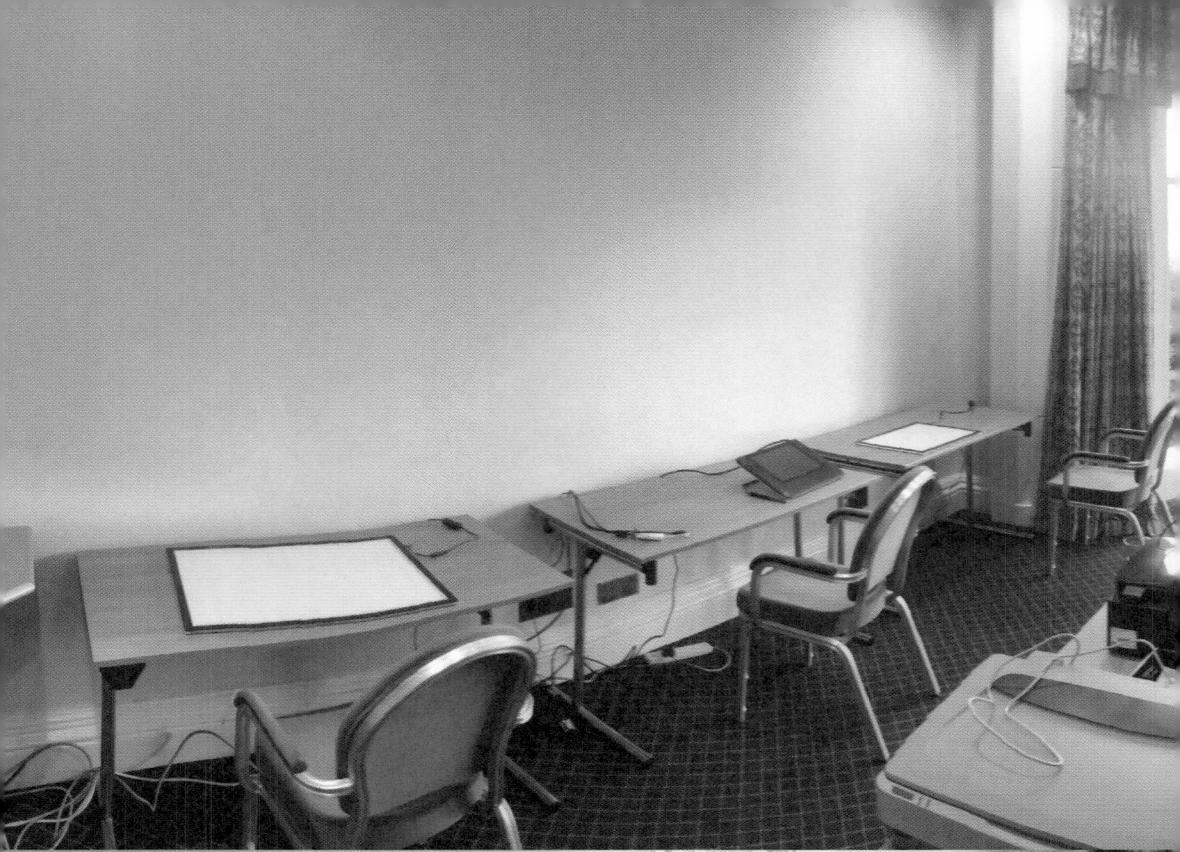

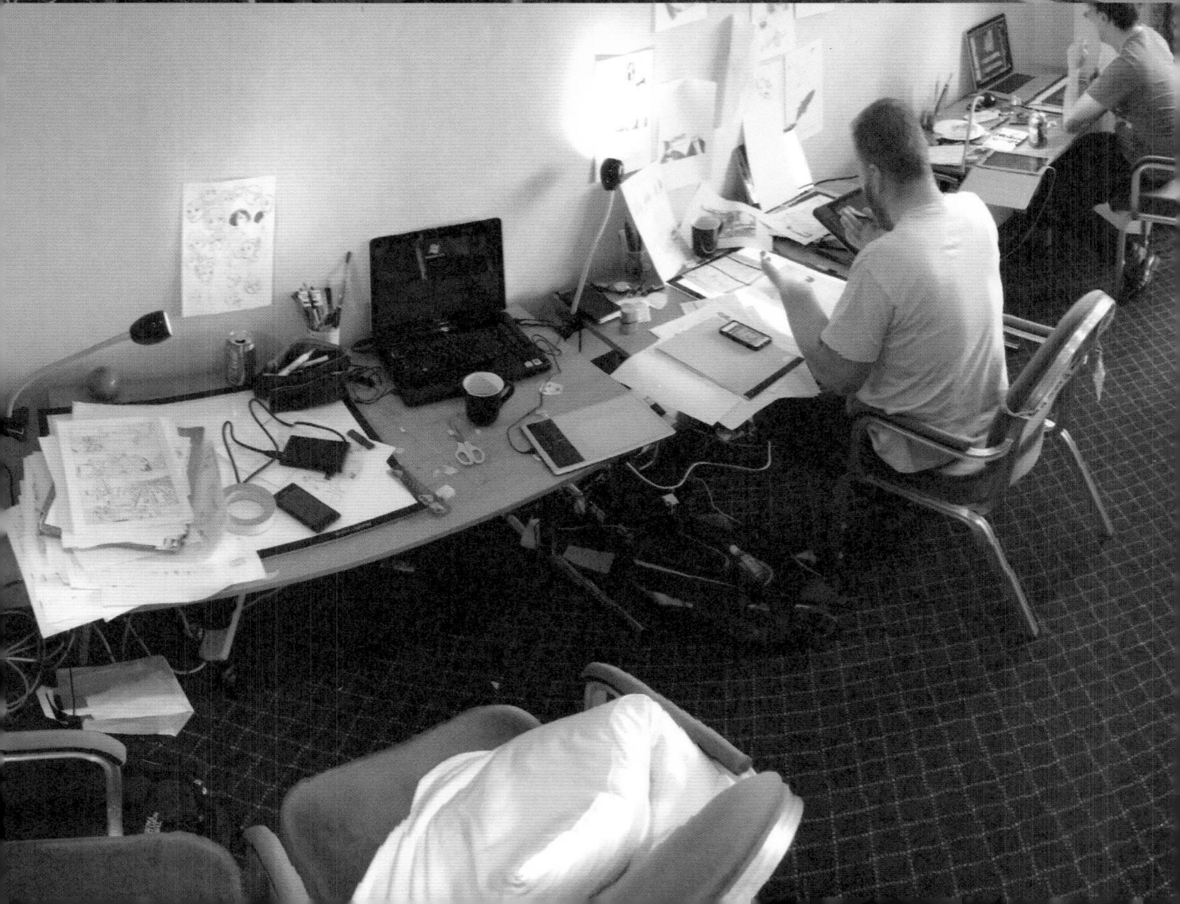

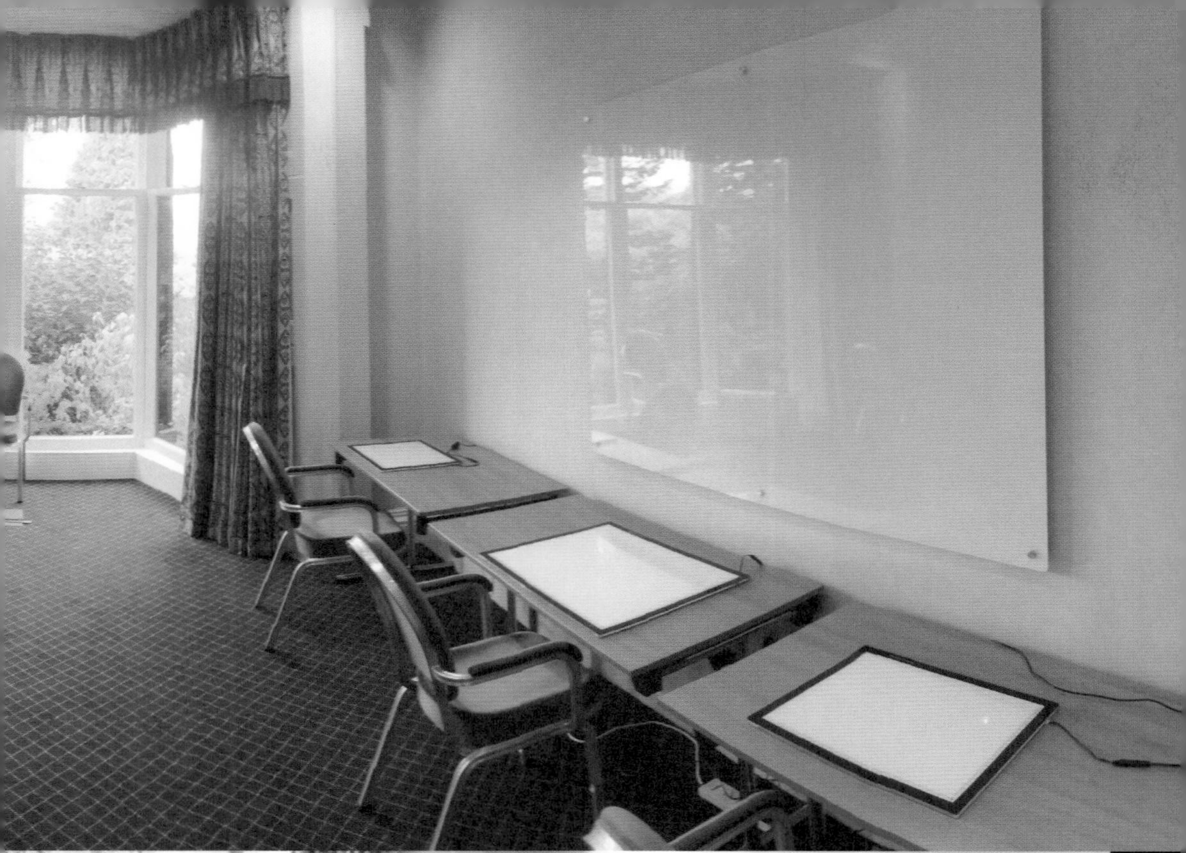
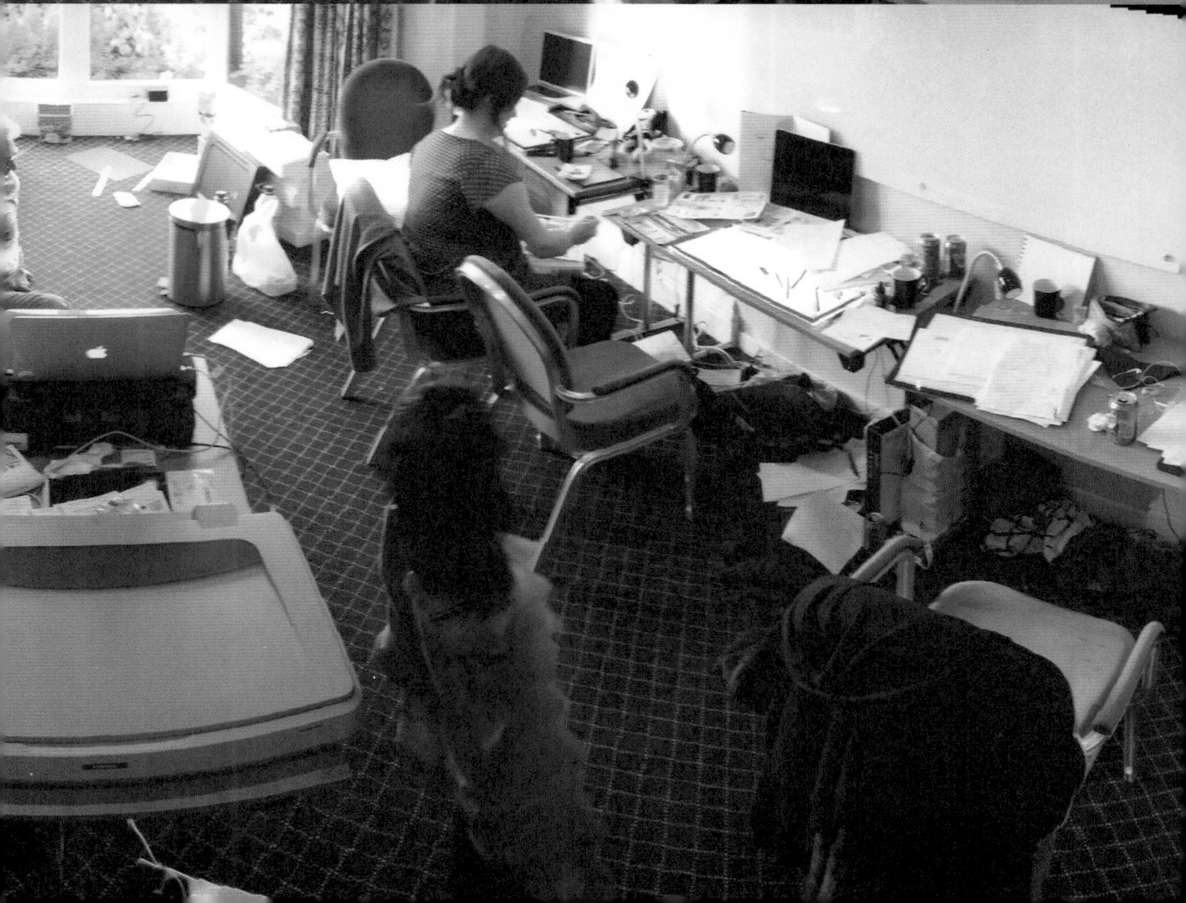

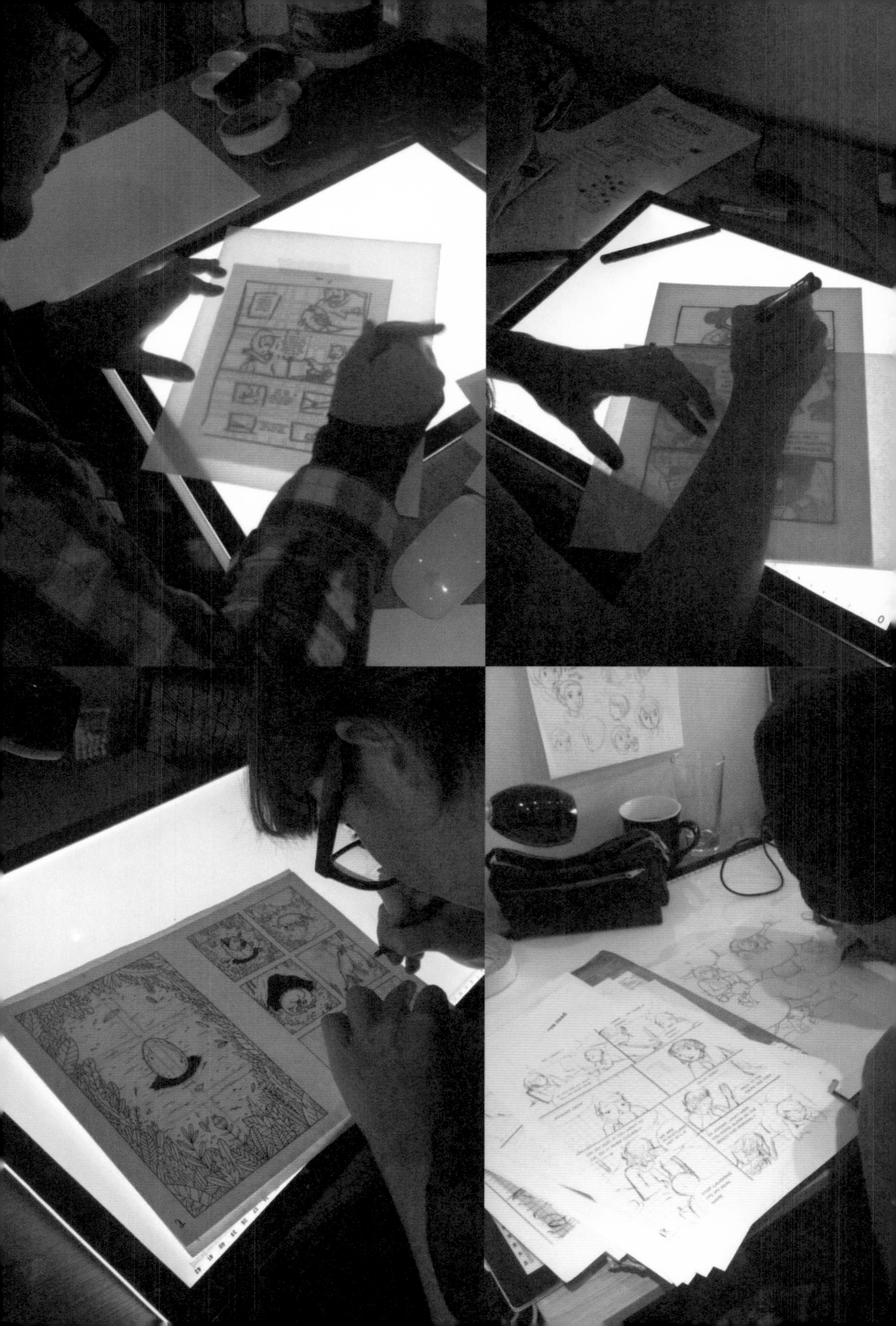

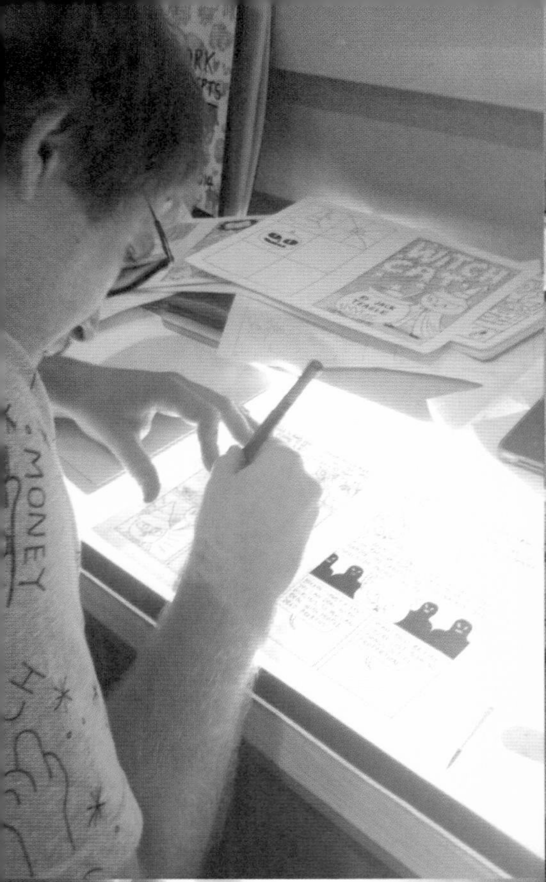
MONEY

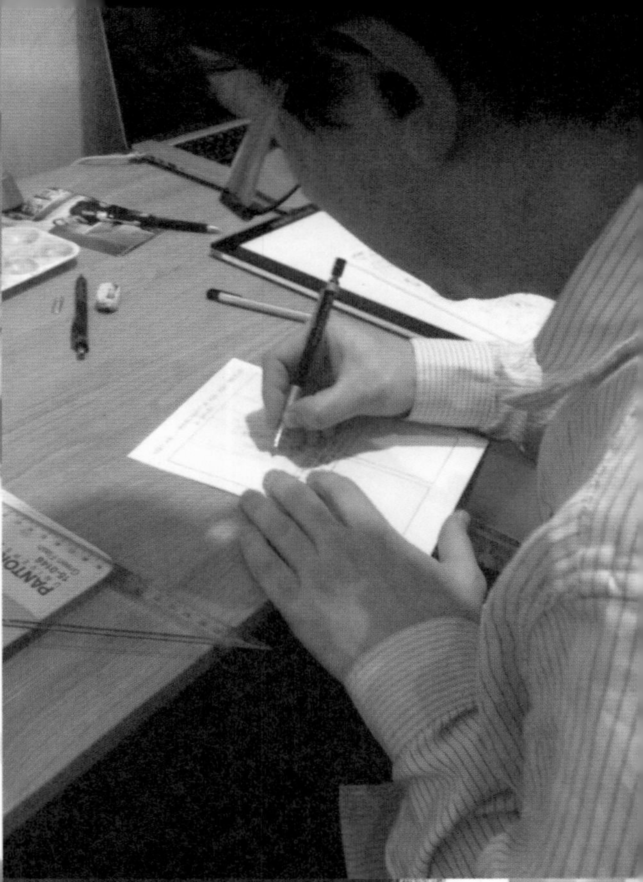

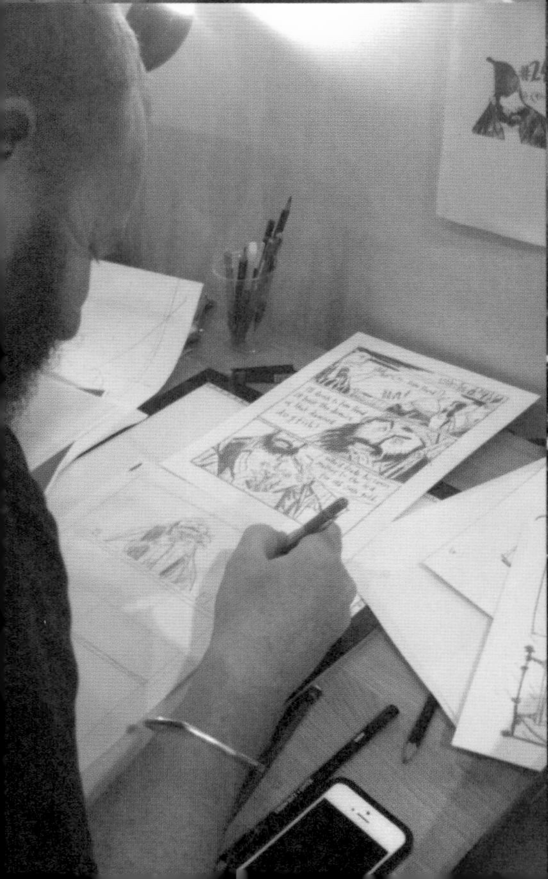

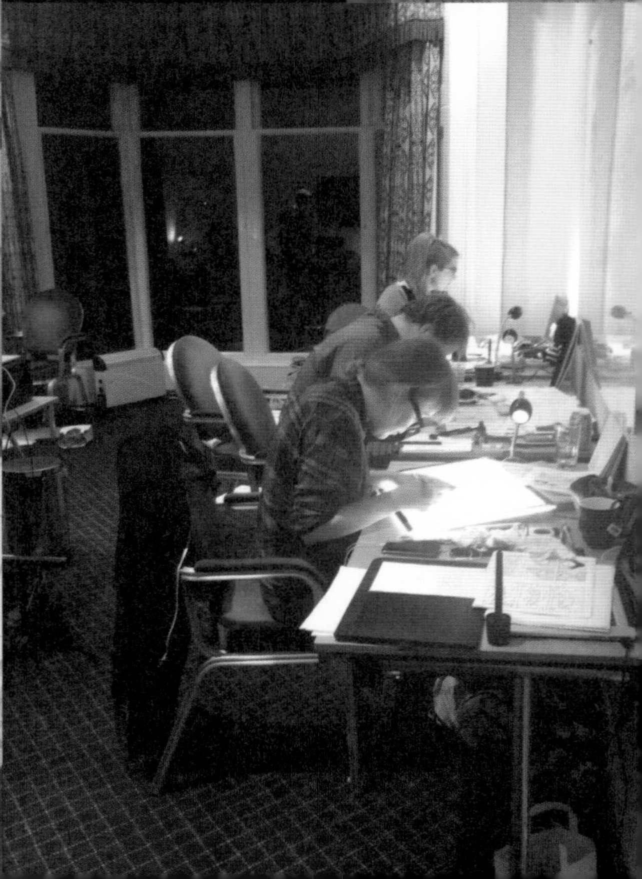

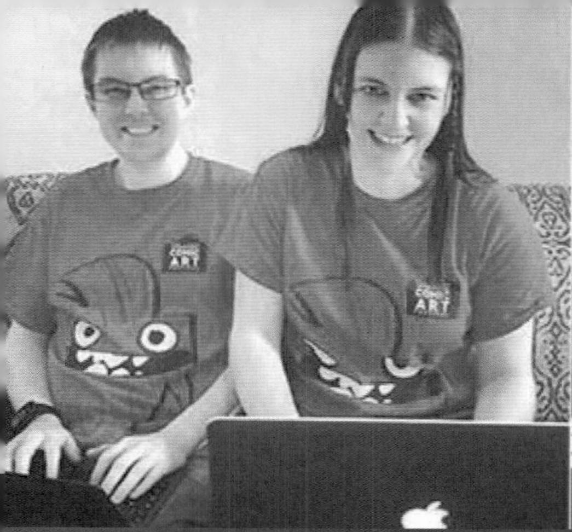
ART
ART

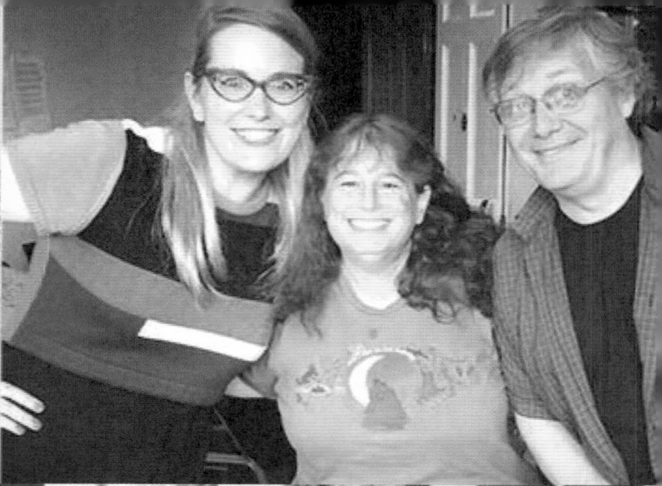

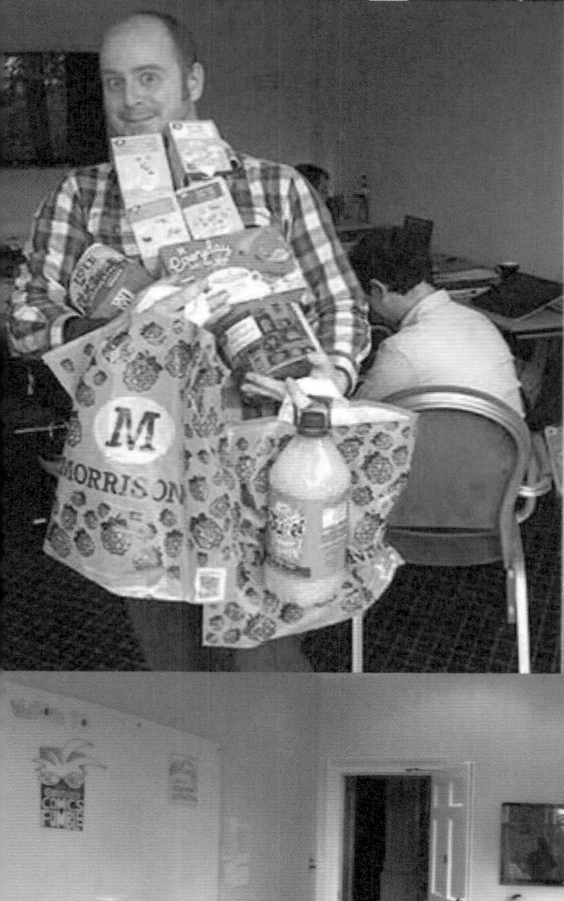
M
MORRISON

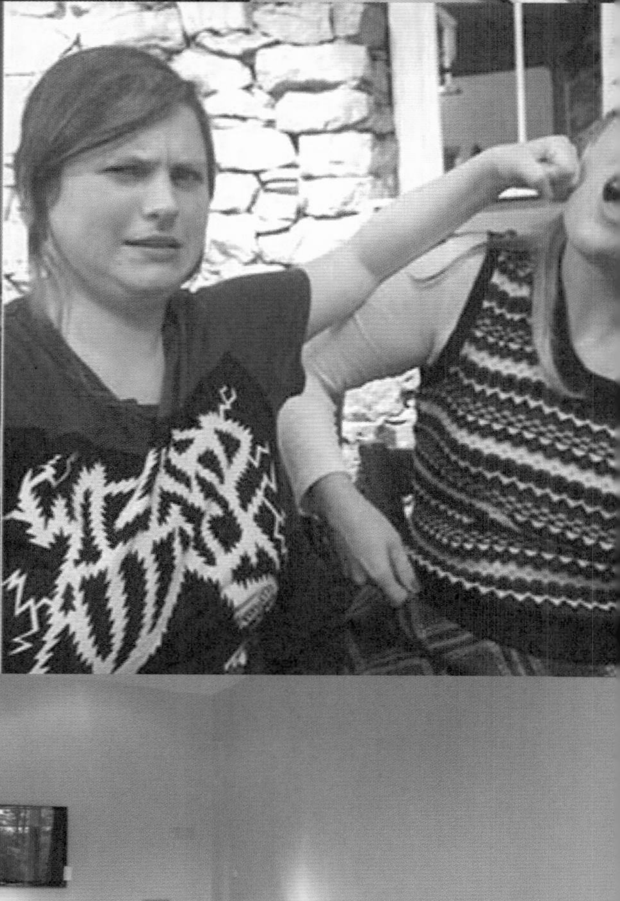

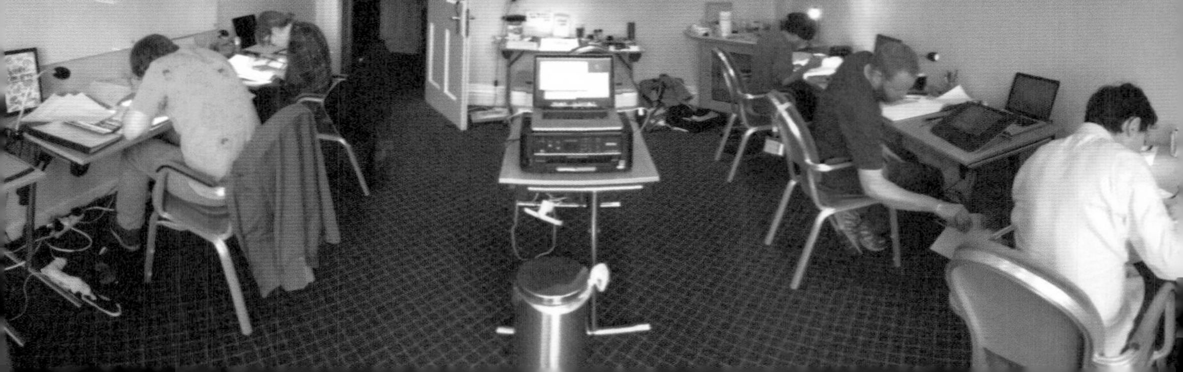

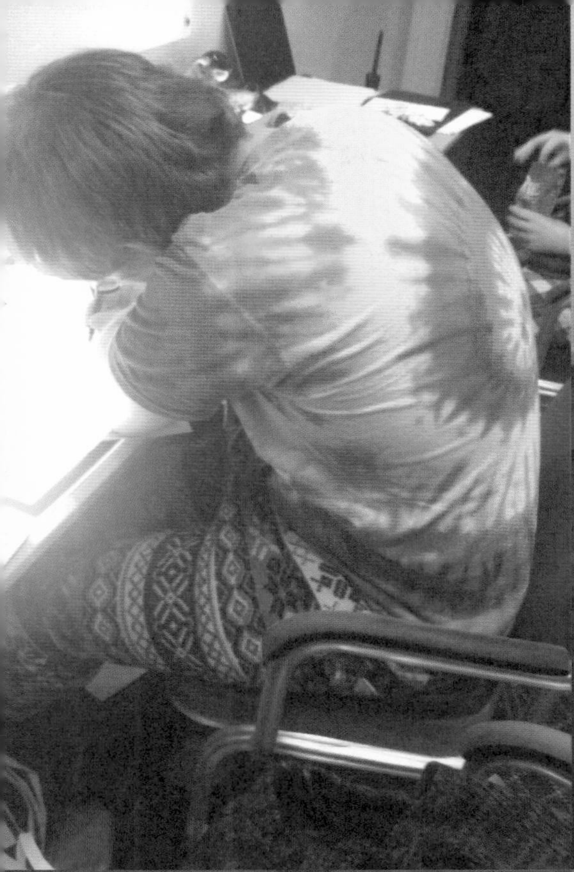
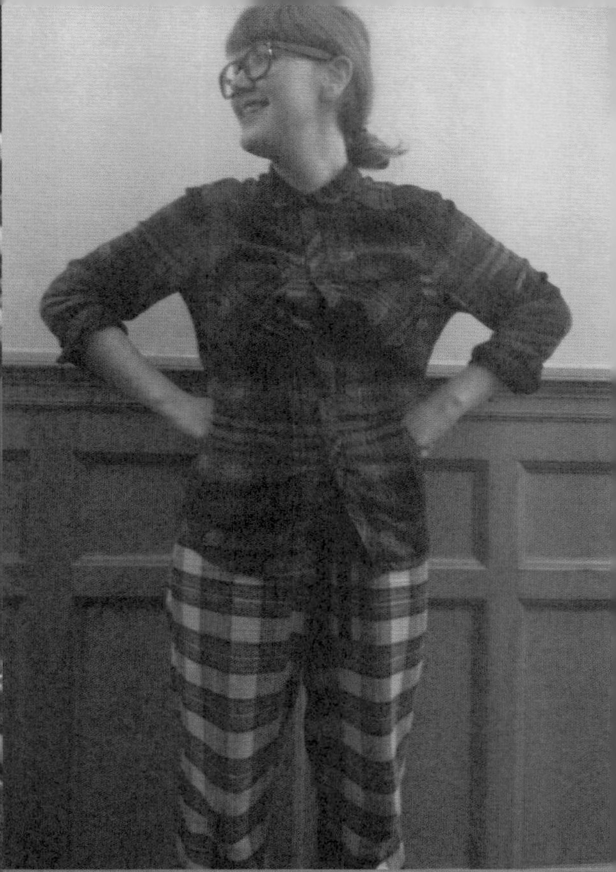
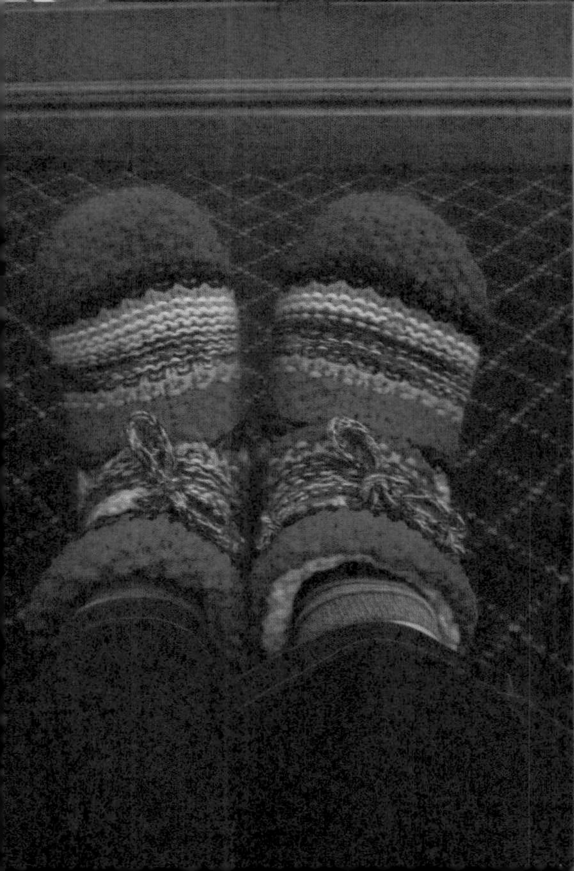
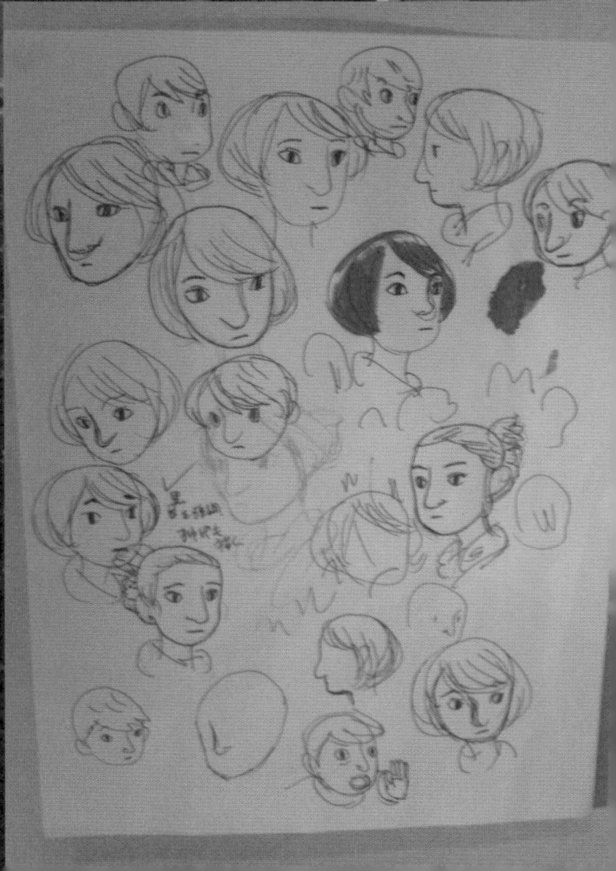

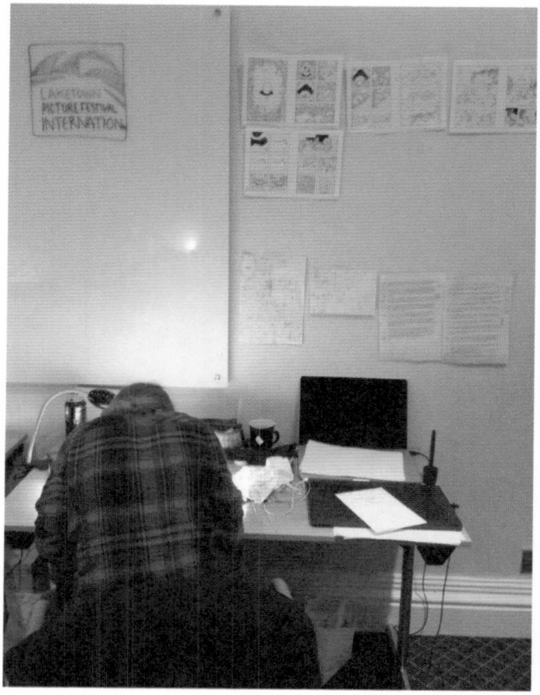
PICTURE FESTIVAL
INTERNATION

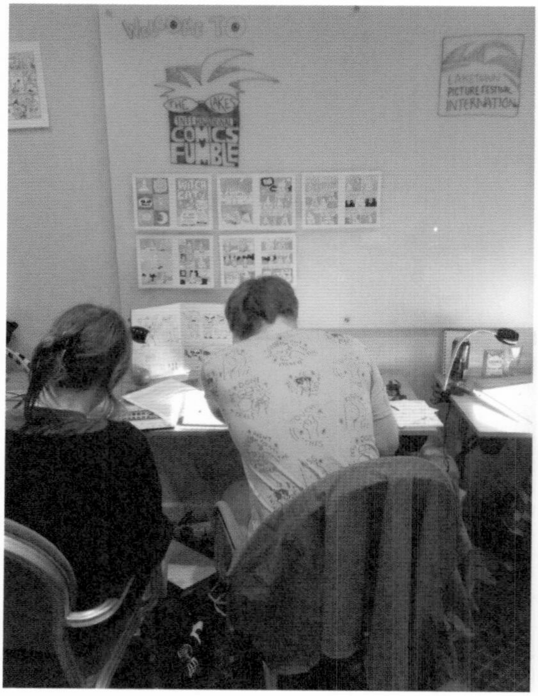
COMICS
FUMBLE
PICTURE FESTIVAL
INTERNATION

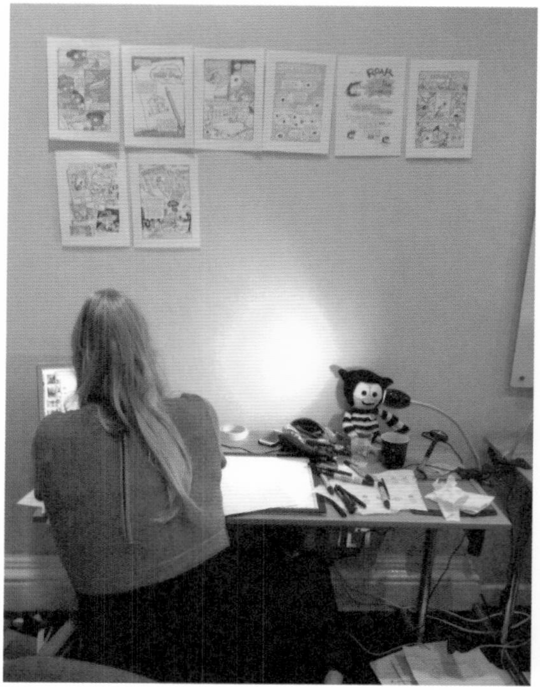

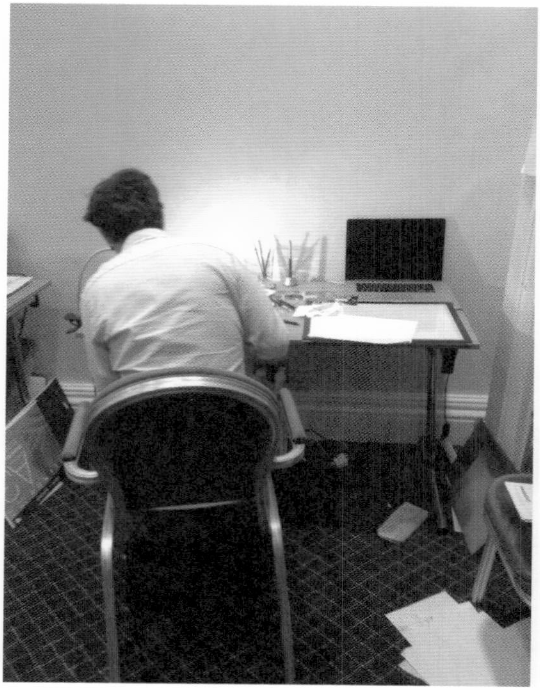

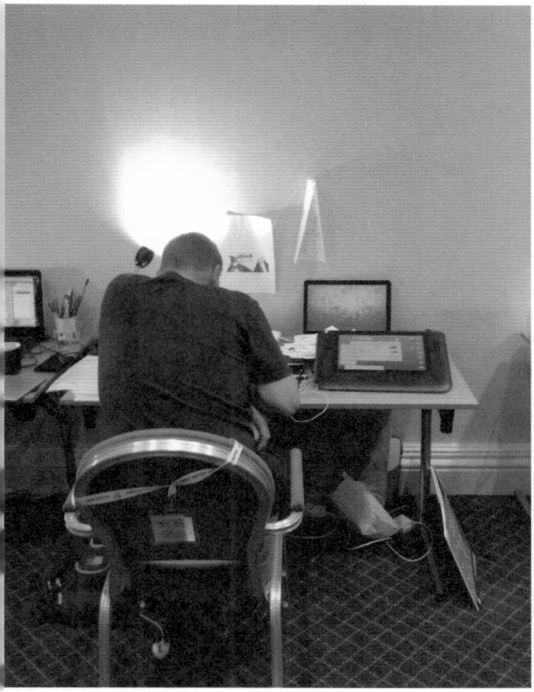

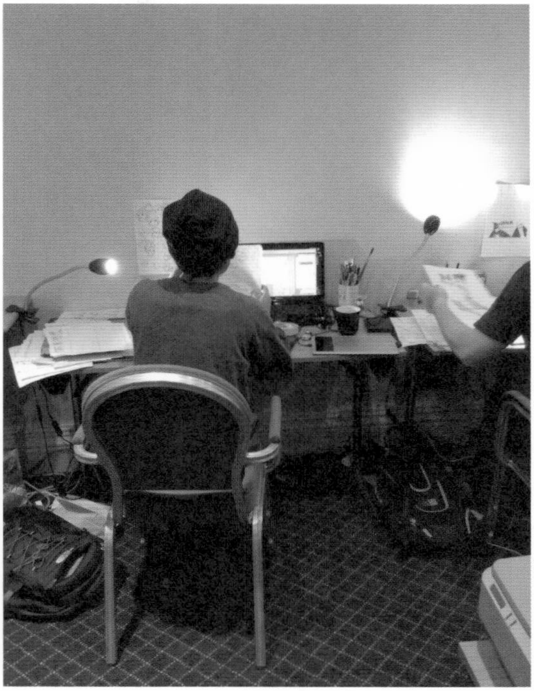

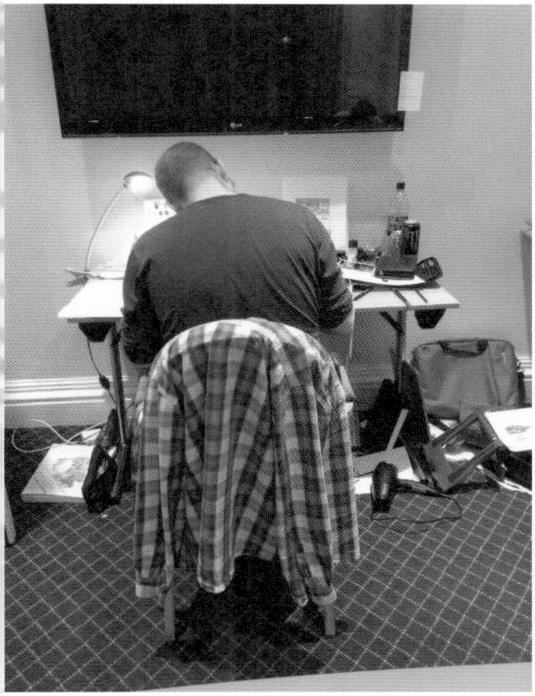

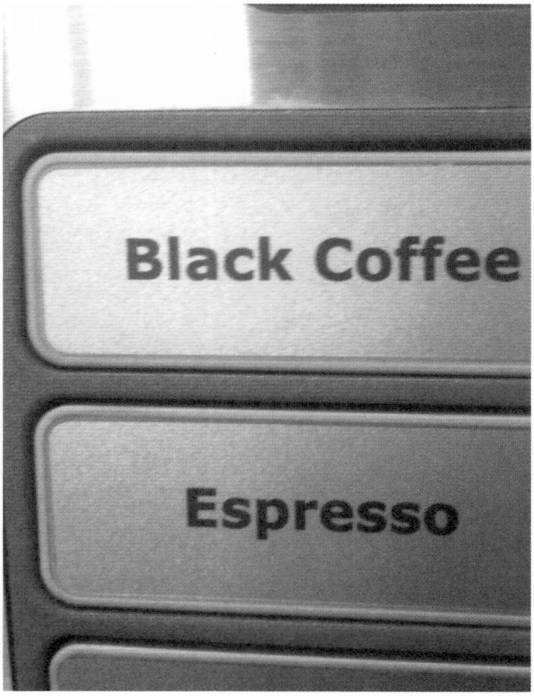
Black Coffee
Espresso

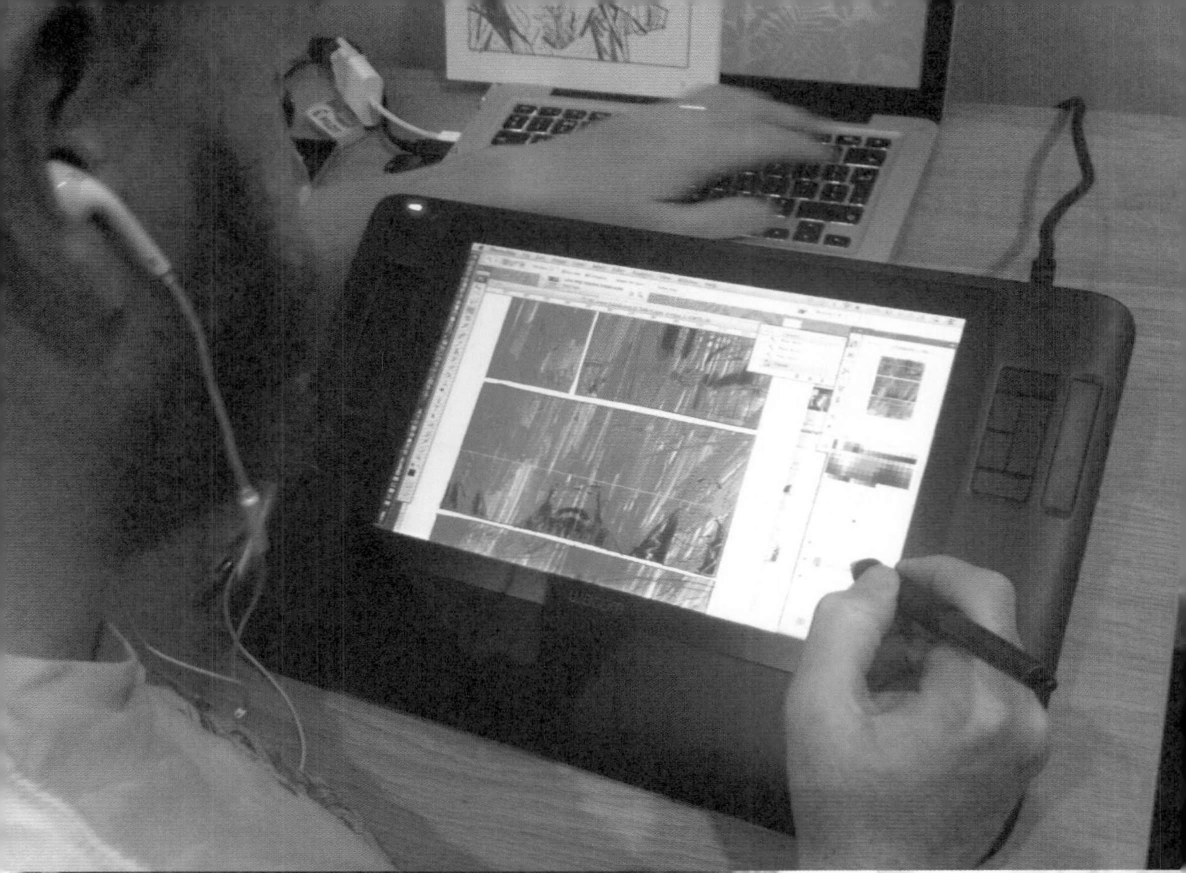

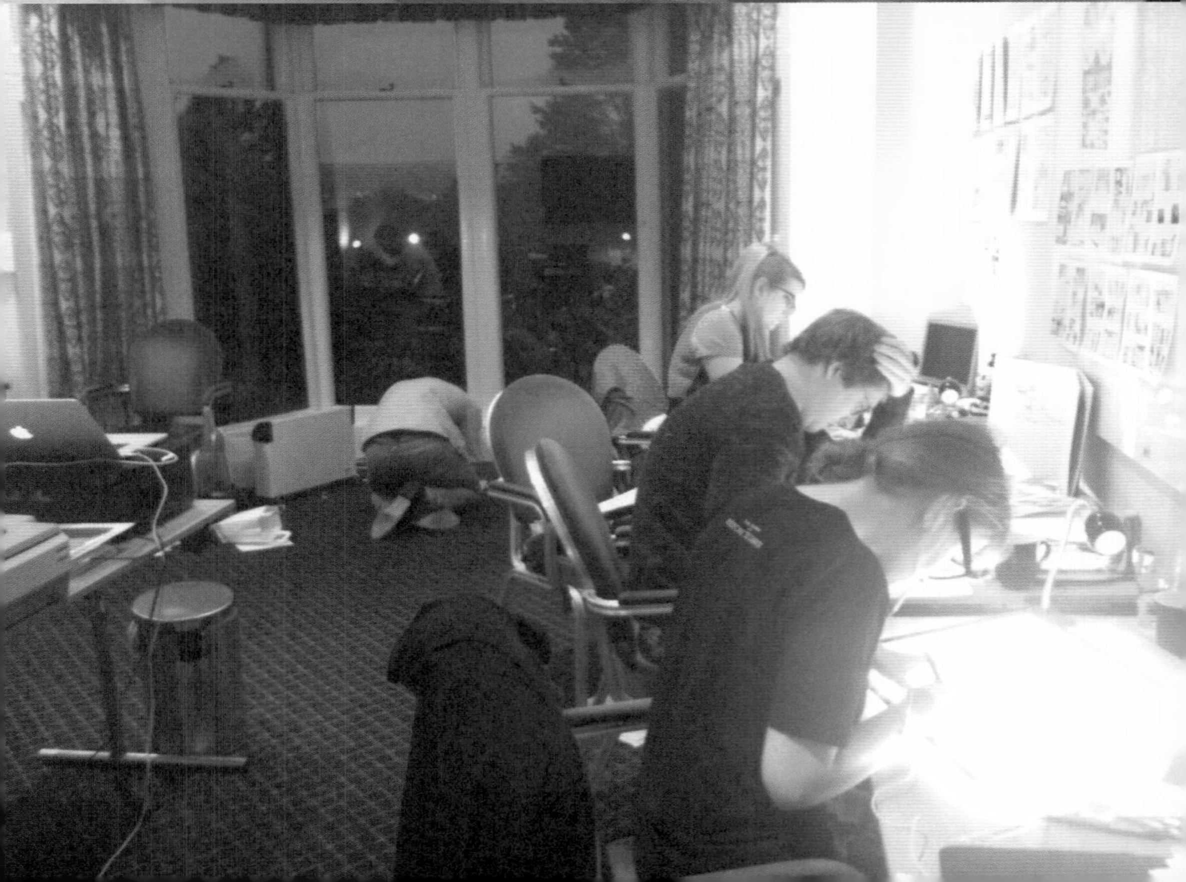

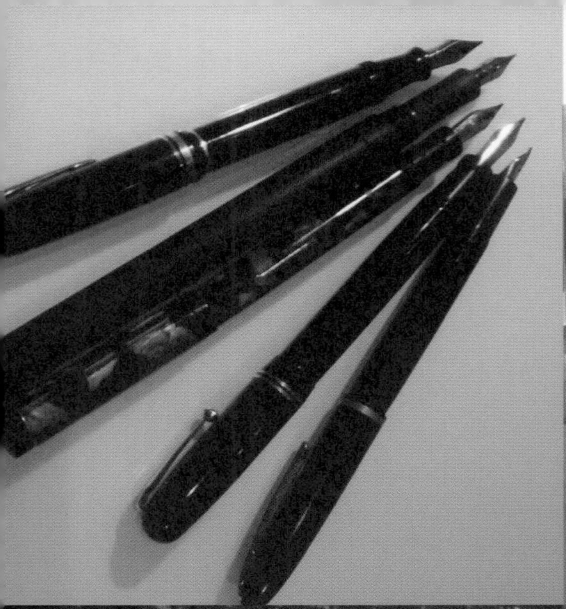

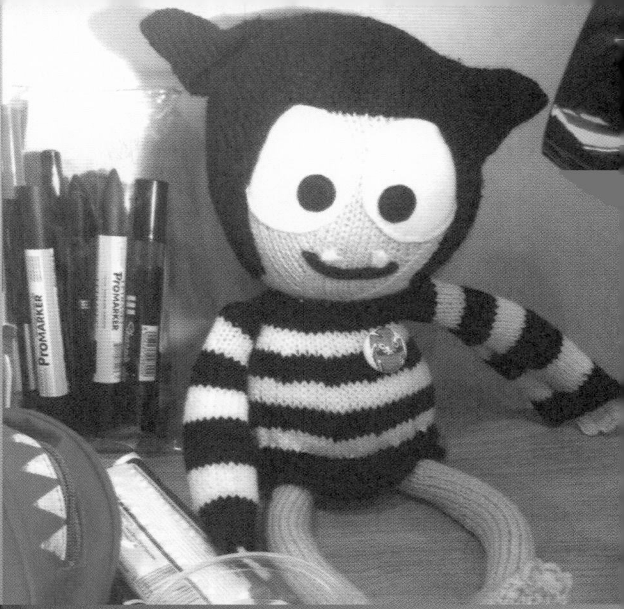
PROMARKER
PROMARKER

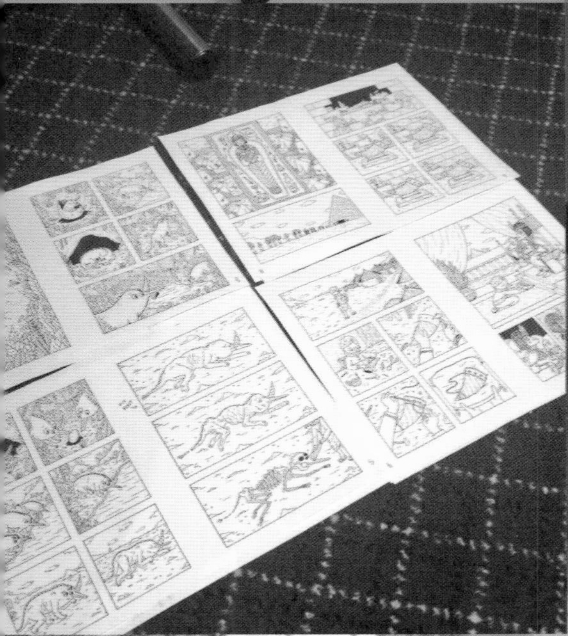

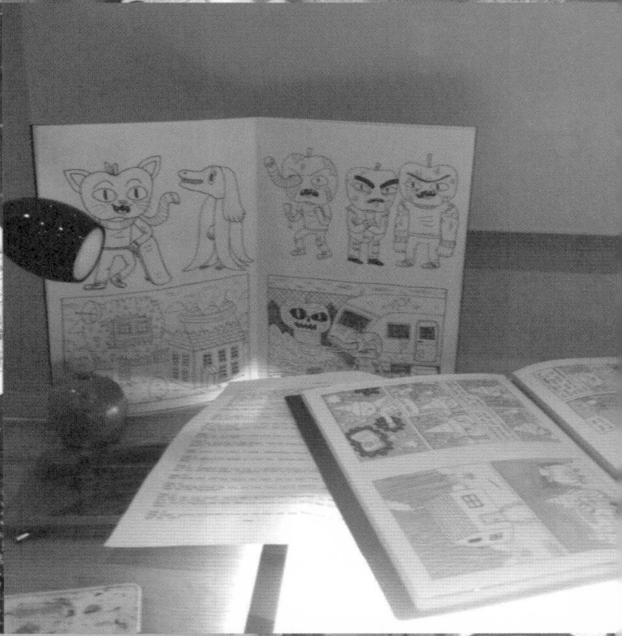

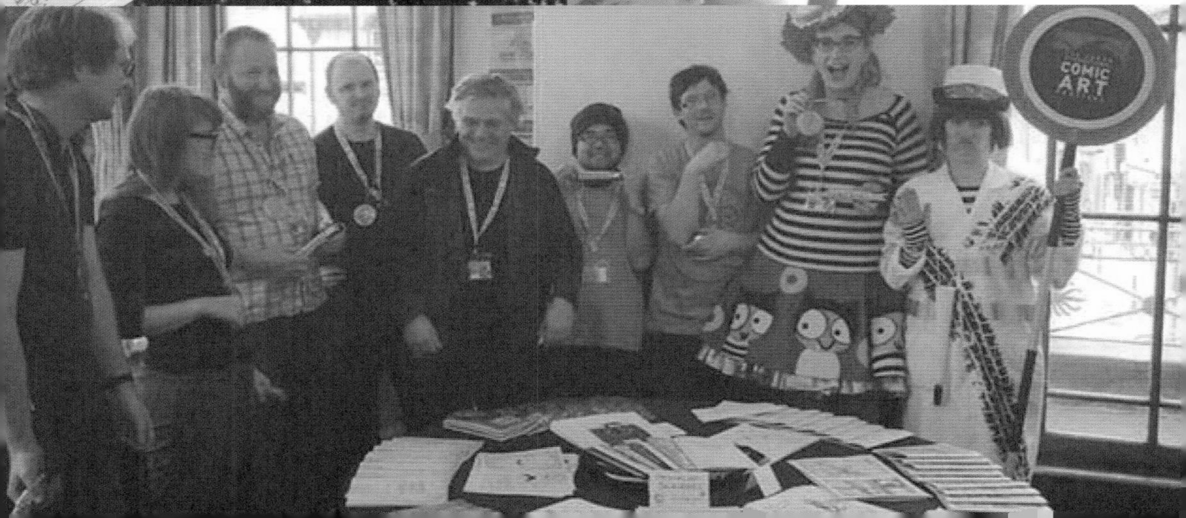
COMIC
ART

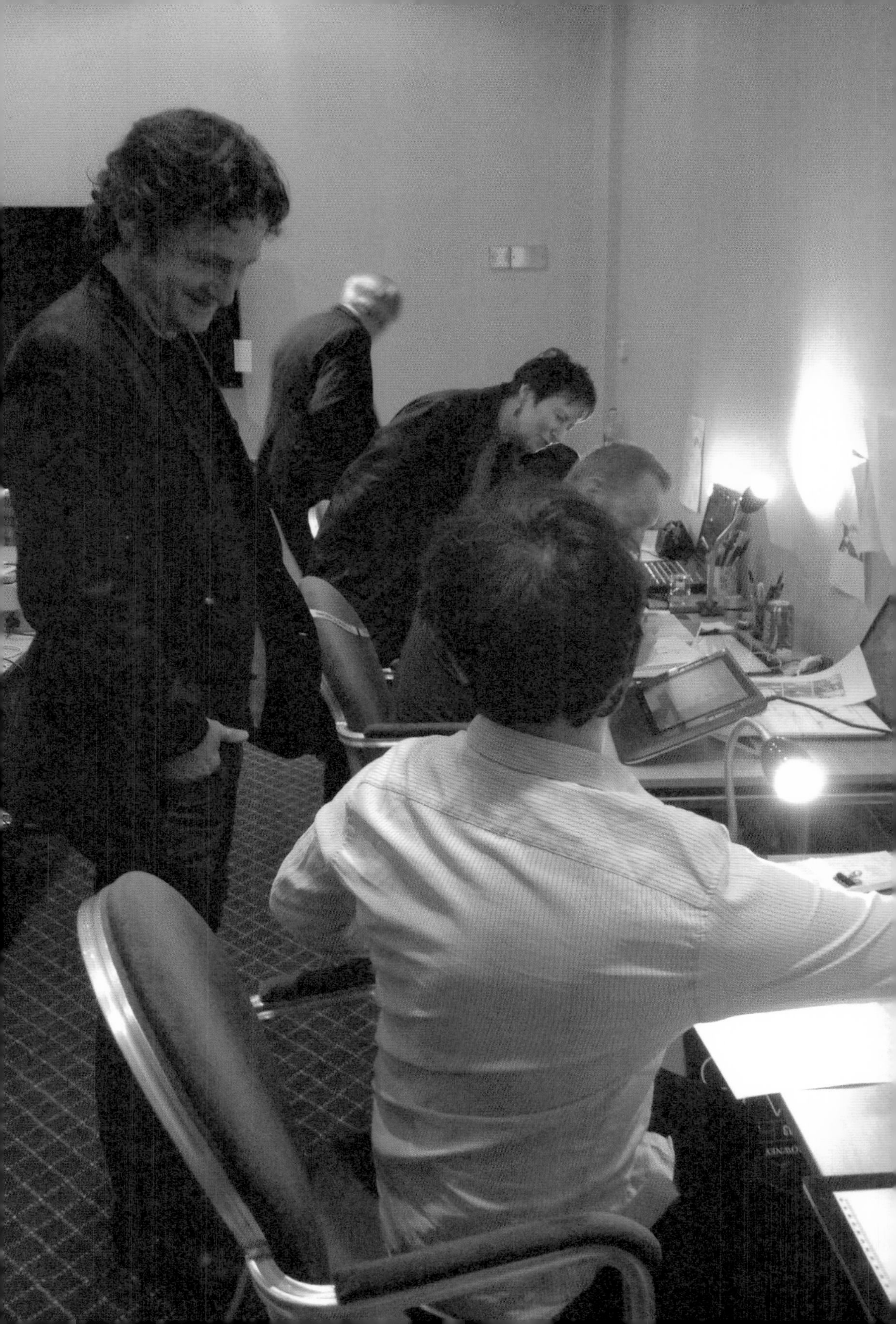